Lecture Notes in Computer Science 15996

Founding Editors

Gerhard Goos
Juris Hartmanis

Editorial Board Members

Elisa Bertino, *Purdue University, West Lafayette, IN, USA*
Wen Gao, *Peking University, Beijing, China*
Bernhard Steffen ⓘ, *TU Dortmund University, Dortmund, Germany*
Moti Yung ⓘ, *Columbia University, New York, NY, USA*

The series Lecture Notes in Computer Science (LNCS), including its subseries Lecture Notes in Artificial Intelligence (LNAI) and Lecture Notes in Bioinformatics (LNBI), has established itself as a medium for the publication of new developments in computer science and information technology research, teaching, and education.

LNCS enjoys close cooperation with the computer science R & D community, the series counts many renowned academics among its volume editors and paper authors, and collaborates with prestigious societies. Its mission is to serve this international community by providing an invaluable service, mainly focused on the publication of conference and workshop proceedings and postproceedings. LNCS commenced publication in 1973.

Bart Coppens · Bruno Volckaert ·
Vincent Naessens · Bjorn De Sutter
Editors

Availability, Reliability and Security

ARES 2025 International Workshops
Ghent, Belgium, August 11–14, 2025
Proceedings, Part III

Springer

Editors
Bart Coppens
Ghent University
Ghent, Belgium

Vincent Naessens
KU Leuven
Ghent, Belgium

Bruno Volckaert
Ghent University
Ghent, Belgium

Bjorn De Sutter
Ghent University
Ghent, Belgium

ISSN 0302-9743   ISSN 1611-3349 (electronic)
Lecture Notes in Computer Science
ISBN 978-3-032-00637-0   ISBN 978-3-032-00635-6 (eBook)
https://doi.org/10.1007/978-3-032-00635-6

© The Editor(s) (if applicable) and The Author(s), under exclusive license
to Springer Nature Switzerland AG 2025
Chapter "Combining Different Existing Methods for Describing Steganography Hiding Methods" is licensed under the terms of the Creative Commons Attribution 4.0 International License (http://creativecommons.org/licenses/by/4.0/). For further details see license information in the chapter.

This work is subject to copyright. All rights are solely and exclusively licensed by the Publisher, whether the whole or part of the material is concerned, specifically the rights of translation, reprinting, reuse of illustrations, recitation, broadcasting, reproduction on microfilms or in any other physical way, and transmission or information storage and retrieval, electronic adaptation, computer software, or by similar or dissimilar methodology now known or hereafter developed.
The use of general descriptive names, registered names, trademarks, service marks, etc. in this publication does not imply, even in the absence of a specific statement, that such names are exempt from the relevant protective laws and regulations and therefore free for general use.
The publisher, the authors and the editors are safe to assume that the advice and information in this book are believed to be true and accurate at the date of publication. Neither the publisher nor the authors or the editors give a warranty, expressed or implied, with respect to the material contained herein or for any errors or omissions that may have been made. The publisher remains neutral with regard to jurisdictional claims in published maps and institutional affiliations.

This Springer imprint is published by the registered company Springer Nature Switzerland AG
The registered company address is: Gewerbestrasse 11, 6330 Cham, Switzerland

If disposing of this product, please recycle the paper.

ARES Workshops 2025 Foreword

Alongside the main track of the 20th International Conference on Availability, Reliability and Security (ARES), the organizers received 17 regular workshop proposals, of which eventually 15 were accepted as workshops. A total of 173 papers were submitted over these workshops, of which 79 were accepted for publication and presentation at ARES 2025. All papers that were not desk rejected received a minimum of 3 double-blind reviews by TPC members, and in the case of conflicts of interest with the workshop organizers, the workshop chairs assigned reviewers and decided on the paper review ranking. As organizers, we believe the resulting workshops will allow for insightful discussions and interesting exchanges of ideas on advances made within the security field.

As workshop chairs we would like to use this space to thank all organizers for their hard work on promoting and managing their workshops. We'd also like to give a special thank you to the TPC members who provided—under strict time constraints—constructive reviews for both accepted and rejected papers. We sincerely believe the workshop programs contribute a lot to maintaining a vibrant ARES community. Therefore, from us to you, a massive thank you.

August 2025

Bart Coppens
Bruno Volckaert
Vincent Naessens
Bjorn De Sutter

ARES Workshops 2025 Organization

General Chair

Bjorn De Sutter — Ghent University, Belgium

General Workshop Chairs

Bart Coppens — Ghent University, Belgium
Bruno Volckaert — Ghent University, Belgium

Proceedings Chairs

Vincent Naessens — KU Leuven, Belgium
Michiel Willocx — KU Leuven, Belgium

Workshop Chairs

Aleksandra Mileva — Goce Delcev University, North Macedonia
Alessandro Aldini — University of Urbino, Italy
Amir Sharif — Fondazione Bruno Kessler, Italy
Amna Shifa — University of Galway, Ireland
Anastasija Collen — University of Geneva, Switzerland
Andrea Saracino — Scuola Superiore Universitaria Sant'Anna di Pisa, Italy
Andrew Marrington — Zayed University, UAE
Angelo Consoli — Scuola Universitaria Professionale della Svizzera Italiana (SUPSI), Switzerland
Artur Janicki — Warsaw University of Technology, Poland
Christoph Schmittner — Austrian Institute of Technology, Austria
Costas Lambrinoudakis — University of Piraeus, Greece
Daniela Pöhn — Universität der Bundeswehr München, Germany
Daniele Canavese — IRIT-CNRS, France
Gregorio Martinez Pérez — University of Murcia, Spain
Günther Pernul — University of Regensburg, Germany
Habtamu Abie — Norwegian Computing Center, Norway

Halvor Holtskog	Norwegian University of Science and Technology, Norway
Hamida Seba	University Lyon 1, France
Helge Janicke	Edith Cowan University, Australia
Javier Lopez	University of Malaga, Spain
Joerg Keller	FernUniversität in Hagen, Germany
Jorge Maestre Vidal	Indra, Spain
Kacper Gradoń	Warsaw University of Technology, Poland
Katarzyna Kamińska	Warsaw University of Technology, Poland
Kim-Kwang Raymond Choo	University of Texas at San Antonio, USA
Leandros Maglaras	De Montfort University, UK
Leonardo Regano	University of Cagliari, Italy
Luca Caviglione	CNR – IMATI, Italy
Mamoona Asghar	University of Galway, Ireland
Mansoor Ahmed	Maynooth University, Ireland
Marco Antonio Sotelo Monge	Indra, Spain
Marco Rasori	National Research Council, Italy
Markus Helfert	Maynooth University, Ireland
Marta Irene García Cid	Indra, Spain
Martin Husák	Masaryk University, Czech Republic
Martin Steinebach	Fraunhofer Institute SIT|ATHENE, Germany
Mauro Conti	University of Padua, Italy
Meriem Benyahya	University of Geneva, Switzerland
Mohamed Ali Kandi	IRIT-University of Toulouse, France
Mohamed-Lamine Messai	University Lyon 2, France
Muhammad Irfan Khalid	University of Agder, Norway
Nadia Kanwal	Keele University, UK
Nils Gruschka	University of Oslo, Norway
Pedro R. M. Inácio	Universidade da Beira Interior, Portugal
Peter Kieseberg	FH St. Pölten, Austria
Philipp Amann	Europol EC3, The Netherlands
Richard Overill	King's College London, UK
Richard Smith	De Montfort University, UK
Salvador Llopis Sanchez	Universitat Politècnica de Valencia, Spain
Sandeep Pirbhulal	Norwegian Computing Center, Oslo, Norway
Simone Fischer-Hübner	Karlstad University, Chalmers University of Technology & Gothenburg University, Sweden
Sokratis Katsikas	Norwegian University of Science and Technology, Norway
Stephen Fisher Davies	Airbus, UK
Steven Furnell	University of Nottingham, UK
Thomas Brandstetter	Limes Security/FHSTP, Austria

Virginia N. L. Franqueira	University of Kent, UK
Wojciech Mazurczyk	Warsaw University of Technology, Poland

WSDF 2025 Preface

Cybercrime evolves rapidly, with offenders adapting to technological and social changes, operating globally, and targeting financially lucrative areas. It has become a major industry, with underground marketplaces offering illegal goods, stolen data, and cybercriminal services. Forensic research is vital for collecting admissible evidence, identifying perpetrators, and analysing attack methods to strengthen defences and prevent future crimes. Scientific workshops like WSDF foster collaboration among experts, helping to identify threats, refine forensic methods, and address legal challenges. They drive innovation, improve prevention strategies, and enhance global efforts against cybercrime.

The International Workshop on Digital Forensics (WSDF) aims to bring together experts from academia, industry, government and law enforcement who are interested in advancing the state of the art in digital forensics by exchanging their knowledge, results, ideas, challenges, best practices and experiences. The intention of the workshop, as in previous years, is to provide a relaxed atmosphere that promotes discussion and free exchange of ideas while providing a sound academic backing.

WSDF 2025 was the eighteenth edition of the workshop, which has run without interruption at ARES since 2007. This year, WSDF had 16 submissions, of which 8 were accepted for presentation at the workshop and included in the proceedings, leading to an acceptance rate of 50%. The technical program committee included 19 researchers from 11 different countries and the review process involved 14 additional experts who acted as sub-reviewers. In line with the main conference guidelines, the peer-review process was double-blinded, with every paper undergoing three reviews and, where required, a short deliberation between reviewers to support the final decision.

The best paper award for WSDF 2025 was sponsored by the Institute of Cyber Security for Society (iCSS), University of Kent, UK.

August 2025

Kim-Kwang Raymond Choo
Virginia N. L. Franqueira
Andrew Marrington
Richard Overill
Martin Steinebach

WSDF 2025 Organization

Workshop Chairs

Kim-Kwang Raymond Choo	University of Texas at San Antonio, USA
Virginia N. L. Franqueira	University of Kent, UK
Andrew Marrington	Zayed University, UAE
Richard Overill	King's College London, UK
Martin Steinebach	Fraunhofer Institute SIT|ATHENE, Germany

Program Committee

Frank Breitinger	University of Augsburg, Germany
Ching Bon Raymond Chan	Singapore Institute of Technology, Singapore
Kam-Pui Chow	University of Hong Kong, China
Sarah De'Ath	De Montfort University, UK
Patricio Domingues	Polytechnic Institute of Leiria, Portugal
Weihan Goh	Singapore Institute of Technology, Singapore
George Grispos	University of Nebraska, USA
Chris Hargreaves	HARGS Solutions Ltd., UK
Katerina Kanta	University of Portsmouth, UK
Erisa Karafili	University of Southampton, UK
Áine MacDermott	Liverpool John Moores University, UK
Chiara Pero	University of Salerno, Italy
Mark Scanlon	University College Dublin, Ireland
Stavros Shiaeles	University of Portsmouth, UK
Hudan Studiawan	Institut Teknologi Sepuluh Nopember, Indonesia
Nina Sunde	Norwegian Police University College, Norway
Harm van Beek	Netherlands Forensic Institute, The Netherlands
Jeroen van den Bos	Infix Technologies, The Netherlands
Vincent van der Meer	Zuyd University, The Netherlands

Additional Reviewers

Marc Leon Agel
Hamda Al Breiki
Jeong-Eun Choi

Yasamin Fayyaz
Nicola Galante
Farkhund Iqbal
Richard Adeyemi Ikuesan
Aaron Jarrett
Jimmy McGibney
Lutta Pantaleon
K. Prabhu Rajasekar
Paige Tynan
Alexandros Vasilaras
Klara Weiand

IWCC 2025 Preface

The societies of today's world are becoming increasingly dependent on online services, where commercial activities, business transactions, government services, and biomedical diagnostics are realized. This tendency has been evident during the recent COVID-19 pandemic. These developments, along with the growing number of military conflicts worldwide (Ukraine, Israel, etc.), have led to the fast development of new cyber threats and numerous information security issues exploited by cybercriminals. The inability to provide trusted, secure services in contemporary computer network technologies has a tremendous socio-economic impact on global enterprises and individuals.

Moreover, the frequently occurring international frauds impose the necessity to conduct investigations spanning multiple domains and countries. Such examination is often subject to different jurisdictions and legal systems. A good illustration of the above is the Internet, which has made it easier to prepare and perpetrate traditional – but now cyber-enabled – crimes. It has acted as an alternate avenue for criminals to conduct their activities and launch attacks with relative anonymity, a high degree of deniability, and the opportunity to operate in a border-agnostic environment. Worrying developments in the abuse of artificial intelligence and machine learning technologies lead to the increased capabilities of malign actors who leverage these tools to design and propagate disinformation, which is especially dangerous (and effective) during emergencies and crises of all kinds. The developments in Generative Artificial Intelligence have also enabled the increase of criminal capabilities in the production, dissemination, and weaponization of high-quality, convincing fake content (text, audio, images, and videos), which translates not only to the truth and trust decay among the affected societies but also to the enhanced capabilities in orchestrating the sophisticated cyber crimes.

Furthermore, nowadays, the majority of life-science-based techniques and resulting data hinge on information technologies. Despite their considerable advantages, dependence on cyber technologies also exposes vulnerabilities. Various threats in the digital realm could target biomedical systems, leading to adverse consequences. The field of CyberBioSecurity was established to assist bio-related sciences in comprehending potential cyber threats and formulating defense approaches, recovery protocols, and resilience strategies.

The increased complexity of communications and the networking infrastructure is making the investigation of these new types of crimes difficult. Traces of illegal digital activities are difficult to analyze due to large volumes of data. Nowadays, the digital crime scene functions like any other network, with dedicated administrators functioning as the first responders. This poses new challenges for law enforcement and intelligence communities and forces computer societies to utilize digital forensics to combat the increasing number of cyber crimes. Forensic professionals must be fully prepared to provide court-admissible evidence. Forensic techniques should keep pace with new technologies to make these goals achievable. Prevention, mitigation, and interdiction of new and emerging threats necessitate an increasingly thorough and multidisciplinary approach. They also require the collaboration of all relevant actors and stakeholders in designing the technology regulation and cyber governance measures.

This year, our 14th International Workshop on Cyber Crime (IWCC 2025) received ten submissions, out of which we selected the five best ones. They cover various topics, starting from deep fake images: their generation and collection (papers: "Generating Deepfakes with Stable Diffusion, ControlNet and LoRA" and "Towards Creating a Darknet Image Database"), through protecting anonymity ("Hello, won't you tell me your name?: Investigating Anonymity Abuse in IPFS") and a paper on the analysis of malicious financial transactions ("Countering Financial Cyber Crime: New Method for Subsequent Steps Analysis in Large Complex Graphs of Financial Transactions"), ending with a review of darknet marketplaces ("From Sign-Up to Multi-Million Revenues: A Deep Dive into Vendors on Darknet Marketplaces"). The reviewing process was double-blind; each of the submissions was assessed by at least three experts. We would like to thank all the authors who contributed to our workshop and all the reviewers who helped with the selection process.

August 2025

Artur Janicki
Kacper Gradoń
Katarzyna Kamińska

IWCC 2025 Organization

Workshop Chairs

Artur Janicki	Warsaw University of Technology, Poland
Kacper Gradoń	Warsaw University of Technology, Poland
Katarzyna Kamińska	Warsaw University of Technology, Poland

Program Committee

Yulliwas Ameur	CNAM, France
Jędrzej Bieniasz	Warsaw University of Technology, Poland
Luca Caviglione	CNR - IMATI, Italy
Eric Chan-Tin	Loyola University Chicago, USA
Michał Choraś	Bydgoszcz University of Science and Technology, Poland
Jana Dittmann	Otto-von-Guericke-Universität Magdeburg, Germany
Stefan Katzenbeisser	University of Passau, Germany
Christian Kraetzer	Otto-von-Guericke-Universität Magdeburg, Germany
Roberto Magán-Carrión	University of Granada, Spain
Gerard Memmi	Telecom Paris, France
Mariusz Sepczuk	Warsaw University of Technology, Poland
Ewa Syta	Yale University, USA
Stefan Wendzel	University of Ulm, Germany

CUING 2025 Preface

It is our great pleasure to introduce research papers presented at the 9th International Workshop on Cyber Use of Information Hiding (CUING 2025), co-located with the 20th International Conference on Availability, Reliability, and Security (ARES 2025). The conference was held in Ghent, Belgium on August 11–14, 2025.

The CUING 2025 workshop focuses on the analysis and countermeasures of information hiding techniques used in cyber attacks, addressing the growing sophistication of threat actors in leveraging stealthy methods to evade detection. As information hiding – such as steganography, covert channels, obfuscation, and anti-forensics – becomes more prevalent in cybercrime, CUING brings together researchers, practitioners, and law enforcement to examine emerging threats and develop novel detection and mitigation strategies. The workshop welcomes work on a wide range of related topics, including AI-enabled hiding methods, privacy-enhancing technologies, stegomalware, traffic obfuscation, and the misuse of legitimate platforms like social media and cloud services. CUING 2025 also encourages discussion on the dual-use nature of these technologies, such as their role in both enabling privacy and facilitating cybercrime.

This year CUING received 14 submissions, of which 50% were accepted. Each paper was peer-reviewed by our experts from the Technical Program Committee (TPC) and, on average, received 3.5 reviews. This year, our TPC consisted of 25 experts from 11 countries around the world (Austria, China, France, Germany, Italy, Israel, Japan, Macedonia, Poland, Spain, and the USA). The whole review process was conducted using double-blind methodology, and assisted by all Workshop Chairs.

August 2025

Philipp Amann
Luca Caviglione
Angelo Consoli
Joerg Keller
Peter Kieseberg
Wojciech Mazurczyk

CUING 2025 Organization

Workshop Chairs

Philipp Amann	Europol EC3, The Netherlands
Luca Caviglione	CNR – IMATI, Italy
Angelo Consoli	Scuola Universitaria Professionale della Svizzera Italiana (SUPSI), Switzerland
Joerg Keller	FernUniversität in Hagen, Germany
Peter Kieseberg	FH St. Pölten, Austria
Wojciech Mazurczyk	Warsaw University of Technology, Poland

Program Committee

Giacomo Benedetti	Institute of Applied Mathematics and Information Technologies, Italy
Krzysztof Cabaj	Warsaw University of Technology, Poland
Michał Choraś	Bydgoszcz University of Science and Technology, Poland
Rémi Cogranne	Troyes University of Technology, France
Marco Cremonini	University of Milan, Italy
Jana Dittmann	Otto-von-Guericke-Universität Magdeburg, Germany
Massimo Guarascio	Institute of HPC and Networking, Italy
Mordechai Guri	Ben-Gurion University, Israel
Stefan Katzenbeisser	University of Passau, Germany
Zbigniew Kotulski	Warsaw University of Technology, Poland
Christian Kraetzer	Otto-von-Guericke-Universität Magdeburg, Germany
Minoru Kuribayashi	Tohoku University, Japan
Daniel Lerch-Hostalot	Universitat Oberta de Catalunya, Spain
David Megías	Universitat Oberta de Catalunya, Spain
Aleksandra Mileva	University Goce Delcev, Macedonia
Marek Pawlicki	Bydgoszcz University of Science and Technology, Poland
Paweł Rajba	University of Wroclaw, Poland
Tobias Schmidbauer	Nuremberg Institute of Technology, Germany
Reza Soosahabi	Keysight Technologies Inc., USA

Avinash Srinivasan	United States Naval Academy, USA
Martin Steinebach	Fraunhofer SIT, Germany
Milad Taleby Ahvanooey	Warsaw University of Technology, Poland
Hui Tian	National Huaqiao University, China
Steffen Wendzel	University of Ulm, Germany
Tanja Zseby	Vienna University of Technology, Austria

Contents – Part III

Proceedings of the Eighteenth International Workshop on Digital Forensics (WSDF 2025)

Forensic Insights into Windows 11's Capability Access Manager Artifacts 5
   Patricio Domingues, Miguel Frade, and Miguel Negrão

Reconstructing File Versions and Timestamps: Challenges and Guidelines
in Network Forensics 23
   Axel Mahr, Jan-Niclas Hilgert, and Martin Lambertz

Measuring the Effectiveness of Keyword Lists in Digital Forensics 42
   Aikaterini Kanta and Christopher Hargreaves

Money on My Mind: Forensic Investigation of Venmo Payment App 60
   Trevor Spinosa, Abdur Onik, Joshua Rovira, and Ibrahim Baggili

Forensic Analysis of AI Applications - A Replika "AI Companion" Example . . . 78
   Christopher Hargreaves and Dan Drury

An AI-Based Network Forensic Readiness Framework
for Resource-Constrained Environments 96
   Syed Rizvi, Mark Scanlon, Jimmy McGibney, and John Sheppard

Mapping the Research Landscape - An Exploratory Analysis of AI
Applications in Digital Forensics 113
   *Gokila Dorai, Pouria Rad, Frank Breitinger, Rajon Bardhan,
and Vijayalakshmi Ramasamy*

The Impact of Anti-forensic Techniques on Data-Driven Digital Forensics:
Anomaly Detection Case Study 131
   Zuzana Hennelová, Eva Marková, and Pavol Sokol

Proceedings of the Fourteenth International Workshop on Cyber Crime (IWCC 2025)

Generating Deepfakes with Stable Diffusion, ControlNet, and LoRA 153
   Stefano Bistarelli, Francesco Santini, and Edoardo Toma Tavassi

Towards Creating a Darknet Image Database 171
   York Yannikos, Marc Leon Agel, Julian Heeger, Lukas Graner,
   and Martin Steinebach

Hello, Won't You Tell Me Your Name?: Investigating Anonymity Abuse
in IPFS 187
   Christos Karapapas, Iakovos Pittaras, George C. Polyzos,
   and Constantinos Patsakis

Countering Financial Cyber Crime: New Method for Subsequent Steps
Analysis in Large Complex Graphs of Financial Transactions 205
   Rafał Kozik, Piotr Gocał, and Michał Choraś

From Sign-Up to Multi-million Revenues: A Deep Dive Into Vendors
on Darknet Marketplaces 221
   Julia Kramer, Anne Streicher, and Marcus Niemietz

Proceedings of the Ninth International Workshop on Cyber Use of Information Hiding (CUING 2025)

Contextual Coherence Evaluation of Perfectly Secure Steganography
in Text Documents 243
   Katsuyuki Umezawa, Toshikatsu Kashima, Sven Wohlgemuth,
   and Kazuo Takaragi

Robust Hashing Meets Inpainting 255
   Martin Steinebach and York Yannikos

Combining Different Existing Methods for Describing Steganography
Hiding Methods 271
   Steffen Wendzel, Christian Krätzer, Jana Dittmann, Luca Caviglione,
   Aleksandra Mileva, Tobias Schmidbauer, Claus Vielhauer,
   and Sebastian Zander

Calyptography: Secure Secret Storage Inspired by Cryptography
and Steganography 290
   Daniel Lerch-Hostalot, Jordi Puiggalí, and David Megías

An Independent Secure Authentication System Against False
Positive/Negative Attacks in SVD-Based Watermarking: Design
and Implementation 309
   Tanya Koohpayeh Araghi and David Megías

Entropy-Aware Secret Data Embedding for Network Storage Channels 327
   Paweł Rajba, Jörg Keller, and Wojciech Mazurczyk

ReWaP: Reversible Watermarking and Paillier Encryption Approach
for Privacy-Preserving Smart Meter 346
   Farzana Kabir, Krzysztof Cabaj, Tanya Koohpayeh Araghi,
   and David Megías

Author Index 365

Proceedings of the Eighteenth International Workshop on Digital Forensics (WSDF 2025)

WSDF 2025 Preface

Cybercrime evolves rapidly, with offenders adapting to technological and social changes, operating globally, and targeting financially lucrative areas. It has become a major industry, with underground marketplaces offering illegal goods, stolen data, and cybercriminal services. Forensic research is vital for collecting admissible evidence, identifying perpetrators, and analysing attack methods to strengthen defences and prevent future crimes. Scientific workshops like WSDF foster collaboration among experts, helping to identify threats, refine forensic methods, and address legal challenges. They drive innovation, improve prevention strategies, and enhance global efforts against cybercrime.

The International Workshop on Digital Forensics (WSDF) aims to bring together experts from academia, industry, government and law enforcement who are interested in advancing the state of the art in digital forensics by exchanging their knowledge, results, ideas, challenges, best practices and experiences. The intention of the workshop, as in previous years, is to provide a relaxed atmosphere that promotes discussion and free exchange of ideas while providing a sound academic backing.

WSDF 2025 was the eighteenth edition of the workshop, which has run without interruption at ARES since 2007. This year, WSDF had 16 submissions, of which 8 were accepted for presentation at the workshop and included in the proceedings, leading to an acceptance rate of 50%. The technical program committee included 19 researchers from 11 different countries and the review process involved 14 additional experts who acted as sub-reviewers. In line with the main conference guidelines, the peer-review process was double-blinded, with every paper undergoing three reviews and, where required, a short deliberation between reviewers to support the final decision.

The best paper award for WSDF 2025 was sponsored by the Institute of Cyber Security for Society (iCSS), University of Kent, UK.

August 2025

Kim-Kwang Raymond Choo
Virginia N. L. Franqueira
Andrew Marrington
Richard Overill
Martin Steinebach

WSDF 2025 Organization

Workshop Chairs

Kim-Kwang Raymond Choo	University of Texas at San Antonio, USA
Virginia N. L. Franqueira	University of Kent, UK
Andrew Marrington	Zayed University, UAE
Richard Overill	King's College London, UK
Martin Steinebach	Fraunhofer Institute SIT|ATHENE, Germany

Program Committee

Frank Breitinger	University of Augsburg, Germany
Ching Bon Raymond Chan	Singapore Institute of Technology, Singapore
Kam-Pui Chow	University of Hong Kong, China
Sarah De'Ath	De Montfort University, UK
Patricio Domingues	Polytechnic Institute of Leiria, Portugal
Weihan Goh	Singapore Institute of Technology, Singapore
George Grispos	University of Nebraska, USA
Chris Hargreaves	HARGS Solutions Ltd., UK
Katerina Kanta	University of Portsmouth, UK
Erisa Karafili	University of Southampton, UK
Áine MacDermott	Liverpool John Moores University, UK
Chiara Pero	University of Salerno, Italy
Mark Scanlon	University College Dublin, Ireland
Stavros Shiaeles	University of Portsmouth, UK
Hudan Studiawan	Institut Teknologi Sepuluh Nopember, Indonesia
Nina Sunde	Norwegian Police University College, Norway
Harm van Beek	Netherlands Forensic Institute, The Netherlands
Jeroen van den Bos	Infix Technologies, The Netherlands
Vincent van der Meer	Zuyd University, The Netherlands

Additional Reviewers

Marc Leon Agel
Hamda Al Breiki
Jeong-Eun Choi
Yasamin Fayyaz
Nicola Galante
Farkhund Iqbal
Richard Adeyemi Ikuesan
Aaron Jarrett
Jimmy McGibney
Lutta Pantaleon
K. Prabhu Rajasekar
Paige Tynan
Alexandros Vasilaras
Klara Weiand

Forensic Insights into Windows 11's Capability Access Manager Artifacts

Patricio Domingues[1,2]((⊠)) , Miguel Frade[1,3] , and Miguel Negrão[1,3]

[1] School of Technology and Management, Polytechnic Institute of Leiria, Leiria, Portugal
{miguel.frade,miguel.negrao,
patricio.domingues}@ipleiria.pt
[2] Instituto de Telecomunicações, Leiria, Portugal
[3] Computer Science and Communication Research Centre, Leiria, Portugal
https://www.ipleiria.pt

Abstract. This paper presents a digital forensic methodology for investigating application access to sensitive hardware resources through Windows 11's Capability Access Manager (CAM) service. The CAM maintains detailed logs of requests and accesses by applications to devices and services such as microphones, cameras, and locations, as well as operations such as screen capture and contacts access. Data kept by CAM can provide timeline information to investigators in privacy-related cases. We analyze the structure, location, and evidentiary value of CAM artifacts in Windows 11 23H2 and 24H2 versions, documenting registry keys and database entries that record hardware access permissions, timestamps, and identifiers for accounts, namely secure identifiers (SIDs), and applications. Our research demonstrates how these artifacts can establish application behavior patterns and provide an additional path to detect the execution of applications and their access to privacy-sensitive devices and services. Additionally, we introduce WLEAPP-CAM, a module for the WLEAPP (Windows Logs Events And Properties Parser) forensic software. This module streamlines the examination of the CAM SQLite 3 database, enabling investigators to filter, interpret, and export the most pertinent evidence. Tests performed on Windows 11 versions 23H2 and 24H2 confirm the reliability of CAM artifacts for forensic purposes, although with some limitations due to the 30-day retention window and the restriction to applications that effectively request access to CAM managed resources and services.

Keywords: Digital forensics · Windows 11 · Capability Access Manager · SQLite 3

1 Introduction

The COVID-19 pandemic led to an increased and normalized use of video conferencing applications like ZOOM and Microsoft TEAMS, which resulted in a heightened demand for computers and devices with video conferencing capabilities [1]. Currently, practically all laptops on the market come equipped with built-in microphones and webcams, making them suitable for video conference usage. Even desktop systems without native video-conferencing features can be easily upgraded with affordable external USB webcams that provide both audio and video functionalities. The proliferation of devices with microphones and cameras coupled with the increasing sophistication of privacy-invasive software, has elevated concerns about unauthorized surveillance. Microsoft's Windows 11 operating system implements the Capability Access Manager (CAM) as a central mechanism for controlling and logging application access to sensitive resources, such as microphone, camera and screen capture, as well as to some user's private data such as contacts and location. In fact, CAM exists to prevent applications from accessing sensitive resources and services without explicit knowledge and consent of the user.

The CAM system is both a privacy tool for users and a possible source of digital evidence for forensic investigators. Indeed, some digital forensic examinations can benefit from establishing the timeline of device access such as microphone, webcam, and location access. Examples include corporate espionage investigations, cases of suspicious partner surveillance [10], and analysis of Remote Access Trojans (RAT) attacks [6].

In the Windows operating system, forensic investigations often rely on application-specific logs, timestamps of files, and system event records such as Prefetch [13] and Amcache [12] to reconstruct such activity. The centralized nature of Windows 11 CAM offers an alternative path, providing records of some hardware and services access across all applications. CAM data can be useful to complement other forensic artifacts, or when dealing with cases implicating privacy-sensitive devices, such as microphone and webcam access. Additionally, as it is account-oriented, that is, capability operations are linked to the user's account that ran the requesting software, CAM's forensic artifacts can help to pinpoint the account involved, thus complementing other digital forensic sources.

1.1 Motivation and Goals

This work was inspired by the excellent four-part study published on the Medium platform by the user *Cyber Sundae DFIR*, which documents the working and the main digital forensic artifacts of CAM for Windows 11, versions 22H2 and 23H2 [4]. The aim of this paper is not only to confirm the findings presented in those posts for version 23H2, but also to extend the study to version 24H2 of Windows 11, noting that version 24H2 introduced significant changes to the CAM service. Furthermore, a software tool named WLEAPP-CAM, developed as a module of WLEAPP [3] (Windows Logs Events And Properties Parser), was built with the intention of facilitating the parsing, analysis, and presentation of the main forensic artifacts associated with the CAM service in Windows 11, supporting both versions 23H2 and 24H2. The module includes capabilities for filtering, listing, and exporting CAM-related data.

1.2 Contributions

The main contributions of this work include: i) Examination of the digital forensic artifacts associated with the CAM service, which validates the comprehensive findings reported by Medium's post [4] for Windows 23H2, while also broadening the scope to encompass Windows 24H2; ii) Development of a module for the Windows Logs Events And Protobuf Parser (WLEAPP) able to process the main data from the CAM service, thus easing access to the CAM digital forensic artifacts. The software is open-source and available at https://github.com/PatricioDomingues/WLEAPPCAM.

The remainder of this paper is structured as follows: Sect. 2 explores work related to this study; Sect. 3 presents a discussion on the CAM service of Windows 11. Section 4 details both the materials used and the methodology employed in this research. In Sect. 5, an analysis on the forensic significance of the CAM SQlite3 database is conducted. Section 6 elaborates on the WLEAPP-CAM forensics software module and presents several results. The study is then analyzed in Sect. 7. Finally, Sect. 8 concludes the paper.

2 Related Work

To the best of our knowledge, the sole study of Windows 11 Capability Access Manager is available on the Medium platform, through the @cyber.sundae.dfir account [4]. This well done 4-part study covers with some details both the behavior of the CAM service, as well the available digital forensic artifacts, for the version 22H2 and 23H2 of Windows 11. Our work confirms the findings published by @cyber.sundae.dfir, and extends the knowledge to the 24H2 version of Windows 11, highlighting the novelties of the CapabilityAccessManager.db SQLite 3 database, namely the addition of four new tables, as well as other minor changes.

The use of a SQLite 3 database by the CAM service aligns with a broader trend within the Windows OS ecosystem, where several built-in services and Microsoft applications have adopted SQLite 3 databases for data storage. For instance, Windows services like the Windows 10 Timeline [8], Windows Push Notification service [5], and Windows Search Indexer, which switched from the Extended Storage Engine (ESE) in Windows 10 to SQLite 3 in Windows 11 [11], exemplify this shift. Additionally, Microsoft applications such as Phone Link (formerly Windows Phone), Microsoft Photos [9], and Microsoft Package Manager are among those utilizing SQLite 3.

3 The Capability Access Manager Service

We now describe the main components of Windows 11's Capability Access Manager service (CAM). We begin with a concise overview of the service, then review the graphical interface that exposes a subset of the CAM functions to the users, and briefly examine the concept of capability within the CAM domain. We then focus on the underlying components (binaries and registry keys) that support the service. Due to its relevance for digital forensics, the SQLite 3 `capabilities.db` and associated files are reviewed in a section of their own.

3.1 Background

Since Windows 10, management of access permissions to a wide range of device capabilities and system resources is performed by the Capability Access Manager Service (`camsvc`). In the Windows service interface, `camsvc` is described as follows: *Provides facilities for managing UWP apps access to app capabilities as well as checking an app's access to specific app capabilities*. This description focuses on Universal Windows Platform (UWP) applications, referring to Windows applications designed to operate on various devices, including PCs, tablets, and Xbox, under stringent access restrictions, utilizing a unified code base and an adaptable user interface. In fact, `camsvc` manages access permissions for both UWP and non-UWP applications, although as we shall see later, it does differentiate between the two types of applications as it process and logs data separately for both types of applications, naming UWP applications as *Packaged* and non-UWP, also designated as desktop applications, as *NonPackaged*. UWP applications are subject to meticulous regulation, necessitating that they explicitly specify in their manifest file (`AppXManifest.xml`) any intended access to resources and services such as webcams, microphones, location data, and screen capture. Conversely, Windows oversees non-UWP or desktop applications with a comprehensive control method, where the CAM service administers them as a whole: permissions for a specific capability are universally applied to all non-UWP applications. Thus, capabilities such as location, camera, and others are configured for the entire collection of such applications.

3.2 Graphical User Interface

In Windows 11, users have significant control over application permissions via the `Privacy&Security` section within the `Settings` application. This user interface is partially shown in Fig. 1a . CAM is the underlying service powering the permission functionality.

The interface is organized by so-called *capabilities*, and allows users to view and modify permissions for various capabilities on a per-app basis for UWP applications. For example, the user interface (UI) to control camera access is partially shown in Fig. 1b. The interface lists the UWP applications that might require camera access, identified as apps, allowing the user to allow/negate access per application to the camera. In the UI, non-UWP applications, are listed after the UWP ones (bottom of Fig. 1b) and can only controlled as a whole: either all are allowed to access the camera, or none. The user interface of Windows 11 CAM showcases 25 capabilities. However, in our study, we only found entries for the following five capabilities: contacts, location, microphone, webcam, and *graphicsCaptureWithoutBorder*, with the latter referring to capturing screenshots.

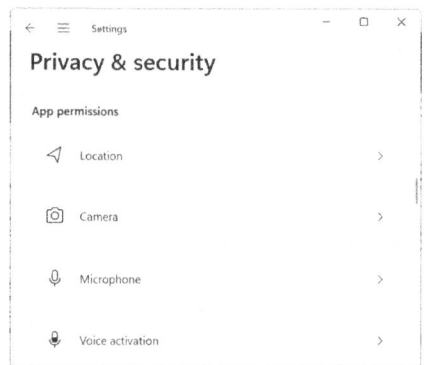 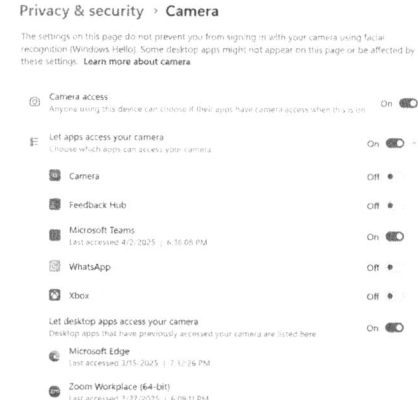

(a) Partial view of the user interface to access some CAM service functions

(b) View of the camera access permissions user interface

Fig. 1. Partial views of Windows 11's CAM service user interface.

3.3 Executable and Dynamic Link Library Files

The `camsvc` service is hosted, as many other Windows services, by the `svchost.exe` binary (`C:\Windows\System32\svchost.exe`). It is run with the `-k osprivacy -p` command line parameters, while its main functions are in the `CapabilityAccessManager.dll` DLL, which is located in `C:\Windows\System32\`. Another DLL, `CapabilityAccess Managerclient.dll`, exposes the Capability Access Manager API, and it is used by applications to interact with the capability access manager. This DLL also implements the prompt mechanism that is triggered the first time that an application requests a certain capability.

4 Materials and Methods

This research involved the use of two 64-bit Windows 11 x86_64 personal computers. The first was operating on version 23H2 with build 22631.5819, while the second was utilizing version 24H2, build 26100.3775. The main software applications employed in this study are provided in Table 1. The `AmCacheParser.exe` utility by Eric Zimmerman was utilized to interpret the data from Windows' `AmCache` for comparison against entries in the CAM service database. To detect the DLLs linked to the CAM service we resorted to Sysinternals' command line tools `handle.exe`, and `strings.exe` to examine the strings in these DLLs.

Both computers were utilized for regular routine operations. Additionally, a variety of applications, encompassing both UWP and conventional desktop apps (denoted as *non-packaged* in the CAM service context), were used to request essential functionalities – *location, microphone, webcam, graphicsCaptureWithoutBorder* – from the CAM service and to assess their effect on its data structures. Examples of these applications are browsers like Brave, Edge, and Firefox;

Table 1. Software tools used in the study

Name	Version	Name	Version
Eric Zimmerman's AmCacheParser.exe	1.5.1.10	Python	3.9.13
DB Browser for SQLite	3.12.2	Strings.exe (SysInternals)	2.5.4
Handle (SysInternals)	5.0	Eric Zimmerman's RegistryExplorer.exe	2.0.0

videoconferencing tools such as Microsoft Teams and Zoom; and multimedia utilities like Microsoft's Snipping Tools, OBS Studio, and the portable version of Audacity. We also utilized certain features within Microsoft Office that necessitate the use of specific capabilities: Word's *dictate* for microphone activation, and PowerPoint's *cameo* for initiating webcam use. Moreover, we crafted various Python scripts to access the webcam, microphone, and location services, thereby prompting requests for these functionalities.

4.1 Registry

As many other Windows services and applications, the CAM service interacts with the Windows Registry to save system and user-controlled configurations such as the allowed/denied state per capability/application, as well as logging the date/time of the last request of any registered applications to a managed capability.

In the Registry, CAM-related data are kept within the user's hive, and therefore are physically stored in the `NTUSER.DAT` file, which is located in the user's directory. This registry hive is mapped to `\HKEY\_USERS\SID` , where SID (Secure ID) is the user's numerical identifier within Windows. When the user is logged in, this registry hive is linked to the `\HKEY\_CURRENT\_USER` key, which often shortened to `HCKU`.

A set of keys related to CAM are kept in the registry path: `$\backslash$HKEY\USERS\SID\Software\Microsoft\Windows\CurrentVersion \CapabilityAccessManager \ConsentStore` . This registry path holds one subkey named after capabilities (e.g., *location*, *microphone*). Each of this subkeys contain values listing the AppIDs or PackageFamilyNames (PFNs) of applications granted consent. Figure 2 shows the *microphone* key and its subkeys. There is one subkey per UWP applications whose manifest file requests microphone access. The highlighted subkey `MSTeams\_8wekyb3d8bbwe` corresponds to the Microsoft Teams application, whose relevant pairs key/value are `LastUsedTimeStart`, `LastUsedTimeStop`, and `Value`. The first two hold, in Microsoft Filetime64 format, the last times usage of microphone was started and ended, respectively. An additional entry, referred to as *value*, can contain one of three possible strings: "Prompt", "Allow", or "Deny". In "Prompt" mode, an application's request to access the capability triggers a user authorization prompt. Meanwhile, "Allow" automatically permits access to the requested resource without requiring user confirmation. On the other hand, "Deny" prevents access to the resource in question.

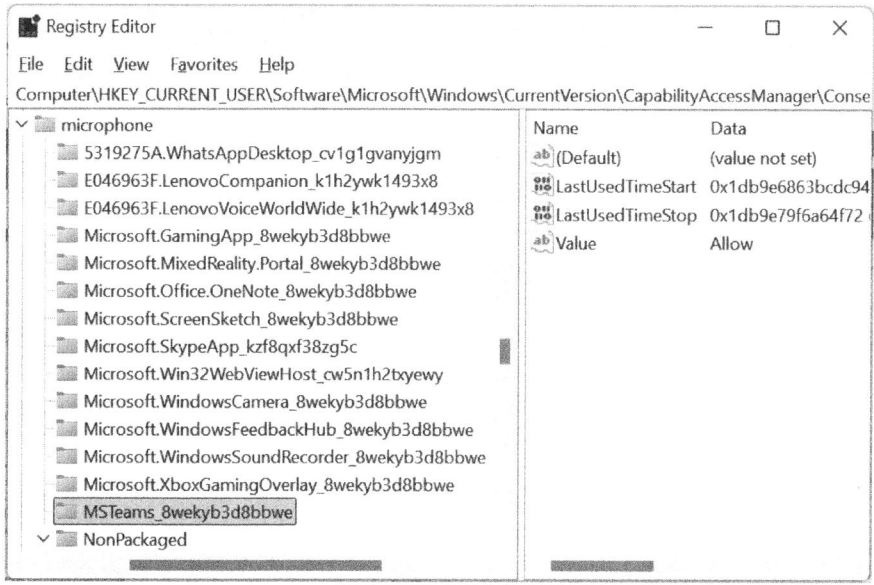

Fig. 2. Partial view of the registry Key CapabilityAccessManager/ConsentStore.

Figure 3 displays the same registry path of Fig. 2, but focuses on so-called *non-packaged* applications, that is, desktop applications. Similar to Registry entries for UWP applications, data for each non-packaged applications include the *LastUsedTimeStart*, *LastUsedTimeStop*, and *value*, as can be seen for the Microsoft Edge application. Figure 3 also shows an entry for Microsoft Teams corresponding to the so-called *Classic Teams* version of the application. In contrast to non-UWP applications, capability permissions for UWP applications can be tailored specifically for each application. Non-UWP applications, on the other hand, have a unified approach where the same permission – either deny, prompt, or allow – applies to all of them collectively.

Registry Update. In the Windows 11–24H2 update (build 26100.3775), released with Microsoft's April 2025 patch, we noted the addition of three new fields to the registry keys associated with application capability management. These fields consist of: *i*) LastSetTime, *ii*) PersistedInDatabase, and *iii*) LastUserAnnotatedLabel. LastSetTime is a 64-bit filetime timestamp that records when the current permission was assigned as "allow", "prompt", or "deny". The PersistedInDatabase takes the value 1 to signify that an access request has been recorded in the CapabilityAccessManager.db database, and 0 if not. Lastly, we were unable to decipher the LastUserAnnotatedLabel, which consistently held the value 2 in our observations. These modifications to the registry data serves as further proof of transformations in evolving digital environments that impact forensic artifacts, as observed by Spichiger et al. [14].

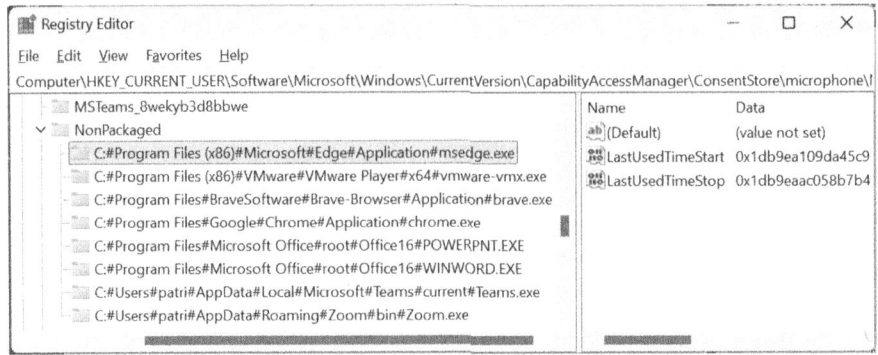

Fig. 3. Registry view of microphone entry focusing on non-packaged applications.

Note that while useful for determining the current allowed/denied state, CAM's registry keys generally lack historical access data, as they only keep the last usage timestamps. Moreover, under Windows 10, CAM service main digital forensics artifacts are restricted to the Registry, while in Windows 11, besides the Registry, CAM also maintains a SQLite 3 database with access requests from the last 30 days.

5 The CapabilityAccessManager.db Database

We proceed to discuss Windows 11's `CapabilityAccessManager.db` database, wherein the CAM service records its data. Initially, we provide an overview of the database. Following this, we explore the specifics of the database as it appears in Windows 11 $23H2$ and subsequently in the $24H2$ version. This differentiation is necessary because the $24H2$ version introduces four additional tables compared to version $23H2$.

5.1 Overview

The initial versions of the CAM service, present in Windows 10, mainly recorded user consent details in the Windows Registry. Although Windows 11 continues to keep some CAM data in the registry, it also employs a dedicated SQLite 3 database, with its main file called `capabilityAccessManager.db`, complemented by a write-ahead log file (WAL). This database retains comprehensive historical access logs for up to 30 days.

The `CapabilityAccessManager.db` database is located in the directory `where the environment variable typically corresponds to` `C:\ProgramData`. Configured with Write Ahead Log (WAL) journaling, the folder not only contains the primary database file but also includes the WAL file `CapabilityAccessManager.db-wal` and the Shared Memory (SHM) file `CapabilityAccessManager.db-shm`.

Next, we offer a detailed examination of the `CapabilityAccessManager.db` database tailored for Windows 11 23H2. Afterward, we focus on the updates integrated into the CAM version released with Windows 24H2. It is important to note that the mp `CapabilityAccessManager.db` database logs timestamps in Universal Time Coordinated (UTC), recorded in the Filetime 64 format.

5.2 Windows 11 Version 23H2

As previously noted, CAM differentiates between UWP and non-UWP applications, maintaining stricter oversight on UWP applications. This differentiation is apparent in the `CapabilityAccessManager.db` database, where UWP applications are labeled as packaged and non-UWP applications as non-packaged. This distinction is mirrored in the database, with some tables dealing with packaged applications, and others with non-packaged ones.

In Windows 11/23H2, the database comprises nine tables. Table 2 enumerates the tables for both versions 23H2 and 24H2, highlighting the significance of each table for both packaged and non-packaged applications.

Table 2. Tables of for W11-23H2 and W11-24H2. The center column classifies whether the table is related to Packaged, NonPackaged, or both types of applications. Tables marked with (*) were empty.

Table Name	Packaged / Non-Packaged	W11-23H2 W11-24H2
BinaryFullPaths	Packaged	Both
Capabilities	Both	Both
FileIDs	NonPackaged	Both
NonPackagedIdentityRelationship	NonPackaged	Both
NonPackagedUsageHistory	NonPackaged	Both
PackagedUsageHistory	Packaged	Both
PackageFamilyNames	Packaged	Both
cre ProgramIDs	NonPackaged	Both
Users	Both	Both
AccessGUIDs (*)	Both	24H2
AppNames	Both	24H2
NonPackagedGlobalHistory (*)	NonPackaged	24H2
ServiceNames (*)	Both	24H2

Data-wise, there are three relevant tables that hold the main CAM data. They are `NonPackagedUsageHistory` and `NonPackagedIdentityRelationship` for non-UWP applications, and `PackagedUsageHistory` for UWP ones.

The other six tables simply contain referenced data, which are referenced by the three main tables through foreign keys. For example, the

Capabilities table has two fields: an numeric field ID, which acts as the primary key, and a string field called StringValue holding a capability name, such as microphone, or webcam. Then, both tables PackagedUsageHistory and NonPackagedUsageHistory have a field named Capability that holds the numeric ID of the respective capability string. For example, an entry in PackagedUsageHistory with the Capability field equal to nine refers to the webcam capability. In fact, all six reference tables have the same two fields: the numeric ID and the string StringValue.

Packaged Applications. Table 3 presents the columns of the PackagedUsageHistory table. As discussed previously, this table consolidates the core information regarding the capability access for UWP applications. When an application's access to a capability is denied, indicated by a value of 1 in the AccessBlocked field, the LastUsedTimeStart timestamp is set to zero, while the LastUsedTimeStop field captures the timestamp of the access attempt. On the other hand, when access is granted, LastUsedTimeStart logs the commencement time of the access, while LastUsedTimeStop captures the completion time.

The UWP application is identified by the PackageFamilyName field, which holds, as the name implies, the Package Family Name (PFN). This identification is indirect, as the field is a foreign key related to the PackageFamilyNames. An example of a *family name* is MSTeams_8wekyb3d8bbwe , which refers to Microsoft Teams, with the suffix 8wekyb3d8bbwe identifying Microsoft as the publisher of the application.

The field UserSid refers, through the Users table, to the Security Identifier (SID) of the account under which the application was running when the capability access was requested. This allows for the explicit attribution of the application execution to a specific account, an important property for a digital forensic artifact. Moreover, the pair LastUsedTimeStart/SID can further be used to attribute account identification to other digital forensics that do not record the account SID, and which occurs in a timeframe compatible with events recorded in the CapabilityAccessManager.db database. This is the case for the Windows Prefetch artifact, which records the last eight execution timestamps of any applications but does not provide any mean to identify the user account. As it will be elaborated upon later, the SID is also incorporated in records for non-packaged applications, thus broadening the opportunities for timestamp/SID usage.

Non-packaged Applications. Table NonPackagedUsageHistory has nine fields, as shown in Table 4. It follows a model similar to the PackagedUsageHistory table. Indeed, it has some fields with the same name and function that the ones found in PackagedUsageHistory table. These include the timestamps fields LastUsedTimeStart and LastUsedTimeStop, which behave as described earlier in Sect. 5.2: LastUsedTimeStart is zero whenever an access attempt is blocked.

Table 3. Fields of the `PackagedUsageHistory` table (PK: Primary Key; FK: Foreign Key)

Field	Description
ID	Automatic integer (PK)
LastUsedTimeStart	Timestamp when last access to capability started
LastUsedTimeStop	Timestamp when last access to capability ended
AccessBlocked	0 = access granted; 1 = access blocked
Capability	Capability (FK from Capabilities table)
PackageFamilyName	UWP family name (FK from PackageFamilyNames table)
UserSid	SecureID of user (FK from Users table)

As indicated by its name, the `BinaryFullPath` field specifies the complete path of the binary file and serves as a foreign key in the table `BinaryFullPaths`. For instance, `C:\Program Files (x86)\Microsoft \Edge\Application\msedge.exe` is associated with the Microsoft Edge browser. Additionally, two fields, `FileID` and `ProgramID`, pertain to the application file, with both functioning as foreign keys that connect to the field `StringValue` in the tables `FileIDs` and `ProgramIDs`, respectively. Moreover, as highlighted in the detailed study of the CAM service and database by Medium's user *Cyber Sundae* [4], these two fields linked with `StringValue` match two other fields in the AmCache, a well-known source of digital artifacts on Windows [12,15]. Specifically, the `ProgramIDs:StringValue` field is equal to the `ProgramID` field of the AmCache, while `FileIDs:StringValue` corresponds to the 160-bit SHA1 hash of the binary program prefixed with two null bytes. Note that the `ProgramIDs:StringValue` is 22-byte long, with the first two bytes being 0x0000 for programs that are labeled as OS components, and with the pair 0x0006 otherwise.

Table 4. Fields of the `NonPackagedUsageHistory` table

Field	Description
ID	Automatic integer (PK)
LastUsedTimeStart	Timestamp when last access to capability started
LastUsedTimeStop	Timestamp when last access to capability ended
AccessBlocked	0 = access granted; 1 = access blocked
Capability	Capability (FK from Capabilities table)
FileID	File numeric identifier (FK from FileIDs table)
ProgramID	ProgramID (FK from ProgramIDs table)
BinaryFullPath	Full path of the binary file (FK from BinaryFullPaths table)
UserSid	SecureID of user (FK from Users table)

As studied by Medium user *Cyber Sundae* [4], and confirmed by our observations, the `NonPackagedIdentityRelationship` table, shown in Table 5, records the first occurrence of a non-UWP application using the CAM service, during the 30-day period the data is retained in the `CapabilityAccessManager.db` database. This initial interaction's timestamp is stored in the misleadingly named `LastObservedTime` field. Applications are identified via the foreign keys `BinaryFullPath`, `FileID`, and `ProgramID`. It is important to mention that an application may appear multiple times in this table, as each new version originates a new record. This scenario occurs with applications that update automatically, such as Microsoft Edge or Google Chrome.

Table 5. Fields of the `NonPackagedIdentityRelationship` table

Field	Description
ID	Automatic integer (PK)
LastObservedTime	Timestamp of the first capability request of the application (last 30 days)
BinaryFullPath	Full path of the application (FK from BinaryFullPaths table)
FileID	FileID (FK from FileIDs table)
ProgramID	ProgramID (FK from ProgramIDs table)

5.3 Windows 11 Version 24H2

In the 24H2 release of Windows 11, the `CapabilityAccessManager.db` database underwent updates, as shown in Table 2. The new version includes four additional tables, three of which are reference tables named `AccessGUIDs`, `AppNames`, and `ServiceNames`. Much like other already described tables, each reference table contains two fields: `Id` and `StringValue`. The `Id` field is used in the updated `PackagedUsageHistory` and `NonPackagedUsageHistory` tables. During our tests, we observed that only the `AppNames` table contained values, which represented the application names. Examples include `Dropbox`, `Adobe Acrobat 64`, and `Snipping Tool` to name just a few.

The designation of the fourth supplemental table, `NonPackagedGlobalPromptHistory`, and its essential fields–`Id`, `ShowTime` (timestamp), `Capability`, `FileID`, `ProgramID`, and `UserSid`–suggest that it is meant for logging user consent prompt interactions in non-UWP applications. Despite the experiments conducted, this table remained without any collected data. Upon examining the strings within Windows's `CapabilityAccessManager.dll`, we found SQL commands related to creating and removing entries from this particular table. We suggest that this table is currently under development and might become operational in an upcoming Windows update.

6 The WLEAPP-CAM Forensics Module

We now describe our software contribution: the *WLEAPP Capability Access Manager* software module, henceforth WLEAPP-CAM. As WLEAPP-CAM is built as a module of WLEAPP, we first overview the LEAPP ecosystem, and then describe WLEAPP-CAM.

6.1 The LEAPP Ecosystem

WLEAPP-CAM is a module for the WLEAPP software [2]. WLEAPP is integrated within the LEAPP ecosystem [3], which is a collection of Python and Javascript-driven open-source initiatives led by Alexis Brignoni, designed to parse and extract digital forensic artifacts. Each LEAPP initiative is designed for a specific platform, offering software parsers capable of extracting and analyzing particular types of digital forensic artifacts. Specifically, the LEAPP ecosystem comprises several specialized tools: ALEAPP for Android, iLEAPP for iOS, VLEAPP for vehicles, RLEAPP for cloud-based archives of services, and WLEAPP, which focuses on forensic artifacts related to Windows OS. The LEAPP projects provide their functions through distinct modules, each operating as a script designed to handle a particular category of artifacts. For instance, in WLEAPP, the `dropbox.py` module is responsible for processing Dropbox artifacts on Windows, while the `windowsNotification.py` module evaluates the Windows Notifications database, `wpndatabase.db` .

As with other LEAPP projects, WLEAPP does not support direct processing of forensic images. Instead, it traverses through input files provided by the forensic analyst, which may have been extracted from a Windows forensic image. These files can be input as an archive, with WLEAPP supporting TAR, ZIP, and GZIP formats, or as an uncompressed directory tree. Each module in WLEAPP is a Python script that is called by the main WLEAPP code and is given a list of paths to all files in the input data. The module then examines the files relevant to its purpose, extracting the digital forensic artifacts.

As with other LEAPP projects, results are presented through reports. These reports are basic HTML files that display forensic artifacts extracted by the module in a table format. A central HTML file serves as an index for all reports and functions as the main entry point for the module's output. LEAPP projects offer Python functions that handle the complexities of report creation, requiring the module to only supply the data in various input forms like lists or SQL queries. In addition to HTML reports, LEAPP projects also facilitate data export via Tab-Separated Values (TSV) files, making it easy to import forensic artifacts into other tools.

6.2 WLEAPP-CAM Usage

Due to the alteration in the open-source licensing terms of the graphical user interface (GUI) module PySimpleGUI[1], which WLEAPP utilizes for its GUI

---
[1] https://www.pysimplegui.com/.

input, we have decided to restrict input functionality to the command line. It is important to mention that graphical output remains unaffected as its solely relies on HTML and associated technologies, as well as, on Tab Separated Values (TSV) files.

Command Line Options. The primary script of WLEAPP, `wleapp.py`, is shared among all modules. To prevent interference with other modules, we added a new command line option to the existing set: `-m/--modules`. This option enables users to select the specific module(s) they want to apply to the digital forensic input data. To execute a module, including the `capabilityAccessManager` module, users need the following options: i) `-t` to define the input type, which can be `fs` (file system), `tar`, `zip`, or `gz` (gzip); ii) to designate the input path for the data to process; and iii) to specify the path where the results, such as HTML reports and TSV files, will be saved.

Listing 1.1 demonstrates how to execute WLEAPP's CAM module from a specific file system path, using a ZIP archive as input. The file `IN.zip IN.zip` refers to a ZIP archive comprising a directory structure. Within this framework, a directory titled `CapabilityAccessManager` must be present and should include the file `CapabilityAccessManager.db`. As an example, `IN.zip` may either be a complete ZIP archive of the entire Windows drive intended for analysis (e.g., `C:\`) or merely contain the `CapabilityAccessManager` directory along with its contents. Finally, `OUT` indicates the target directory where the created files are stored, including HTML reports and TSV files.

Listing 1.1. Executing the CAM module from the command line
```
wleapp.py -t zip -i IN.zip -o OUT -m WindowsCapability
```

In addition to the command-line parameters, WLEAPP-CAM can be configured using a JSON file named `wleap-capabilityAccess.json`. This configuration file enables users to set three primary options: i) Optionally defining a date range for filtering the CAM database, using `start\_date` and `end\_date` fields; ii) Utilizing the `order\_by\_date` option for sorting results by date; iii) Applying the `merge\_WAL\_file\_to\_DB` option to manage the incorporation of the Write Ahead Log (WAL) file into the main SQLite 3 database. It is important to highlight that, by default, WLEAPP-CAM accesses the `CapabilityAccessManager.db` database in read-only mode. Furthermore, there are additional JSON options meant for debugging. For example, the \texttt{debug.show_SQL} option can be activated to reveal the SQL queries employed for generating HTML reports during the tool's operation.

Reports. WLEAPP-CAM produces up to seven HTML reports, each one focusing on a specific aspect of the CAM database. The reports are accessible through the left menu of the `index.html` file, as shown in Fig. 4.

For easier reference, each report's name starts with a capital letter, ranging from A to G. The reports are succinctly described in Table 6. Note that the

Fig. 4. WLEAPP-CAM main window (cropped due to space constraints).

E_CAM_CountPerApps E_CAM_CountPerApps and E_CAM_CountPerApps G_IDs_in_amcache reports have no forensic value. Indeed, the E report displays the number of records per capability, while the G report shows the matches between the FileID field of the NonPackagedIdentityRelationship table and the FileID that exists in Windows' AmCache, allowing to verify the correspondence between both FileIDs. The G report is only produced if the option amcache.csv_filename of the JSON configuration file is set to a CSV file of the AmCache. This CSV file needs to correspond to the *_UnassociatedFileEntries.csv file created by Eric Zimmerman's AmCacheParser forensic tool [7].

Figure 5 shows a partial view of a D_CAM_AllApps report. This report comprises the capability requests of both packaged and non-packaged applications, as can be seen in the figure: while Microsoft Edge is a non-packaged application, StartExperiences, which is the start menu, is a packaged application. Note, as visible at the top of Fig. 5, the data range of the report was set to [2025.04.15, 2025.05.03].

D_CAM_AllApps report

Total number of entries: 1105 (Date(s) [2025-04-15,2025-05-03])
D_CAM_AllApps located at: C:\Temp\WLEAPP-main\R24H2\WLEAPP_Reports_2025-05-02_Friday_162713\temp\CapabilityAccessManager\CapabilityAccessManager.db

LastUsedTimeStop	Access	Capability	AppIdentifier	AppName
2025-04-19 01:24:37	Access OK	location	C:\Program Files (x86)\Microsoft\Edge\Application\msedge.exe	Microsoft Edge
2025-04-19 01:51:48	Access OK	location	Microsoft.StartExperiencesApp_8wekyb3d8bbwe	Start Experiences App

Fig. 5. WLEAPP-CAM D_CAM_AllApps report (cropped).

Table 6. HTML reports created by the WLEAPP-CAM

Report	Application Types	Description
A_CAM_PackagedApps	Packaged	List the capability access requests made by packaged apps
B_CAM_NonPackagedApps	NonPackaged	List the capability access requests made by non-packaged apps
C_CAM_NonPackagedId	NonPackaged	List the table NonPackagedIdentityRelationship
D_CAM_AllApps	All	List the capability access requests of both packaged and nonpackaged apps
E_CAM_CountPerApps	All	Count the number of records per capability
F_CAM_NonPackagedPrompt	NonPackaged	List the content of the NonPackagedGlobalPromptHistory table (not available for W11-23H2)
G_IDs_in_amcache	NonPackaged	List table NonPackagedIdentityRelationship whose FileID also exists in Windows' AmCache

7 Discussion

From a forensic perspective, the `CapabilityAccessManager` database is a potential source of digital forensic artifacts in Windows 11. It can provide a timeline of application usage, thereby complementing other detailed artifacts related to application execution, like the `Windows Prefetch` and `AppCompat` services (`ShimCache, AmCache`). An important property of CAM data, from a digital forensic perspective, is the fact that the database records are associated with a Secure Identifier, which unequivocally identifies an account. Additionally, CAM data can also be crucial in examining possible malicious software that attempts to access or target sensitive privacy resources, such as webcams, microphones, and the location on a Windows 11 computer.

CAM data also allows to study the behavior of applications regarding the usage of services and resources managed by CAM. For instance, in our experiments, we observed that the field `AppName` in CAM database entries related to the Microsoft Teams desktop application had three distinct descriptions: 1) *Microsoft Teams*; 2) *Microsoft Teams: Emergency calling (if available) and regional call compliance*; 3) *Microsoft Teams: Telemetry to improve call quality*. For example, in one instance of the CAM database spanning 30 days, in a machine where the location service was enabled for all applications, we surprisingly observed that the top number of requests for geographical location were from the Dropbox client (780 times), and Microsoft Teams (301 times). This might be associated with the requirement for these cloud-based services to choose the most appropriate servers.

Limitations. One significant limitation of CAM in digital forensics is its retention period, with data in the database being only available for 30 days. However, the CAM database is backed up by the Windows Volume Shadow Copy Service (VSS). Consequently, previous versions of the CAM database, with records older than 30 days may potentially be retrieved from VSS instances. An additional limitation is that the CAM database exclusively logs details of application execution when the application seeks to access a resource or service that is managed by CAM. Another issue is the logging of only the application binary, neglecting any command line parameters: This is critical for scripts run through `Python` or `PowerShell`, where solely the interpreter is logged as the binary. In fact, given `PowerShell`'s frequent use in malware [16], the absence of command line parameter data reduces the effectiveness of CAM records in such scenarios.

8 Conclusion

The Capability Access Manager is crucial in Windows as it manages privacy permissions. It ensures applications seek user consent before accessing sensitive data like location, camera, or contacts. Furthermore, it enables users to review and manage these permissions through the `Privacy&Security` section within the Windows Settings.

In Windows 11, the data storage for the CAM service was improved to include a SQLite 3 database, which can keep up to 30 days' worth of application permission request records. As a result, this database becomes an important repository for digital forensic artifacts, especially useful for gathering information like timestamps of permission requests made by active applications monitored by the CAM service. CAM's dataset can also assist in recognizing applications that aim to access pivotal devices and services such as webcams, microphones, screen capture, and location services, and whether these requests were consented or denied. Additionally, a crucial feature of CAM's database is the association of the access requests with the SID of the account operating the requesting application.

Our study confirms the findings of the in-depth analysis by *Cybser Sundae* [4], extending the knowledge to the 24H2 version of Windows 11. In this version, some relevant changes from the digital forensic perspective occurred within the SQLite 3 database of the CAM service, namely with the addition of four tables, although three of these table were consistently empty in our experiments. Our contribution also includes the WLEAPP-CAM software, a Python module for the WLEAPP forensic framework. The goal is to facilitate the parsing and analysis of the CAM database through the production of HTML-based reports, and data export in TSV format. As future work, we aim to continue to monitor the evolution of the CAM service and of its inner data, and to correspondingly adapt the WLEAPP-CAM software.

Acknowledgments. This work was supported by Fundação para a Ciência e a Tecnologia (FCT) and MCTES through national funds and when applicable co-funded by EU funds under projects UIDB/EEA/50008/2020 (DOI:10.54499/UIDB/50008/2020), LA/P/0109/2020 (DOI:10.54499/LA/P/0109/2020), and UIDB/04524/2020.

Disclosure of Interests. The authors have no competing interests to declare that are relevant to the content of this article.

References

1. Baraniuk, C.: No end to Covid-19 webcam shortage, July 2020, https://www.bbc.com/news/technology-53506401, Accessed 02 Apr 2025
2. Brignoni, A.: GitHub - abrignoni/WLEAPP: WLEAPP is an open source project that aims to parse Windows OS artifacts for the purpose of triage analysis (2023), https://github.com/abrignoni/WLEAPP, Accessed 26 Apr 2025
3. Brignoni, A.: Abrignoni (brigs) - github, Apr 2024, https://github.com/abrignoni, Accessed 26 Apr 2025
4. CyberSundae-DFIR: CapabilityAccessManager.db - Deep Dive, Part 1 (Medium Post), November 2024, https://medium.com/@cyber.sundae.dfir/capabilityaccessmanager-db-deep-dive-part-1-ff49f69c58af, Accessed 11 Apr 2025
5. Domingues, P., Andrade, L., Frade, M.: A digital forensic view of Windows 10 notifications. Forensic Sci. **2**(1), 88–106 (2022)
6. El-Metwaly, A.E.S., et al.: Remote access trojan (RAT) attack: a stealthy cyber threat posing severe security risks. In: 2024 International Telecommunications Conference (ITC-Egypt), pp. 1–5 (2024)
7. Eric, Z.: GitHub - EricZimmerman/AmcacheParser: Parses amcache.hve files, but with a twist!, January 2025, https://github.com/EricZimmerman/AmcacheParser, Accessed 02 May 2025
8. Horsman, G., Caithness, A., Katsavounidis, C.: A forensic exploration of the microsoft Windows 10 timeline. J. Forensic Sci. **64**(2), 577–586 (2019)
9. Jovanović, L., Adamović, S.: digital forensics artifacts of the microsoft photos application in Windows 10. In: Sinteza 2022 - International Scientific Conference on Information Technology and Data Related Research, pp. 427–434 (2022)
10. Karwayun, R., Sharma, P., Sainger, M., Joshi, N., Manna, S.: Role of spyware in the intelligent digital age: a comparative analysis. In: 2024 4th International Conference on Advancement in Electronics & Communication Engineering (AECE), pp. 1058–1066 (2024). https://doi.org/10.1109/AECE62803.2024.10911775
11. Labs, A.C.: Windows search index: the forensic artifact you've been searching for | Aon, https://www.aon.com/cyber-solutions/aon_cyber_labs/windows-search-index-the-forensic-artifact-youve-been-searching-for/, Accessed 04 May 2025
12. Singh, B., Singh, U.: Leveraging the Windows amcache.hve file in forensic investigations. J. Digit. Forensics Secur. Law **11**(4), 7 (2016)
13. Singh, B., Singh, U.: Program execution analysis in Windows: a study of data sources, their format and comparison of forensic capability. Comput. Secur. **74**, 94–114 (2018)
14. Spichiger, H., Adelstein, F.: Preserving meaning of evidence from evolving systems. Forensic Sci. Int. Digit. Invest. **52**, 301867 (2025), DFRWS EU 2025 - Selected Papers from the 12th DFRWS Europe
15. Tokarev, A., Tokareva, V.: Comparative analysis of Amcache trace formation mechanisms in Windows 10 and Windows 11. In: 2023 IEEE Ural-Siberian Conference on Biomedical Engineering, Radioelectronics and Information Technology (USBEREIT), pp. 289–292 (2023)
16. Tsai, M.H., Lin, C.C., He, Z.G., Yang, W.C., Lei, C.L.: PowerDP: de-obfuscating and profiling malicious PowerShell commands with multi-label classifiers. IEEE Access **11**, 256–270 (2022)

Reconstructing File Versions and Timestamps: Challenges and Guidelines in Network Forensics

Axel Mahr(✉), Jan-Niclas Hilgert, and Martin Lambertz

Fraunhofer FKIE, Zanderstr. 5, 53177 Bonn, Germany
axel.mahr@fkie.fraunhofer.de

Abstract. Extracting files from a network capture file sounds like an easy task solved by modern network analysis and forensic tools. Upon closer examination, however, it becomes evident that numerous highly relevant forensic aspects remain unaddressed or inadequately explored. The apparent lack of awareness regarding this issue is even more problematic. Our paper intends to address and close this gap.

We provide a systematic presentation of current challenges in extracting and reconstructing files from network traffic in the context of digital forensics, along with their causes. Moreover, we discuss solutions and guidelines to overcome these challenges. While some of our proposed approaches generally hold for all protocols, some are protocol-dependent. Hence, we use the SMB protocol as an example illustrating how several challenges can be addressed using protocol-inherent information. This discussion is accompanied by a ready-to-use implementation, which we incorporated into an open-source network forensic tool.

Our paper highlights current research and tooling gaps and provides directions to tackle them. Hence, we hope to spawn and foster new research in this area. Moreover, we are confident that our paper helps practitioners conduct network forensic analyses and provides important guidelines and considerations for analysts and investigators. Finally, our paper highlights facets that current commercial and open-source tools consider not sufficiently enough, hoping that they incorporate these aspects in future developments.

Keywords: network forensics · file extraction · challenges · metadata · timestamps · digital forensics

1 Introduction

Network forensics is a large area in digital forensics and incident response. The analyses carried out during investigations differ in the required data and techniques, depending on the use case and goals. For some tasks, metadata in the form of network flow information is sufficient [6]. However, there are use cases where it is crucial to know which data has been transmitted over the network [13].

The type and format of data transmitted as payload over a network is highly protocol-dependent. Hence, there is no universal way to extract and interpret the payload data. A suitable approach can be to first group network protocols into classes of the same functionality. For instance, there are protocols for chat messages, like XMPP and Tox, which implement the same high-level concepts in different technical ways. The same holds for high-level concepts, like video and audio streaming, which are implemented by protocols like RTP or RTSP.

Another high-level class is file transfer. Protocols like SMB or NFS allow users to access a shared file system of a remote system, and FTP and WebDAV allow users to copy files to and from a server. Finally, accessing a website using HTTP is also a transfer of several files from a server to a client.

This class is significant in digital forensics and incident response, as file transfers are involved in various typical investigation scenarios involving network communication. The download of illegal or malicious files plays a role in child sexual abuse cases as well as in cyberattacks. The upload of files to remote storage servers is a key component in data loss or espionage cases. Finally, being able to track which files have been transferred between systems helps draw conclusions about the activity on these systems.

This paper reconsiders a seemingly solved problem: extracting files transferred over the network. From a practical perspective, several tools already support this task. Among the most prominent are Wireshark[1] and NetworkMiner[2], which enable analysts to export files transferred via protocols such as SMB, HTTP, or FTP. In some situations, this is entirely sufficient and all we need. Consider the child sexual abuse material example from above. Finding such material in the network traffic of a computer system is sufficient to warrant further investigations. However, we argue that extracting files from network traffic scratches the surface only. In fact, we miss a vast amount of relevant forensic data and information if we stop there.

First, we disregard valuable information the network protocol might contain. This includes metadata about transferred files or entire files that are not present on the client or server system, such as dynamically generated content sent over HTTP. Moreover, even though some approaches support the parsing of metadata and the extraction of file contents, the combined analysis and correlation of these elements are often minimal. For instance, while extracted file names are frequently used for recovered files, other information such as file paths, timestamps, or permissions is generally disregarded. In addition, available timestamps may stem from different sources, requiring careful correlation to ensure accurate interpretation. Second, network traffic related to file transfers contains not only metadata about the transferred files but sometimes also about the communicating systems, like the accounts that initiated the transfers, providing more detailed insights during an analysis. Finally, there are simply protocols for which file extraction is not implemented in modern tools. Examples are the protocols distributed file systems use or peer-to-peer protocols.

---

[1] https://www.wireshark.org/.
[2] https://www.netresec.com/?page=NetworkMiner.

Our work provides a discussion of challenges that arise when we want to extract transferred files in a forensically sound manner. We discuss challenges in acquiring, extracting, interpreting, and presenting the relevant data. After that, we present various solutions and approaches to tackling the challenges. While some facets are protocol-dependent, we also identified fundamental aspects that are generally applicable. Notably, we examine and apply the concepts of *file versions* and *time dimensions* to network forensics.

In summary, our paper contributes to the area of digital forensics and incident response by

- highlighting overlooked challenges when reconstructing files from network captures,
- proposing general approaches to tackle these challenges based on different protocol examples,
- showing how *file versions* and *time dimensions* help addressing two of the most crucial challenges, and
- providing an implementation for the SMB protocol addressing the identified challenges

Our work does and can not solve all the challenges we identified. However, we provide important hints and guidelines for practitioners conducting investigations involving file transfers and vendors providing corresponding solutions. At the same time, we hope our work fosters further research in this area and provides guidelines for future tool development.

After summarizing related work in Sect. 2 and presenting our methodology in Sect. 3, we discuss the challenges we identified in Sect. 4. We continue with approaches to tackle the challenges in Sect. 5 before we conclude our paper in Sect. 6.

2 Related Work

In the academic literature, file reconstruction from network traffic has received relatively little attention. In 2017, Lee et al. [8] introduced an indexing architecture for extracting files from network traffic, focusing on challenges related to the large amounts of data typically encountered in network captures. FileTSAR [3], proposed in 2018, is a toolkit for file analysis and reconstruction from network traffic that supports protocols such as HTTP or FTP. Although it improves file extraction in a forensic context by incorporating cryptographic hashing, the authors do not examine any challenges or opportunities arising from network-based file extraction. Similarly, Netfox Detective [11] is an open-source network forensic analysis tool capable of extracting files transferred via various protocols. Although these tools facilitate and improve file extraction from network traffic, the authors do not discuss any intricacies of the extraction process in the context of digital forensics.

A more recent work [5] that highlights this gap examines the feasibility of reconstructing entire file systems from SMB network traffic. The authors argue that analyzing network traffic offers advantages compared to isolated file system analysis, including retrieving historical file versions, and emphasize the importance of correctly reconstructing metadata embedded in a protocol. However, they do not provide a general overview of challenges within this domain. For peer-to-peer file sharing networks, Liberatore et al. [9] conducted a forensic investigation focusing on Gnutella and BitTorrent, discussing forensic and legal issues. Although they detail how file downloads work in such protocols, they do not explore additional metadata that these protocols might carry. Regarding distributed file systems, Hilgert et al. [4] highlight forensic challenges but do not specifically address network traffic aspects. Other studies on distributed file systems, such as those targeting the Hadoop Distributed File System, center on persistent artifacts (e.g., logs) rather than network-related information [1].

A key component of possibly overlooked metadata in network protocols is timestamps. While the role of timestamps in network-based file reconstruction remains underexplored, the identification and correlation of timestamps is a longstanding research concern within digital forensics. Stevens [14] underlines the challenges that arise when merging data from multiple sources, stressing the importance of understanding different clock behaviors, time zones, and potential clock errors. Similarly, Weil [16] proposed correlating MAC file system timestamps with those contained in the files themselves to identify clock skews. Schatz et al. [12] investigated challenges in merging timestamps from diverse sources and introduced algorithms for correlating timestamps across web browsers and proxy records. Most recently, Vanini et al. [15] revisited timestamp interpretation, discussing concepts like anchors to address its inherent complexities.

In summary, current research on file extraction from network protocols reveals two major gaps. First, most existing approaches and tools focus solely on reconstructing file content, often overlooking valuable metadata such as timestamps. Moreover, the subsequent interpretation and correlation of extracted information are underexplored. Second, forensic analysis of certain network protocols themselves—especially those used in distributed file systems—is still limited.

3 Methodology

To provide a comprehensive overview of challenges, we systematically examined a range of scenarios involving network protocols that transmit file-system-related data and the entities involved in these communications. As a collective term, we henceforth use *file transmission protocols* to refer to network protocols designed to facilitate the transfer of files and their associated metadata between systems. This term includes traditional file-sharing protocols (e.g., SMB, NFS), file transfer protocols (e.g., FTP, SFTP), the network layers of distributed file systems (e.g., CephFS, HDFS), as well as protocols used to deliver dynamically generated or volatile files, such as HTTP and HTTP/2.

By analyzing multiple scenarios and reducing them to their essential elements, we derived a simplified yet generalized model, as illustrated in Fig. 1. In this model, network captures of file transmission protocols involve multiple components: the *network* as a communication medium, a *protocol* that governs the communication format, and three main entity types: *accessing entities*, *serving entities*, and *recording devices*. Accessing entities interact with serving entities over the network to request or transmit file content and metadata. In distributed file systems that span multiple servers, communication can also occur between serving entities. Potential intermediate components such as caches or proxies are conceptually grouped with the accessing or serving side. The third entity type, recording devices, captures this communication. Multiple recording devices may be deployed and positioned anywhere between or at the accessing and serving entities.

Notably, accessing and serving entities are not strictly bound to the roles of clients and servers, respectively. However, we refer to them as clients and servers for simplicity and readability throughout this work.

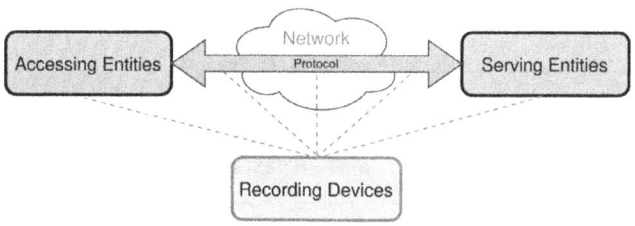

Fig. 1. Generalized scenario for file transmission protocols.

Given this generic model, different characteristics emerge, reflecting peculiarities in system configurations, network environments, and protocol behaviors. These characteristics directly give rise to specific challenges in reconstructing file content and metadata from network captures. Importantly, the challenges are not isolated: they often stem from multiple underlying characteristics, are interrelated, or may trigger additional challenges.

4 Characteristics and Challenges

Figure 2 provides an overview of the identified characteristics and their resulting challenges. The following sections are structured according to these characteristics.

4.1 Plurality of Entities

Several characteristics arise from the fact that multiple entities are involved. The characteristics are described in the following sections.

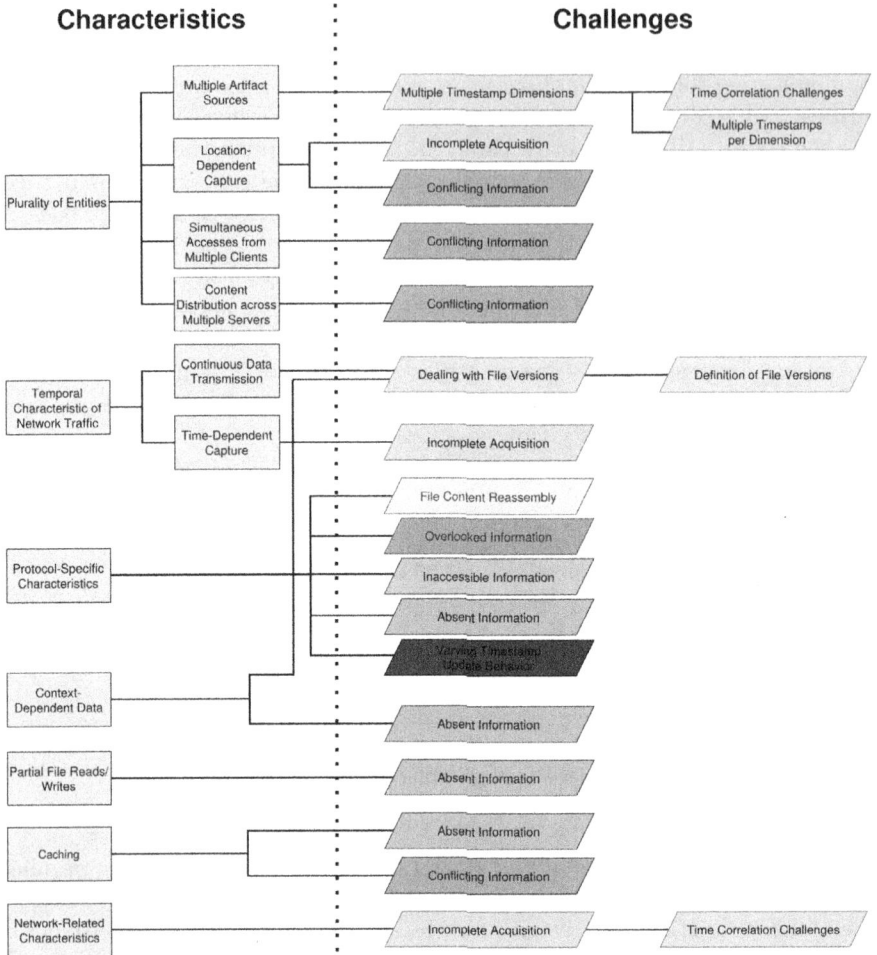

Fig. 2. Summary of challenges and their origins.

4.1.1 Multiple Artifact Sources

Since multiple entities participate in a network recording, the captured information originates from different sources, including clients, servers, and recording devices. This plurality of sources introduces inconsistencies and challenges for reconstruction.

A key aspect that can vary between entities and impacts reconstruction is timestamps. In general, each entity operates on its own time axis, predetermined by its internal system clock. Consequently, multiple time dimensions exist:

– *Network time*: The time axis of the recording device, where each recorded packet is assigned a timestamp.

– *Client-side time*: The time dimension of the client, which may also vary across clients in multi-client scenarios. Client-side time is reflected in *file system timestamps* as well as *protocol-internal timestamps*, either embedded in messages or implicitly used in the protocol's logic.
– *Server-side time*: The time dimension representing the server's view of file operations, which may also differ across servers in distributed systems. Analogous to client-side time, it manifests in file system timestamps and protocol-internal timestamps embedded or implied in network communication.

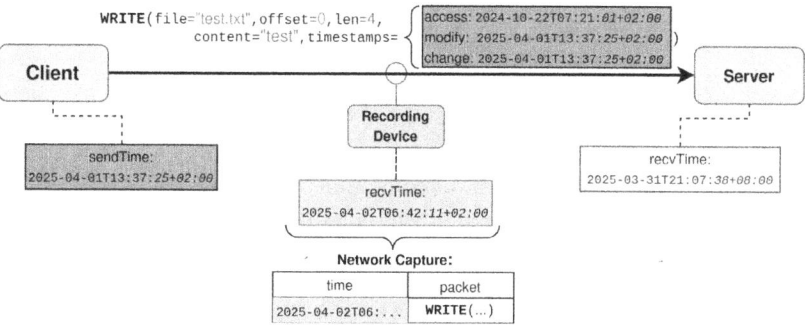

Fig. 3. Exemplary illustration of the different time dimensions. In this example, the time axes of all entities are misaligned.

To illustrate the problems arising from these multiple time dimensions, we consider a scenario in which a single client writes to a file, updating its timestamps, as depicted in Fig. 3. A single server receives this operation and must handle two sources of timestamps: the client-provided timestamps set in the protocol message (*file system time*, highlighted in blue), and its own internally generated timestamps, such as the moment it receives the packets (*server-internal time*, highlighted in gray). The recording device is positioned between client and server. The corresponding network capture thus records the file system timestamps contained in the message and the network timestamps of the transmitted packets (*network time*, colored green). As a result, three distinct time dimensions coexist and must be considered during analysis.

⟹ *Resulting Challenge: Multiple Timestamp Dimensions*

The analyst must decide which time dimension to use as a reference axis during reconstruction and how to align the underlying time dimensions. As the time dimensions of all entities involved in the network capture exist simultaneously and are potentially misaligned, this introduces further challenges. The broader issue of correlating time information across multiple artifact sources has been extensively studied in prior research [2,12,14,15]. However, these works do not specifically address a network-based perspective.

Differences in clock settings across clients, servers, and recording devices can lead to timestamp misalignment. As in the previous example, the network time(s) and the local times of the accessing and serving entities can be skewed. The time skews can vary between different entity pairs and may also fluctuate over time, making precise adjustments difficult. Based solely on the network capture, skews may either be not determinable at all or only inaccurately. Similarly, all entities may operate in different time zones, potentially leading to ambiguities in interpreting absolute timestamps.

$\Longrightarrow$ *Resulting Challenge:* Time Correlation Challenges

Moreover, a single file operation can generate multiple timestamps within the same time dimension. For example, a file write operation may span multiple network packets, each with its own network timestamp. Similarly, a file could be written to multiple destinations in a distributed environment with multiple servers, resulting in multiple, potentially divergent, server-side timestamps.

$\Longrightarrow$ *Resulting Challenge:* Multiple Timestamps per Dimension

4.1.2 Location-Dependent Capture

Traffic may not be captured from all communication sides. For example, if traffic is recorded solely from a single client, modifications made by other clients remain invisible unless they can be inferred indirectly. This incomplete acquisition entails missing information in the network capture that could be included with an improved recording strategy.

$\Longrightarrow$ *Resulting Challenge: Incomplete Acquisition*

Conversely, incomplete acquisition may also lead to conflicting information. For example, suppose that a file is marked as read-only, but a successful write operation is observed. In that case, the discrepancy may stem from an unrecorded event—such as a permission change—that occurred before the write. Without visibility into this intermediate step, the reconstruction process may yield misleading conclusions.

$\Longrightarrow$ *Resulting Challenge:* Conflicting Information

4.1.3 Simultaneous Accesses from Multiple Clients

Concurrent access by multiple clients to the same files increases reconstruction complexity. Related issues are closely intertwined with network-specific problems and protocol-specific behaviors described later.

Since clients may issue overlapping or conflicting operations, different protocols employ different conflict prevention and resolution strategies, manifesting differently in the network captures. For instance, file-sharing protocols like SMB use file leases and locks to manage concurrent access, whereas distributed file systems often resolve conflicts retrospectively using strategies like last-writer-wins. In scenarios involving conflicting writes, where different content for the same file is transmitted over the network, the file transmission protocol implementation may internally decide which content to actually apply. This decision may not be explicitly reflected in the network trace, making it difficult for the investigator to determine which version of the file ultimately prevailed.

The investigator's challenge is correctly interpreting the contradictory information in the network capture, discerning which content was actually committed

and distinguishing genuine operational conflicts from inconsistencies caused by location-dependent captures.
⟹ *Resulting Challenges:* Conflicting Information

4.1.4 Content Distribution Across Multiple Servers
Similar to scenarios involving multiple concurrently operating clients, additional challenges arise when files are distributed across multiple servers, particularly when network recording occurs on the side of serving entities.

For redundancy or performance, a file may be replicated across several servers. When such a file is modified, the servers hold different versions if synchronization is delayed or does not occur. Depending on the nature and timing of modifications, these versions may contradict each other. The resulting inconsistencies can be reflected directly in the captured network traffic.

During synchronization, conflicts may arise when merging divergent file states. These conflicts may not be directly observable in network traffic, making reconstructing the correct file version from captured data challenging.
⟹ *Resulting Challenge:* Conflicting Information

4.2 Temporal Characteristic of Network Traffic

In addition to challenges arising from the plurality of involved entities and location-dependent capture, network traffic captures possess a temporal dimension that gives rise to two characteristics, discussed in the following two subsections.

4.2.1 Continuous Data Transmission
Unlike traditional file systems, where a file usually exists in a single, current state, network captures allow multiple versions of the same file to be observed over time. As file operations are transmitted over the network, different captured packets may reflect distinct states of a file, including variations in content and metadata. This creates several challenges in defining, identifying, and reconstructing file versions from network traffic.

In general, multiple instances of the same file can emerge in network traffic due to various factors:

– *Repeated transfers:* The same file may be transferred multiple times between different entities, either without any changes or potentially with alterations in metadata or content.
– *Replication and synchronization:* File synchronization mechanisms, including those influenced by caching, can create different states across distributed nodes.
– *Transient data:* Some read/write transmissions may contain temporary data that actually never existed on disk, such as Remote Procedure Calls (RPCs) or dynamically generated content.

– *Simultaneous file operations:* Concurrent file operations from multiple clients can result in conflicting file versions being observed. Some of these may not have been committed in the final file state, but are still present in the network capture.

A core challenge in file reconstruction is determining what constitutes a distinct file version. The definition has significant implications for forensic analysis, affecting how versions are reconstructed and interpreted. In addition to defining file versions, caching mechanisms complicate version tracking, potentially leading to incorrect assumptions about the timeline and order of file versions.
$\Rightarrow$
Resulting Challenges: Dealing with File Versions , Definition of File Versions

4.2.2 Time-Dependent Capture

In addition to location-dependent capture, time-related gaps in the network capture pose challenges. The desired reconstruction point may fall outside the recording period, introducing significant uncertainty. As events occurring before or after the captured interval remain unknown, the amount of confident file information at the desired reconstruction point is severely limited because arbitrary modifications could have happened. Nevertheless, metadata such as timestamps can sometimes aid partial reconstruction, allowing analysts to determine whether a file existed at a given time or remained unchanged over a specific period.
$\Rightarrow$ *Resulting Challenge: Incomplete Acquisition*

4.3 Protocol-Specific Characteristics

File-sharing mechanisms are implemented using various protocols, each with distinct functionalities and different approaches to achieving the same operations. These protocols define how files are accessed, read, and written and how information is transmitted. However, this also involves further mechanisms—such as file replication, synchronization, caching, and management of simultaneous file accesses—which are mentioned in the other sections.

First, file transmission protocols implement file content transfer differently, with variations in chunking, ordering, and encoding. In distributed setups, a file may be split across multiple servers or include parity data, making it difficult to determine the role and order of each chunk. This creates challenges in correctly reassembling the file content.
$\Rightarrow$ *Resulting Challenge: File Content Reassembly*

Second, a common observation is that file transmission protocols embed a wealth of information in network traffic, but the full potential is often not exhausted during analysis. The sheer volume of recorded data and protocol complexity may lead to overlooking relevant details. Implicit dependencies between operations or less obvious protocol messages may hold critical insights yet remain unnoticed. Effective reconstruction requires systematically examining all available data, ensuring no meaningful details are disregarded. Fundamentally, however, such analysis is only possible if the network protocol itself is supported—otherwise, its information remains entirely overlooked.

⟹ Resulting Challenge: Overlooked Information

Moreover, certain factors, such as encryption, restrict access to file information, as data transmitted via encrypted channels cannot be reconstructed without access to the corresponding key material. Depending on the protocol, encryption may be partially applied—for example, by encrypting file transfers but leaving commands in plaintext. While partial encryption allows some level of reconstruction, it also introduces risks of misinterpretation when incorrect assumptions are made about the encrypted traffic. The resulting challenge is the inaccessibility of information, meaning that—unlike incomplete acquisition—the information is technically present in the network capture but remains inaccessible without further effort or knowledge.

⟹ Resulting Challenge: Inaccessible Information

Furthermore, file transmission protocols do not transmit all information that is required for full reconstruction. Typically, only a subset of the content and metadata that exists on the accessing and serving entities is actually transmitted and thus observable in the capture. For instance, due to the existence of multiple time dimensions, protocol implementations may lead to timestamps of one dimension (e.g., client-side timestamps) not being available in another (e.g., network traffic). This type of missing data is referred to as *absent information*. In contrast to *incomplete acquisition* and *inaccessible information*, *absent information* is not present in the network capture and also cannot be acquired through an improved recording strategy due to the nature of the protocol and its implementation.

⟹ Resulting Challenge: Absent Information

Finally, a further challenge arising from protocol diversity is timestamp update behavior, as different file-sharing protocols and their specific implementations handle timestamp updates in distinct ways. The concrete behavior (i.e., which file operation causes which timestamps to be updated) can vary based on client/server applications, protocol settings, and the specific operation being performed. In addition to automatic timestamp modifications due to specific file operations, protocols might also allow timestamps to be manually updated by a user or application.

⟹ Resulting Challenge: Varying Timestamp Update Behavior

4.4 Context-Dependent Data

Some file transmission protocols, particularly those used for web-based content delivery, serve data dynamically, generating file content on demand based on contextual factors. These factors may include the user's authentication state, session attributes, permission levels, query parameters, or even the timing of the request. As a result, the same file identifier (e.g., a URL or API endpoint) may yield different content and metadata depending on the specific request context.

This behavior gives rise to two key challenges. First, multiple versions of a single file may legitimately coexist within a network capture at a single point in time, each corresponding to a different contextual state of access.

$\Longrightarrow$ *Resulting Challenge:* Dealing with File Versions

Second, and more fundamentally, not all potential variants of a context-sensitive file may be requested or triggered during the observed period. As a result, some incarnations of a file are never transmitted over the network and thus remain completely absent from the capture.

$\Longrightarrow$ *Resulting Challenge:* Absent Information

4.5 Partial File Reads/Writes

Reads and writes captured in network traffic do not necessarily correspond to the entirety of a file. In many cases, only a part of a file is read or written, which can lead to misleading conclusions about a file's overall state. Reconstructing a file in distributed file systems may require multiple network captures, as file content is often split across servers for load balancing, with different chunks transferred over various connections, at different times, or to different destinations.

$\Longrightarrow$ *Resulting Challenge:* Absent Information

4.6 Caching

Caching can occur on client and server sides as well as anywhere in between and introduces significant challenges in serializing file operations from network traffic, as operations captured in the traffic may not reflect real-time file modifications or refer to outdated file versions. The consequences of caching mechanisms resonate with several of the previously explained challenges.

Client-side caching can delay the transmission of file modifications, meaning that, for instance, write operations may not appear in the network capture until the cache is flushed or synchronized with the server.

Server-side caching can cause discrepancies, where a read operation captured in network traffic does not necessarily reflect the latest file content. In environments with multiple distributed servers, caching-induced asynchronous update mechanisms may lead to inconsistent propagation of file modifications across servers. For example, some distributed systems update file metadata and file content separately, which can result in situations where the metadata suggests a file has been modified while the content update has not yet reached all servers.

$\Longrightarrow$ *Resulting Challenges:* Absent Information , Conflicting Information

4.7 Network-Related Characteristics

Several challenges arise from the nature of the communication medium and network-related specifics of the capture process. One such issue is packet loss, which can result from network congestion, unreliable connections, or limitations in the capture process. Network traffic is captured in discrete packets, and if some packets are lost or arrive out of order, crucial file operations may be inaccurately reconstructed or lost entirely. For instance, if a write operation or file deletion is performed but the corresponding packet is lost, the file modification may be absent from the reconstruction, resulting in an incomplete or inaccurate view of the file's history.

Latency, especially in congested networks, introduces further complications, such as out-of-order packets and timestamp inaccuracies. This can occur if traffic is captured at multiple network interfaces with differing delays or, in general, when large files are transmitted. For example, if a write operation takes a significant amount of time and the updated file timestamps reflect only the end of the operation, correlating this with other events becomes difficult, especially if the goal is to determine when the write actually began.

In addition, file transmission protocols usually produce a high volume of network traffic. Because of that and due to potential bandwidth constraints, full packet capture is often infeasible [13]. Hence, selective logging is often employed, recording only a portion of the traffic. This inevitably leads to missing file information in the capture.

$\implies$
Resulting Challenges: Incomplete Acquisition , Time Correlation Challenges

5 Guidelines

This section presents protocol-agnostic strategies to address the challenges discussed earlier. We distinguish between two complementary perspectives: *acquisition guidelines*, which focus on preparing and conducting network captures, and *analysis guidelines*, which address interpreting and evaluating the recorded data.

5.1 Acquisition Guidelines

Focusing on aspects of forensic readiness and technical considerations for effective and reliable network traffic recording, we identified the following recommendations to address the challenges. Several of them are also advised by NIST's *Network Infrastructure Security Guide* [7] and in the *Network Infrastructure Security Guidance* [10] by the NSA.

– *Define the temporal scope:* Determine the appropriate start and end times for network capture.
– *Define capture locations:* Capture traffic at all relevant communication points—ideally on both client and server sides—to avoid selective visibility.
– *Assess and prepare the recording environment:* This includes stress-testing for packet loss under high-throughput conditions (e.g., large file transfers) and identifying potential performance bottlenecks and processing lags.
– *Plan for encrypted traffic:* If encrypted protocols are used, assess whether decryption is feasible. This may involve collecting session keys, configuring key logging, or enabling visibility via proxies.

– *Ensure time synchronization:* All recording devices and communicating entities should be synchronized to a reliable, authenticated time source (e.g., via NTP). This prevents inconsistencies due to clock skew, drift, or time zone differences.
– *Capture supporting context:* When available, collect metadata such as DHCP lease records, ARP tables, or DNS resolutions. This data supports traffic interpretation and IP-to-hostname resolution during analysis.
– *Document the capture configuration:* Maintain a detailed record of the capture setup, including interface locations, applied filters, system performance metrics, and any preprocessing steps. This information is essential for interpreting gaps or distortions in the recorded traffic.

5.2 Analysis Guidelines

The challenges that can be addressed through algorithmic means boil down to two key aspects: managing the different time dimensions and handling file versions. The following subsections elaborate on these focal areas, underpinning each point with concrete examples for SMB, as implemented in our analysis tool[3]. In addition, we address general considerations regarding knowledge about and awareness of specific behaviors of file transmission protocols and their manifestation in network captures.

5.2.1 Handling of Timestamps and Time Dimensions

First, we recommend that all time dimensions are considered and preserved independently throughout the reconstruction process. This enables analysts to trace the evolution of file states across different temporal axes. Reconstructed files should, therefore, support separate views concerning the following time dimensions:

For a *network-based time view*, reconstructed files should be equipped with the timestamp of the last associated file operation in the capture. For operations spanning multiple packets (e.g., reads or writes), it is advisable to utilize the final data-carrying packet's network timestamp consistently.

For a *file system time view*, analysts should use the timestamps reported in protocol messages (e.g., file metadata returned by the server). If only a single file version is observed, the most recent file system timestamp should be applied. When multiple versions are observed, timestamps should be selected per version based on the corresponding operation: for read operations, use the most recent file system timestamp before the read; for write operations, use the next available file system timestamp following the write. A null or placeholder value may be used if no timestamp is available.

In addition, we propose a third time dimension: *hybrid timestamps*, which combine network and file system time into a unified, enriched timeline. This is based on the work of Dreier et al. [2], who introduce the generalized notion of

---

[3] https://github.com/fkie-cad/pcapFS.

hyper timelines to combine time information from different artifact sources for forensic investigations. Hybrid timestamps aim to enhance analytical clarity and semantic expressiveness and serve as an overlay that integrates available time data into a coherent timeline, mitigating inconsistencies caused by skew, delay, protocol-specific behaviors, or not considering all available information.

Constructing and managing hybrid timestamps involves several steps. First, the time offset between the server's file system clock and the recording device's clock must be calculated for each connection. Depending on the protocol, this may be inferred by comparing messages containing the server's system time with the corresponding network packet timestamps.

Second, for each file read/write operation, the previously last known file system (or hybrid) timestamps need to be updated using the network timestamp adjusted by the previously calculated skew. This process should follow consistent rules—e.g., updating access time on reads and modify/change time on writes. This use of reference timestamps aligns with the *time anchors* concept by Vanini et al. [15] and supports synchronization under inconsistent circumstances caused by caching and time shifts.

SMB-Specific Implementation. To obtain a file system time view in SMB, the timestamps in the preceding SMB2 CREATE response can be used for read operations. For writes, the relevant timestamps can be extracted from the subsequent SMB2 CLOSE response or from later SMB2 CREATE or metadata query responses.

For hybrid time management in SMB reconstructions, the clock skew can be computed by subtracting the network timestamp of the SMB2 NEGOTIATE response from the server-reported system time contained in that message. Reference timestamps used to update hybrid values can be drawn from the most recent related SMB2 CREATE response preceding the specific operation or from the previous hybrid timestamps set for the corresponding file.

5.2.2 Handling of File Versions

To define what constitutes a file version, several strategies can be applied:

- *Network-event-based versioning* treats every instance of a file being accessed or transmitted as a new version, regardless of whether the content or metadata has changed.
- *Content-based versioning* focuses exclusively on changes to the file content. A new version is created only if the file content differs from the previous observation, ignoring metadata updates.
- *Metadata-based versioning* considers any update to file metadata (e.g., access time changes) sufficient to constitute a new version, even if the content remains the same.
- *Exclusion of transient data* involves filtering out artifacts that do not correspond to persistent files, such as content transmitted via pipes, Remote Procedure Calls, or other dynamically generated data not stored on disk.

To manage file versions, we suggest the following steps: First, the investigator has to decide on one versioning strategy. We recommend using content-based versioning, optionally supplemented with transient data for a broader reconstruction scope. An advantage of this strategy—and of considering all observable file versions in general—is the ability to reconstruct files that never actually existed on disk, such as those resulting from conflicting writes or dynamically generated content. This enables a more comprehensive reconstruction, surpassing the limitations of traditional file recovery methods.

Second, all file operations—reads, writes, and metadata exchanges—should be tracked in detail. A new file version should be instantiated for every coherent set of read or write operations that change the file content. Each file version should be represented with the following attributes:

- *File name:* Depending on the protocol, resolving file handles to their corresponding names may be required.
- *Absolute file path:* If available (e.g., in file shares), this enables reconstruction of directory hierarchies.
- *File content:* The data as written or read during the file operation.
- *Operation type(s):* Indicates whether the version resulted from read, write, or combined operations.
- *Client identifiers:* Information such as IP address and port of the client(s) accessing this version.
- *Access timestamps:* Network time(s) when the version was read/written.
- *Timestamp mappings:* Correlations between network time, file system time, and hybrid time, documenting when which timestamps were present and requested for this file version. This approach also accounts for metadata updates independent of file content modifications.
- *Additional metadata:* Any further available metadata, such as file permissions.

Reassembling the file content must be done carefully: Only successful operations should be considered for reconstruction. In addition, the investigator should be aware that due to partial reads/writes, the extracted file content may be incomplete, representing only a part of the entire file.

Ultimately, the explained versioning strategy should lead to the ability to see the history of all file versions over time. In addition, it can be valuable to generate snapshot views that reflect the concrete state of all reconstructed files at specific points in time. Files whose contents are unknown but are known to have existed (e.g., inferred from metadata messages) should also be considered. In such cases, empty placeholder files with available metadata (e.g., name, timestamps, permissions) should be created to preserve the record of their existence.

SMB-Specific Implementation. Our implementation of file version handling and extraction for SMB extends the approach outlined by Hilgert et al. [5]. During a preprocessing phase, two essential mappings must be resolved to interpret the recorded network traffic: First, tree identifiers must be mapped to their corresponding share names using information from SMB2 TREE_CONNECT requests and responses. Second, file handles must be resolved to their associated file names and absolute paths within the respective share. This mapping can be established by analyzing `SMB2 CREATE` messages, which are issued for any file or directory access—not just file creation.

Then, the tracking of file operations can be conducted in the following way: The existence of files and their associated timestamps can be inferred from `SMB2 CREATE` messages and from directory listings obtained via `SMB2 QUERY_DIRECTORY`. This is already enough to represent the files as empty placeholder files. In order to populate extracted files with content, `SMB2 READ` and `SMB2 WRITE` messages are analyzed. These operations must be associated with prior `SMB2 CREATE` messages to link the data to the correct file. Any read or write action that results in a content change should trigger the creation of a new file version.

Metadata updates, particularly timestamp modifications, can be derived from various SMB messages, including `SMB2 CREATE`, `SMB2 QUERY_DIRECTORY`, `SMB2 QUERY_INFO`, `SMB2 SET_INFO`, and `SMB2 CLOSE`. Each newly obtained piece of metadata should be stored alongside the network timestamp of the packet in which it was observed. This enables precise tracking of when certain metadata was communicated and known for a file, contributing to a complete and temporally grounded version history.

5.2.3 Background Knowledge and General Awareness
Beyond algorithmic guidance, effective analysis requires a solid foundation of domain expertise and awareness of the behaviors exhibited by file transmission protocols and the artifacts they produce.

Investigators should be familiar with common principles employed by file transmission protocols, as well as the specifics of how particular protocols implement file access and modification operations—including moves, renames, and deletions—and how these actions manifest in network traffic. This also includes understanding further protocol-specific features such as caching mechanisms, file synchronization strategies, and conflict prevention or resolution techniques. All protocol-specific information present in network captures should be leveraged during analysis.

We further emphasize the following awareness-related considerations:

– Do not leap to conclusions that file operations observed in network traffic are *user-initiated* or performed directly on the *on-disk version* of a file at that time.
– Vice versa, the *absence* of certain operations in a network capture does not necessarily indicate that those operations did not occur—they may have taken place *outside the scope or time frame* of the recording.
– In *multi-client scenarios*, remember that the *actual order* of file operations may have been different from how they appear in the capture, and that *file states may differ* between client and server.

6 Conclusion

In this paper, we have systematically identified critical yet often overlooked challenges in extracting files from network traffic in the context of digital forensics. These challenges are often inadequately addressed in existing literature and forensic methodologies. We posit that one contributing factor lies in the previously limited awareness of the existence of these challenges. To bridge this gap, we presented not only the challenges and their causes but also actionable guidelines and best practices tailored to mitigate these obstacles.

Several challenges can be addressed by implementing proper forensic readiness. This procedure includes capturing traffic at strategically important points to minimize absent information as well as spatial and resource issues.

Other challenges can be addressed by incorporating all available information. On the one hand, vendors of forensic tools have to make the information available to the investigator. On the other hand, they have to enhance the correlation of different data and metadata sources. At the same time, investigators must be aware of common pitfalls and challenges and know how to tackle them.

However, not all challenges can be solved efficiently or at all. Issues caused by caching and absent or inaccessible information, e.g., due to encryption or packet losses, can be reduced but likely remain and demand disproportionate resources for uncertain outcomes. Here, a promising approach is to combine network forensics with storage forensics and correlate artifacts from both sources.

Our paper showed intrinsic difficulties in reconstructing files or activities from network traffic—a process far more involved than commonly assumed. We hope our work has demonstrated both the challenges and potential opportunities inherent in implementing a systematic and comprehensive approach to extracting files from network traffic to foster new research and better tooling in this area. As an illustration, we provide an implementation of an enhanced file extraction from SMB traffic[4], which we provide to the community as a starting point for future work.

References

1. Asim, M., McKinnel, D.R., Dehghantanha, A., Parizi, R.M., Hammoudeh, M., Epiphaniou, G.: Big data forensics: Hadoop distributed file systems as a case study. In: Handbook of Big Data and IoT Security, pp. 179–210 (2019)
2. Dreier, L.M., Vanini, C., Hargreaves, C.J., Breitinger, F., Freiling, F.: Beyond timestamps: integrating implicit timing information into digital forensic timelines. Forensic Sci. Int. Digit. Invest. **49**, 301755 (2024)
3. Hansen, R.A., et al.: File toolkit for selective analysis & reconstruction (filetsar) for large-scale networks. In: 2018 IEEE International Conference on Big Data (Big Data), pp. 3059–3065. IEEE (2018)
4. Hilgert, J.N., Lambertz, M., Baier, D.: Forensic implications of stacked file systems. Forensic Sci. Int. Digit. Invest. **48**, 301678 (2024)

---

[4] https://github.com/fkie-cad/pcapFS

5. Hilgert, J.N., Mahr, A., Lambertz, M.: Mount smb.pcap: reconstructing file systems and file operations from network traffic. Forensic Sci. Int. Digit. Invest. **50**, 301807 (2024)
6. Hofstede, R., Čeleda, P., Trammell, B., Drago, I., Sadre, R., Sperotto, A., Pras, A.: Flow monitoring explained: from packet capture to data analysis with NetFlow and IPFIX. IEEE Commun. Surv. Tutorials **16**(4), 2037–2064 (2014)
7. Kent, K., Chevalier, S., Grance, T., Dang, H.: Guide to integrating forensic techniques into incident response. Technical Report, NIST SP 800-86, National Institute of Standards and Technology (2006)
8. Lee, P.T., Yang, B.: Indexing architecture for file extraction from network traffic. In: Proceedings of the 6th Annual Conference on Research in Information Technology, pp. 17–21 (2017)
9. Liberatore, M., Erdely, R., Kerle, T., Levine, B.N., Shields, C.: Forensic investigation of peer-to-peer file sharing networks. Digit. Invest. **7**, S95–S103 (2010)
10. National Security Agency: Network infrastructure security guide. Technical Report, National Security Agency (2023)
11. Pluskal, J., Breitinger, F., Ryšavý, O.: Netfox detective: a novel open-source network forensics analysis tool. Forensic Sci. Int. Digit. Invest. **35**, 301019 (2020)
12. Schatz, B., Mohay, G., Clark, A.: A correlation method for establishing provenance of timestamps in digital evidence. Digit. Invest. **3**, 98–107 (2006)
13. Sikos, L.F.: Packet analysis for network forensics: a comprehensive survey. Forensic Sci. Int. Digit. Invest. **32**, 200892 (2020)
14. Stevens, M.W.: Unification of relative time frames for digital forensics. Digit. Investig. **1**(3), 225–239 (2004)
15. Vanini, C., Hargreaves, C.J., van Beek, H., Breitinger, F.: Was the clock correct? exploring timestamp interpretation through time anchors for digital forensic event reconstruction. Forensic Sci. Int. Digit. Invest. **49**, 301759 (2024)
16. Weil, M.C.: Dynamic time & date stamp analysis. Int. J. Digit. Evidence **1**(2) (2002)

Measuring the Effectiveness of Keyword Lists in Digital Forensics

Aikaterini Kanta[1](✉)[iD] and Christopher Hargreaves[2][iD]

[1] PAiDS Research Centre, School of Computing, University of Portsmouth, Portsmouth, UK
`katerina.kanta@port.ac.uk`
[2] Department of Computer Science, University of Oxford, Oxford, UK
`christopher.hargreaves@cs.ox.ac.uk`

Abstract. Keyword searching is fundamental to digital forensics and therefore there is a clear need to validate results. This paper demonstrates an approach that can be used to measure the effectiveness of generic wordlists used for specific crime types (e.g. drugs, child abuse, terrorism) that complement specific keywords chosen for individual cases. This approach allows measurement of error associated with this use of case-type based wordlists, and facilitates development of a new research area in digital forensics: optimising keyword lists. The paper demonstrates this experimentally and shows that this important technique can now be evaluated in a scientific manner and concludes with a proposed implementation for deploying this within a forensic lab.

Keywords: Digital Forensic Science · Keyword Searching · Keyword Lists · Validation · Error Rates · Digital Forensics · Datasets

1 Introduction

Digital forensics involves a variety of techniques to assist in locating relevant evidence [16] and there is existing work considering how to improve many of them, e.g. entity extraction [12], hashing [28], data reduction [26], and timelines [19]. The DFPulse 2024 Practitioner Survey suggests that keyword searching is one of the most important techniques [17].

A core part of the keyword searching process is selecting which words to search for. While it may be intuitive that some keyword lists perform better than others, evaluating their effectiveness is not easy. This work examines the use of keyword lists and develops tools and techniques to facilitate evaluation in a systematic manner and therefore makes the following contributions:

- a method for evaluating keyword list effectiveness, which could be integrated into validation strategies and tools, and to construct more effective lists,
- an Autopsy plugin and accompanying script that allows keyword results to be exported and compared with a ground truth dataset,

- three experiments, and accompanying datasets that demonstrate the use of the tool and techniques to measure keyword list effectiveness,
- a fourth experiment that shows how the method can be used to evaluate a recently proposed AI-based keyword list generation method.

2 Background and Related Work

A discussion of keyword searching in digital forensics can be broken down into three main areas: coverage and correctness of the keyword search function within tools, selection of keywords, and presentation and ordering of the results.

2.1 Keyword Search Function of Forensic Tools

Many digital forensics tools offer the option to search by keywords, either by manually entering a list of keywords or using pregenerated lists. Some examples of the capabilities of commercial and non-commercial tools include searching for exact matches, substrings, and regular expressions (both custom and pre-configured). A summary of string search tool functionality is available in NIST's Computer Forensic Tools and Techniques Catalog[1], and [15] examines open source tools in detail.

There are many challenges with keyword searching. For tools, many are documented in [1], which provides an example of testing forensic tools' keyword searching function, described as "one of the most complex implementations in developing a forensic tool". It reported the need to account for case sensitivity, fragmentation of keywords, compound sentences (substring matches), compound containers e.g. compressed files, keywords in unallocated space, slack space, or alternate data streams, and keywords located in metadata of files rather than content. [13] goes further and provides a 'requirements specification' for searching, including additional concepts such as character encoding. In addition, there is the related challenge of correctly or comprehensively creating and managing the index of text on a disk.

2.2 Selection of Keywords

There are also challenges unrelated to text extraction, e.g. how variations of words can be identified (permutations, synonyms, misspellings, etc.) [14,25]. Since keyword searching is an important technique in finding relevant artefacts, it is important to know what set of keywords to use to maximise retrieval of relevant evidence, while minimising irrelevant hits.

Aside from the functionality of forensic tools allowing searches for individual words or regular expressions, custom word lists can be used which are usually assembled manually by the investigator or forensic lab [30]. Sites such as *dfir.training* host example lists of keywords for various crimes e.g. arson, drugs,

---
[1] https://toolcatalog.nist.gov.

weapons, sex trafficking etc.[2] There is some academic work in this area too, which proposed case domain modelling, adding a step in which the case concepts and entity relationships are selected, attributes extrapolated, and used to create search goals and keyword lists [4]. While this assists in selecting keywords, and there was anecdotal evidence that the method was useful, a structured validation method was not possible.

Generation, optimisation, and evaluation of wordlists have been performed in related areas such as password cracking. Unlike keyword searching, information from leaked lists of passwords can aid in the assembly of robust wordlists [20,22]. There are metrics associated with assessing the guessability of the passwords [31] as well as the quality of password-cracking wordlists [21]. This ability to evaluate the impact of a wordlist on password cracking performance allows for the optimisation of the process and the creation of bespoke wordlists [23].

In domains like password cracking and unrelated areas such as Search Engine Optimisation (SEO), the success of a query or a password cracking attempt can be verified by an absolute result, i.e. whether a piece of data was decrypted, or the rank of the page in the search results. In other cases the 'retrieval effectiveness' of keyword searching is measured by user perception and experience [32]. This may also be the case within digital forensics, since lists are likely to have evolved organically based on terms or websites that have been identified within different case types over many years.

2.3 Presentation and Ordering of Results

There is also work considering the presentation and ordering of results after keyword searches are carried out. Work by [2,3] presents a method referred to as 'post-retrieval clustering' for grouping the results using natural language processing and string matching algorithms and presenting them according to evidence type and location. This does demonstrate measurements related to keywords for this 'post-retrieval' stage of the process, but does not focus on initial selection of an optimised list.

2.4 Summary

Formal assessment of keyword list effectiveness within digital forensics is a challenge because usually, the examined data has no ground truth since it comes from those under investigation. Currently, there are no methods of gaining objective metrics on the effectiveness of different keyword lists. However, there is a need for method validation in digital forensics and for tools to have measurable error rates [11], especially as digital forensics comes under more scrutiny as part of forensic science e.g. [9].

---

[2] https://www.dfir.training/downloads/search-terms.

3 Methodology for Keyword Evaluation

This research aims to provide a step towards improving keyword lists to more quickly identify relevant evidence. It addresses the precursor challenge to this improvement, which is that no method is available for evaluating the effectiveness of keyword lists used, and therefore to measure improvements. There are several aspects to explore to address this problem: metrics, test data, and tooling.

3.1 Defining Metrics for Keyword Evaluation

The first challenge is identifying the metrics that could be used to determine if an updated keyword list offers an improvement. Terms such as false positive and false negative are described in a digital forensic tool context in [6], and a hashing context in [5]. However, if consideration is given specifically to what a keyword search needs to achieve, and this is applied to these metrics, the following are derived: True Positives ("TP") are the *number of relevant files that appear in keyword search results*, False Positives ("FP") are the *number of non-relevant files that appear in keyword search results*, True Negatives ("TN") are the *number of non-relevant files that do not appear in keyword search results*; and False Negatives ("FN") are the *number of relevant files that do not appear in keyword search results*.

Based on the above definitions, common metrics such as precision and recall can be calculated, but there is difficulty in obtaining the values needed. First, it is necessary to measure the proportion of the total relevant files that are identified with the keywords used. This can be calculated as: *identified relevant/total relevant results* (recall). This is different to the metrics used in [3], which noted that "the true total number of relevant hits in the dataset is not known", and therefore the total number of hits found by the respective tool was used, rather than the total relevant results. However, this is not sufficient for this work, since the 'results found' is exactly what needs to be measured. Therefore, here, 'total relevant results' *is* used, and a means of determining this is necessary, which is discussed in Sect. 3.2.

It is also important how many of the results within the total set of results returned by the keyword search, are actually relevant. This is important because they will need to be time-consumingly reviewed, so the higher this proportion is, the less time needs to be spent reviewing non-relevant files. This can be calculated as: *identified relevant/total returned results* (precision).

3.2 Datasets

So, given the need to measure true and false positives, and true and false negatives, which form the basis of recall and precision calculations, there is a need for ground truth data. Existing work on ground truth datasets can be found e.g. [10], but it often focuses on a set of actions carried out with documentation of those actions, or on details such as expected output from file system parsing[3]. The following possibilities have been identified that could be used for this keyword-based approach:

- **Build a custom data set** - This involves building a collection of files associated with a particular topic or scenario and adding some additional 'noise files', with annotation as to whether they are relevant or not.
- **Use a data set and add additional annotation** - There are existing digital forensic scenario datasets, and some do have 'solutions' [10]. The problem is that they are not annotated to the level required for evaluating keyword search results. However, they can be reviewed and new annotation data can be added.
- **Extract relevant files from historic cases** - Partnership with an organisation that conducts real investigations is another option. This involves extracting bookmarked evidence from historical cases and using these as the basis for files that should return matches. This is problematic as only the evidence that has been found using existing methods would be included in the dataset. However, this is discussed further in Sect. 5.4.
- **Experiment with real investigators on live case data** - This approach would involve providing an updated keyword list to investigators and asking them to run the old and new lists in parallel and return high-level results as to the success of each approach, once the results are reviewed for relevance. This is highly inefficient in terms of investigator time.

For this paper, the approach chosen is to focus on the synthetic dataset approaches (1 and 2). At this stage in the research, the real data approaches are not used, given the overheads that would be pushed onto front-line investigators, which is challenging to justify at this stage. Therefore, a more synthetic approach is chosen, and if promising results are obtained then the higher-overhead but more realistic approaches can be pursued. Given the successful results described later, a proposed method for applying this in a lab environment in future is described later in Sect. 5.4.

3.3 Tooling

It is also necessary to consider practically how an analysis of the datasets could be conducted so that metrics could be computed. It was deemed most appropriate to use existing digital forensic tools to perform keyword searching of the datasets. Autopsy was chosen as it is freely available without restrictions and provides the best opportunity for results to be replicated. Also, since it has a plugin framework, it can be customised to export keyword results in a specific format. It also provides text indexing, and the option to load custom keyword lists.

---

[3] https://cfreds.nist.gov/search/author/HollyDuns%2FDSTL.

3.4 Building a Keyword Evaluation Method

With the three building blocks of the method established it is possible to discuss the overall approach for performing keyword list evaluation. In this paper an iterative approach is presented, to introduce how measurement of the effectiveness of keywords and keyword lists is possible. Four examples are given, each building towards a method that in future could be used within digital forensic labs to evaluate the keyword lists used in active digital forensic investigations. For this paper, four experiment sets were conducted:

- **A basic keyword example:** This first experiment set introduces the idea and how measurement and improvements can be made. It looks at single keywords against an annotated dataset, the use of regular expressions, and then moves to the use of keyword lists. For each of these examples, the metrics are calculated and presented such that improvements or deterioration of results can be seen. This is discussed in Sect. 5.1.
- **Keyword list improvements:** This second experiment set uses a labelled subset of the Enron dataset. This is used to show how keyword lists can be updated and the results measured to provide a keyword list that improves and has a measurable error rate against a specific dataset. This is discussed in Sect. 5.2.
- **Use of scenario data to evaluate lists:** This third experiment uses a custom data set and shows how given a 'scenario-based' dataset that has known relevant artefacts, it is possible to use this to measure the effectiveness of a keyword list. This is discussed in Sect. 5.3. The end of this section also includes future use within a lab environment.
- **Evaluating novel keyword list improvement techniques:** This final experiment set considers a novel method of keyword list generation. In [29] ChatGPT is presented as an idea for keyword list generation. However, it states that no evaluation method for the effectiveness of the approach exists. Since a method has now been developed in this paper, the proposed method for keyword list generation is tested against each of the three previous datasets. This is discussed in Sect. 5.5

For each of these experiment sets a dataset is created, either through annotating an existing dataset or creating a new one. Specific methods of annotation are discussed in each section. That dataset is ingested and indexed by Autopsy and keyword searching is used to obtain results. For each set of results, these are exported and compared with the ground truth annotation, allowing metrics to be calculated. Datasets, tools, keyword lists and raw results are available in the project Git repository[4].

4 Tool Development

This section outlines the Autopsy plugin that was created and the data formats that were used to capture keyword results. Furthermore, the annotation

---

[4] https://github.com/sys001/keyword-searching-DF.

format for the ground truth associated with datasets is presented along with the additional code used to perform comparisons and calculate metrics.

4.1 Autopsy Plugin Development

While Autopsy and other tools do allow export of keyword results[5], it was deemed more generalisable to create a standard output for keyword results that would allow this method to be extended to other tools in future. It also provided consistency between different search methods, i.e. keywords and regular expressions. The plugin itself is written in Python and is available on GitHub. It extracts data from the tables *tsk_files*, *blackboard_artifacts* and *blackboard_attributes* from the Autopsy case database to recover keyword hits and associated details. It then exports all of the keyword results from the case into a standard format in JSON. The export format is discussed in Sect. 4.2.

4.2 Data Formats Created

Two formats were created to support this research:

Keyword Export Format: As discussed earlier a plugin was created to allow the export of keyword results in a consistent structure and format (JSON). The fields included in this format are described below:

- **search_type**: Whether the term is a simple keyword or a regular expression.
- **search_term**: The term that was searched for. This could be a regular keyword or a regular expression.
- **match_term**: The term that was matched. For regular keywords, this will be the same as the search term, but may be different for regular expressions.
- **keyword_list_name**: The name of the keyword list that enabled the match (not applicable for individual keyword results).
- **match_path**: A path to the file containing the match. This uses Autopsy terminology for the path description.

There are other potential fields that could be included in a more general format, for example, a link to a 'keyword index' object which would contain settings and technologies used to create the index from which results are derived.

Dataset Annotation Format: For annotation of the datasets, a simple CSV format was used with the file path, followed by whether the file was relevant (r) or not relevant (nr), i.e. should this file be matched by the set of keywords used. At present, it does not record the specific keywords that should match, only that the file should be found. This is adequate for the purposes of this paper, as will be demonstrated, but could be expanded in future.

---

[5] source name, keyword preview, keyword, keyword regular expression (if that was used), modified time, access time, change time, file path.

4.3 Additional Scripts

In addition to the Autopsy plugin, code was also created that would calculate result metrics as described in Sect. 3.1 from the exported keyword lists and the annotated expected results. It is important to note that the exported keyword results report the *files* that contain matches. Therefore what is described and calculated is the ability of a *keyword list* to match a file, rather than checking that all occurrences of a keyword are indexed, which is deemed an important tool validation challenge, but out of scope for this paper. Furthermore, in the metric calculation scripts, there are flags for --ignoreslack, due to Autopsy behaviour related to slack space where all zero files include the file name in the indexed text, which affects results, and --ignoreunalloc, since there is no practical, systematic way to tag parts of unallocated space as relevant or non-relevant.

5 Results

5.1 A Basic Case Study

Construction of Dataset: This initial set of experiments derives a dataset from an existing dataset from Kaggle that contains all the airports across the world[6]. The original dataset contains the names of 5,095 airports. In order to construct the ground truth 5,095 files were created, each containing the name of one of the airports. An annotation file was constructed, annotating those files as 'relevant', as discussed in Sect. 4.2.

For the first variation of the experiment, named from now on 'airport_basic', a further 5,095 files were created, each containing a random English word which were annotated as non-relevant files. Padding was added to all files to ensure they would exist as discrete files and not be resident data within the MFT if an NTFS file system was used. The second variation contained the same set of relevant files but this time the non-relevant files contained passages from the novel *The Picture of Dorian Gray*, to measure the effect of adding a larger and broader set of text to the image as random "noise" and consider the effect on the metrics. Referred to as 'airport_books'. The third variation was created using the same 'airport files', but this time they were added to a full Windows 11 installation, hereby referenced as 'airport_windows'.

Keyword List Results: For each dataset described above, a case was created and the disk image was ingested; the keyword search plugin was run to index the disk image, and a set of searches with individual keywords, regular expressions, and keyword lists were executed. Once complete, the results were exported using the developed plugin and analysed using the developed tool.

The results are shown in Table 1 and illustrate the basic operation of the tools and techniques and demonstrate that results can be measured and reported. As can be observed from Table 1, and as would intuitively be expected, the results of

---

[6] https://www.kaggle.com/datasets/timmofeyy/all-the-airport-across-the-world-dataset/versions/1.

Table 1. Results for the different single keywords, regular expressions and keyword lists across the different 'airport' datasets. 'Three-word list' refers to a list containing 'airport', 'heliport' and 'aerodrome'. Other list names are self-explanatory.

	airports_basic						airports_books						airports_windows					
	\multicolumn{18}{c}{Single Keywords}
	TP	FP	TN	FN	R	P	TP	FP	TN	FN	R	P	TP	FP	TN	FN	R	P
aerodrome	7	0	5,095	5,088	0.001	1	7	0	5,095	5,088	0.001	1	7	0	113,274	5,088	0.001	1
airport	4,989	0	5,095	106	0.979	1	4,989	0	5,095	106	0.979	1	4,989	36	113,238	106	0.979	0.993
heliport	5	0	5,095	5,090	0.001	1	5	0	5,095	5,090	0.001	1	5	0	113,274	5,090	0.001	1
	\multicolumn{18}{c}{Regular Expressions}
	TP	FP	TN	FN	R	P	TP	FP	TN	FN	R	P	TP	FP	TN	FN	R	P
[a-zA-Z]{1,}port	4,999	3	5,092	96	0.981	0.999	4,999	35	5,060	96	0.981	0.993	4,999	25,136	88,138	96	0.981	0.166
[a-zA-Z]{3,4}port	4,999	1	5,094	96	0.981	1	4,999	8	5,087	96	0.981	0.998	4,999	22,424	90,850	96	0.981	0.182
(air—heli)port	4,995	0	5,095	100	0.98	1	4,995	0	5,095	100	0.98	1	4,995	79	113,195	100	0.98	0.984
	\multicolumn{18}{c}{Keyword Lists}
	TP	FP	TN	FN	R	P	TP	FP	TN	FN	R	P	TP	FP	TN	FN	R	P
Three-Word List	5,001	0	5,095	94	0.982	1	5,001	0	5,095	94	0.982	1	5,001	36	113,238	94	0.982	0.993
100 largest cities	165	2	5,093	4,930	0.032	0.988	165	40	5,055	4,930	0.032	0.805	165	1,178	112,096	4,930	0.032	0.123
500 largest cities	569	2	5,093	4526	0.112	0.996	569	52	5,043	4,526	0.112	0.916	569	2,036	111,238	4,526	0.112	0.218
1,000 largest cities	906	3	5,092	4189	0.178	0.997	906	64	5,031	4,189	0.178	0.934	906	3,757	109,517	4,189	0.178	0.194
World capitals	300	1	5,094	4,795	0.059	0.997	300	50	5,045	4,795	0.059	0.857	300	1,161	112,113	4,795	0.059	0.205

airport_windows, which contains the full windows installation showcase one of the main problems of keyword today: the large number of false positives that often need to be manually reviewed. Secondly, looking at the results in more detail, it is possible to see how even regular expressions can be measured and compared. Considering the first and second regular expressions for the airports_windows dataset shows that a simple change from [a-zA-Z]{1,}port to [a-zA-Z]{3,4}port - which reduces the number of characters in front of the substring port to only 3 or 4, results in no change in true positives, but reduces the number of false positives by 2,712. The next regular expression is more specific, focusing on just 'air' or 'heli' followed by 'port', and this returns just 79 false positives, compared with false positives in the thousands, but does reduce true positives by 4. The necessity of such trade-offs in refining keyword lists will become much more apparent later.

Thirdly, the data also shows the importance of comprehensive and representative datasets. For example, when considering the keyword list for the 1,000 world's largest cities, while the recall rate in all datasets is the same (0.178), the precision in the airports_basic, and airports_books datasets is 0.997 and 0.934. However, in the Windows 11 installation, the precision is just 0.194, which is significantly worse, with 3,757 false positives that would need to be reviewed. Therefore, these results demonstrate the importance of the use of recall and precision metrics in understanding the performance of a keyword, regex, or keyword list, since otherwise comparing performance across the different sized datasets is difficult. Nevertheless, seeing the raw number of false positives within a dataset, that is representative of real-world data, can also be valuable to understand the scale of the problem in terms of result reviewing.

5.2 Enron Dataset Keyword List Case Study

The second experiment shows how keyword lists can be evaluated and incrementally updated to improve keyword lists for a given dataset.

Construction of Dataset: For this experiment, a subset[7] of the Enron dataset [24] was used. This dataset contains 1,700 labelled email messages focusing on business-related emails and the California Energy Crisis. Several broad categories are used, including business documents, news articles, legal documents, and personal emails with categories such as humour/jokes.

This experiment used content of a legal nature, and using the labels, files were considered relevant (91), or non-relevant (1611). This is a small subset but considered acceptable for an illustration of keyword list progression using ground truth data. This is also in line with what is observed in real casework, where only a small subset of the findings are relevant to the case. It is therefore also expected that precision would be low. The two category labels were "2.8 - legal documents (complaints, lawsuits, advice) in included/forwarded information", and "3.10 - legal advice if the primary category was company business, strategy, etc.". A new annotation was created as per the format in Sect. 4.2.

Keyword List Results: For this experiment, existing legal lists from the Internet were evaluated to determine how well they could identify legal content. Results are shown in Fig. 1.

The first list was created from the 'Glossary of Legal Terms' from encyclopedia.com[8], and did poorly in both recall and precision, since many of the terms were too general, e.g. 'articles'. Other similar glossaries from the American Bar Association (ABA)[9], the U.S. Department of Justice (DoJ)[10], and the UK Law Society[11], were also evaluated. Surprisingly, the best-performing internet list was from the UK Law Society, even though Enron is an American company.

After a review of the results, a custom list was created to improve recall and precision, using several iterations. The four lists above were considered and individual keyword performance was reviewed. Often, words that did not have inherently legal content were in these lists and generally did not perform well, e.g. "maintenance". Also, many words that are inherently legal did not return relevant hits, e.g. "defendant", since the specific dataset contains mostly selected emails reflecting the Energy Crisis. With this information, the keywords in the lists were roughly classified into four categories depending on their performance. They were also further divided by whether they were inherently legal or not. Based on this rough classification four iterations of the new experimental list were created. The first included the keywords that returned good results and were legal. The second added those legal words that offered a good trade-off between relevant and non-relevant hits. The third included the previous two

---

[7] https://bailando.berkeley.edu/enron_email.html.
[8] www.encyclopedia.com/law/legal-and-political-magazines/glossary-legal-terms.
[9] www.americanbar.org/groups/legal_services/flh-home/flh-glossary/.
[10] www.justice.gov/usao/justice-101/glossary.
[11] www.americanbar.org/groups/legal_services/flh-home/flh-glossary/.

as well as the non-legal words that returned good results. Finally, the fourth category included all the previous as well as those legal words that returned some relevant but also many irrelevant hits. The results of these four new keyword lists can be seen in Fig. 1.

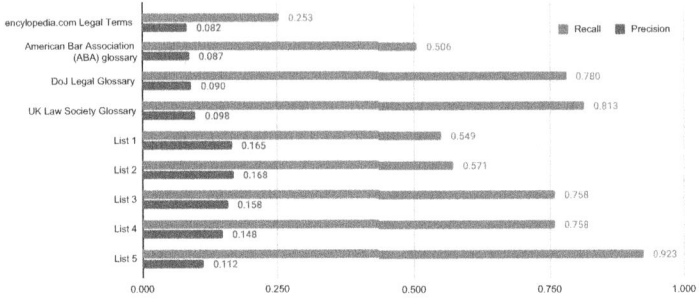

Fig. 1. Results from List Development for the Enron Example.

As can be seen in Fig. 1, even the combination of the most relevant keywords from all four internet lists, in various iterations with the goal to maximise recall and precision, did not offer significant gains. *List 1*, which contained the best-performing keywords from all four lists, had a lower number of true positives than 2 of the 4 internet lists. Every new list after that increased the number of true positives while also increasing the number of false positives, bringing forth the question of trade-off once again. List 3, the best-performing of the four manual lists, had a worse recall (0.758) than the best-performing internet list, UK Law Society (0.813), but had better precision (0.098→0.158).

This suggests that the internet lists do not sufficiently cover the Enron case. The internet lists contain terms that are too broad and generic and can only take the results so far, all the while significantly increasing the number of false positives i.e. the number of irrelevant files an investigator will have to sift through. Therefore, after a review of the relevant emails, a small selection of curated keywords was added to List 3 (the best-performing one of the 4), creating List 5, with the goal of increasing recall. As can be observed in Fig. 1, the new list has a recall of 0.923, while UK Law Society had a recall of 0.813 while also managing to improve on the precision rate (0.098 → 0.112).

This demonstrates that Internet word lists may not have the performance expected and through experiments and measurement, this can be determined, and potentially custom lists can be created that improve results and ultimately save investigators' time. However, improved datasets are needed to produce a truly improved generalised "legal terms" list, since with this experiment, a list is created and optimised for this Enron dataset only.

5.3 Wifi Hacking Scenario Case Study

This extended example provides the building blocks for how these tools and techniques can be used practically to measure and improve the comprehensiveness of keyword lists in digital investigations.

Construction of Dataset: For this example, rather than taking an existing dataset and creating a suitable annotation, a custom dataset was created. A basic scenario was created involving a suspect researching how to break into wireless networks. To create this, a series of actions were carried out and documented in a new Windows installation, including Google searches, program downloads, installations, and saving of instructional material.

To create an annotated version of this dataset the resulting disk image was processed using Autopsy, although without using the keyword searching capabilities. Using a combination of the documentation of the actions performed, Autopsy plugins such as *Recent Activity*, timelines, and additional tools such as MZCacheView, a manual analysis of the disk image was carried out and files that were potentially relevant to a WiFi hacking case were bookmarked. Several iterations of this were necessary to ensure an accurately annotated dataset. These bookmarked paths were exported and converted into the dataset annotation format using a custom script.

There are limitations to this approach, as it is possible to miss files that should be flagged as relevant. It is also possible that files that would never result in a keyword hit are flagged as relevant, for example, images from within the Wireshark user guide. For the purposes of improving keyword lists, failing to bookmark some relevant files will increase the false positive rate. However, during the process of keyword list improvement, that error is consistent and can be at least partially factored out.

Keyword List Results: For this example, it is important to remember that files bookmarked were any potentially related to WiFi hacking, even if the chance of a keyword hit was low. For instance, the aircrack-ng package found in the Downloads folder resulted in bookmarking every file in its folder, including makefiles and licenses. There are two ways to evaluate the results. The first is **relative**, where improvements in recall or precision indicate a better list. The second is **absolute**, where recall shows what proportion of bookmarked files were found with a keyword search. Since many files aren't suited to keyword searches, achieving 100% recall is not feasible, and highlights when other techniques such as hash matching or timelines are needed.

The results from these experiments are shown in Fig. 2. **List 1** used basic terms like 'wifi' and 'wi-fi', resulting in poor recall and precision. **List 2** added 'ssid' and 'packet', improving both. **List 3** focused on names of tools from a hacking website, improving recall (0.22→0.35) and precision (0.18→0.86). **List 4** added terms like 'SSID', 'hacking', 'cracking', and 'hashcat', improving recall slightly (0.35→0.37) but reducing precision (0.86→0.63). **List 5** added 'packet', which increased recall (0.37→0.45), finding 236 extra relevant files, but decreased precision (0.63→0.41), with 1,229 false positives.

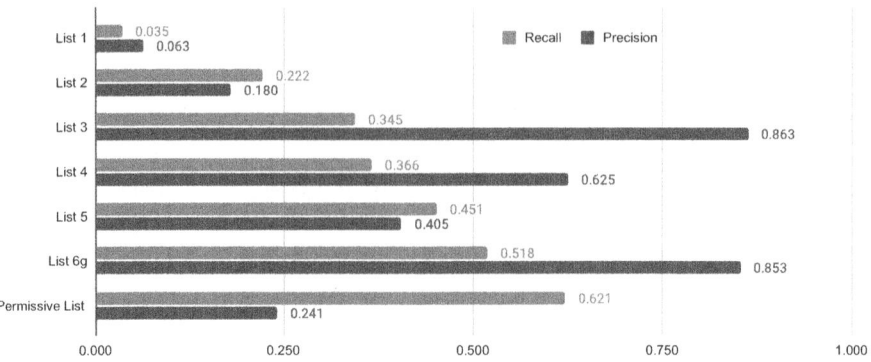

Fig. 2. Results from list development for WiFi Hacking Example. *List1-6g* Represent Iterative Improvements. *P* Represents the most permissive list created.

To achieve further improvements, a new approach was necessary. The tool used to calculate the statistical results also outputs the full list of files in each category (FN, TP, TN, FN), allowing for a qualitative review of where the list went wrong. Focusing on false negatives, the list can be loaded into `Autopsy` for review. False positives can also be analysed to identify keywords generating hits in irrelevant files, typically those from the Windows installation. These keywords can then be evaluated and potentially removed or replaced.

List 6g is the result of this review process and provides an optimised list for this dataset (recall 0.518, precision 0.853). It includes 68 keywords, which is larger than previous lists, but the inclusion of more specific terms proved more effective than using fewer, more general keywords. However, further datasets are needed to evaluate this approach.

The recall rate of **List 6g** (0.518) is relatively low by machine learning standards. However, it's crucial to remember that keyword searching has an upper limit, as some files will not be found with this approach, and that it works in conjunction with other digital forensic techniques. One challenge is knowing when to stop refining the list, given achieving 100% recall is impossible. To explore the upper limit of keyword searching, a broad, permissive list was created with 87 general terms such as 'wifi', 'packet', 'beacon', and 'monitor'. This permissive list achieved a precision of 0.24 (with 5,415 false positives) but a recall of 0.621, indicating that 62% of the bookmarked files were recoverable using very broad keywords. This sets a practical upper bound for keyword search effectiveness.

While further refinements to the list are possible, the goal should be to add richer datasets on the same topic to evaluate and generalise the results, rather than optimising for this specific dataset. For the purposes of this paper, **List 6g** represents a balanced, optimised list, made possible by the measurement tools and techniques discussed earlier.

5.4 Optimising Keyword Searching in a Digital Forensic Lab

The previous sections have shown how a dataset can be constructed from scratch and used to create, measure and improve keyword lists. The main limitation of the results is due to the limited scale and variety of the constructed datasets. However, within a digital forensic lab with a large number of previous cases, there is additional potential for this measurement technique using the same procedure. Assuming the availability of data from previous cases, and assuming the use of bookmarking of artefacts within those cases, it would be possible to create a measurement dataset using existing data. Therefore, knowledge gained from previous cases can be applied to newer cases of the same topic by way of using already refined keyword lists.

As shown in the previous section, paths to bookmarked files can be exported and used to create an annotation for the data. This would allow a lab's keyword lists to be evaluated and determine the level of coverage provided by case type-specific keyword searching alone. If some artefacts were identified through techniques other than keyword searching, the adoption of this technique allows inspection of files that did not get a keyword hit, and then improvement of keyword lists to account for this. Such an approach would seem to be permitted, at least in the UK, where validation "may include the testing of a method in a series of more demanding ways using casework material." [8]. Therefore, this example demonstrates that measurement of error rate is possible, that keyword searching techniques can be improved, and that there is a practical method to apply this to real lab data to ensure results are representative.

5.5 LLM (ChatGPT) List Case Study

This final experiment set demonstrates how this technique can be used to evaluate future-developed methods for keyword list generation. For example, in [29], ChatGPT is presented as an idea for keyword list generation. However, it states that no evaluation method for the effectiveness of the approach exists. This section uses the method developed for evaluation and shows the results against the three datasets used. This is not meant as a thorough evaluation of ChatGPT-generated lists, since the datasets are limited, but rather to illustrate that evaluation is now possible. Results are all shown in Table 2.

For the airports' dataset (Windows disk only), it shows that the first list generated by ChatGPT performed well in terms of recall, but precision could not match the specifics of the custom lists or regular expressions targeted at the problem, and the second list was very specific but did not return as many files. For Enron, the two ChatGPT lists are shown with the best manual result (List 5), and while the manual list does perform better, the ChatGPT list results are close in recall and precision. For the WiFi example, the best manual list (List 6g) is shown alongside the ChatGPT results (25 and 26 keywords each respectively). Here, the precision is very good, and therefore the terms were specific enough to return mostly useful hits, but they did not provide as good coverage as the curated list, indicated by lower recall.

So there is certainly promise for this as a technique, as suggested in [29], and with future, more extensive datasets, this generative AI approach for keyword lists can be more comprehensively evaluated.

Table 2. Results for ChatGPT generated lists for each of the three datasets against the best manual list.

Airports	TP	FP	TN	FN	R	P
(air—heli)port	4,995	79	113,195	100	0.980	0.984
Three Word List	5,001	36	113,238	94	0.982	0.993
Chat-GPT 1	5,021	5,102	108,172	74	0.985	0.496
Chat-GPT 2	968	11	113,263	4,127	0.190	0.989
Enron	TP	FP	TN	FN	R	P
List 5	84	665	946	7	0.923	0.112
Chat-GPT 1	79	651	960	12	0.868	0.108
Chat-GPT 2	78	543	1,068	13	0.857	0.126
WiFi	TP	FP	TN	FN	R	P
List 6g	1,436	247	115,798	1,336	0.518	0.853
Chat-GPT 1	488	23	116,022	2,284	0.176	0.955
Chat-GPT 2	482	22	116,023	2,290	0.174	0.956

6 Discussion

The results in the previous sections demonstrate that it is now possible to measure the effectiveness of keyword lists within the context of a digital investigation using a variety of test datasets. Section 5.3 contains the most realistic example and also discusses how this process could be applied effectively within digital forensic laboratories using existing case data. This could firstly be used to assist with validation, since the 'keyword search technique' now has a measurement method, and error rates can be computed, which is an issue of great importance for the digital forensics community. The recent SOLVE-IT knowledge base [16] specifically highlights a weakness in the keyword searching technique (T1049) of *W1057: Relevant results not captured by the keyword or keyword list used*, with a suggested mitigation of *M1032: Validation of selected words used in keyword lists*. This work provides a practical demonstration of this conceptual mitigation, and operationally, there is now a method by which the performance of keyword lists, which are fundamental for digital investigations, can be measured and therefore improved. By utilising this method on existing, already concluded investigations, valuable insights can be gained to improve keyword searching for future investigations.

In terms of the statistics that are calculated in this paper, only recall and precision are presented, along with the raw numbers of found artefacts. F-scores are calculated but not included. The decision as to which of these to prioritise is an operational issue as to whether there is a need to get as many hits as possible, or false positives are considered more problematic since they are time-consuming to review. However, F-scores are included in the tool output, so any of these measurements can be selected based on operational priorities and strategy.

6.1 Limitations of this Approach

There are limitations to this work. First, it is assumed that the keyword indexing and search within the tool are operating correctly. This method provides evaluation only of *keyword lists* and does not address limitations of indexing [27] or tool errors that may result in missed keywords. This needs addressing but is a different challenge and requires a different methodology.

Another limitation of this paper is the datasets used and the annotation performed. Most significantly, this relates to the WiFi scenario example since the first two are more illustrative than 'real-world'. As explained in Sect. 5.3, the way the dataset was annotated was systematic but simplistic, where anything that possibly related to wireless hacking was bookmarked. This effectively gives results based on the question "Which keyword list finds the most items related to WiFi hacking?". However, in an investigative context, a better question may be "Which keyword list finds the most items that can be used to determine if WiFi hacking took place?". This is subtly, but importantly different, and the files relevant to that question would be different. To assess this, and other questions, the method is still possible to use, but the annotation process needs to bookmark only data that can be used to answer that specific question. Lists can then be optimised accordingly from results based on that annotation.

6.2 Future Work

There is also significant further work that this paper facilitates. This work has focused on the development of a measurement technique and has demonstrated some basic list optimisations. However, more extensive work can now begin to optimise lists and gain access to actionable evidence as quickly as possible.

For the purpose of this paper, plugins and annotation scripts have been created for Autopsy. However, the statistical calculation tool and the keyword export format presented in Sect. 4.2 are generic and could be adopted by any other tools such as X-Ways Forensics and AXIOM, allowing the use of those tools for keyword list evaluation. Also, further updating the annotation format to allow the inclusion of not only the file that matches but also the keyword matches that should occur in each file would facilitate a different type of validation, where the comprehensiveness of the disk image parsing and indexing capabilities of forensic tools could be assessed. This would require very different, edge-case, error-focused datasets to be constructed [18], but this would allow tool results to be validated more effectively.

Finally, because this work has identified useful information to store within a 'keyword hit' data structure, this could form the basis for adding a 'keyword result' representation to the CASE ontology [7]. This would further facilitate validation via cross-tool comparison, although other data would need to be preserved such as settings for indexing, character encoding, etc.

7 Conclusions

As digital forensic science is now rightly subjected to the same scrutiny as traditional forensic science, ways to evaluate techniques that are used as part of investigations become increasingly important. Keyword searching is a common and significant method within digital forensic science, and this paper has developed and demonstrated a method for measuring the effectiveness of case-type-specific keyword lists used as part of investigations. Hopefully, with this method, confidence in the results can be increased, and new methods to improve list development can now be effectively measured and optimised, resulting in an overall improvement of results in digital forensic science.

References

1. Beckett, J., Slay, J.: digital forensics: validation and verification in a dynamic work environment. In: 2007 40th Annual Hawaii International Conference on System Sciences (HICSS 2007), pp. 266a–266a. IEEE (2007)
2. Beebe, N., Dietrich, G.: A new process model for text string searching. In: Advances in Digital Forensics III, pp. 179–191 (2007)
3. Beebe, N.L., Clark, J.G., Dietrich, G.B., Ko, M.S., Ko, D.: Post-retrieval search hit clustering to improve information retrieval effectiveness: two digital forensics case studies. Decis. Support Syst. **51**(4), 732–744 (2011)
4. Bogen, A.C., Dampier, D.A.: Preparing for large-scale investigations with case domain modeling. In: 5th DFRWS Conference Proceedings, pp. 1–10 (2005)
5. Breitinger, F., Roussev, V.: Automated evaluation of approximate matching algorithms on real data. Digit. Investig. **11**, S10–S17 (2014)
6. Carrier, B.: Open source digital forensics tools: the legal argument (2002)
7. Casey, E., Barnum, S., Griffith, R., Snyder, J., van Beek, H., Nelson, A.: Advancing coordinated cyber-investigations and tool interoperability using a community developed specification language. Digit. Investig. **22**, 14–45 (2017)
8. Forensic Science Regulator, UK: Forensic science providers: validation (FSR-G-201) (2020), https://www.gov.uk/government/publications/forensic-science-providers-validation
9. Forensic Science Regulator, UK: Method Validation in Digital Forensics FSR-G-218 (2020), https://www.gov.uk/government/publications/method-validation-in-digital-forensics
10. Garfinkel, S., Farrell, P., Roussev, V., Dinolt, G.: Bringing science to digital forensics with standardized forensic corpora. Digit. Investig. **6**, S2–S11 (2009)
11. Garfinkel, S.L.: Digital forensics research: the next 10 years. Digit. Investig. **7**, S64–S73 (2010)
12. Garfinkel, S.L.: Digital media triage with bulk data analysis and bulk_extractor. Comput. Secur. **32**(C), 56–72 (2013)

13. Guo, Y., Slay, J., Beckett, J.: Validation and verification of computer forensic software tools—searching function. Digit. Investig. **6**, S12–S22 (2009)
14. Hansen, J.: The study of keyword search in open source search engines and digital forensics tools with respect to the needs of cyber crime investigations. Master's thesis, NTNU (2017)
15. Hansen, J., Porter, K., Shalaginov, A., Franke, K.: Comparing open source search engine functionality, efficiency and effectiveness with respect to digital forensic search. In: Proceedings of the 11th Norwegian Information Security Conference, 19–20, September 2018. NISK Journal, e-ISSN 1894-7735 (2018)
16. Hargreaves, C., van Beek, H., Casey, E.: SOLVE-IT: a proposed digital forensic knowledge base inspired by MITRE ATT&CK. FSI: Digit. Investig. **52** (2025)
17. Hargreaves, C., Breitinger, F., Dowthwaite, L., Webb, H., Scanlon, M.: Dfpulse: the 2024 digital forensic practitioner survey. FSI: Digit. Investig. **51** (2024)
18. Hargreaves, C., Nelson, A., Casey, E.: An abstract model for digital forensic analysis tools-a foundation for systematic error mitigation analysis. FSI: Digit. Investig. **48** (2024)
19. Hargreaves, C., Patterson, J.: An automated timeline reconstruction approach for digital forensic investigations. Digit. Investig. **9**, S69–S79 (2012)
20. Imhof, G., Kanta, A., Scanlon, M.: Context-based password cracking dictionary expansion using generative pre-trained transformers. In: 2024 Cyber Research Conference - Ireland (Cyber-RCI), pp. 1–6 (2024)
21. Kanta, A., Coisel, I., Scanlon, M.: PCWQ: a framework for evaluating password cracking wordlist quality. In: Gladyshev, P., Goel, S., James, J., Markowsky, G., Johnson, D. (eds.) Digital Forensics and Cyber Crime, pp. 159–175. Springer, Cham (2022)
22. Kanta, A., Coisel, I., Scanlon, M.: Harder, better, faster, stronger: Optimising the performance of context-based password cracking dictionaries. FSI: Digit. Investig. **44** (2023)
23. Kanta, A., Coisel, I., Scanlon, M.: A comprehensive evaluation on the benefits of context based password cracking for digital forensics. J. Inf. Secur. Appl. **84**, 103809 (2024)
24. Klimt, B., Yang, Y.: Introducing the Enron Corpus. In: CEAS, vol. 45 (2004)
25. Nizam, S.H.S., Ab Rahman, N.H., Cahyani, N.D.W.: Keyword indexing and searching tool (kist). IJoICT **6**(1), 23–30 (2020)
26. Quick, D., Choo, K.K.R.: IoT device forensics and data reduction. IEEE Access **6**, 47566–47574 (2018)
27. Richard, I., Roussev, V.: Digital forensic tools: the next generation. In: Digital Crime and Forensic Science in Cyberspace, pp. 75–90. IGI Global (2006)
28. Roussev, V.: An evaluation of forensic similarity hashes. Digit. Investig. **8**, S34–S41 (2011)
29. Scanlon, M., Breitinger, F., Hargreaves, C., Hilgert, J.N., Sheppard, J.: ChatGPT for digital forensic investigation: the good, the bad, and the unknown. FSI: Digit. Investig. October 2023
30. Shaw, A., Browne, A.: A practical and robust approach to coping with large volumes of data submitted for digital forensic examination. Digit. Investig. **10**(2), 116–128 (2013)
31. Ur, B., et al.: Measuring real-world accuracies and biases in modeling password Guessability. In: 24th USENIX Conference Proceedings, pp. 463–481 (2015)
32. Webber, W.: Evaluating the effectiveness of keyword search. IEEE Data Eng. Bull. **33**, 54–59 (2010)

Money on My Mind: Forensic Investigation of Venmo Payment App

Trevor Spinosa[✉], Abdur Onik[✉], Joshua Rovira, and Ibrahim Baggili[✉]

Baggili(i) Truth (BiT) Lab, Center of Computation and Technology, Division of Computer Science and Engineering, Louisiana State University, Baton Rouge, LA, USA
{tspinosa1,aonik1,jrovira1,ibaggili}@lsu.edu

Abstract. The current state of fintech (financial technology) security, while well developed, still has significant vulnerabilities. In this paper, we analyze Venmo, a widely used fintech application, by examining its functionalities through network traffic inspection and logical data acquisition on a mobile phone. We present PyMent, a forensic tool that leverages Venmo Application Programming Interfaces (APIs) to remotely log into user accounts, bypass multifactor authentication (MFA), and retrieve comprehensive transaction histories. Using a Man-in-the-Middle (MitM) attack scenario, we intercepted and parsed API calls, user information, critical session cookies, and token values from the Venmo application. Building on these findings, PyMent further demonstrates how investigators can extract sensitive data that is not available in the application interface. Additionally, we highlight several Key Findings indicating that other cloud-based fintech services may share server-centric vulnerabilities, that session management tokens could represent a primary point of failure in these platforms, and that network-based forensics will likely outpace traditional device imaging as the industry moves further toward cloud services. Based on these observations, we identify a research gap concerning the need to systematically test a broader range of fintech systems, examining these issues across various mobile payment applications. We also provide an in-depth analysis of Venmo's HTTPS architecture, offering insights that can guide more robust cybersecurity measures in fintech.

Keywords: Venmo · Payment Applications · Cloud Acquisition · Digital Forensics · Network Analysis · Fintech

1 Introduction

Personal banking, finances, and payments have been steadily transitioning towards a mobile environment, undeniably marked by the global mobile payment market surpassing an estimated 72.5 billion dollars, with global digital wallet transactions valued at 9 trillion dollars in 2023. With the integration of digital wallets and fintech applications, mobile transactions have reportedly accounted for 49% of all transactions. With over 60% of the world's population expected to use some type of digital wallet application by 2026, the world increasingly depends on online and mobile payment options [4].

Consumers in the western market have turned to services that prioritize convenience. Venmo is one of these services, and it exceeded 80 million users in 2023 [6]. Venmo allow users to send and receive money instantaneously, link personal bank accounts, and even offers its own credit cards, debit cards, stock payment, and cryptocurrency managers.

Despite the attention that the mobile payment market requires, many of these applications are not as secure as consumers may expect. With 38% of U.S. adults having used Venmo, 11% of users across this and other similar payment platforms reported that their account has been hacked [2]. What's more, Venmo's integrated social media features create a pathway for potential attacks and data scraping. For instance, all transactions are set to public access by default, meaning anyone who views a users profile while logged in can see the transaction. A user must opt out of this default setting during each payment process by changing the privacy setting to "friends only" in which any user who is added as a friend may see the payment or "private" wherein only the payer and the recipient may see evidence of the transaction. Accounting for user social data, financial data, and personal information being transferred across the internet, it follows that the security of these fintech services is essential.

However, individual users aside, Venmo has been a recent victim of attacks and data leakage, namely, a reported tripling of fraud rates in Venmo from 2020 to 2022 in certain regions [15]. To mitigate this, several platforms, including Venmo, have imposed strict authentication and security measures which verify users, restrict maximum transaction amounts, and review abnormal transactions and account behaviors. These responses, while helpful, are not all encompassing, and there still lies a great potential for bypassing these security measures.

Although searching for these security flaws may potentially put system availability and normal users at risk, it will certainly provide a necessary step forward in forensic investigations and cybercrime response. While explicitly forbidden by the Terms of Service agreement, there have been numerous instances of digital wallet and payment transactions being used for criminal exploits, one of which effectively tied a U.S. House Representative to a sex trafficking investigation based on his previous Venmo payments [20]. Even on smaller scales, a precedent for illicit use of these services begets a method by which law enforcement can respond and combat such activities. By utilizing the Application Programming Interface (API) calls of fintech and digital wallet services in a targeted manner, we have develop a tool, PyMent, that can supply law enforcement agencies with potentially essential forensic evidence.

This paper aims to contribute to the protection of user financial data by probing and analyzing the network traffic of the Venmo application via a Man in the Middle (MitM) attack while providing a foundation for combating cybercrimes. In this work, we strive to answer these research questions:

RQ1 What private user data is available in the Venmo application network traffic through API calls?

RQ2 How can we systematize an approach that helps investigators acquire and analyze digital artifacts produced by Venmo?

RQ3 Is the data shown on the application interface the same as the data found using the corresponding APIs?

Our contributions during this research are as follows:

1. We leveraged cloud-based data from the Venmo fintech application as a source for digital forensic investigations, enhancing the accuracy of transaction histories.
2. We developed a tool, PyMent, for Venmo which makes use of Venmo's authorization APIs to remotely log in, potentially bypass Multi-factor Authentication (MFA), and pull any user's transaction history. PyMent can extract more data from the servers than is shown in the application, including more accurate transaction timestamps.
3. We provide an in-depth analysis of Venmo's network architecture, describing certain mitigations and limitations regarding several sensitive API calls.
4. We demonstrated a criminal investigation scenario to showcase our tool's potential to assist examiners in real-world cybercrime situations.

The remainder of this paper is structured as follows: In Sect. 2, we provide and review a comprehensive collection of related works. In Sect. 3, we present and explain the methodology used in this study. In Sect. 4, we describe the network analysis and API functionality of Venmo. In Sect. 5, we supplement our findings with results from logical data acquisitions of a mobile phone's usage of Venmo application. In Sect. 6, we analyze the outcomes and consequences of our findings with regard to the research questions, constructing a framework for use in cybercrime investigations and applying it in a case study. In Sect. 7, we describe the limitations encountered and lay the groundwork for future work, and in Sect. 8, we conclude with final remarks.

2 Related Work

Digital payment applications have become a key focus of forensic investigations due to the sensitive nature of their data. Although numerous studies have analyzed these applications, there has been limited in-depth exploration of network traffic and API analysis for the Venmo application. This section reviews related works that employ similar methodologies, highlighting the distinct approach of our investigation. The studies are organized chronologically, with the most recent and relevant works presented first.

2.1 Payment Application Forensics

The growing significance of mobile payment applications in forensics stems from their sensitive nature. However, research on network traffic and API analysis for fintech applications like Venmo remains limited. Below is a review of works applying digital forensics to payment apps, arranged chronologically.

Zhou and Karabiyik [27] analyzed WeChat's payment feature, demonstrating full recovery of contact transactions and partial data from credit card registrations, but no data from the official WeChat Pay account. Magnet Axiom tools were used for image extraction and artifact analysis. Despite providing valuable insights, the study lacks a network traffic-based forensic framework like PyMent. Nicholson et al. [16] examined Apple Pay's payment card and transaction data, focusing on cross-device syncing and the effects of data deletion, which are relevant to criminal investigations. Salamh et al. [23] conducted a forensic analysis of Venmo to retrieve artifacts such as usernames, messages, and transaction data across iOS and Android systems.

Ezennaya-Gomez et al. [7] assessed the security of online payment systems by analyzing the data flows of PayPal, Klarna-Sofort, and Amazon Pay, identifying vulnerabilities in some APIs and employing semi-automated traffic analysis. Nikkel [17] introduced fintech forensics as a sub-discipline, emphasizing the role of digital forensics in combating fraud and money laundering in financial technologies. Lwin and Aung [13] found that several Burmese mobile money apps store sensitive data, such as usernames, passwords, and account information locally, sometimes in plain text, raising security concerns. Kier et al. [11] highlighted the vulnerabilities of Near Field Communication (NFC)-enabled transactions and proposed forensic strategies to detect fraudulent activities.

2.2 Network Traffic Analysis and Forensics

Network traffic analysis is essential for examining application functionality and the associated APIs. Berrios et al. [3] analyzed 15 two-factor authentication apps and revealed the storage of sensitive data like secret keys and timestamps in various forms. Mahr et al. [14] conducted a forensic study on Zoom, extracting chat messages and user credentials using network captures, highlighting anti-forensic techniques used by the platform. Yarramreddy et al. [26] pioneered forensic analysis of Virtual Reality (VR) systems, recovering usernames, profile pictures, and system details from platforms such as Oculus Rift and HTC Vive. Walnycky et al. [25] reconstructed messages from 16 instant messaging apps via network and device forensics, recovering passwords, pictures, videos, and other artifacts.

Karpisek et al. [10] decrypted WhatsApp's calling feature traffic, extracting forensic artifacts such as phone numbers and call durations, and developed a tool to visualize WhatsApp protocol messages. Pichan et al. [22] explored the challenges of cloud computing, discussing strategies such as log frameworks and resource tagging to aid investigations. Huber et al. [9] demonstrated how web crawling and social media APIs could be used to create a snapshot of a target user, a method that could potentially be applied to fintech applications.

Onik et al. [1] developed an open-source Python tool to extract data from the Progressive cloud that could not be accessed through the mobile interface. By applying network forensic techniques, they successfully uncovered driving data, including location, speed, dangerous maneuvers, and distracted driving events.

Another study examined the forensic potential of Internet of Thing (IoT) devices, specifically the iRobot Roomba. Their research identified undocumented APIs in Roomba's cloud infrastructure, leading to the development of PyRoomba, an open-source Python tool [18].

2.3 Mobile Banking Forensics

Mobile banking security has become increasingly important with the rise of online fraud, yet forensic research remains limited. Thomas et al. [24] developed FORESHADOW, a framework for extracting artifacts such as public keys and transaction histories from cryptocurrency wallets. Osho et al. [19] investigated 12 Nigerian mobile banking apps, revealing that most retained sensitive data in memory and failed to enforce strong device security policies. Haigh et al. [8] focused on crypto wallet apps, providing insight into code obfuscation, reverse engineering, and forensic artifact recovery. Kuncoro et al. [12] conducted static forensic analysis on mobile banking apps to extract logs and transaction records, identifying robust security measures designed to prevent unauthorized access.

3 Methodology

Our methodology follows five phases, based on the digital forensic framework proposed by [5].

Table 1. A Detailed list of hardware and software utilized in the experimental setup for forensic analysis. The table includes essential apparatus categorized by type, purpose, company, and specific version or model. The hardware and software were selected to ensure comprehensive data acquisition, analysis, and network traffic interception during the forensic investigation.

Hardware/Software	Use	Company	Software/Model Version
Galaxy s10+	Device Acquisition	Samsung	Android 13.0.0
Windows PC	MitM Attack to analyze network traffic	Microsoft Corporation	Windows 10.0.22621
Venmo Application	Application analysis	PayPal	Version-10.35.0
Mitmproxy	Network Traffic Analysis Application	Open Source	Version 10.2
Magnet Acquire	Device Acquisition	Magnet Forensics	Version 2.73.0.38909

3.1 Experiment Setup

The preparation phase for analyzing Venmo application involved acquiring the necessary hardware and installing the required software (Table 1). We used an Android smartphone (Samsung Galaxy S10+) and employed the apk-mitm tool, a Command Line Interface (CLI) tool, to prepare the Android Application Package (APK) files for HyperText Transfer Protocol Secure (HTTPS) traffic inspection. Since modern Android applications employ certificate pinning to prevent

MitM attacks, apk-mitm was used to modify the Network Security Configuration, disable certificate pinning, and re-sign the APK without affecting functionality. This modification allowed us to monitor encrypted traffic in plaintext. The modified Venmo APK was installed on a test phone with burner accounts, enabling HTTPS traffic analysis.

To capture Venmo's network traffic, we used *mitmproxy*, an open-source HyperText Transfer Protocol (HTTP) proxy tool, installed on a Dell XPS 13 laptop. The mobile phone's network was configured to route traffic through the proxy, and the *mitmproxy* certificate was installed on the Android phone to bypass encryption. Both devices were connected to the same network using a mobile hotspot to ensure seamless traffic monitoring. Finally, we deposited sufficient funds into the accounts to facilitate the testing and analysis of real transaction activities. This setup provided us with comprehensive access to network traffic, allowing detailed analysis of both applications' API calls and transaction history.

We also installed Magnet Acquire, a digital forensic tool, on the Dell XPS 13 to acquire logical images of the mobile device during our analysis.

3.2 Data Acquisition

We obtained data in the form of network traffic flows by conducting a MitM attack using mitmproxy, as shown in Fig. 1. By generating a Certificate Authority (CA), we bypassed Transport Layer Security (TLS) encryption and recorded all sent and received HTTP packets between the application servers and the mobile application. Mitmproxy includes a web-based GUI that displays each packet's headers, cookies, data, and metadata across a recorded session. These sessions were saved and referenced later during analysis. For the Venmo application, we recorded packets sent during log in, receipt of money, sending of money, access and modification of settings options, retrieval of transaction history, general site exploration, and logout. We took several separate captures of the traffic related to Venmo on the same network and laptop. Throughout our captures, we modified only two criteria to compare changes in site functionality: sign-in options – username, phone number, or email – and the browser profile – guest user or our personal browser account.

Parallel to these captures, we acquired logical data from the Galaxy S10+ to determine what data remained on it. During this acquisition, the computer was connected to a USB port to conduct payments and edit profile information. The information was downloaded in compressed .zip files[1].

---

[1] https://github.com/natonomous/Acquisition.

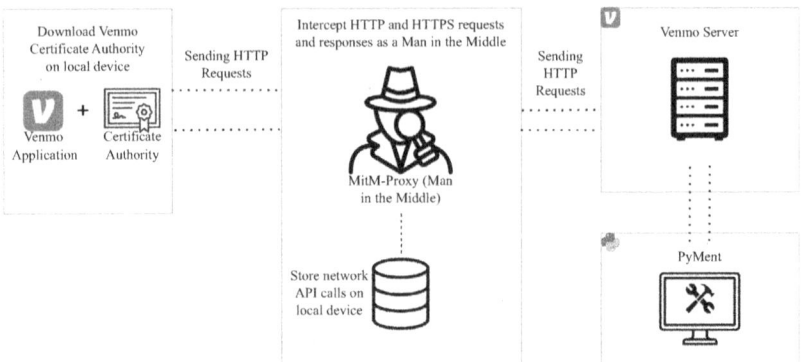

Fig. 1. The figure illustrates a Man-in-the-Middle (MitM) attack designed to intercept and monitor network traffic, uncovering hidden APIs, and extract transaction details, including timestamps. The process begins by employing apk-mitm to bypass certificate pinning, followed by MITM-proxy to capture communication between the Venmo application and its server. Leveraging these intercepted APIs, the Pyment tool was developed to acquire information during forensic investigations. This approach demonstrates the forensic potential of network interception techniques in app-server communications.

3.3 Data Analysis

We analyzed the acquired data by loading the traffic captures into mitmproxy and manually examining each HTTP request. Using this approach, we evaluated the relationship between the payloads and headers of important requests, categorizing API calls and responses to assess the security of each operation. We recorded the order in which the APIs were called, the method of calling the APIs, the associated cookies and headers, the destination URLs, the response payloads, and any other notable changes in the response packets. By analyzing the traffic from various sessions, including those from guest browsers, we identified several key APIs and used them to build our tool.

3.4 Tool Development

We developed PyMent (see Fig. 2), a forensic tool designed to support investigations involving Venmo by leveraging our insights into Venmo's authentication process and undocumented APIs. PyMent uses these findings to provide a structured approach that assists law enforcement in retrieving a user's transaction history with minimal user information.

While PyMent was developed with a broader vision for fintech services, its current implementation is specific to the Venmo application. The tool allows investigators to seamlessly access detailed transaction histories, including accurate timestamps and associated user information. Unlike the Venmo application interface, which provides only limited transaction history, PyMent directly extracts data from Venmo's cloud, offering a more comprehensive view. Furthermore, the timestamps extracted through PyMent are more precise than those available in the mobile application interface, enhancing the accuracy and reliability of forensic analysis.

The development of PyMent was partially inspired by prior work conducted by [1,18], including the repository[2], which explored similar investigative approaches. However, PyMent advances beyond existing methodologies by implementing an independent investigative framework and introducing a graphical user interface (GUI). This GUI is specifically designed to streamline the investigative process, enabling investigators to utilize the application more efficiently. These enhancements ensure that PyMent is not only a powerful tool for data retrieval but also an accessible and user-friendly solution for forensic analysis in real-world scenarios.

3.5 Forensic Simulation: Evaluating PyMent

We tested our tool in a simulated real-world scenario to demonstrate its effectiveness in forensic investigations. By constructing a mock crime scene, we used our tool for investigation and successfully retrieved the complete transaction history of a Venmo user involved in illicit activity.

3.6 Ethical and Legal Considerations

This study followed to strict ethical and legal guidelines to ensure compliance with established standards for cybersecurity research. Techniques such as MitM attacks and MFA bypass were employed exclusively within a controlled lab environment using accounts created specifically for this research. No real user data or accounts were accessed or manipulated.

4 Venmo

We conducted network captures, each time replicating conditions such as devices, network, transaction amount, and the order and exploration of accounts. The network traffic was collected using mitmproxy for all iterations, with the only changes being the switching between normal browser accounts and the "guest" account, which visits the websites of the services without any cache or cookies, and using alternate methods to sign in. This was done to verify the network traffic even in cases involving unfamiliar devices or when using a phone number as opposed to email. Throughout our captures, we observed that Venmo calls its API via POST requests to https://api.venmo.com/graphql. The request payloads typically include the field "operationName:", followed by a value that dictates the desired function. These functions vary and are discussed further below. Calls to these functions are accompanied by distinguishing fields that

---

[2] https://github.com/mmohades/venmo

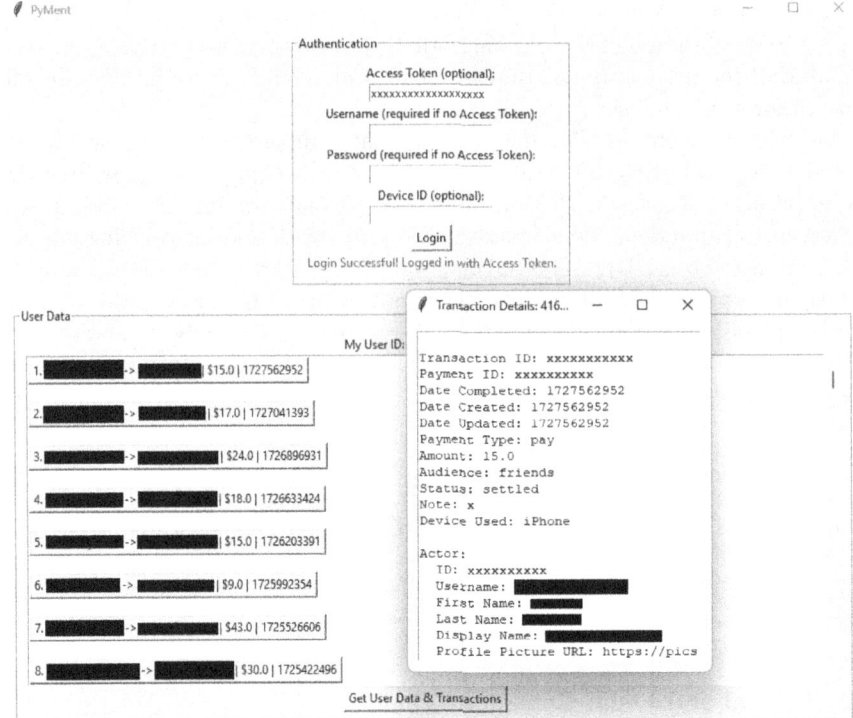

Fig. 2. Interface of our developed tool, PyMent. After logging in with valid credentials, the investigator can view a list of all previous transactions. Each transaction can be selected to display the full set of details available on the server.

pass necessary information to the call as well as certain header values which, depending on the function, authenticate or otherwise enable the execution of the process. The undocumented APIs we discovered are listed in Table 2.

4.1 Authenticated Requests

Throughout our investigation, we found that Venmo protects some of its API calls and functionalities with an authorization header. This header is a constant value tied to the user. The same value can be used across multiple sessions and is passed to the user upon verification. This authorization token is originally denoted by the header "*api_access_token*." This is the sole method of authorized packet signing.

4.2 Login

Venmo uses a multi-layered authentication process, including MFA with SMS-based One-Time Passwords (OTPs), to verify users. During our study, we

Money on My Mind: Forensic Investigation of Venmo Payment App 69

Table 2. Mapping of Venmo API Endpoints and Their Forensic Relevance. This table outlines key Venmo API endpoints, their associated request URLs, authorization headers, and forensic significance in an investigative context. Each API endpoint provides specific functionalities critical for user authentication, payment transactions, and multi-factor authentication (MFA). The forensic relevance section highlights how these endpoints can be analyzed to detect unauthorized access, verify device activity, and track financial transactions.

No.	API Name	Request URL	Authorization Header	Forensic Relevance
1	Login to Get Access Token	https://api.venmo.com/v1/oauth/access_token	device-id, Content-Type	Analyze login attempts, detect unauthorized access, track devices used.
2	Request OTP for 2FA	https://api.venmo.com/v1/account/two-factor/token	device-id, venmo-otp-secret, Content-Type	Track OTP requests, verify legitimate access, analyze 2FA enforcement.
3	Verify OTP & Get Access Token	https://api.venmo.com/v1/oauth/access_token?client_id=1	device-id, venmo-otp-secret, Venmo-Otp, User-Agent	Identify successful or failed OTP verification, trace device activity.
4	Make a Payment or Request Money	https://api.venmo.com/v1/payments	Authorization (Bearer Token), Content-Type	Analyze transaction history, verify sender/recipient, detect unauthorized payments.
5	MFA SMS Request	https://account.venmo.com/en/account/mfa/sms	sec-ch-ua, sec-ch-ua-mobile, sec-ch-ua-platform, user-agent	Provides insight into authentication attempts, including timestamped MFA activities, which are key for verifying legitimate user access or detecting anomalies.

observed that Venmo allows trusted devices to bypass the MFA step after initial recognition, simplifying access for subsequent logins. We identified this trusted status using the "d_id" value, a set-cookie returned after the first login attempt, enabling us to replicate trusted device conditions. We discovered that during login, Venmo's MFA process could be bypassed entirely by capturing a unique MFA token (e.g. "d_id") from the network traffic from the trusted device, thereby removing the need for the SMS OTP. By using this token, we gained direct access to the web application, highlighting a significant vulnerability in the MFA mechanism.

In addition, Venmo uses several tokens, such as the "api_access_token" and "deviceID", for session verification. These tokens are repeated across sessions, tying them to a specific user. Through network interception (e.g., MitM attacks), these tokens can be used to impersonate a user, revealing weaknesses in session handling.

From a forensic perspective, capturing tokens like "d_id", 'api_access_token', and MFA bypass values is highly relevant. These artifacts allow investigators to trace unauthorized access, understand session vulnerabilities, and identify weaknesses in authentication that could be exploited for persistent unauthorized access.

4.3 Transaction History

The transaction history API request requires the Authorization header and returns the transaction information in JSON format for the month specified in the request payload. Interestingly, the API call specifies the account to be transacted by means of a "profileID" field, which is a unique identifier assigned to each account. We found that this API responds to any valid profile ID, allowing someone to pull the transaction data of another user. The range of transactions pulled is determined by two fields, "startDate" and "endDate", which correspond to the beginning and ending of each month in the format YEAR-MONTH-DAY.

4.4 Change Password

To change a user's password, the "operationName:" "changePassword" request requires only the API key in the form of an authorization bearer, the device ID, and the client ID, with the payload containing a single variable "input" which includes the current password and the new password. This is sent following a preliminary preflight request that checks for permission to use the POST method and the pertinent headers.

4.5 Payments

Payments differ from other API calls in that they do not follow the "operationName" schema. Venmo does not dynamically update the balance or transaction history when receiving payments; and a manual refresh or window change is required to see the effect. The sending of payments is executed over the course of multiple packets. First, a POST request is sent to the path "/api/eligibility" with the transaction type, transaction amount, note, target user's ID, and the distinction of the type of user that it is being sent to, all included in the payload. This information is sent to obtain an eligibility token, which is used in the subsequent POST request to "/api/payments." This POST request is sent with the api_access_token, but it is not listed as an authorization header. The payload contains the same information as the initial request but includes additional fields: audience and fundingSourceID – a unique ID identifying the payment method used for the transaction.

5 Device Acquisition and Analysis

In addition to network analysis, we also conducted a logical device acquisition of a Samsung Galaxy S10+ to determine what sensitive data is stored on the user's device. We aimed to find any verification-dependent data, such as username, user ID, device ID, password, keys, or tokens associated with Venmo, using only the device. However, any data found associated with these applications would be useful for forensic analysis.

To acquire the data, we conducted both independent captures and parallel captures alongside our network traffic analysis. During these captures, we authenticated, performed transactions, received payments, and navigated through the application using the mobile device. Additionally, we edited personal user settings, such as changing the suername and password within the application. Finally, we pulled and viewed the transaction histories and user information of the account. All of these actions were performed using the normal and intended functionality of the Venmo application.

To prepare the device for acquisition, we obtained root access of the device. After priming the device, we extracted a logical device acquisition using Magnet Acquire, a free tool provided by Magnet Forensics. We manually examined the application files but uncovered no information regarding Venmo. We then used the "findstr" command to search through all retrieved files for the username, password, and other pertinent data used for API calls or account verification. We found no strings matching our search criteria. Based on this investigation, we believe that sensitive client information is only stored on Venmo servers. Official Venmo documentation does not specify what, if any, sensitive data is stored client-side versus server-side, but they do, however, stress that server-side information is encrypted [21].

After exploring all our avenues for physically acquiring account information, we searched for other potentially useful forensic data. We successfully uncovered timestamps for application use in the logs. While not significant on its own, during a forensic investigation, timestamps can be mapped to transaction history to confirm and identify a criminal suspect's involvement in illegal acts via payments.

It is important to note that while device acquisition remains a common practice in forensic investigations, one of the key findings of our study is that not all applications, such as Venmo, store significant amounts of sensitive data on user devices. Specifically, Venmo retains very limited data on the device itself. Therefore, cloud-based data acquisition is needed in such cases, particularly for fintech applications. Our work demonstrates the importance of leveraging cloud resources in digital forensic investigations, offering investigators a more effective approach for extracting pertinent information when traditional device acquisition yields limited results. Some of the files found in our acquisition can be found on GitHub[3].

6 Evaluation and Discussion

In this section we review the experiments conducted during our methodology to answer the research questions (RQs) stated in the introduction. We analyzed network traffic APIs, created a tool for calling these APIs to use them for forensic investigations, and prepared a scenario to test our tool.

6.1 Network Traffic Analysis

RQ1: What private user data is available in Venmo network traffic through API calls?

---

[3] https://github.com/natonomous/Acquisition.

We intercepted and decrypted TLS-encrypted network traffic using a MitM proxy. This allowed us to view user information that would otherwise be securely encrypted during transmission. Furthermore, with proper access tokens and the API calls, we were able to access sensitive information, perform payments, and even edit user account information.

6.2 Tool and Approach

RQ2: How can we systematize an approach that helps investigators acquire and analyze the digital artifacts produced by Venmo?

To assist in the identification of evidence against criminals using Venmo for illegal activities, we developed *PyMent*. PyMent is designed to quickly retrieve a target user's transaction history given minimal personal information about the user. We used the Venmo APIs to access transaction history and developed the code to ensure that no payments or payment requests can be made, thereby maintaining forensic integrity. We created a user interface, shown in Fig. 2, to simplify the process of logging in with credentials and displpaying transaction details. As presented in Fig. 3, PyMent shows more precise timestamps for transactions. We conducted five transactions using the application and compared the times shown in the interface with those displayed by PyMent. The application interface always rounds up to the next minute, making the times less accurate. PyMent is open source, free to use, and can be found on GitHub[4].

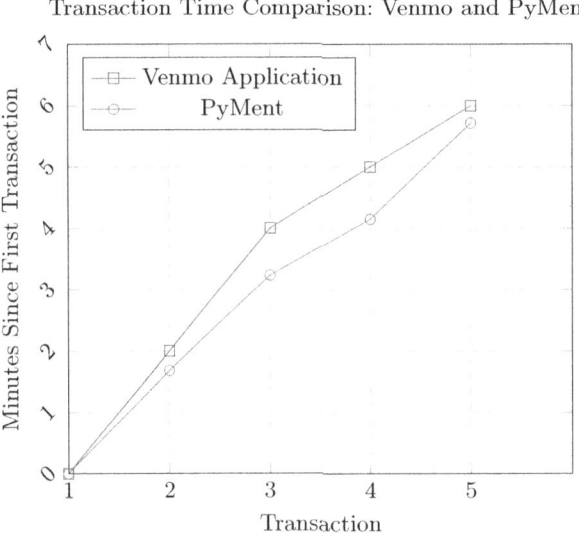

Fig. 3. We performed five successive transactions using the Venmo Application and then compared the difference in times shown by the application interface and PyMent.

---

[4] https://github.com/natonomous/PyMent.

The exact method of using PyMent to obtain all transaction details is shown in Algorithm 1. In lines 2 through 8 of the algorithm, the investigator uses the user credentials to obtain the account access token. In lines 10 through 18, the investigator retrieves all transaction details from the Venmo server. If no access is given, re-authenticate and try again.

One of the main benefits of PyMent is that it shows more transaction history than the Venmo application. Therefore, if a transaction was completed many years ago, it might not be available on the official application, but it will be available using PyMent.

Algorithm 1. PyMent Transaction History Retrieval

1: **Start** PyMent forensic tool
2: **Authenticate** user with access token or credentials
3: **if** access token is available **then**
4:     Use access token for API communication
5: **else**
6:     Prompt user for credentials
7:     Perform MFA bypass if trusted device id is available
8:     Retrieve access token from server
9: **end if**
10: Send transaction history request with API token
11: **if** response is valid **then**
12:     Parse transaction data
13:     Extract relevant fields: transaction IDs, amounts, timestamps
14:     Store data for forensic analysis
15: **else**
16:     Handle errors or request re-authentication
17: **end if**
18: **End** PyMent process

6.3 Transaction Reconstruction: Analyzing Illicit Payments Using PyMent

RQ3: Is the data shown on the application the same as the data found using the corresponding APIs?

In this section, we reconstruct two small-scale transactions to demonstrate PyMent's capabilities in forensic analysis. The goal is to highlight how the tool extracts hidden data from Venmo transactions, assisting investigators in uncovering critical details that would otherwise remain hidden.

We explore a scenario involving a payment transaction made through Venmo. This transaction was conducted using an Android device by a user named Trevor Spinosa who sent a payment to another user, Josh Rovira. The transaction, involving an amount of $1.00 and was noted as "illicit substances," was successfully completed and settled. The transaction specifics, including unique identifiers such as transaction_id and payment_id, provide a foundational data set for forensic examination.

Through the forensic examination of the transaction history via our tool, we observed that the timestamps recorded in the device's acquisition logs matched the timestamps retrieved from the transaction history. This synchronization of data timestamps serves as an important verification step in digital forensic investigations, ensuring the reliability of the data being analyzed.

Furthermore, the user profiles provide additional layers of information. Both users had their profile pictures and basic information publicly accessible, which could be used to verify identities in a forensic context. The visibility of the transaction to friends only, as specified by the audience parameter, raises questions about privacy settings and their implications for digital forensic practices.

This case study highlights the complexity of digital forensic investigations involving mobile payment applications such as Venmo. It demonstrates the necessity of comprehensive forensic tools and frameworks that can adapt to the dynamic nature of digital transactions and the evolving landscape of mobile payment environments. The ability to correlate device and application logs critically supports forensic analysts in constructing a coherent narrative during investigations, especially when dealing with sensitive transaction details.

7 Limitations and Future Work

Our research into the security and privacy vulnerabilities of mobile payment platforms, specifically the Venmo application, while extensive, has several limitations. Venmo's API calls and network traffic structure may change as a result of software updates. That being said, Venmo's API structure has remained in place since 2016, so it is unlikely to change for a significant period, making this limitation somewhat moot. However, if changes do occur, updating PyMent to work with new API modifications would be trivial, following our methodology, making this a minor issue.

There is a need for a comprehensive and focused tool that can support the protocols of multiple fintech applications to retrieve a user's transaction history. The nature of our analysis has brought us closer to achieving an automated process for acquiring past payments for use as evidence in real-world criminal investigations.

8 Conclusions

In this work, we conducted a network forensic analysis of the Venmo application, uncovering vulnerabilities and providing insights into its operational structure. Using a MitM attack we bypassed key security mechanisms such as MFA, captured sensitive API calls, and extracted user information not available through the official application interface. Our research shows that Venmo's reliance on APIs, which store critical tokens across sessions, presents potential weaknesses that could be exploited to access transaction data.

PyMent was developed to illustrate how law enforcement and forensic analysts can leverage these vulnerabilities to acquire evidence during investigations. By accessing more precise transaction timestamps and detailed histories than what the Venmo application interface provides, PyMent enhances accuracy in reconstructing transaction records.

Our findings highlight key considerations for the security of fintech applications and recommend stronger security protocols, including improved multi-factor authentication and session management. In future work, we will focus on expanding the tool to cover multiple fintech applications, automating vulnerability identification across different APIs, and ensuring adaptability to future application updates. These developments would provide a more effective tool for forensic investigators and deeper insights into the strengths and weaknesses of fintech applications.

References

1. Hit and run: Forensic vehicle event reconstruction through driver-based cloud data from progressive's snapshot application. Forensic Sci. Int. Digit. Investig. **49**, 301762 (2024). https://doi.org/10.1016/j.fsidi.2024.301762
2. Anderson, M.: Payment apps like venmo and cash app bring convenience – and security concerns – to some users (2022), https://www.pewresearch.org/short-reads/2022/09/08/payment-apps-like-venmo-and-cash-app-bring-convenience-and-security-concerns-to-some-users/
3. Berrios, J., Mosher, E., Benzo, S., Grajeda, C., Baggili, I.: Factorizing 2fa: forensic analysis of two-factor authentication applications. Forensic Sci. Int. Digit. Investig. **45**, 301569 (2023). https://doi.org/10.1016/j.fsidi.2023.301569
4. CapitalOne, S.R.: Digital wallet statistics (2024), https://capitaloneshopping.com/research/digital-wallet-statistics/#:~:text=Digital
5. Carroll, O.L., Brannon, S.K., Song, T.: Computer forensics: digital forensic analysis methodology. US Att'ys Bull. **56**, 1 (2008)
6. Daniel, C.: Venmo revenue and growth statistics (2024) (2023), https://www.usesignhouse.com/blog/venmo-stats#:~:text=As
7. Ezennaya-Gomez, S., Kiltz, S., Kraetzer, C., Dittmann, J.: A semi-automated http traffic analysis for online payments for empowering security, forensics and privacy analysis. Association for Computing Machinery, New York, NY, USA (2021). https://doi.org/10.1145/3465481.3470114
8. Haigh, T., Breitinger, F., Baggili, I.: If i had a million cryptos: cryptowallet application analysis and a trojan proof-of-concept. In: Digital Forensics and Cyber Crime: 10th International EAI Conference, ICDF2C 2018, New Orleans, LA, USA, 10–12 September 2018, Proceedings 10., pp. 45–65. Springer (2019)
9. Huber, M., Mulazzani, M., Leithner, M., Schrittwieser, S., Wondracek, G., Weippl, E.: Social snapshots: digital forensics for online social networks. In: Proceedings of the 27th Annual Computer Security Applications Conference, pp. 113–122 (2011)

10. Karpisek, F., Baggili, I., Breitinger, F.: Whatsapp network forensics: decrypting and understanding the whatsapp call signaling messages. Digit. Investig. **15**, 110–118 (2015). https://doi.org/10.1016/j.diin.2015.09.002, special Issue: Big Data and Intelligent Data Analysis
11. Kier, C., Madlmayr, G., Nawratil, A., Schafferer, M., Schanes, C., Grechenig, T.: Mobile payment fraud: a practical view on the technical architecture and starting points for forensic analysis of new attack scenarios. In: 2015 Ninth International Conference on IT Security Incident Management & IT Forensics, pp. 68–76 (2015). https://doi.org/10.1109/IMF.2015.14
12. Kuncoro, A.P., Riadi, I., Luthfi, A.: Mobile forensics development of mobile banking application using static forensic. Int. J. Comput. Appl. **975**, 8887 (2017)
13. Lwin, H.H., Aung, W.P.: Forensics analysics of mobile financial applications used in Myanmar. Ph.D. thesis, MERAL Portal (2020)
14. Mahr, A., Cichon, M., Mateo, S., Grajeda, C., Baggili, I.: Zooming into the pandemic! a forensic analysis of the zoom application. Forensic Sci. Int. Digit. Investig. **36**, 301107 (2021). https://doi.org/10.1016/j.fsidi.2021.301107
15. Mendoza, J.: Over 8 million cash app users possibly affected by data breach from a former employee (2022), https://www.usatoday.com/story/money/2022/04/06/cash-app-data-breach/9490327002/
16. Nicholson, T., Hayes, D., Le-Khac, N.A.: Forensic analysis of the ios apple pay mobile payment system, pp. 3–19. Springer, Cham (2023)
17. Nikkel, B.: Fintech forensics: criminal investigation and digital evidence in financial technologies. Forensic Sci. Int. Digit. Investig. **33**, 200908 (2020). https://doi.org/10.1016/j.fsidi.2020.200908
18. Onik, A.R., Alsmadi, R., Baggili, I., Webb, A.M.: So fresh, so clean: cloud forensic analysis of the amazon irobot roomba vacuum. Forensic Sci. Int. Digit. Investig. **48**, 301686 (2024)
19. Osho, O., Mohammed, U.L., Nimzing, N.N., Uduimoh, A.A., Misra, S.: Forensic analysis of mobile banking apps. In: Misra, S., et al. (eds.) ICCSA 2019. LNCS, vol. 11623, pp. 613–626. Springer, Cham (2019). https://doi.org/10.1007/978-3-030-24308-1_49
20. Pagliery, J.: Gaetz paid accused sex trafficker, who then venmo'd teen (2021), https://www.thedailybeast.com/gaetz-paid-accused-sex-trafficker-who-then-venmod-teen
21. PayPal, I.: About venmo security (2024), https://help.venmo.com/hc/en-us/articles/360035844973-About-Venmo-Security
22. Pichan, A., Lazarescu, M., Soh, S.T.: Cloud forensics: technical challenges, solutions and comparative analysis. Digit. Investig. **13**, 38–57 (2015)
23. Salamh, F.E., Mirza, M.M., Hutchinson, S., Yoon, Y.H., Karabiyik, U.: What's on the horizon? an in-depth forensic analysis of android and ios applications. IEEE Access **9**, 99421–99454 (2021)
24. Thomas, T., Piscitelli, M., Shavrov, I., Baggili, I.: Memory foreshadow: memory forensics of hardware cryptocurrency wallets-a tool and visualization framework. Forensic Sci. Int. Digit. Investig. **33**, 301002 (2020)
25. Walnycky, D., Baggili, I., Marrington, A., Moore, J., Breitinger, F.: Network and device forensic analysis of android social-messaging applications. Digit. Investig. **14**, S77–S84 (2015). https://doi.org/10.1016/j.diin.2015.05.009, the Proceedings of the Fifteenth Annual DFRWS Conference

26. Yarramreddy, A., Gromkowski, P., Baggili, I.: Forensic analysis of immersive virtual reality social applications: a primary account. In: 2018 IEEE Security and Privacy Workshops (SPW), pp. 186–196 (2018). https://doi.org/10.1109/SPW.2018.00034
27. Zhou, J., Karabiyik, U.: Watch your wechat wallet: digital forensics approach on wechat payments on android. In: Goel, S., Gladyshev, P., Nikolay, A., Markowsky, G., Johnson, D. (eds.) Digital Forensics and Cyber Crime, pp. 97–110. Springer, Cham (2023)

Forensic Analysis of AI Applications - A Replika "AI Companion" Example

Christopher Hargreaves[1(✉)] and Dan Drury[2]

[1] Department of Computer Science, University of Oxford, Oxford, UK
christopher.hargreaves@cs.ox.ac.uk
[2] DSTL, Salisbury, UK
ddrury@mail.dstl.gov.uk

Abstract. Many applications now incorporate or make use of AI models to some degree, making them AI-dependent or AI-supported. This paper provides an analysis of the app Replika, which provides an AI companion to users. The AI capabilities are hosted remotely and are not accessible for analysis, but this research shows the results of analysing the local app on iOS that interacts with the server-side AI-system and finds that effective analysis is possible, without necessarily needing to analyse the AI model itself.

Keywords: Digital Forensic Science · AI Forensics · Generative AI · Chat Bot · Replika · Mobile Forensics · iOS

1 Introduction

Recent years have seen major increases in the use of AI, with one in six UK businesses implementing at least one of the AI applications asked about in a survey (Office of National Statistics, UK 2023). Digital forensics has also seen increasing interest in the use of AI for digital forensics, and is discussed in more detail in Sect. 2.1. However, the application of digital forensic techniques to AI-based software systems has been studied to a lesser degree in the academic literature, and is discussed in Sect. 2.2. This paper falls into the second category and offers example research into a mobile app in the 'AI companion' category and shows that there is substantial evidence that can be recovered, despite lack of access to server-side artefacts, or the AI model in use. This paper therefore makes the following contributions:

- Digital forensic research into the 'AI companion' app *Replika* on iOS.
- A discussion of the types of artefacts recoverable from this app category.
- Open source scripts to demonstrate the data extraction from the Replika mobile app artefacts, with example data[1].

---

[1] https://github.com/chrishargreaves/replika-ai-forensics.

- Addition of an 'AI chat app examination' technique to the SOLVE-IT digital forensics knowledge base (Hargreaves et al. 2025), along with potential weaknesses associated with the technique.
- Further discussion of the categorisations within the new 'AI Forensics' subdomain, highlighting different roles of AI within crime, and therefore within digital investigations.

The remainder of this paper is structured as follows: background and related work is discussed in Sect. 2, followed by the methodology in Sect. 3. Results of the app analysis are provided in Sect. 4, followed by discussion and conclusions in Sects. 5 and 6.

2 Background and Related Work

2.1 Use of AI in Digital Forensics

Several recent papers have discussed how digital forensics could make use of AI technologies to assist with investigations. Du et al. (2020) contains an overview of work up to 2020, with more recent papers continuing the discussion and including the advances made since the launch of ChatGPT in 2022. (Scanlon et al. 2023) provided early work on the potential applications of LLMs to digital forensics, using ChatGPT as a demonstrator. Many other pieces of work focus on more detailed applications within digital forensics, e.g. reporting (Michelet and Breitinger 2024), or even generating teaching scenarios (Voigt et al. 2024). There is some overall analysis of where AI can be applied within a digital forensic investigation, with Wickramasekara et al. (2025a) considering applications at different phases of a digital forensics process model (Casey 2011), and one of the applications of the recent SOLVE-IT knowledge base (Hargreaves et al. 2025), which breaks digital forensics into specific objectives and techniques, was to consider the application of AI to each specific technique, with 5 techniques identified as already implemented within digital forensic tools, 7 in academic work with an implementation, 11 in academic work as ideas, 26 where some application could be envisaged, and 51 where a non-AI-based technique is likely sufficient. Other work has focused on addressing issues particularly important to digital forensics, e.g. explainability (Solanke 2022), or measuring the correctness of results (Wickramasekara et al. 2025b).

2.2 Forensic Analysis of AI Supported Systems: Categorisation

Another topic is the use of digital forensic techniques to analyse systems that make use of AI. The arxiv paper from Baggili and Behzadan (2019) defines AI Forensics as "scientific and legal tools, techniques, and protocols for the extraction, collection, analysis, and reporting of digital evidence pertaining to failures in AI-enabled systems", which restricts to a specific use-case of investigating failures in AI systems. This explanation has a useful component of describing the need to analyse the entire AI-enabled system, but adds a restriction as to the purpose of the investigation. Many AI systems will not have failed, but still contain evidence that is highly relevant to investigations, e.g. queries or conversations typed into ChatGPT. The work also differentiates 'AI Application Forensics' from 'AI model forensics'[2], although practically the model may be part of the application, but the separation is useful, regardless of the precise relationship between those components.

Schneider and Breitinger (2023) highlights the 'failure-based' restriction in Baggili and Behzdan (2019) but introduces a different limitation, which is to focus on "systems designed for a malicious act", which again, not all analysis of AI-enabled systems would have this investigative objective, and could be examining 'off the shelf' systems that are not 'malicious by design' or tampered with, but could contain evidence of criminal acts.

2.3 Forensic Analysis of AI Supported Systems: Implementations

In addition to the classification exercises, there is practical work examining the artefacts left by some specific implementations. Early work on Cortana was undertaken in Singh and Singh (2017), considering Windows 10 and predating the recent advances in LLM based applications. Dragonas et al. (2024) reports on the artefacts left by the ChatGPT mobile app on iOS and Android, and integrates the findings into the open source tools ALEAPP and iLEAPP. Cho et al. (2025) consider 'conversational AI services' including ChatGPT, Gemini, Copilot and Claude, examining a mixture of mobile app data, desktop data, and data recovered from the cloud e.g. Google Takeout. Similar work also covers ChatGPT, Copilot and Gemini apps on iOS and Android (Tyagi et al. 2025).

In forensic tools, as noted above, iLEAPP[3] and ALEAPP[4] now support analysis of ChatGPT apps. However, the status of support in commercial tooling is unclear, as without full licenses, it is difficult to ascertain the level of support for specific apps, making identification of research gaps difficult.

These examples illustrate the need for digital forensic research into applications that make use of AI, either as the core feature, such as ChatGPT, or as a secondary feature, e.g. Cortana as part of MS Windows). These could be differentiated as AI-dependent, and AI-supported. However, it remains to be seen if there are any practical analysis differences between the two.

2.4 AI Supported Systems: AI Companions

The previous work described in the previous section focused largely on 'conversational AI' apps, e.g. ChatGPT etc. However, there are other classes of AI apps that could be interesting to digital forensic investigations, for example image generation, deep fake software, nudify apps, and voice cloning.

Another relevant category is referred to as 'Companion AI' apps, which are reported to be growing in popularity (De Freitas and Cohen 2024) and differ

---

[2] It also includes: 'AI Training Forensics': forensics of AI training processes and datasets, and 'AI substrate forensics': meaning the systems on which AI systems run.
[3] https://github.com/abrignoni/iLEAPP.
[4] https://github.com/abrignoni/ALEAPP.

from the general conversational apps described above as they are designed to be 'friend-like' or even romantic. This class of app has been referred to in real cases, where individuals have discussed their criminal intent with these companion apps, for example in the UK, plans to break into Windsor Castle with a crossbow to assassinate the Queen were discussed and the individual had reportedly exchanged 5,000 messages with the bot (BBC News 2023).

Given the gap in research in this area, the novelty of this app type, and the use in real cases, this paper reports the results of experiments into the 'AI companion' category, specifically the Replika chatbot. This was chosen as it has good market penetration[5], offers multimodal interaction methods, and has been mentioned as relevant in real-world cases (BBC News 2023).

2.5 Replika Overview

Replika is described as an 'AI companion' and is one of many available on the App Store and Google Play. It is available for iOS, Android and the Meta Quest VR headset[6]. A screenshot from the iOS App Store is shown in Fig. 1. The features of the app are discussed in Sect. 3.

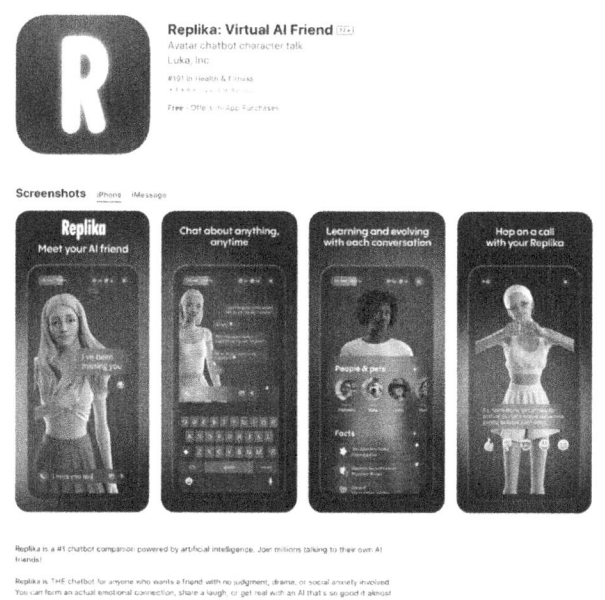

Fig. 1. Screenshot of the Replika app, advertised on the Apple App Store.

---

[5] It has 18K reviews on the Apple App Store, and has 504K reviews, and is in the '10M+ downloads' category on Google Play.
[6] https://replika.com.

3 Methodology

3.1 Overview

The aim of the research was to both determine the artefacts left from a specific AI companion app, but also to determine the features and artefacts that may result from this category of app. The methodology used for this work is largely experimental. The app was installed, and features determined from both documentation and the user interface of the app. Based on those features, probable investigative objectives were extrapolated and a series of experiments conducted to populate the app with data, and then examine the resulting data to determine if forensic artefacts are recoverable. The objectives selected for this research were:

- to identify user accounts associated with the app,
- to identify configuration parameters used to set up the AI companion,
- to recover the chat messages to and from the AI companion.

3.2 Experimental Method

The experiments focused on the iOS version of the app. Since the aim of the research was to determine what an AI chatbot's capabilities and features are, and how they manifest as digital forensic artefacts, an example is sufficient for this. iOS was chosen as it was reported as being encountered in 83.6% of cases (compared to 73.8% for Android) in the DFPulse 2024 Practitioner Survey (Hargreaves et al. 2024).

The app was installed on a test device, an account set up, an AI companion configured (referred to as a Replika) and various chat interactions carried out. The tests were conducted with the free version of the app to examine the features available to the majority of users. Iterative iOS backups and file system extractions were performed.

Setting up the app triggers a series of questions for configuration: email address, name, pronouns, age bracket, familiarity with AI technology, first contact with AI, main reason to download Replika, how Replika should adapt over time, movies the user is a fan of (from *Her*, *Blade Runner*, *Ex-Machina*), how the user spends their free time, how they perceive solitude, coping mechanisms for loneliness, what they are interested in doing with the Replika, quality that attracts them most to a companion, desired gender for companion, their ideal companion, how their Replika should treat them, what is their 'love language', how adventurous they are, major 'turn offs', character type for their Replika, how they would like their Replika to interact (texting, video chat, AR, audio calls and messages). Further configurations and features are shown in Table 1:

It is also possible to upload photos as part of the text chat, and to receive images from the AI companion.

Table 1. Configurations and features of a Replika chatbot.

Feature	Details
Relationship	What the defined relationship is with the Replika. The default is 'friend', but girlfriend/boyfriend, wife/husband, sister/brother, and mentor are also options
Memories	These are 'facts' extracted from conversations with the Replika but can also be edited by the user
Diary	This is record of the Replika's day from their perspective. It can contain general topics it has been "thinking about" but can also contain summaries about interactions with the user
Traits	These are customisable aspects of the Replika's personality e.g. confident, shy, energetic, mellow, caring, sassy, practical, dreamy, artistic, and logical
Interests	These are things that the Replika 'knows about' and has an interest in, e.g. board games, comics, manga, history, philosophy, cooking and baking, anime, basketball, football, sci-fi, sneakers, gardening, skincare and makeup, cars, space, soccer. K-pop, fitness, physics, and mindfulness. This is configurable by the user
Voice	Defines the voice used by the Replika from a set
Backstory	This is a free text field that can be populated by the user

4 Results

Replika 9.35.3 was installed on iOS 15.1, accounts created, and then incremental chat with a bot conducted. The free version of Replika was used (but the 'Pro' version is available for 59 per year subscription). The paid versions (either Pro or ULTRA) provides additional features such as: "a better conversational model, enhanced emotional intelligence, improved continuous self learning" (ULTRA 67.99), or "advanced conversational model, personality customisation, voice messages and video calls, activities for personal growth", also more "relationship options", and more "gems and coins" for purchases (Pro 59.99).

For the experiments, iOS backups were taken, along with file system extractions. Results from both are presented here so the extraction level necessary can be determined depending on the artefacts needed.

The focus of these results is based around the objectives described in the methodology, but the results also first include the structure of the data in the iOS backup and the structure of the data in the file system extraction to provide context for the remainder of the results.

4.1 Structure of the iOS Backup

For an iOS backup, the app data is stored in the folder *Appdomain-ai.replika.app*. The structure of the contents of that folder is shown in Fig. 2.

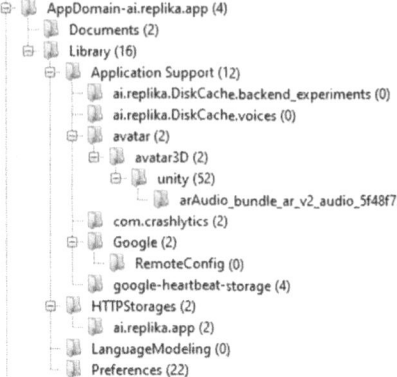

Fig. 2. Folder structure of the *ai.replika.app* from an iOS backup.

4.2 Structure of Data in File System Extraction

To locate the same data from the iOS backup in the full file system extraction, the path to the container needs to be identified. This information can be found in: */private/var/mobile/Library/FrontBoard/applicationState.db*, and is also automatically extracted using tools such as iLEAPP, shown as the 'Sandbox path' field. For this example, it shows that the app itself, and the associated user data, were located in the following paths:

/private/var/containers/Bundle/Application/DF42CDB7-1D6B-4A2A-8DDA-C1741A32009E/Replika.app

/private/var/mobile/Containers/Data/Application/C31CB699-2B97-4304-B261-8C751ED00C7C

Looking at the contents of the container folder (Fig. 3), you can see that the folder structure is, as expected, much more extensive in the full file system extraction than the iOS backup shown earlier.

Only a small subset of files is needed to answer the research questions set for this work. The results are discussed in the following subsections.

4.3 Location of Account Information

Keyword searches were conducted for the ground truth data used to set up the account (in this case the 'Sign in with Apple' feature was used, along with 'Hide my email' which created a random email address linked to the user's Apple email account). There were two locations where this information was located:

- a Realm database[7] (in both iOS backup and file system acquisition)
- a .WAL database file within the Cache subfolder (file system acquisition only)

---

[7] "a relatively new database format built as a potential replacement for SQLite" (Cobley and Geneste 2022).

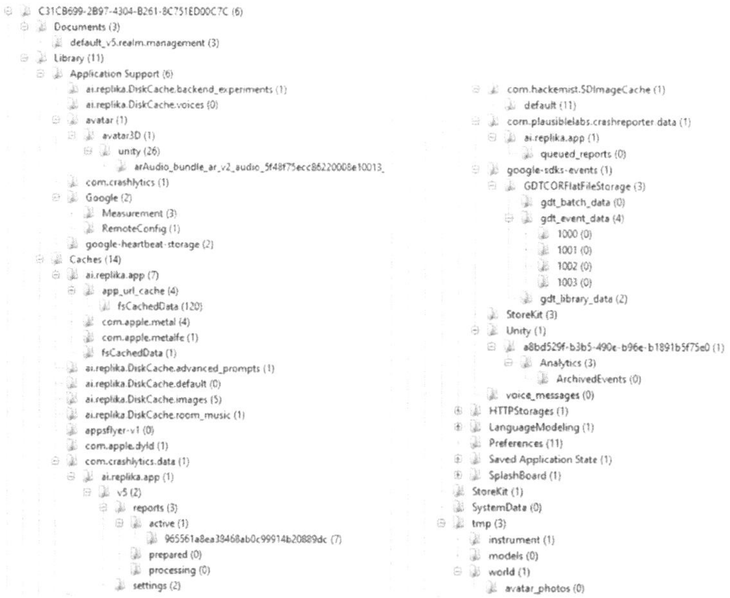

Fig. 3. Folder structure from a file system extraction.

Realm Database. The Realm database is located in these different locations depending on the data source:

- /AppDomain-ai.replika.app/Documents/default_v5.realm (iOS backup)
- /private/var/mobile/Containers/Data/Application/C31CB699-2B97-4304-B261-8C751ED00C7C/Documents/default_v5.realm (file system)

From either source, the Realm database can be viewed with Realm Studio[8], and example data is shown in Fig. 4. The database has 54 'tables' (to use usual database terminology) but only relevant tables for the research objectives are discussed in this paper due to space constraints. A full table list is available in the project repository.

For the question of account information, the table `GRUserProfileEntity` includes the fields: *ageRange*, *firstName*, *lastName*, *phoneNumber*, *email*, and *emailVerified*. The full list of fields for this table are in the project repository, and an example is shown in Fig. 5, which shows the user's name provided (a first name only was supplied), the age range supplied, and the Apple 'hide my email' address is also shown. It can also be seen that the email address was verified. This acts as a reminder that use of this app can also be inferred from the presence of verification emails extracted in the usual manner. There is also a user ID which is used later in message analysis.

---

[8] https://docs.realm.io/sync/realm-studio.

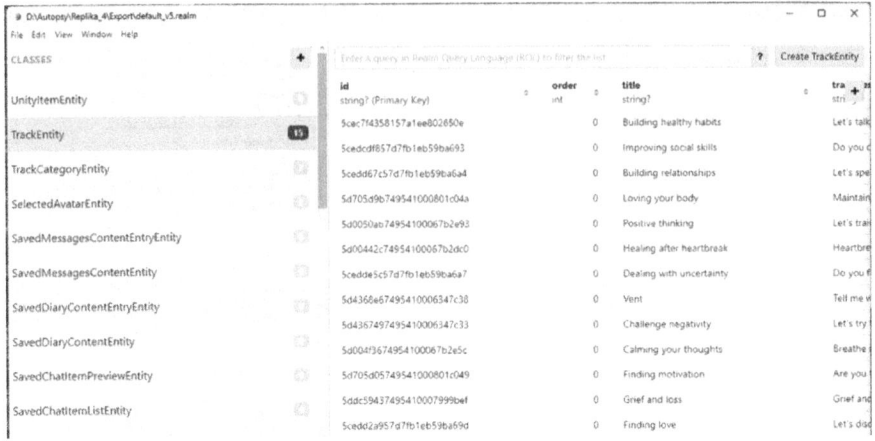

Fig. 4. An example of viewing Realm database data in Realm Studio.

Fig. 5. Example data extracted from the GRUserProfileEntity 'table'.

Cache.db-Wal. Data related to the user account was also found in the app cache, specifically keyword hits in the WAL file for the Cache.db database described below (in file system acquisition only):

/private/var/mobile/Containers/Data/Application/C31CB699-2B97-4304- B261-8C751ED00C7C/Library/Caches/ai.replika.app/app_url_cache/Cache .db-wal

To parse this information, the *app_url_cache* folder was extracted, and code developed in Python was used to extract information from the Cache.db SQLite database, allowing data from the WAL to integrate into the main database.

This shows that within the cache, for data cached from the URL *https://replika.ai/api/mobile/1.5/profile*, there is JSON data stored within the cache, which can be parsed with the developed code. An example of the cached profile information is shown in Fig. 6. It shows the same information, including user ID, name, supplied age range, and email information, including the verified status.

4.4 AI Companion Configuration

As discussed in the introduction, on initial setup of the app, the user provides settings and preferences to the app for their AI companion. Much of the configuration information is available in files within the app cache. The Python code discussed earlier was modified to recover content from requests to the URLs shown below for the Replika bot details, and as a result reconstructing many of the initial and subsequent configuration settings.

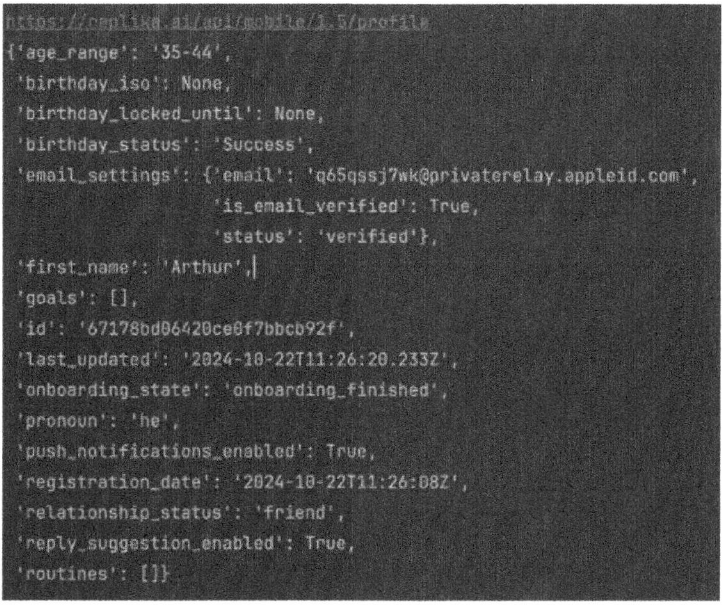

Forensic Analysis of AI Applications - A Replika "AI Companion" Example 87

Fig. 6. An example of the cached JSON data from the url: *https://replika.ai/api/mobile/1.5/profile*

Replika Bot Details: Some details of the created bot can be recovered from the Realm database in the table: GRBotEntity. Relevant fields include the Replika name, gender, a link to items in their room (*roomItems*), a link to the id of the avatar used (*avatar*, linked to SelectedAvatarEntry table).

Details can also be recovered from the app cache. The name assigned to the Replika AI bot can be recovered from the cache by examining the cached objects for the URL: *https://replika.ai/api/mobile/1.5/core_description*. This can also be found in *https://replika.ai/api/mobile/1.5/personal_bot*, under the field *name* along with gender, and an ID. It may also be possible to extrapolate customisations to the body shape of the basic avatar models, but this has not been explored.

Other information provided such as the 'backstory' which is free text from the user, can be recovered by looking at the content within the cache from accesses to: *https://replika.ai/api/mobile/1.5/core_description/backstory*. This is recovered by the developed Python script.

In terms of traits and interests that have been selected for the AI Replika bot, this can also be determined from the cache, from the URL: *https://replika.ai/api /mobile/1.5/store/actions/buy_user_items*. These traits usually need to be purchased with 'coins' or 'gems' inside the app. Some coins are provided, but useful amounts of coins and gems can be purchased with real currency via in-app purchases. From the cached data, Fig. 7 shows that the 'physics' interest has been bought, and is enabled. This information was not recovered from the Realm database, and keyword searches did not return hits, but it may still be present in encoded data within fields of the database, but without the development of better tooling, this is difficult to conclusively demonstrate either way.

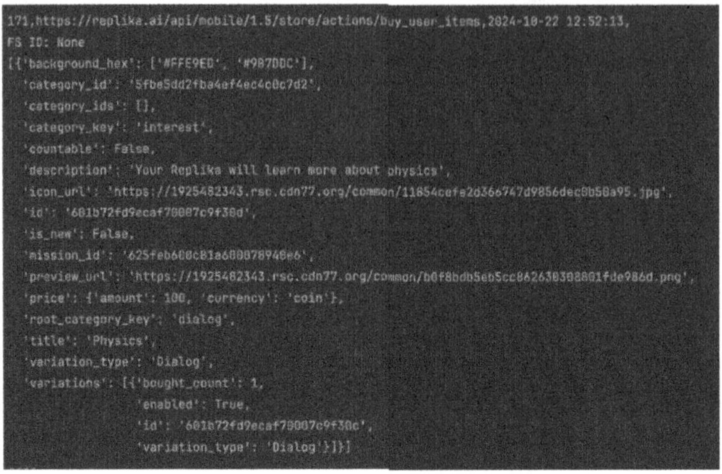

```
171,https://replika.ai/api/mobile/1.5/store/actions/buy_user_items,2024-10-22 12:52:13,
FS ID: None
[{'background_hex': ['#FFE9E0', '#987DDC'],
 'category_id': '5fbe5dd2fba4ef4ec4c0c7d2',
 'category_ids': [],
 'category_key': 'interest',
 'countable': False,
 'description': 'Your Replika will learn more about physics',
 'icon_url': 'https://1925482343.rsc.cdn77.org/common/11854cefe2d366747d9856dec0b56a95.jpg',
 'id': '601b72fd9ecaf79007c9f38d',
 'is_new': False,
 'mission_id': '625feb600c81a680078948e6',
 'preview_url': 'https://1925482343.rsc.cdn77.org/common/b0f8bdb5eb5cc862638308a01fde986d.png',
 'price': {'amount': 100, 'currency': 'coin'},
 'root_category_key': 'dialog',
 'title': 'Physics',
 'variation_type': 'Dialog',
 'variations': [{'bought_count': 1,
                 'enabled': True,
                 'id': '601b72fd9ecaf79007c9f38c',
                 'variation_type': 'Dialog'}]}]
```

Fig. 7. Shows that the 'physics interest' has been bought and is enabled.

There is also some information in the preferences files:

- *AppDomain-ai.replika.app/Library/Preferences/personal.defaults.67178bd06 420ce0f7bbcb92f.plist* (iOS Backup)
- */private/var/mobile/Containers/Data/Application/C31CB699-2B97-4304- B261-8C751ED00C7C/Library/Preferences/personal.defaults.67178bd06420 ce0f7bbcb92f.plist* (file system)

This binary property list has several fields, one of which is onboarding-*personalization.personalization-v3-context*, which contains binary data that is Base64 encoded. This can be extracted and decoded in various ways, e.g. converting the plist to XML and using CyberChef[9] with a combination of an XPath expression to extract the data from the key[10], followed by 'Base64 decoding' and 'JSON Beautify', it is possible to see configuration parameters such as adventurousMeter, interaction modes selected (i.e. text, audio etc.), and answers to onboarding questions discussed earlier e.g. movies, ideal companion, preferred bot gender etc. Alternatively, the binary data can be copied from the plist and just the 'Base64 decoding and 'JSON Beautify recipes in CyberChef used.

---

[9] https://gchq.github.io/CyberChef/.
[10] //key[text()='onboarding-personalization.personalization-v3-context']/
following-sibling::data[1]/text().

4.5 Location of Chat Data

Recovery of chat is possible from the Realm database, available in both iOS backups and full file system extractions. However, reconstruction of this data from the Realm database is a bit more complex than the previous examples and there are details extracted from several of the tables to make sense of the data.

The tables needed to make sense of the chat are:

- `GRMessageEntity`,
- `GRMessageContentEntity`,
- `GRMessageReactionEntity`,
- `GRUserProfileEntity`.

One note is that within the table `GRUserProfileEntity`, the ID of the user can be found. This will be used shortly and in this example the id is: 67178bd06420ce0f7bbcb92f.

Starting from the table `GRMessageEntity`, there are various fields available with key fields shown in Table 2.

Table 2. Key fields from `GRMessageEntity`

Field	Notes
date	The time of the message
authorID	Linked to `GRUserProfileEntity:id` the author of the message (null if it is the bot)
botID	Linked to `GRBotEntity:id` the bot that is being interacted with
authorship	Seems to be: 0=user, 2=bot
content	If type 0, indicates text of message in Realm Studio but also links to `GRMesssageContentEntity:text` . If type 2 it indicates a picture, with link to AWS content (access denied if link is accessed). Type 9 indicates a voice message with the text of the message in the text field, but see below in `GRMesssageContentEntity` table details for more.

Within the `GRMesssageContentEntity` table (linked from `GRMessageEntity` by the text field), while most fields were not populated in the experiment data, other potential fields of interest include those shown in Table 3:

In terms of automated parsing of this content, this is certainly possible in future, but there are some challenges, and this has not been implemented for this project. Some options include:

- There is some Python code for Realm on GitHub but nothing official. The code that is available is experimental and therefore not considered production ready.

Table 3. More detailed fields from `GRMessageEntity`

Field	Notes
type	Repeats the message type discussed earlier. 0:text, 2: image, 9: voice message
images	Links to content on AWS, but not accessible without credentials
voiceMessageLink	Contains a link to the audio of a voice message. This is accessible online without credentials. However, the text of the audio message is also available in the text field earlier
duration	Length of the voice message

- Another option is that Realm Studio will export JSON. However, since Realm Studio 13, the JSON export is quite complex, with numeric references for content of fields and is difficult to parse. This is because the developers needed to handle circular references inside of the Realm database which do not translate if the data were to be exported to 'flat JSON . A reformatter for this JSON export into something more suitable for forensics is a more likely option to explore first.

Some aspects of the chat have also been recovered from the cache, but not all, so the Realm database is more reliable. However, some images can be found in the cache (important if the AWS links cannot be accessed). For these images, the cached items for the following URLs can be examined (coded into the `dump_replika_cache_info.py` script): URLs starting with: *https://replika. ai/api/mobile/1.5/images?image_url* allow images sent to and received from the bot to be recovered from the cache. The term 'botimage' in the file name indicates the image was sent from the bot.

4.6 Memories

Another key aspect of how the Replika AI bot functions is via the use of 'Memories. These can be viewed within the app and can include the random 'thoughts of the Replika, but also extracted pieces of information obtained through interaction with the user. Information regarding memories can be recovered from the Realm database. The majority of the useful information can be found in the table `MemoryV3FactEntity`, which include the fields shown in Table 4:

Some 'memories' information can also be recovered from the cache: */private /var/mobile/Containers/Data/Application/C31CB699-2B97-4304-B261-8C751 ED00C7C/Library/Caches/ai.replika.app/app_url_cache/Cache.db*

Extracting cache content for URLs starting with: *https://replika.ai/api/ mobile/1.5/memory/v3/* will recover JSON data separated into customer_facts and robot_facts. It appears from the dataset created that the customer_facts relate to 'memories of what the user has done, whereas robot_facts relate to 'memories produced by the Replika.

Table 4. Fields from the table `MemoryV3FactEntity`

Field	Notes
id	ID for the entry
Text	The text of the memory
creationDate	The creation date of the memory. An important note is that this is not the time of the text input or output that is the basis for the memory, rather the time of a seemingly separate 'memory forming process
isRead	Whether the memory has been read by the user
isUserEdited	Whether the memory has been edited by the user
categoryid	A category ID that links into the id field in the table MemoryV3ItemCategoryEntity. That table provides the text name for the category that the memory is in
rawSubject	Unknown

5 Discussion and Future Work

5.1 Objectives

Reviewing the objectives set for the research:

Provide an example of the capabilities and artefacts from an AI 'companion app: This work has shown an example of how a synthetic 'companion can be created in an AI companion app and some of the features that are offered. It has also identified broad categories of artefacts that can be present: user accounts, configuration of the AI bot, chat messages, and shared images and other media.

Identify User Accounts Associated with the App: The user account information for Replika has been recovered from a Realm database that is available in both iOS backups and file system extractions. This includes the provided users name, email address, and 'verified status of the email address. This information is also available in cached artefacts in JSON form, accessible in file system extractions only.

Identify Configuration Parameters Used to Set up the AI Companion: For Replika data, it is possible to recover details about the personality traits, interests, appearance (only via images sent at present, but theoretically possible from configuration parameters) and backstory provided for the AI bot. This is again via the Realm database and cached JSON artefacts. Without further work it is difficult to know how these specific configurations and customisations generalise to other chatbot apps, but it is likely that some degree of customisability is a required feature for bots created in any system.

Recover the Chat Messages to and From the AI Companion: The chat messages sent to and from the AI bot have been recovered from the Realm database, which, again is accessible via both iOS backups and file system extractions. This has also included accessible links online to voice messages from the

Replika bot (although the text of the message is stored locally). Parts of the conversation are also recoverable from the cached JSON data, which may be useful if messages are deleted and no longer available in the Realm database. This also can include copies of images sent to and from the Replika.

5.2 Future Work

In terms of future work, while this work has looked at Replika in reasonable detail, there is still further work that could be done on this AI companion app, e.g. experiments used the free version only, and more longitudinal data would reveal any limits to the persistence of artefacts recoverable.

It may be necessary in some circumstances to identify if the free or paid for version was in use, but further work will be necessary to establish that. However, the paid features relevant to digital forensics have been explored already e.g. image, voice, and text recovery, and setting the bot's traits and memories. Examination of different relationship types for the bot has not been explored, but assessing the capabilities of different persona is more of a social science experiment than a digital forensics one so has not been prioritised.

From a technical perspective, regarding Realm databases, the forensic capabilities in this area are not very satisfactory. There is some work on recovering deleted data from Realm databases: (Kim et al. 2018) (in Korean), Cobley and Geneste (2022), and 2022, but has not advanced much since, with only a brief discussion in Omsha (2024). Also, basic forensic tool support for Realm does not seem to exist, and exporting data from Realm Studio is not adequate for forensic reporting. Another file type encountered are UnityFS files; while not essential for this report, no satisfactory method of deconstructing them was found, or to identify the assets within. All of these would be sensible and generalisable further work.

This work has shown the nature and capabilities of an example 'AI companion app. It has shown how to recover account information, details about the configuration of the AI companion, and chat history. There are many of this style of app now available for iOS and Android, and as more people interact with virtual companions, they could be a valuable data source for users ideas, plans, thoughts, and motivations, which are sometimes difficult things to definitively infer from existing data sources. Further work mapping more of these apps would likely be of potential benefit to future investigations, and would determine the extent to which the results in this paper can be generalised.

More generally, it is likely that there is further work to do on categories within the subdiscipline of 'AI Forensics', a shorthand for 'digital forensics of AI systems', and there may be differences between AI-dependent (i.e. does very little without the AI component, e.g. ChatGPT) and AI-supported systems (still has core features but AI offers additional capabilities, e.g. iOS). It may also be worth reapplying work summarised in Brenner (2010) referring to the roles that computers could play in crime (target, tool, incidental). Considering the same idea with AI, we can see that:

- AI systems could be the target of the offence,
- AI systems could be used as a tool for an offence,
- AI systems could play an incidental role in the commission of the offence

It may be that a fault in an AI system as described in Baggili and Behzadan (2019), could fit into 'incidental' as they capture information related to some criminal negligence in the development of the system, or a new category may be needed. The work in Schneider and Breitinger (2023) would mean that AI could be both the *target*, if it has been maliciously compromised, or is the *tool* if designed for malicious intent, or perhaps both simultaneously. It remains unclear if this categorisation is useful without substantially more examples, which will accrue as the subdomain matures.

Other general work would be to add the different implementations of AI-supported or dependent systems to future iterations of the DFPulse Practitioner Survey (Hargreaves et al. 2024) so that trends can be tracked over time and determine the extent of the digital forensic challenge. Also, Replika, and other implementations of AI-dependent systems have models that are not locally accessible and could change over time at the behest of the service provider. The recent work in Spichiger and Adelstein (2025) captures this concept as 'evolving systems' and highlights the need to preserve reference data not just from local devices, but also from servers at the time of the incident. This would also cover APIs changing that are used in the cache analysis in this work, but how to how to achieve reference data preservation specifically for AI-systems remains an open question.

6 Conclusions

This research has contributed to the new subdomain of AI forensics, focusing on applications where the AI-system may be 'incidental' to the crime carried out rather than the target, or a tool. It has focused on a specific example of AI companions, which are missing from academic research, and used Replika as an example given its relevance to real cases. The artefacts related to the use of Replika on iOS have been highlighted, but more broadly it has shown the need to monitor app offerings for AI-dependent and AI-supported apps, and also that traditional digital forensic artefact research is valuable and may still be effective within this new subdomain.

References

Baggili, I., Behzadan, V.: Founding the domain of AI forensics. arXiv preprint arXiv:1912.06497 (2019)

BBC News: how a chatbot encouraged a man who wanted to kill the queen (2023). https://www.bbc.co.uk/news/technology-67012224

Brenner, S.W.: Cybercrime: Criminal Threats from Cyberspace. Bloomsbury Publishing USA (2010)

Casey, E.: Digital Evidence and Computer Crime: Forensic Science, Computers, and the Internet. Academic Press (2011)

Cho, K., Park, Y., Kim, J., Kim, B., Jeong, D.: Conversational AI forensics: a case study on ChatGPT, Gemini, Copilot, and Claude. Forensic Sci. Int. Digit. Investig. **52**, 301855 (2025)

Cobley, P., Geneste, G.: Chapter 8, Realm, in Mobile Forensics – The File Format Handbook, chap. 8. Springer (2022)

De Freitas, J., Cohen, I.G.: The health risks of generative AI-based wellness apps. Nat. Med. **30**(5), 1269–1275 (2024)

Dragonas, E., Lambrinoudakis, C., Nakoutis, P.: Forensic analysis of OpenAI's ChatGPT mobile application. Forensic Sci. Int. Digit. Investig. **50**, 301801 (2024)

Du, X., Hargreaves, C., Sheppard, J., Anda, F., Sayakkara, A., Le-Khac, N.A., Scanlon, M.: SOK: exploring the state of the art and the future potential of artificial intelligence in digital forensic investigation. In: Proceedings of the 15th International Conference on Availability, Reliability and Security, pp. 1–10 (2020)

Hargreaves, C., van Beek, H., Casey, E.: Solve-it: a proposed digital forensic knowledge base inspired by mitre att&ck. Forensic Sci. Int. Digit. Investig. **52**, 301864 (2025)

Hargreaves, C., Breitinger, F., Dowthwaite, L., Webb, H., Scanlon, M.: DFPulse: the 2024 digital forensic practitioner survey. Forensic Sci. Int. Digit. Investig. **51**, 301844 (2024). ISSN 2666-2817, https://doi.org/10.1016/j.fsidi.2024.301844

Kim, J., Han, J., Choi, J.H., Lee, S.: The method of recovery for deleted record of realm database. J. Korea Instit. Info. Secur. Cryptol. **28**(3), 625–633 (2018)

Kim, S., et al.: Methods for recovering deleted data from the realm database: case study on Minitalk and Xabber. Forensic Sci. Int. Digit. Investig. **40**, 301353 (2022)

Michelet, G., Breitinger, F.: ChatGPT, llama, can you write my report? An experiment on assisted digital forensics reports written using (local) large language models. Forensic Sci. Int. Digit. Investig. **48**, 301683 (2024)

Office of National Statistics, UK: Understanding AI uptake and sentiment among people and businesses in the UK: June 2023 (2023). https://www.ons.gov.uk/businessindustryandtrade/itandinternetindustry/articles/understandingaiuptakeandsentimentamongpeopleandbusinessesintheuk/june2023

Omsha, B.: A comparative study of .net MAUI and Avalonia in cross-platform mobile application development (2024)

Scanlon, M., Breitinger, F., Hargreaves, C., Hilgert, J.N., Sheppard, J.: ChatGPT for digital forensic investigation: the good, the bad, and the unknown. Forensic Sci. Int. Digit. Investig. **46**, 301609 (2023)

Schneider, J., Breitinger, F.: Towards AI forensics: did the artificial intelligence system do it? J. Info. Secur. Appl. **76**, 103517 (2023)

Singh, B., Singh, U.: A forensic insight into windows 10 Cortana search. Comput. & Secur. **66**, 142–154 (2017), ISSN 0167-4048, https://doi.org/10.1016/j.cose.2017.01.007

Solanke, A.A.: Explainable digital forensics AI: towards mitigating distrust in AI-based digital forensics analysis using interpretable models. Forensic Sci. Int. Digit. Investig. **42**, 301403 (2022)

Spichiger, H., Adelstein, F.: Preserving meaning of evidence from evolving systems. Forensic Sci. Int. Digit. Investig. **52**, 301867 (2025)

Tyagi, S., Gong, Y., Karabiyik, U.: Forensic analysis and privacy implications of LLM apps: a case study of ChatGPT, Copilot, and Gemini (2025). https://papers.ssrn.com/sol3/papers.cfm?abstract_id=5209937

Voigt, L.L., Freiling, F., Hargreaves, C.J.: Re-imagen: generating coherent background activity in synthetic scenario-based forensic datasets using large language models. Forensic Sci. Int. Digit. Investig. **50**, 301805 (2024)

Wickramasekara, A., Breitinger, F., Scanlon, M.: Exploring the potential of large language models for improving digital forensic investigation efficiency. Forensic Sci. Int. Digit. Investig. **52**, 301859 (2025)

Wickramasekara, A., Densmore, A., Breitinger, F., Studiawan, H., Scanlon, M.: AutoDFBench: a framework for AI generated digital forensic code and tool testing and evaluation. In: Proceedings of the Digital Forensics Doctoral Symposium, pp. 1–7 (2025b)

An AI-Based Network Forensic Readiness Framework for Resource-Constrained Environments

Syed Rizvi[1(✉)], Mark Scanlon[2(✉)], Jimmy McGibney[1(✉)], and John Sheppard[1(✉)]

[1] South East Technological University, Waterford, Ireland
Syed.Rizvi@postgrad.wit.ie, {Jimmy.McGibney,John.Sheppard}@setu.ie
[2] School of Computer Science, University College Dublin, D04 V1W8 Dublin, Ireland
mark.scanlon@ucd.ie

Abstract. In recent years, the adoption of Internet of Things (IoT) devices has transformed industries and daily life. However, the integration of real-time services and internet connectivity increases the risk of attackers exploiting network vulnerabilities. Investigating such vulnerabilities in Resource-Constrained Environments (RCEs) poses challenges due to limited computational capacity, power constraints, and the heterogeneity of IoT-generated data and traffic. To address these issues, this study proposes a framework integrating optimised artificial intelligence models trained on the CICIoT2023 and CSE-CIC-IDS2018 datasets. A Docker-based simulation replicates constrained environments and captures network traffic in real time. The framework continuously monitors resources and dynamically selects the most suitable AI model for attack detection. Once an attack is detected, the system captures and preserves digitally signed critical forensic artefacts, categorised into system metadata, event/resource logs, network data, and processes. The AI-based framework aligns with ISO/IEC 27043:2015 Digital Forensic Readiness principles, automating many manual procedures and reducing both time and human effort. The quantitative evaluation demonstrates the effectiveness of the proposed network forensic readiness framework to address the specific challenges of RCEs.

Keywords: Network Forensic Readiness · IoT Forensics · Artificial Intelligence · Resource-constrained Environments

1 Introduction

The ubiquitous nature of Internet of Things (IoT) devices makes them vulnerable to attack. Investigating these attacks can be difficult because IoT devices have limited processing capabilities, power constraints, and storage, and different types of devices pose significant challenges for forensic investigation [2,18].

IoT devices can be the source of potentially pertinent digital forensic evidence and are a common focus of digital forensic research [3]. However, IoT activities are often short-lived and their associated data can be volatile. This presents challenges to trace security breaches, as the collection of evidence from IoT devices that are no longer connected to the network is complicated [7]. Data Integrity and Authenticity (DIA) are important in IoT forensics due to tampering risks and the transient nature of IoT data. Traditional digital forensic models developed for post-incident investigations struggle to adapt to the heterogeneous and complex nature of IoT devices. This limitation has complicated forensic investigations after security incidents, highlighting the need for a proactive approach.

Network Forensic Readiness (NFR) provides a proactive method to prepare for security incidents. NFR focusses on the identification, collection, and preservation of network evidence to support compliance and investigations [5]. The complexity of IoT networks necessitates a robust framework NFR approach to minimise human involvement in data collection, processing, and preservation while reducing investigative costs and latency. The framework proposed as part of this paper is aligned with the ISO/IEC 27043:2015 standard [23] to ensure that appropriate and effective Digital Forensic Readiness (DFR) methods are in place before an incident occurs.

The integration of Artificial Intelligence (AI) into network forensics has transformed attack detection and forensic readiness. The deployment of AI models in Resource-Constrained Environments (RCEs) poses significant challenges due to limited computational capabilities, energy constraints, and limited network bandwidth [16,21]. A Network Intrusion Detection System (NIDS) serves as the first line of defence. An AI-based NIDS has significant demands on device resources and network bandwidth. It requires mechanisms to dynamically prioritise or delay detection based on resource availability. The transient nature of events in RCE, where evidence can vanish after network access, highlights the need for efficient and scalable frameworks.

1.1 Key Contributions

In this paper, an AI-based optimised NFR framework is proposed to improve forensic readiness in RCE. The framework facilitates real-time network traffic capture and processing at the source. The new insights from the work highlight the trade-off between resource utilisation, throughput, and detection accuracy in RCE. The framework introduces dynamic model selection in real time based on available computational resources to ensure optimal performance. It supports comprehensive evidence acquisition to help forensic investigation by collecting system metadata, logs, and memory snapshots at the time of the incident. The effectiveness of the framework is validated through extensive real-time attack simulations involving seven different types of attack across five distinct devices, providing a quantitative evaluation of its performance. The framework performs multiclass attack classification and detects attacks in just 0.3 ms per packet, making it suitable for real-time use. The suggested framework achieved the highest 99.58% and 99.91% accuracy in the CICIoT2023 and CSE-CIC-IDS2018 datasets, respectively.

2 Related Work

Several studies have explored various aspects to improve attack detection, evidence acquisition, preservation, and analysis while addressing the limited computational nature of RCE.

Sadineni et al. [19] presented Ready-IoT, a forensic-readiness model that gathers data at both the network and application layers. The workflow spans scenario definition, device setup, event detection, evidence acquisition, preservation and readiness configuration. Experiments in Contiki-NG's *Cooja* emulator assessed the model against jamming and synchronisation attacks in the Time-Slotted Channel Hopping (TSCH) layer. Evidence is retained in a secure database, maintaining the chain of custody.

Recently, Waguespack et al. [25] introduced the Memory Anomaly Recognition System (MARS), a host IDS that monitors device memory within a Trusted Execution Environment (TEE). A Convolutional Neural Network (CNN) deployed on a remote server analyses n-gram sequences from memory dumps to detect deviations from the memory baseline. These sequences are also converted into audio spectra to extract features such as MFCCs, Mel spectrograms, and chroma variants for intrusion detection. MARS uses a watchdog timer to enforce periodic memory capture, triggering a device reset upon anomaly detection. This mechanism mitigates basic malware, while a secure boot process protects firmware integrity against advanced threats. Evaluations of the STM32 controller demonstrated scalability, trustworthiness, accuracy, and robustness.

Kebande et al. [8] introduced a comprehensive forensic model for IoT devices based on the ISO/IEC 27043 standard. The model spans the entire forensic lifecycle through three phases: forensic readiness (proactive), forensic initialisation (incident), and forensic investigation (reactive). The proposed model eliminates the need for ad hoc approaches, supports diverse IoT applications, and provides a customisable and configurable framework. Rizal et al. [15] also introduced a framework by integrating the Gated Recurrent Unit (GRU) model to improve forensic readiness in an IoT environment based on the ISO/IEC 27043 standard. The framework includes a smart repository and a sophisticated storage system designed to organise evidence using metadata and contextual information. The repository automates tasks, recognises patterns, and provides intelligent insights.

Many researchers have explored and highlighted the capabilities of AI for digital forensics, network forensics, and NFR. However, RCEs face persistent challenges such as data diversity, proliferation, integrity, authorisation issues, resource constraints, and the volatile nature of data [17]. The black-box nature and high computational demands of AI models complicate their application for NFR within RCE. This study aims to address these challenges through the design and deployment of an optimised AI-based framework for NFR within RCE, aligned with the ISO/IEC 27043:2015 standard.

3 Methodology

This section provides a detailed overview of the design and architecture of the proposed framework. This study follows the Design Science Research (DSR) methodology [11]. The DSR focusses on the development of a framework that addresses real-world problems and contributes to scientific knowledge.

3.1 Framework Design

The proposed approach extends beyond algorithmic or conceptual models through a framework design and implementation for NFR, aligned with the ISO/IEC 27043:2015 standard. The architecture of the proposed AI-based optimised NFR framework is shown in Fig. 1.

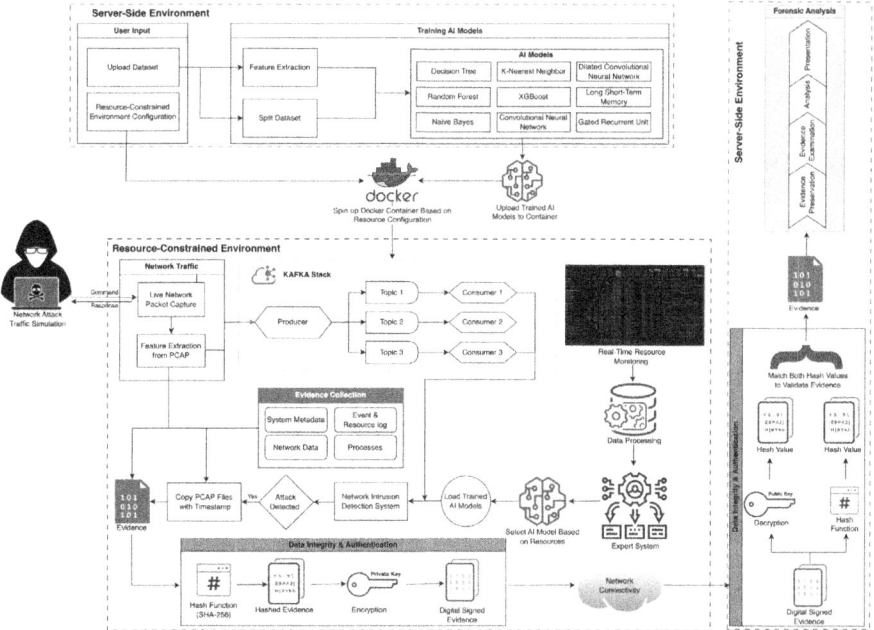

Fig. 1. The Proposed AI-based Optimised Network Forensic Readiness Framework Architecture for Resource-Constrained Environments

The NIDS component is the core feature of the proposed framework. This component utilises optimised AI models to enhance attack detection capabilities in RCE. AI models that incorporate both ML and DL approaches were trained using the CICIoT2023 [13] and CSE-CIC-IDS2018 [4] datasets. Both datasets were pre-processed using NumPy, Matplotlib, and Pandas by removing duplicates, handling missing/inconsistent values, and removing irrelevant features, which reduced the number of instances per attack class.

The use of dynamically interchangeable AI models instead of a single conventional model stems from the recognition that each model has its unique characteristics and corresponding performance-to-resource ratio under RCEs. These trained models are deployed within the RCE, where the framework continuously monitors resources such as power, memory, and CPU usage. An integrated expert system dynamically selects the most appropriate AI model based on available resources to ensure optimal trade-offs between real-time attack detection and resource utilisation. Upon detection of the attack, the framework activates evidence acquisition components to collect relevant data for forensic analysis. The DIA component secures the acquired evidence, which is then transmitted to a server-side environment for validation and secure preservation. Each component is elaborated in detail in the following subsections.

3.2 Network Intrusion Detection System

The framework's NIDS component used five ML and four DL algorithms to train models on the CICIoT2023 and CSE-CIC-IDS2018 datasets. Both ML and DL approaches were considered after reviewing relevant research that demonstrated their effectiveness for NIDS within RCE. The ML algorithms used for NIDS include Decision Tree (DT), Random Forest (RF), Naïve Bayes (NB), Extreme Gradient Boosting (XGBoost), and K-Nearest Neighbours (KNN). For DL, the models included CNN and Recurrent Neural Networks (RNNs). To optimise these models for RCEs, extensive experiments were conducted by systematically tuning key hyperparameters such as tree depth, number of estimators, learning rate, maximum features, number of layers, filter sizes, kernel sizes, activation functions, dropout rates, and dilation rates to achieve the best performance.

Convolutional Neural Networks. The CNN models, 1D Convolutional Neural Network (1D-CNN) and 1D-Dilated Convolutional Neural Network (1D-DCNN), were used to develop DL-based NIDS. These models account for the sequential nature of network traffic and extract spatial features from hierarchical structures such as TCP connections, flows, sessions, services, and hosts. 1D-DCNN captures a broader context that helps to reduce processing time without significantly increasing computational costs. This characteristic of 1D-DCNN makes it suitable for real-time NIDS in RCE.

The 1D-CNN architecture begins with convolutional layers using 32 filters to capture localised patterns that result in a tensor shape (None, 10, 32). A max-pooling layer was added to reduce the dimensions while keeping key features. This results in an output shape of (None, 5, 32) for better computational efficiency. Another convolutional layer with 64 filters was added to extract complex features that help to enhance feature representation and classification accuracy, reducing the sequence length to 3 and generating an output shape of (None, 3, 64). A flattening layer then converts the output into one-dimensional vectors. In the end, a dense layer was added along with a *softmax* activation function to perform classification.

The 1D-DCNN includes a convolutional layer with 32 filters, kernel size 1, and dilation rate of 2 to extract patterns and expand contextual scope, followed by another convolutional layer with 64 filters, kernel size 1, and dilation rate 8. These layers effectively handle feature extraction and representation. A flattening layer was added to reshape the output for integration with a dense layer, which uses *softmax* activation for classification. The *Adam* optimiser is used to minimise the loss function during neural network training.

Recurrent Neural Networks. RNNs extend the feedforward networks with a hidden recurrent state. This includes temporal information through backpropagation over time. However, challenges such as vanishing gradients and high computational costs arise when processing long sequences. To address these, the Long Short Term Memory (LSTM) introduces a gating mechanism for longer memory and better control over weight updates. Another model is called GRU, a simpler variant of LSTM. GRU uses fewer parameters, making it faster and less computationally expensive. GRU utilises two gates: the update gate and the reset gate, which enable efficient retention of long-term dependencies in data. This design overcomes the limitations of traditional RNNs in handling sequential information. After an in-depth analysis of both mechanisms, the proposed optimised architectures used a reduced number of layers. This ensures computational efficiency and scalability for real-time applications.

The LSTM architecture is composed of an LSTM layer with the shape of (None, 64), where *None* indicates the variable batch size and *64* represents the number of output units. This layer has a total of 19,712 trainable parameters. Considering resource constraints, the architecture does not feature more hidden layers; instead, it is composed of a dense layer with an output shape of (None, 10) and 650 trainable parameters. The dense layer used the *softmax* activation function, which converts the learnt information into class probabilities.

The optimised GRU model followed an architecture similar to that of the proposed LSTM model, which is a single hidden layer and a dense layer. However, it used fewer trainable parameters compared to LSTM. The hidden GRU layer with a shape of (None,64) has 14,976 trainable parameters. This layer determines whether to retain or discard information from previous steps. The dense layer has an output shape (None, 10) with 650 parameters. This layer performs the attack classification based on the features learnt through the previous GRU layer.

Machine Learning Algorithms. A systematic experimental methodology was implemented that involved training and evaluation of the most widely used algorithms, such as DT, RF, NB, KNN, and XGBoost, on both CICIoT2023 and CSE-CIC-IDS2018 datasets. Many ML models, including Logistic Regression, Linear Regression, K-means, and Support Vector Machine (SVM) were excluded from consideration during the experiments due to suboptimal performance or excessive detection time in preliminary testing on RCEs. Hyperparameter tuning and feature selection are important to achieve desirable results. Hyperparameter tuning for the selected ML algorithms was performed using the

GridSearchCV function. *GridSearchCV* performs a search through a predefined grid of hyperparameters using cross-validation. This process identifies optimal parameter combinations that maximise model performance while mitigating the risk of overfitting. The process involved defining relevant hyperparameters for each model, such as regularisation parameters, scaling values, solver algorithms, tree depth, and the number of neighbours. For example, in hyperparameter tuning of the RF model, key parameters that are considered to achieve the best results are the number of estimators, the maximum features per split and the splitting criteria that were systematically optimised. The models were evaluated on the datasets after hyperparameter tuning.

3.3 Evidence Acquisition

The evidence acquisition component of the framework is used to collect timestamped critical evidence upon attack detection. The collected evidence is organised into the following four categories: 1) system metadata containing the operating system and its version, architecture, processor cores, system uptime, timestamp, log-in history, and user information; 2) event and resource logs including memory dumps, system logs, event timelines, application logs, scheduled tasks, and resource usage; 3) network data comprising active network connections, network activity, network statistics, network connectivity, connected devices, device location, ARP tables, and captured network traffic (PCAP files); and 4) processes lists containing associated commands and user data, page tables, and kernel modules.

3.4 Data Integrity and Authentication

The DIA component of the proposed framework ensures compliance with legal requirements and forensic principles for admissible evidence, according to the ISO/IEC 27043:2015 standard. After the acquisition of evidence, a hash value is generated from the collected evidence using SHA-256 [12]. The hash value is then encrypted using a Rivest-Shamir-Adleman (RSA) private key [14]. On the server side, the DIA component verifies the digitally signed evidence using the corresponding public key, confirming that the evidence has not been tampered with and originates from a trusted source.

3.5 Forensic Analysis

The forensic analysis component of the framework is responsible for preserving evidence on a server after implementing DIA To examine the preserved evidence, Volatility and Wireshark were used to perform memory forensics and network traffic analysis.

4 Implementation and Results

The experiments comprehensively evaluate the framework on different RCEs and network attack scenarios. The evaluation involves a conscientious alignment of the proposed framework with the ISO/IEC 27043:2015 standard. As depicted in Fig. 1, the proposed framework uses two environments, the server-side environment and RCE.

Server-Side Environment. The server environment uses macOS 14.0 with a 3.49 GHz ARM-based processor and 16GB LPDDR5 RAM. AI models were developed in Python 3.11.5 using Keras, TensorFlow, and scikit-learn. All models were trained, optimised, and tested on the server prior to deployment in RCEs. The server also acted as a secure repository for evidence preservation using digital signing to ensure data integrity and authenticity (DIA), and supported forensic examination and analysis.

Resource Constrained Environments. Multiple RCEs were emulated via Docker containers [10], replicating five devices: Raspberry Pi Zero 2 W, Raspberry Pi 3B+, ODROID-C2, Orange Pi 4, and NVIDIA Jetson Nano. All devices used Linux-based operating systems, as detailed in Table 1.

Table 1. Hardware specifications of devices used for simulation

Device Name	Memory (MB)	Storage (GB)	CPU (GHz)	Power Usage (W)	Processor
Raspberry Pi Zero 2 W	512	8	1.00	1.50	ARM Cortex-A53
Raspberry Pi 3B+	1024	16	1.40	5.00	ARM Cortex-A53
ODROID-C2	2048	16	1.50	3.00	ARM Cortex-A53
Orange Pi 4	3072	16	1.80	7.00	Cortex-A72 + Cortex-A53
NVIDIA Jetson Nano	4096	16	1.43	10.00	Cortex-A57 MPCore

To evaluate the robustness of the proposed framework, various attack traffic scenarios were simulated and transmitted to RCEs. The deployment of the proposed framework was implemented using Python 3.9.2, supported by various libraries such as Keras, TensorFlow, Scikit-learn, Pandas, Pyshark, Scapy, LiME, and cryptography. The Kafka stack was integrated to facilitate real-time streaming data pipelines and enable the deployment of a real-time NIDS.

4.1 Simulated Network Attack Traffic

Real-time network attack traffic generated using *Scapy*. Scapy was used to construct, decrypt, send, capture, and analyse packets using various protocols. The experiment replicated seven attack types from the CICIoT2023 dataset: DDoS, Brute Force, Spoofing, DoS, Reconnaissance, Web-based, and Mirai. Each attack category included multiple scenarios. For example, web-based attacks included SQL injection, command injection, and Cross-Site Scripting (XSS).

In addition, a composite attack scenario randomly simulated seven attack types, automating the process to reveal the most effective method mix for broader and more potent threats. This setup assessed AI models and RCE behaviour when multiple attackers launched diverse assaults from different sources.

4.2 Network Intrusion Detection System

The first line of defence of the framework is the NIDS, where AI models were initially trained and evaluated within a server-side environment to develop optimised models. DL models were evaluated by monitoring accuracy and loss in both training and validation sets at each epoch. This facilitates effective anomaly detection within RCE in real-time data.

The model is compiled with an *Adam* optimiser and sparse categorical *cross-entropy* loss function. Adam optimiser was selected due to its adaptive estimation capabilities and low memory requirements, whereas cross entropy accurately evaluates the divergence between various attack types. Early stopping, a regularisation technique, was used to improve the ability of the DL model to generalise by avoiding excessive adaptation to the training data. This technique is integrated to determine the optimal point at which to stop the training process. The early stopping approach monitors the model's performance using a holdout validation set and a metric, such as loss, to ensure training stops when there is no further improvement.

In general, the RF model demonstrated the best performance among the selected models on the CICIoT2023 dataset. It achieved 99.58% accuracy, with precision and recall scores of 0.996 and an F1 score of 0.996. RF required 222.205 s to train with a prediction time of 2.243 s. However, considering resource utilisation and bandwidth constraints within RCE, the DT model outperformed RF. DT achieved an accuracy of 99.47% along with precision, recall, and F1 scores of 0.995. The DT model required significantly less time compared to RF. DT used 13.154 s to train the model and just 0.032 s for prediction, as shown in Table 2.

Among the DL models on the CICIoT2023 dataset, GRU outperformed the other DL models. GRU achieved 99.03% accuracy, with precision, recall, and F1 scores of 0.990. GRU required 202.856 s for training and 8.157 s for prediction across different attack types. LSTM model followed closely and achieved a slightly better accuracy of 99.05% with precision, recall, and F1 scores of 0.990, 0.991, and 0.990, respectively. However, LSTM demanded 226.543 s for training and a slightly longer prediction time of 9.001 s compared to GRU. The prediction time is crucial to deploy AI models for real-time NIDS within RCE.

On the CSE-CIC-IDS2018 dataset, DL models outperformed ML models across all evaluation metrics, including accuracy, precision, recall, and F1 score. Among the DL models, the 1D-DCNN demonstrated the best performance, achieving an accuracy of 99.99%, a precision of 1.000, recall of 0.991, and an F1 score of 0.996. ML models generally require less time for both training and

Table 2. Performance Comparison of Optimised AI Models on CICIoT2023 and CSE-CIC-IDS2018 Datasets

Model	CICIoT2023						CSE-CIC-IDS2018					
	Acc. (%)	Prec.	Recall	F1	Train (s)	Pred (s)	Acc. (%)	Prec.	Recall	F1	Train (s)	Pred (s)
DT	99.47	0.995	0.995	0.995	13.154	0.032	96.89	0.969	0.968	0.969	5.506	0.008
RF	99.58	0.996	0.996	0.996	222.205	2.243	97.11	0.969	0.971	0.970	43.776	0.417
KNN	99.19	0.992	0.992	0.992	0.339	1250.771	95.42	0.944	0.954	0.945	0.073	45.346
NB	78.40	0.685	0.784	0.712	0.821	0.466	16.20	0.851	0.162	0.216	0.147	0.062
XGB	99.49	0.995	0.995	0.995	138.793	0.991	98.03	0.980	0.980	0.978	23.133	1.045
LSTM	99.05	0.990	0.991	0.990	226.543	9.001	99.88	1.000	0.998	0.999	26.559	0.909
GRU	99.03	0.990	0.990	0.990	202.856	8.157	99.88	1.000	0.998	0.999	26.559	0.858
1D-CNN	98.91	0.989	0.989	0.988	978.648	17.634	99.87	0.998	0.998	0.998	213.575	2.896
1D-DCNN	98.98	0.990	0.990	0.989	461.419	15.248	99.99	1.000	0.991	0.996	80.651	1.694

prediction. KNN had the shortest training time at 0.073 s but exhibited the highest prediction time 45.346 s, due to its instance-based architecture that relies on distance calculations during inference. NB followed, with a training time of 0.147 s and prediction time of 0.062 s; however, it achieved the lowest accuracy among all models, with only 16.20%. Among the DL models, GRU stood out for its efficiency, requiring just 26.559 s for training and 0.858 s for prediction while still delivering strong performance, as shown in Table 2.

4.3 Framework Deployment

The proposed framework was deployed on various simulated devices to determine its performance within RCE.

The proposed framework was deployed on various simulated devices to evaluate its performance within RCE. Network attack traffic was generated using seven distinct attack types, with each attack simulated on different devices. For consistency, each attack type included 500 network packets of uniform packet size to allow a controlled evaluation of the performance of the framework in terms of attack detection, evidence acquisition, and resource utilisation. Extensive experiments were conducted to gather the essential knowledge for the development of the expert system, which is integrated as a component of the proposed framework. This knowledge enables the expert system to identify the most appropriate AI model based on the available resources within RCE. The results of the simulated reconnaissance attack on 5 different devices are shown in Table 3. Similar results were obtained when simulating other attacks on various devices.

The primary objective of these experiments is to dynamically select the most appropriate AI model based on the available resources. If sufficient resources were not available, the framework refrained from engaging AI-based NIDS and allowed the RCE to prioritise its primary task.

In general, the DT model demonstrated better performance in terms of resource utilisation, detection time, and evidence collection. DT required only

Table 3. AI Models Resource Utilisation on Raspberry Pi-3B+ Device for Reconnaissance Attack on 500 Network Packets

Model	Device			Model			Time		
	CPU Usage (%)	Memory Usage (MB)	Power Usage (mW)	CPU Usage (%)	Memory Usage (MB)	Power Usage (mW)	Detection Time per Packet (s)	Total Detection Time (s)	Memory Dump Time (s)
DT	18.8	597	114.0	16.5	276	57.1	0.0003	0.1659	2.91
RF	28.3	638	95.0	24.4	398	55.1	0.0014	0.9287	3.46
KNN	87.2	857	267.0	84.5	694	138.0	0.0674	38.1184	4.07
NB	22.1	597	89.7	16.9	269	47.1	0.0003	0.1833	3.59
XGB	20.3	590	104.0	17.1	279	54.2	0.0004	0.2401	3.10
LSTM	53.3	588	103.0	47.7	315	65.4	0.0371	20.6388	3.00
GRU	52.4	582	106.0	47.6	320	65.2	0.0455	20.3733	2.98
1D-CNN	51.7	576	95.8	47.0	319	57.0	0.0393	20.3423	5.32
1D-DCNN	53.6	598	80.2	46.9	314	50.9	0.0404	20.2980	2.98

16.5% of CPU usage and 276 MB of memory to process 500 network packets associated with suspicious activity. In addition, the DT model presented exceptional real-time capabilities by detecting a single attack packet in 0.3 ms and 0.1659 s for 500 network packets with high accuracy. DT also consumed minimal power during attack detection, which makes it highly efficient for RCEs. The RF model followed DT in performance but required slightly more computational resources. RF consumed 24.4% of CPU and 398 MB of memory while achieving a detection time of 0.0014 s per packet and 0.9287 s for 500 network packets. Although RF required more computational resources, its performance remained competitive, making it suitable for scenarios where additional resources are available.

In the case of DL models, resource utilisation and detection times were relatively similar across all models. However, the 1D-DCNN model outperformed other DL models in terms of efficiency. It utilised 46.9% CPU and 314 MB of memory, consuming 50.9 mW of power to detect a network attack packet. On average, 1D-DCNN required 0.0404 s per packet and processed 500 packets in 20.2980 s.

These findings highlight the trade-offs between computational efficiency and detection capabilities in different models, providing valuable insights into selecting the most appropriate AI model based on the available resources in RCE.

Extensive Testing. To evaluate the scalability of the proposed framework, a series of experiments were conducted that analysed its performance based on the varying volume of network packets. The experiments were carried out on the five aforementioned devices, with the number of packets gradually increasing from 500 to 5000. DT and GRU models were selected to evaluate performance, and the results of the experiments are presented in Table 4 and Table 5, respectively.

The experiments considered critical factors such as network traffic, time, computational resources, and bandwidth utilisation, both with and without AI integration. The results demonstrated that as the number of packets increased, the processing time per packet remained relatively similar. The comparative results highlight the ability of the proposed framework to handle larger network traffic efficiently.

Table 4. DT Performance with Various Number of Network Packets on Raspberry Pi-3B+ Real-Time Network Traffic

No of Packets	Features Extraction Time (s)	Packet Size (Bytes)	Detection Time (s)	Total Time With AI (s)	Total Time Without AI (s)	Bandwidth With AI (Mbps)	Bandwidth Without AI (Mbps)	Power Consumption (mW)	Memory Dump (s)	Max Memory Time Utilisation (MB)
500	1.31	417,853	0.20	2.18	0.88	1.45	10.45	107	2.98	687
1000	2.32	864,580	0.33	4.12	1.80	1.60	3.67	205	3.39	717
2000	5.12	1,685,576	0.64	8.68	3.56	1.48	3.61	252	3.84	727
3000	7.74	2,524,791	0.97	12.89	5.15	1.49	3.74	333	4.15	733
4000	10.72	3,357,845	1.31	17.52	6.81	1.46	3.76	350	5.76	740
5000	14.20	4,234,019	2.00	22.97	8.77	1.41	3.68	326	3.67	756

Table 5. GRU Performance with Various Number of Network Packets on Raspberry Pi-3B+ Real-Time Network Traffic

No of Packets	Features Extraction Time (s)	Packet Size (Bytes)	Detection Time (s)	Total Time With AI (s)	Total Time Without AI (s)	Bandwidth With AI (Mbps)	Bandwidth Without AI (Mbps)	Power Consumption (mW)	Memory Dump (s)	Max Memory Time Utilisation (MB)
500	1.34	417,853	20.65	2.22	0.88	1.44	3.64	128	4.01	644
1000	2.25	864,580	42.42	4.05	1.80	1.63	3.67	168	3.11	674
2000	5.10	1,685,576	81.24	8.67	3.56	1.48	3.61	283	3.85	709
3000	9.46	2,524,791	129.16	14.62	5.15	1.32	3.74	340	3.19	708
4000	12.23	3,357,845	175.54	19.04	6.81	1.35	3.76	335	3.08	784
5000	16.79	4,234,019	213.64	25.57	8.77	1.26	3.68	345	3.61	717

The dynamic selection of AI models based on available resources was evaluated through multiple tests. A simulated application was developed using Python that utilised interactive sliders that enable dynamic adjustment of resource utilisation. The testing also validated that if RCE requires exceeded computational resources for its primary task, the framework would bypass attack detection and evidence collection to ensure uninterrupted operation. After the simulated application, different resource-intensive applications were executed within RCE to observe their impact on model selection in real time.

Real-Time Feature Extraction. The feature extraction module in the proposed framework was deployed for real-time feature extraction after network traffic capture. This module is capable of processing network packets from IEEE 802.11 (WiFi), Ethernet, and Zigbee communication standards. These communication standards were selected to ensure real-time compatibility with the IoT network, as the majority of IoT devices use these protocols for data transmission.

The module extracts features from three key protocols: TCP/IP (Transmission Control Protocol/Internet Protocol), UDP (User Datagram Protocol), and ARP, which identify the essential attributes of the network packet data for potential attack detection. After processing PCAP-stored packets, it derives the same 40 features used to train the ML and DL models, structuring them into input vectors according to the expected model input shape. These are streamed in real time via Kafka, where producers transmit them to consumers for AI-based attack detection, which returns a numeric class label representing the predicted attack type. This design ensures minimal impact on network bandwidth during prediction. Upon detection, the Kafka consumer activates the evidence acquisition component.

Evidence Acquisition. Evidence acquisition is the crucial component of the framework to ensure a comprehensive and systematic collection of evidence within the RCE. The process begins with the collection of system metadata that includes evidence files containing user information (active users and login history with timestamps) and system details such as timestamps, operating system specifications, machine architecture, physical cores, and memory statistics (total and available memory). After collecting system metadata, the component collects detailed event and resource logs. These logs include a system log file that records all events, requests, and activities on the system, an event timeline file to establish when specific events occurred, an application log file that provides behavioural information about running software, and a scheduled tasks file that documents tasks set to execute at defined times. Memory-related evidence is also collected, including memory dump files (snapshots of physical memory at a given moment) and a page table file that includes buffered and cached memory, swap memory, active and inactive memory, paging information, kernel memory usage, and system parameters such as *CommitLimit, Committed_AS, VmallocTotal*, and *VmallocUsed*. The memory detail provides valuable insights into the system's run-time state and resource use at the time of evidence collection.

The component also captures network-related data to provide network activity on RCE. This includes PCAP files that sequentially record network packets, a connected device file that contains information about connected devices and details about the kernel IP routing table, an active connection file consisting of IP addresses, port numbers, and the statuses of active connections, and a file of network connectivity that includes IP addresses, subnet masks, and MAC addresses for network interfaces. The geolocation data file provides the longitude, latitude, and address of the devices. In the end, the framework gathers process-related information, including a process list file that provides details of active processes along with their usernames, process IDs (PIDs), names, and command-line arguments, and a kernel module information file that outlines installed modules, their sizes, and dependencies. This comprehensive collection ensures that no critical aspect of the state or activity of the system is overlooked. Once the evidence collection process is complete, the framework triggers the DIA component.

Data Integrity and Authentication. In the RCE, the DIA component generated unique private and public keys after attack detection and evidence collection. SHA-256 was used to create a unique hash for each evidence file mentioned in Sect. 4.3. The private key was used to encrypt the hash to generate digitally signed evidence.

In the server-side environment, the signed evidence was decrypted using the corresponding public key to retrieve the original hash value. Simultaneously, the SHA-256 hash was compared to the received evidence hash value to verify that the evidence had not been tampered with. This process validated the integrity of the evidence to ensure that it was in accordance with the standards and admissibility of the evidence in legal proceedings. After the evidence was validated, it was stored on a server for forensic analysis.

5 Discussion

The adaptability of RCEs is rapidly increasing due to cost-effective hardware and widespread connectivity. However, their inherent vulnerabilities, such as outdated security, weak authentication, minimal security considerations during development, insecure network services, etc., make them more vulnerable to infiltration than traditional computing systems. The evolving threat landscape continues to challenge effective digital forensic investigations in RCEs. Despite existing forensic tools, the complex architecture of RCE demands innovative solutions to bridge the gap between ideal forensic procedures and real-world constraints. AI models have been adopted for the detection and analysis of cybersecurity incidents. However, AI-based forensic readiness faces challenges in RCE due to resource constraints, power consumption, and the effects on network bandwidth. The proposed AI-based optimised NFR framework improves forensic readiness by automating incident detection and response. This reduces response time, minimises human intervention, and improves attack detection, evidence acquisition, preservation, and analysis. Quantitative simulation helps the framework to dynamically select the most appropriate AI model based on the available resources, including CPU, memory, and power. The framework is designed to capture and process network packets to extract features for AI models from different communication standards and protocols in real time. Its versatility and scalability make it compatible with most RCEs. The framework prioritises strategic planning, as discussed in ISO/IEC 27043:2015. It integrates attack detection, evidence acquisition, validity checks, and secure evidence storage to ensure comprehensive tamper-proof digital evidence for legal proceedings.

Real-Time Deployment Feasibility in Resource-Constrained Environment. The effectiveness of real-time NFR depends not only on detection accuracy, but also on its ability to identify attacks promptly, since evidence collection begins immediately after detection. Lightweight AI models that can run on RCEs and detect attacks promptly are essential; any delay can lead to critical packet loss and missed forensic evidence, ultimately compromising the proactive approach. Shoukat et al. [22] reported detection times of 0.079 ms, 0.087 ms, 0.084 ms on N-BaIoT, Edge-IIoTset, and CIC-IDS2017 using a hardware configuration of an Intel Core i5-6200U CPU @ 2.30 GHz, 12 GB RAM. However, this study did not evaluate performance on constrained devices such as the Raspberry Pi Zero 2 W. Wang et al. [27] reported a detection time of 0.0172 ms and achieved an accuracy of 99.90% on the CSE-CIC-IDS2018 dataset. However, the authors did not evaluate their model on low-end devices.

In comparison, the proposed framework achieved detection times of 0.3 ms per packet on real-time traffic and was successfully deployed on a variety of resource constrained devices, as listed in Table 1. The offline evaluation further showed 0.00019 ms and 0.001 ms detection times on CICIoT2023 and CSE-CIC-IDS2018 datasets. The comparison of the proposed framework with the existing state-of-the-art is shown in Table 6.

Table 6. Proposed Model Performance Comparison with Existing Studies

Ref.	Low-End Device	Dataset	Acc. (%)	Train (s)	Detect (ms)	Pwr (mW)	Usage
Shoukat et al. [22]	✗	CIC-IDS2017	98.57	–	0.084	–	
Vellela et al. [24]	✗	CSE-CIC-IDS2018	99.30	882.00	–	–	
Zhang et al. [27]	✗	CSE-CIC-IDS2018	99.90	74.88	0.0172	–	
Seth et al. [20]	✗	CSE-CIC-IDS2018	97.72	5.06	0.13801	–	
ElSayed et al. [6]	✓	CICIoT2023	93.60	–	–	7500	
Kharoubi et al. [9]	✗	CICIoT2023	99.17	–	0.060	–	
Alzahrani et al. [1]	✓	CICIoT2023	99.10	–	6760.00	6040	
Wang et al. [26]	✗	CICIoT2023	93.13	708.40	6.40	–	
Proposed Model ✓		**CICIoT2023**	99.58	222.20	0.00019	114	
Proposed Model ✓		**CSE-CIC-IDS2018**	99.99	80.65	0.00100	635	

5.1 Limitations and Future Work

An AI-based optimised NFR framework was introduced, demonstrating robustness, accuracy, integrity, and authentication. However, certain design and testing limitations should be acknowledged. The framework was not deployed on real devices, so future research should involve implementing and evaluating it on representative devices to validate its performance in realistic settings. The privacy of data collected during forensic investigations is beyond the scope of this study. The time required for dynamic model selection is not addressed and will be explored in future work. Additionally, the proposed approach relied on TensorFlow and Kafka, which require more computational resources than lightweight options, e.g., MQTT and TensorFlow Lite. Future implementations should consider AI frameworks customised for RCEs.

6 Conclusion

This paper introduces an AI-based optimised NFR framework for RCE. The framework integrates five ML and four DL models for attack detection, followed by evidence collection that is categorised into system metadata, event and resource logs, network data, and process information. The proposed framework achieved an optimal balance between the use of computational resources, the bandwidth of the network, and the accurate detection of attacks. The expert system was integrated, which utilised the knowledge of extensive experiments carried out in different simulated environments to find the appropriate AI model for attack detection based on available computational resources on RCE. The DIA component of the framework effectively validated the evidence using a robust digital signing technique. This ensures that the evidence remains unmanipulated and admissible for legal proceedings. The framework was designed and developed to enhance the NFR standard outlined in ISO/IEC 27043:2015 through the application of AI.

References

1. Alzahrani, H., Sheltami, T., Barnawi, A., Imam, M., YASAR, A.: A lightweight intrusion detection system using convolutional neural network and long short-term memory in fog computing **80** (2024)
2. Atlam, H.F., Alenezi, A., Alassafi, M.O., Alshdadi, A.A., Wills, G.B.: Security, cybercrime and digital forensics for IoT, pp. 551–577. Springer International Publishing, Cham (2020)
3. Breitinger, F., Hilgert, J.N., Hargreaves, C., Sheppard, J., Overdorf, R., Scanlon, M.: DFRWS EU 10-year review and future directions in digital forensic research. Forensic Sci. Int. Digit. Investig. **48**, 301685 (2024). https://doi.org/10.1016/j.fsidi.2023.301685
4. Canadian Institute for Cybersecurity: A Realistic Cyber Defense Dataset (CSE-CIC-IDS2018). https://registry.opendata.aws/cse-cic-ids2018/. Accessed 02 June 2022
5. Darabseh, A., Kbar, G., Almulhem, A.: Network forensics readiness: a survey. J. Digit. Forensics Secur. Law **11**(2), 61–76 (2016)
6. ElSayed, Z., Elsayed, N., Bay, S.: A Novel zero-trust machine learning green architecture for healthcare IoT cybersecurity: review, analysis, and implementation. In: SoutheastCon 2024, pp. 686–692 (2024)
7. Fagbola, F.I., Venter, H.S.: Smart digital forensic readiness model for shadow IOT devices. Appl. Sci. **12**(2) (2022). https://doi.org/10.3390/app12020730
8. Kebande, V.R., Mudau, P.P., Ikuesan, R.A., Venter, H., Choo, K.K.R.: Holistic digital forensic readiness framework for IoT-enabled organizations. Forensic Sci. Int. Rep. **2**, 100117 (2020)
9. Kharoubi, K., Cherbal, S., Mechta, D., Gawanmeh, A.: Network intrusion detection system using convolutional neural networks: NIDS-DL-CNN for IoT security. Clust. Comput. **28**(4), 219 (2025)
10. Merkel, D.: Docker: lightweight Linux containers for consistent development and deployment. Linux J. **239**, 2 (2014)
11. Montasari, R., Carpenter, V., Hill, R.: A road map for digital forensics research: a novel approach for establishing the design science research process in digital forensics. Int. J. Electron. Secur. Digit. Forensics **11**(2), 194–224 (2019)
12. National Institute of Standards and Technology: Secure Hash Standard. Federal Information Processing Standards Publication FIPS PUB 180-4, U.S. Department of Commerce (2015)
13. Neto, E.C.P., Dadkhah, S., Ferreira, R., Zohourian, A., Lu, R., Ghorbani, A.A.: CICIoT2023: a real-time dataset and benchmark for large-scale attacks in IoT environment. Sensors **23**(13) (2023)
14. Rivest, R.L., Shamir, A., Adleman, L.: A method for obtaining digital signatures and public-key cryptosystems. Commun. ACM **21**(2), 120–126 (1978). https://doi.org/10.1145/359340.359342

15. Rizal, R., Selamat, S.R., Mas'ud, M.Z., Widiyasono, N.: Enhanced readiness forensic framework for the complexity of internet of things (IoT) investigation based on artificial intelligence. J. Adv. Res. Appl. Sci. Eng. Technol. **50**(1), 121–135 (2025)
16. Rizvi, S., Scanlon, M., Mcgibney, J., Sheppard, J.: Application of artificial intelligence to network forensics: survey Challenges and future directions. IEEE Access **10**, 110362–110384 (2022) Challenges and future directions. IEEE Access **10**, 110362–110384 (2022)
17. Rizvi, S., Scanlon, M., McGibney, J., Sheppard, J.: Deep learning based network intrusion detection system for resource-constrained environments. In: Digital Forensics and Cyber Crime, pp. 355–367. Springer Nature Switzerland, Cham (2023)
18. Rizvi, S., Scanlon, M., McGibney, J., Sheppard, J.: Pushing network forensic readiness to the edge: a resource constrained artificial intelligence based methodology. In: 2024 Cyber Research Conference - Ireland (Cyber-RCI), pp. 1–8 (2024). https://doi.org/10.1109/Cyber-RCI60769.2024.10939120
19. Sadineni, L., Pilli, E.S., Battula, R.B.: Ready-IoT: a novel forensic readiness model for internet of things. In: 2021 IEEE 7th World Forum on Internet of Things (WF-IoT), pp. 89–94 (2021)
20. Seth, S., Singh, G., Kaur Chahal, K.: A novel time efficient learning-based approach for smart intrusion detection system. J. Big Data **8**(1), 111 (2021)
21. Shahin, M., Maghanaki, M., Hosseinzadeh, A., Chen, F.F.: Advancing network security in industrial IoT: a deep dive into AI-enabled intrusion detection systems. Adv. Eng. Inform. **62**, 102685 (2024)
22. Shoukat, S., Gao, T., Javeed, D., Saeed, M.S., Adil, M.: Trust my IDS: an explainable AI integrated deep learning-based transparent threat detection system for industrial networks. Comput. Secur. **149**, 104191 (2025)
23. Valjarević, A., Venter, H., Petrović, R.: ISO/IEC 27043: 2015–role and application. In: 2016 24th Telecommunications Forum (TELFOR), pp. 1–4. IEEE (2016)
24. Vellela, S.S., D, R., Purimetla, N.R., Thalakola, S., Vuyyuru, L.R., Vatambeti, R.: Cyber threat detection in industry 4.0: leveraging GloVe and self-ttention mechanisms in BiLSTM for enhanced intrusion detection. Comput. Electr. Eng. **124**, 110368 (2025)
25. Waguespack, K.M., Smith, K.J., Muliri, O.A., Vijayakanthan, R., Ali-Gombe, A.: MARS: the first line of defense for IoT incident response. Forensic Sci. Int. Digit. Investig. **49**, 301754 (2024)
26. Wang, Z., Chen, H., Yang, S., Luo, X., Li, D., Wang, J.: A lightweight intrusion detection method for IoT based on deep learning and dynamic quantization. Peer J. Comput. Sci. **9**, e1569 (2023)
27. Zhang, H., Zhang, B., Huang, L., Zhang, Z., Huang, H.: An efficient two-stage network intrusion detection system in the internet of things. Information **14**(2) (2023). https://doi.org/10.3390/info14020077

Mapping the Research Landscape - An Exploratory Analysis of AI Applications in Digital Forensics

Gokila Dorai[1]( ), Pouria Rad[1], Frank Breitinger[2], Rajon Bardhan[1], and Vijayalakshmi Ramasamy[3]

[1] School of Computer and Cyber Sciences, Augusta University, Augusta, GA, USA
{gdorai,peslamirad,rbardhan}@augusta.edu
[2] Chair for Cybersecurity, University of Augsburg, Augsburg, Germany
frank.breitinger@uni-a.de
[3] Computer Science, Georgia Southern University, Statesboro, USA
vramasamy@georgiasouthern.edu

Abstract. Artificial intelligence (AI) and machine learning (ML) have great potential to enhance digital forensic investigation, but progress is impeded by challenges in building datasets that meet technical accuracy and legal requirements. We herein compile findings from the latest scholarly literature to identify potential key aspects that are required for building forensic datasets that can effectively support AI-based investigative tools. We examine current practices in dataset building, ranging from representativeness of data, quality of annotation, chain-of-custody documentation, and metadata standardization, and consider their effects carefully on training robust AI models. Results point to key shortcomings that impede advanced AI implementations in digital forensics, which form a strong baseline for developing a standard workflow for building forensic datasets. This work, therefore, forms a stepping stone for future projects to enhance investigation capabilities through a better-structured and legally sound process of dataset building.

Keywords: Machine Learning · Digital Forensics · Datasets · AI Applications · Challenges

1 Introduction

Digital forensics (DF), the backbone of modern criminal investigations and the systematic application of investigative techniques to digital evidence, is increasingly becoming essential in our computing society [6,46,66]. With computing technology pervading all aspects of human life, today's inquiries face an unprecedented volume and complexity of evidence derived from emails, text messages, digital images, system logs, and more [25]. This diverse digital information brought to light the limitations of traditional forensic methods, thereby necessitating the integration of automated means. To that end, the field increasingly turned to artificial intelligence (AI) and machine learning (ML) as valuable means to enhance the efficiency and accuracy of forensic workflows [32,49].

While there is immense promise in AI and ML, effective digital forensic solution development is severely hampered by insufficiently organized, domain-related datasets [19,23]. Most available forensic datasets suffer from limitations of volume, diversity, and representativeness, the qualities required for practical training of models for consistent performance under the uncertainty involved in an investigation. Randomly, examiners are frequently challenged with retrofitting information from various domains, which does not embrace the unique subtlety and operating environments inherent to digital forensic examination. Beyond damaging the generalizability of AI/ML algorithms, this dimension also inhibits their capacity to assist investigative performance under real-world conditions. To tackle this noticeable shortcoming, it is vital to create standardized information frameworks that precisely account for specific digital forensic needs, enabling AI-driven systems to improve investigative effectiveness significantly.

This exploratory study makes the following contributions:

- We map the research landscape in AI-driven digital forensics through an exploratory literature review, categorizing publications into four thematic areas to identify trends and interrelationships.
- We identify recurring challenges across literature categories that limit effective creation and utilization of datasets for AI applications in digital forensics.
- We highlight specific gaps in current dataset practices that should be addressed to improve both the technical performance of AI models and their acceptance in forensic contexts.

In this study, we examine a carefully selected sample of digital forensic datasets by comparing their organization, content, and labeling techniques to determine the key criteria required for training in AI and ML in forensic proceedings. Unlike providing an exhaustive review, our discussion emphasizes the role of dataset attributes in enabling improved, AI-driven investigative capabilities. This focus differentiates our study from previous reviews of forensic datasets (see [19]). The remainder of this paper is organized as follows. In Sect. 2, we provide a concise overview of key machine learning algorithms and outline the essential data criteria that underpin AI applications in digital forensics. Section 3 details our systematic, multi-phase exploratory review methodology, including literature search, screening, thematic coding, and synthesis of findings. In Sect. 4, we present an in-depth narrative analysis of the technical, legal, and practical challenges associated with constructing and using forensic datasets for AI. Section 5 discusses the limitations of our study, and finally, Sect. 6 offers concluding remarks along with future research directions to establish standardized frameworks for forensic dataset development.

2 Preliminaries: Machine Learning Algorithms and Datasets

This section summarizes the key concepts in AI and ML that frame our discussion of forensic datasets and AI-assisted investigative tools. To ensure that the subsequent analysis is comprehensible, we highlight the key principles and techniques in AI and ML that are particularly relevant to digital forensics. While in-depth treatments of these topics exist in leading textbooks (see [4,22,37,51,59]), our focus is on elucidating the factors that enable the construction of sound forensic datasets and analytical models. The major paradigms in machine learning can be broadly classified as follows:

Supervised learning: Involves algorithms being trained on data (examples) that are already labeled; meaning, each input comes with a label. Your training set has example input and output pairs that the algorithm studies to determine the mapping between them. Digital forensics often uses supervised learning techniques for applying malware detection and evidence classification in order to distinguish between known malicious and non-malicious behaviors through examples. Heuristic-based machine learning algorithms such as decision trees can be trained to classify files as suspicious or benign, while support vector machines (SVM) can be employed to different types of digital evidence in order to minimize false positives, with other useful setting options [45,52,60].

Unsupervised learning: In unsupervised learning, there are no labeled targets in the dataset; instead, the aim is to uncover hidden patterns or hierarchies in the data. Clustering and anomaly detection techniques again empower users to detect groups of similar items or flag anomalies that do not conform to expected patterns. Unsupervised approaches in the domain of digital forensics have been utilized for the analysis of network traffic or system logs to uncover latent features that could signify hidden intrusion(s) in cyberspace, where labeled samples are not accessible. This is especially beneficial when new or previously unknown types of evidence may come to light [8,33].

Reinforcement learning: Reinforcement learning is a framework in which an agent learns to make decisions by interacting with its environment and receiving feedback in the form of rewards or penalties. Over time, the agent develops a strategy, or policy, that maximizes the cumulative reward. Although its application in digital forensics is still in its nascent stages, reinforcement learning holds potential for adaptive decision-making processes—for example, in optimizing the allocation of investigative resources or dynamically adjusting analysis strategies during complex cyber incident responses [40]. Its ability to learn through trial and error can be harnessed to handle evolving forensic scenarios.

Deep learning: Deep learning, a subset of machine learning, leverages artificial neural networks with many layers to learn high-level abstractions from data. This approach is particularly effective for handling large amounts of high-dimensional data. In digital forensics, deep learning models have been successfully applied to image and video analysis, such as automating the detection of graphic content in visual evidence, and natural language processing tasks, including document analysis and speech recognition. Convolutional neural networks (CNNs) are used to analyze visual patterns in digital imagery, while recurrent neural networks (RNNs) and transformer architectures are well-suited for processing sequential data like text and audio, contributing to more nuanced and robust forensic analysis [9,14,62].

The efficacy of AI and ML in digital forensics depends on the algorithms' advanced sophistication and the quality of the underlying forensic data sets. When creating models to assist in investigative operations, it is most important that these data sets capture the diversity and richness of the digital evidence in authentic casework. These data sets should meet rigorous technical and legal criteria so that AI-based forensic systems will operate effectively under various conditions. In the field of digital forensics, the following data needs are of the utmost importance:

Labeled data: Supervised learning techniques rely on data sets in which every item of evidence, like email messages, images, or system logs, is labeled with precise details describing its category and significance. Such high-quality, labeled data not only makes it easy to create accurate classifiers (like separating benign files from possible malware) but also preserves the chain-of-custody and admissibility of electronic evidence [17,45,52,60].

Unlabeled data: In most of the scenarios present in forensics, most of the available data will actually be unlabeled and unstructured data. Unsupervised learning techniques, including anomaly detection and clustering, can identify implicit trends, group similar events, and detect anomalies in storage systems or networks of logs. This method is beneficial for revealing unexpected or unknown criminal activity when no pre-labels are available [8,33].

Data diversity: Data diversity in forensics in the digital context extends beyond a diversity of formats. It includes the need for the datasets to capture the whole range of types of evidence encountered in the real world, from differences in device types and operating systems to file structure differences and temporal differences. Diverse data is important when it comes to the development of robust

Table 1. Benchmark Datasets in Related Domains and Their Key Success Factors

Dataset	Domain	Key Characteristics	Success Factors
CIDDS [48]	Network security	Labeled flow-based data with attack vectors	Complete attack scenarios, detailed metadata
PhishingCorpus [41]	Email security	Annotated phishing emails with features	Real-world samples, detailed annotations
KDD Cup'99 [58]	Intrusion detection	Network traffic with attack labels	Comprehensive attack coverage, standardized format
Toxic Comment [30]	Content moderation	Labeled toxic comments	High-quality labels, diverse examples
AVCaesar [3]	Malware analysis	Dynamic and static malware features	Comprehensive metadata, execution traces
CSE-CIC-IDS2018 [55]	Network security	Modern attack profiles with full packets	Realistic network configurations, ground truth

and unbiased AI/ML models. As a result, the models will work effectively when assessing new or dynamic types of digital evidence [19,23].

2.1 Datasets That Power AI in Related Domains

It is imperative to understand what makes a dataset significant to inform the design of high-quality datasets to enable sound AI and ML use. We consider a dataset significant in our analysis if it is broadly cited, cited at least in five distinct studies, and if it has evidently inspired innovation by being a benchmark in its category. Successful datasets in the general AI environment have some of the following general characteristics: comprehensive breadth, representativity, deliberate labeling, standard formats, and public availability. These qualities have facilitated breakthroughs and swift progress in a variety of fields. These attributes include:

1. **Ground truth:** Authoritative labels or annotations developed through rigorous validation processes that provide a reliable reference for training models [17].
2. **Scale:** A sufficiently large number of samples that allows complex models to generalize across diverse scenarios [11].
3. **Diversity:** A representation of a wide range of scenarios, conditions, and edge cases, ensuring models can handle novel or unexpected evidence [23].
4. **Accessibility:** Open availability to the research community under clear licensing terms, which fosters further innovation and reproducibility [61].
5. **Metadata richness:** Detailed contextual information that aids in effective feature engineering and model interpretation [39].
6. **Standardized format:** Consistent data structures that facilitate interoperability between tools and systems [58].
7. **Regular updates:** The capacity to evolve by incorporating new data and emerging patterns to keep pace with the changing domain [55].

In computer vision, ImageNet, for instance, is a prime dataset that includes more than 14 million labeled images across more than 20,000 categories. Its popularity stems from its high diversity, hierarchically structured setup, and uniform labeling standards [11]. Likewise, in natural language processing, the GLUE benchmark offered uniform task-level evaluation underpinned by strong validation procedures, transparent measures of evaluation, and extensive documentation [61]. For security and behavior analysis applications more closely related to digital forensics, several notable datasets have enabled AI/ML advances, which is apparent in the Table 1.

Some datasets are useful for more practical applications, including security and behavior analysis. For use in more practical security and behavior analysis, the CSE-CIC-IDS2018 data set provides complete network traffic capture and labeled attack scenarios, highly realistic networks, and extensive feature extractions, all of which are necessary to create effective intrusion detection systems [55]. In malware analysis, data sets like AVCaesar contain static and dynamic features, such as execution traces and behavioral networking, that facilitate the construction of models that detect and classify malware effectively [3].

3 Context and Scope of the Study

To gain deeper insights into how datasets are cited and applied in AI-driven digital forensics, we carried out an exploratory literature search using a four-phase approach: literature search and identification, screening and selection, thematic analysis, and synthesis of findings. In the search phase, we used ResearchRabbit (a citation network and semantic similarity-based literature mapping software) to cast a broad net across the literature. We also seeded the search using seminal papers in the fields of AI and digital forensics, including seminal studies by Casey et al. and Garfinkel et al. This approach allowed us to capture papers that might not appear using standard keyword searching and map the intellectual landscape of the field using citation links [7,15,47]. Figure 1 presents a four-phase methodology for our exploratory analysis, progressing from a broad literature search through screening, thematic analysis, and culminating in a synthesized research landscape map.

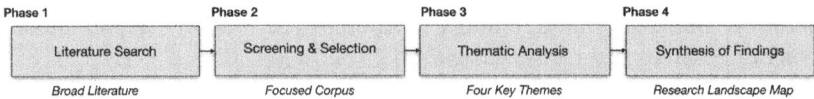

Fig. 1. Research Methodology

In the screening phase, we applied rigorous inclusion criteria: selected publications had to explicitly address AI and ML applications in digital forensics, discuss dataset challenges, applications, or evaluation methods, be peer-reviewed full papers, and be published between 2009 and 2024. Two researchers independently evaluated the candidate publications using these criteria, ultimately selecting 60 papers for detailed analysis.

Fig. 2. Word Cloud of Literature Review.

The subsequent thematic analysis involved systematically coding each publication to identify recurring themes, methodologies, and challenges. Through iterative review and consensus meetings, four dominant research themes emerged: dataset adequacy, ML applications in digital forensics, emerging techniques, and benchmarking and standardization [47]. Figure 2 shows a word cloud of the titles of the publications we selected. This visualization summarizes the most common words in our corpus in a concise manner and shows us the essential concepts and trends in the literature.

Proceeding in our analysis, we conducted a secondary synthesis stage whereby every article was allocated its main thematic category in line with its leading contribution, noting that numerous articles cross many themes. Subsequently, a cross-cutting analysis was conducted to bring out the recurring challenges and gaps common in the four theme areas. Our results bring out the pertinent evolutionary trends in the field of digital forensics studies. Of note, trends show that while the applications of machine learning have had tremendous growth, peaking during the years around 2021–2022, new techniques have had rapid progress in the last couple of years.

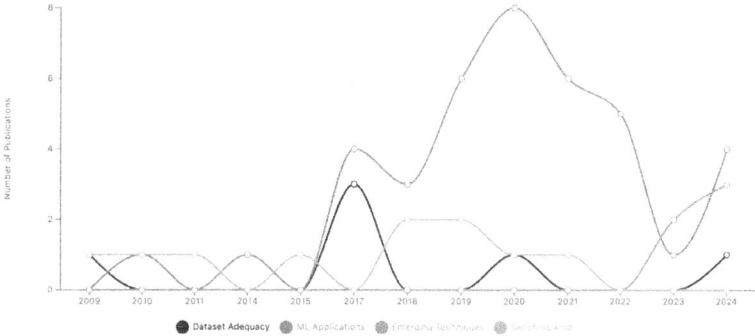

Fig. 3. Trend Analysis of Digital Forensics Research (2009–2024): A visualization of the evolving research focus across four thematic categories, with notable growth in machine learning applications and emerging techniques.

Figure 3 illustrates these trends by charting research themes along the four thematic categories from 2009 to 2024. This trend reinforces the growing use of machine learning and new research techniques in the field of digital forensics, in line with the dynamic and progressive nature of the field. While our methodology is exploratory and not exhaustive, it provides useful insights into the conceptual landscape and development of the research in this new interdisciplinary field.

4 Literature-Based Analysis of AI Dataset Constraints in Digital Forensics

Our literature analysis of AI-based digital forensics uncovered a multitude of ongoing challenges associated with dataset construction and utilization. The literature generally indicates a variety of important constraints keeping effective machine learning-based solutions out of the reach of forensics in general. These challenges can collectively be categorized under four distinct headings. Foremost is a category associated with the intrinsic quality of the dataset, including concerns pertaining to its construction, representativeness, and general reliability.

Category #1. Dataset Construction and Quality: Creation, Representativeness, and Intrinsic Properties: Good dataset development is crucial when creating AI models that work effectively in digital forensic analysis and are also legally sound. Researchers repeatedly emphasized that the lack of standardized forensic corpora restricts reproducibility and prevents meaningful cross-comparisons of studies, thereby slowing scientific development in the discipline [17]. In overcoming these obstacles, several studies have suggested benchmark frameworks of a given forensic area, including mobile device analysis, where a precise standard is paramount in testing the quality of tools under various conditions [65].

Researchers have also proposed controlled datasets that are purpose-specific to facilitate forensic use. Specifically, one work put forward a raw image dataset specifically to benchmark forensic algorithms, creating a scenario where image quality variation and authenticity variation can be analyzed in a systematic manner [10]. The extensive reviews of the available data scenario have also indicated how fragmented the available data is, coupled with the need to address it by having better sharing practices to enable collaborative work [23].

An additional area of effort has focused on increasing dataset realism. Methods have also been created that automatically simulate realistic user activity to produce test images of a forensic nature, thus creating synthetic data that more closely resembles real-world digital evidence [13]. Complementary techniques have also been proposed to create synthetic data that not only models simulated network flows but also artifacts at the operating system and application levels so that high-quality ground truth is present to test and validate in dynamic environments [20].

The challenges in assembling datasets remain very practical. Indeed, previous studies have shown the importance of following stringent best practices in data collection to ensure the reproducibility of forensic experiments [27]. Such efforts would also help produce reliable datasets for different multimedia, pictures, and videos assembled for machine learning analysis to fulfill requirements regarding data diversity when developing strong investigative models [14]. Analyses based on FAIR principles have revealed serious shortcomings within current forensic metadata standards, a priority improvement area under these circumstances to enable proper sharing and repurposing of data [39].

Category #2. ML Applications in Digital Forensics - Challenges and Opportunities: The use of machine learning in digital forensics has great potential to make the investigation much more accurate, qualitatively even better, and finally, make it much easier to implement in practical settings. Researchers have exploited different ML approaches to deal with challenging forensic issues. However, many obstacles still prevent the technology from being fully implemented. One strand of research has focused on developing frameworks that leverage ML for processing large-scale forensic data in emerging domains such as the Internet of Things (IoT). For example, a big data forensic framework has been proposed that harnesses unsupervised and supervised ML techniques to identify abnormal patterns and potential security threats in IoT environments, thereby enabling more effective investigations [8]. Likewise, other studies have demonstrated that dynamic malware detection, through ML-based forensic data analytics, can significantly improve the speed and accuracy of identifying malicious software in rapidly evolving threat landscapes [60].

In network forensics, investigations have benefited from frameworks employing deep learning to analyze network traffic and trace the origin of cyber attacks. Research in this area has shown that ML can identify and track attack behaviors in IoT networks, ultimately assisting in the timely mitigation of security breaches [33]. Complementary reviews have examined ML applications for object detection and classification across digital forensic evidence, highlighting the strengths and limitations of current techniques [21,43].

Further studies have explored the predictive potential of ML in forensic investigations. Researchers have demonstrated how ML algorithms can analyze large forensic datasets to uncover current criminal behaviors and even forecast potential criminal activities, providing valuable intelligence for proactive law enforcement [45]. In parallel, challenges associated with adopting these advanced technologies have been documented, particularly the practical difficulties law enforcement agencies face in integrating ML-based tools into existing forensic workflows [63]. Moreover, investigations into attack classification in cloud forensic environments have employed supervised learning models to improve the categorization and response to cyber attacks [52]. A comprehensive systematic review further highlighted that while ML applications in digital forensics are growing, significant gaps remain in consistent evaluation metrics, interpretability of models, and cross-domain applicability [40].

Category #3. Emerging Techniques: Large Language Models (LLMs), Explainable AI (XAI): The recent developments in AI open doors for fresh approaches. They might change investigations on digital forensics. A mix of explainable artificial intelligence and large language models piques interest. This combination aims to increase knowledge and automation of forensic techniques. Researchers investigate many facets of such approaches. They draw attention to possible advantages apart from challenges in implementation. Studies exploring XAI have focused on enhancing the transparency of AI models within the forensic domain. Researchers have demonstrated that incorporating explainability into forensic analytics enables practitioners to better understand model decisions, a critical requirement for legal admissibility. One investigation emphasized using XAI techniques to improve the interpretability of AI-driven forensic investigations, thereby fostering greater trust in the automated analysis of digital evidence [24]. Complementary work has discussed practical and novel approaches to leveraging XAI for extracting forensically sound artifacts, thereby facilitating the explanation of AI outputs in complex investigative scenarios [56].

Studies have assessed the application of large language models. They have demonstrated a substantial ability to manage and create natural language. This ability is usable for many forensic assignments. One study looked at whether ChatGPT can do digital forensic assignments. These assignments include writing investigative reports and studying textual evidence. Some researchers looked at local large language models like ChatGPT besides Llama for forensic report creation. They noted that this process can lower computation expenses and maintain correctness. Research suggests that if one constrains large language models well, they can improve effectiveness in forensic investigations. This is possible by automating standard analytic assignments.

More studies have been done on how LLMs might help to simplify forensic processes. One paper examined the possibility of automating important components of forensic analysis using LLM integration, generating valuable insights and encouraging a more efficient investigative process [64]. Another line of research looked at the resilience of AI-based forensic tools under adversarial attacks, so stressing the need for resilience in newly developed systems [53] Furthermore, under discussion are approaches for including AI-enhanced forensic techniques—emphasizing automation and efficiency—to support the fast processing and interpretation of digital evidence [31]. In text forensics, other research has shown that LLMs are especially appealing for large-scale investigations since they could perform author profiling with high accuracy at low computational costs, saving costs [9]. With an emphasis on triaging ransomware-related processes, recent research has assessed the use of LLMs in memory forensics, highlighting these advanced techniques' general relevance in many forensic environments [42].

Category #4. Forensic Tool Evaluation and Legal Admissibility: Standards, Testing Frameworks, and Courtroom Requirements: Tools and AI models used in forensic investigations must satisfy stringent legal requirements and provide dependable technical performance. In this regard, scholars have underlined the necessity of exacting assessment procedures that guarantee forensic instruments are both legally admissible and scientifically sound. To evaluate the dependability of forensic tools in a controlled yet realistic setting, research has concentrated on creating dynamic performance testing frameworks based on in-depth empirical observations [29]. Other studies support standardizing forensic procedures and data representations [16] to ensure that the techniques employed in evidence analysis are consistent and defendable in court.

Further research has offered thorough comparisons of forensic tools to aid in directing investigative decisions, allowing practitioners to choose the best tools for particular case requirements [18]. Problems in authenticating digital evidence to present in court have also been explored, stressing the importance of closely studying automation methods to verify whether they comply with legal standards [2]. Studies have suggested standardized frameworks for AI-based methods to streamline the digital evidence mining process, guaranteeing that these systems can efficiently and legally extract and analyze forensic data [56].

Additionally, other studies highlight how machine learning techniques can automate certain aspects of forensic investigations while still meeting legal requirements and upholding compliance [29]. The significance of standardized testing protocols for meaningful evaluation has been reinforced by comparative studies demonstrating differences in accuracy and reliability among various forensic tools [26,36]. A thorough evaluation framework for automated forensic systems has been proposed to guarantee that the instruments utilized in digital forensic investigations are held to the highest standards. This framework integrates technical performance and legal admissibility [5].

Table 2. Matrix of relationships between literature categories (rows) and cross-cutting themes (columns)

	Dataset Quality and Legal Admissibility	Technical Limitations	Interpretability and Trust	Practical Implementation
Dataset Construction	• Chain of custody documentation • FAIR principles • Representativeness [27,39]	• Insufficient sample sizes • Annotation inconsistency • Limited diversity [14,20]	• Dataset provenance transparency • Ground truth establishment [17]	• Privacy regulations • Sharing barriers • Resource requirements [23]
ML Applications	• Legal validation of ML outputs • Standards compliance [52]	• Feature selection challenges • Context preservation • Domain knowledge integration [40,45]	• ML model explainability • Decision justification [8]	• Adoption barriers • Integration with workflows • Training requirements [63]
Emerging Techniques	• Legal precedents for LLM evidence • Procedural validity [54,64]	• Computational demands • Data preprocessing needs [62]	• Black-box model transparency • XAI approaches • Adversarial robustness [24,53,56]	• Deployment challenges • Training requirements • Cost factors [31]
Forensic Tool Evaluation	• Courtroom admissibility standards • Validation frameworks [2,5]	• Evaluation metrics • Benchmarking methodologies [26,44]	• Tool reliability assessment • Output verification methods [56]	• Standardization gaps • Interoperability issues • Comparative frameworks [18,36]

Note: Cell shading intensity indicates strength of relationship between categories and themes, with darker shading representing stronger relationships based on frequency and emphasis in the literature.

To provide essential context for the field's evolution, we also reference several foundational works that established key concepts in digital forensics. Studies by [6,46,66] offer foundational examinations of digital forensic models and definitions, establishing critical conceptual frameworks for the field.

A study by [7] provides a comprehensive overview of digital evidence and computer crime, exploring the intersection of forensic science, computing, and legal considerations. Researchers like [28,38] have contributed specific methodological approaches for forensic analysis of mobile devices, highlighting the evolving technological landscape. Researchers in [1,50,57] further expanded the discourse by examining privacy issues, mobile application forensics, and the broader implications of digital investigations. Technological advancements in machine learning, as discussed by [34,35], have significantly influenced forensic methodologies, enabling more sophisticated analysis techniques. The work of [12] provides a systematic exploration of the state of the art and future potential of AI in digital forensic investigations, offering a forward-looking perspective on the field's technological trajectory. While some of these works fall outside our primary 2009–2024 focus period, they provide valuable historical context that informs current research directions and challenges identified in our thematic analysis.

After categorizing the literature, we conducted a secondary analysis to identify recurring challenges and concerns across the four primary categories. These cross-cutting themes were derived through an iterative coding process where the authors independently analyzed each of the publications, identifying common challenges mentioned across different paper categories, which is illustrated concisely in Table 2. We then consolidated these observations, focusing on issues that appeared in at least three of our four thematic categories. This process revealed several cross-cutting themes that emerge across multiple categories. These themes represent significant challenges facing AI-driven digital forensics research with respect to datasets.

The following subsections synthesize these challenges, drawing connections between publications across our categorization framework to provide a holistic view of the current landscape.

1. Dataset Quality and Legal Admissibility Concerns

Several researchers have highlighted critical issues with dataset quality that directly impact the legal admissibility of AI-driven forensic analysis:

- **Representativeness**: Garfinkel et al. [17] noted that many forensic datasets are not statistically representative of real-world evidence, potentially leading to biased ML models that may not hold up in court.
- **Privacy Concerns**: Grajeda et al. [23] discussed how privacy regulations and ethical considerations severely limit the sharing of authentic forensic data, creating a fundamental tension between dataset utility and privacy compliance.
- **Validation Methodology**: As highlighted by Bollé et al. [5], datasets lack rigorous validation protocols that would establish their fidelity to real-world scenarios, a critical requirement for court proceedings.
- **Chain of Custody**: Horsman et al. [27] emphasized that datasets must maintain proper documentation of their origin and handling to meet legal standards - a requirement rarely addressed in current datasets.
- **Metadata Standards**: Mombelli et al. [39] applied the FAIR principles (Findability, Accessibility, Interoperability, and Reusability) to forensic datasets, finding significant deficiencies in current documentation practices.

2. Technical Limitations for AI Applications

The literature identifies several technical issues that limit the effectiveness of current datasets for training sophisticated AI models:

- **Domain Specificity**: Datasets created for one forensic application (e.g., network forensics) often lack transferability to other domains (e.g., mobile device forensics), hindering the development of comprehensive AI solutions [33].
- **Annotation Inconsistency**: The literature points to a lack of standardized annotation practices, making it difficult to develop a reliable ground truth for supervised learning approaches [14].
- **Context Loss**: Sachdeva et al. [52] highlight how extracted features often lose critical contextual relationships between artifacts that human investigators would utilize.
- **Insufficient Scale**: Unlike datasets that have powered AI advances in other domains, forensic datasets often contain too few samples to train deep learning models effectively, as noted by Nayerifard et al. [40].

3. Interpretability and Trust Challenges

A significant concern across the literature focuses on how datasets impact model interpretability and trustworthiness:

- **Provenance Transparency**: Several researchers note that the opacity of dataset creation processes undermines confidence in models trained on those datasets, particularly when used in high-stakes legal contexts [2].
- **Black-box Models**: Hall [24] and Solanke [56] emphasize that datasets must support the development of explainable AI models, as unexplainable outputs may be rejected in legal contexts.
- **Adversarial Robustness**: Sanna et al. [53] demonstrate that current datasets don't adequately prepare AI models to resist adversarial tampering, raising concerns about the reliability of AI-generated evidence.

4. Practical Implementation Barriers

The final category addresses practical challenges in implementing AI solutions with existing datasets:

- **Standardization Gaps**: Despite efforts like DFXML [15], the lack of standardized data formats hampers interoperability and reproducibility of AI-driven forensic analysis.
- **Evaluation Metrics**: Lovanshi [36] and Ghazinour [18] note inconsistencies in how forensic tool performance is measured, making it difficult to meaningfully compare AI approaches.
- **Resource Requirements**: The computational resources needed to process large-scale forensic datasets can be prohibitive for many forensic practitioners, limiting the practical utility of data-intensive approaches [29].
- **Integration with Existing Tools**: Wilson-Kovacs [63] highlights the difficulties law enforcement faces in adopting new AI technologies that may not integrate seamlessly with established forensic tools and workflows.

5 Limitations of This Study

This exploratory analysis has a few limitations that should be acknowledged. First, our literature selection process was based on specific keywords related to AI in digital forensics, which may have introduced sampling bias by excluding relevant papers that used alternative terminology. The relatively small sample size of publications limits the generalizability of our findings and may not fully represent the breadth of research in this rapidly evolving field. Second, our categorization approach, while systematic, involved subjective judgment in assigning papers to the four thematic categories. Many publications address multiple themes simultaneously, and our assignment to a single primary category may oversimplify the complex interrelationships between dataset adequacy, ML applications, emerging techniques, and benchmarking efforts.

Despite these limitations, this exploratory study provides valuable insights into current research trends and gaps in AI-driven digital forensics. Our approach offers a preliminary landscape mapping that can guide more comprehensive systematic reviews. By recognizing these limitations, we position our work as an initial exploration that contributes to the ongoing conversation about the role of AI in digital forensics rather than a definitive assessment of the field.

6 Conclusion and Future Work

Based on our analysis of dataset challenges in AI-driven digital forensics, we propose several specific recommendations to address the identified limitations.

First, we recommend developing a standardized dataset creation framework for digital forensics. This framework should incorporate mandatory chain-of-custody documentation, clear privacy-preserving anonymization protocols, standardized metadata schemas aligned with FAIR principles, and validation methodologies with statistical significance metrics. Such standardization would enhance legal admissibility and scientific validity of AI-driven forensic analyses. Second, we suggest establishing a multi-stakeholder collaborative dataset initiative involving academic institutions, law enforcement agencies, and industry partners. This consortium would pool resources for creating diverse, high-quality forensic datasets, implement shared access models that balance security with accessibility, develop legal frameworks for dataset sharing that comply with privacy regulations, and create sandbox environments for testing AI models on sensitive forensic data. Collaboration across sectors would address the current fragmentation in forensic dataset development. Third, technical standards for forensic AI training data should be implemented to ensure consistency and reliability. These standards should include minimum diversity requirements across device types, operating systems, and user behaviors; annotation guidelines specifically designed for forensic artifacts; benchmark datasets for specific forensic domains such as network and mobile forensics; and synthetic data generation tools that accurately model real-world forensic scenarios. Fourth, an explainability and legal admissibility framework is essential for forensic AI applications. This framework should develop standardized documentation practices linking dataset characteristics to AI model decisions, create evaluation metrics specifically measuring admissibility criteria, establish verification protocols that maintain evidential integrity, and design dataset attributes that support transparent AI reasoning. Such a framework would address current challenges in explaining AI outputs in legal contexts. These recommendations address the core challenges identified in our analysis and provide concrete steps toward improving dataset availability, quality, and applicability for AI-driven forensic investigations.

Future work should focus on developing standardized forensic datasets that meet the requirements of legal admissibility in investigative and judicial contexts. Additionally, research should explore ways to enhance dataset quality assessment frameworks and explainable AI techniques to improve forensic AI interpretability and reliability. Furthermore, AI models trained on forensic datasets must align with legal and procedural standards to be considered valid in court, addressing issues such as bias in training data, reproducibility of AI outputs, and transparency in forensic decision-making.

References

1. Aminnezhad, A., Dehghantanha, A., Abdullah, M.T.: A survey on privacy issues in digital forensics. IJCSDF **1**(4), 311–323 (2012)
2. Arshad, H., Jantan, A.B., Abiodun, O.I.: Digital Forensics: review of issues in scientific validation of digital evidence. J. Info. Process. Syst. **14**(2), 346–376 (2018)
3. AVCaesar Team: AVCaesar - Malware Analysis Service. https://avcaesar.malware.lu. Accessed April 2025
4. Bishop, C.M.: Pattern Recognition and Machine Learning. Springer (2006)
5. Bollé, T., Casey, E., Jacquet, M.: The role of evaluations in reaching decisions using automated systems supporting forensic analysis. Forensic Sci. Int. Digit. Investig. **34**, 301016 (2020)
6. Carrier, B., et al.: Defining digital forensic examination and analysis tools using abstraction layers. Int. J. Digit. Evidence **1**(4), 1–12 (2003)
7. Casey, E.: Digital Evidence and Computer Crime: Forensic Science, Computers, and the Internet. Academic Press (2011)
8. Chhabra, G.S., Singh, V.P., Singh, M.: Cyber forensics framework for big data analytics in IOT environment using machine learning. Multimedia Tools Appl. **79**, 15881–15900 (2020)
9. Cho, S., Kim, D., Kwon, H.C., Kim, M.: Exploring the potential of large language models for author profiling tasks in digital text forensics. Forensic Sci. Int. Digit. Investig. (2024). https://doi.org/10.1016/j.fsidi.2024.301814
10. Dang-Nguyen, D.T., Pasquini, C., Conotter, V., Boato, G.: Raise: a raw images dataset for digital image forensics. In: Proceedings of the 6th ACM Multimedia Systems Conference, pp. 219–224 (2015)
11. Deng, J., Dong, W., Socher, R., Li, L.J., Li, K., Fei-Fei, L.: ImageNet: a large-scale hierarchical image database. 2009 IEEE Conference on Computer Vision and Pattern Recognition, pp. 248–255 (2009)
12. Du, X., Hargreaves, C., Sheppard, J., Anda, F., Sayakkara, A., Le-Khac, N.A., Scanlon, M.: SOK: exploring the state of the art and the future potential of artificial intelligence in digital forensic investigation. In: Proceedings of the 15th International Conference on Availability, Reliability and Security, pp. 1–10 (2020)
13. Du, X., Hargreaves, C., Sheppard, J., Scanlon, M.: TraceGEN: user activity emulation for digital forensic test image generation. Forensic Sci. Int. Digit. Investig. **38**, 301133 (2021)
14. Ferreira, S., Antunes, M., Correia, M.E.: A dataset of photos and videos for digital forensics analysis using machine learning processing. Data **6**(8), 87 (2021)
15. Garfinkel, S., Farrell, P., Roussev, V., Dinolt, G.: Bringing science to digital forensics with standardized forensic corpora. digit. investig. **9**, S2–S11 (2012)
16. Garfinkel, S.L.: Digital forensics research: the next 10 years. Digit. Investig. (2010). https://doi.org/10.1016/j.diin.2010.05.009
17. Garfinkel, S.L., Farrell, P., Roussev, V., Dinolt, G.W.: Bringing science to digital forensics with standardized forensic corpora. Digit. Investig. (2009). https://doi.org/10.1016/j.diin.2009.06.016
18. Ghazinour, K., Vakharia, D.M., Kannaji, K.C., Satyakumar, R.: A study on digital forensic tools. In: 2017 IEEE International Conference on Power, Control, Signals and Instrumentation Engineering (ICPCSI), pp. 3136–3142. IEEE (2017)
19. Göbel, T., Breitinger, F., Baier, H.: Optimising data set creation in the cybersecurity landscape with a special focus on digital forensics: Principles, characteristics, and use cases. Forensic Sci. Int. Digit. Investig. **52**, 301882 (2025)

20. Göbel, T., Schäfer, T., Hachenberger, J., Türr, J., Baier, H.: A novel approach for generating synthetic datasets for digital forensics. In: Advances in Digital Forensics XVI: 16th IFIP WG 11.9 International Conference, New Delhi, India, January 6–8, 2020, Revised Selected Papers 16, pp. 73–93. Springer (2020)
21. Goni, I., Gumpy, J.M., Maigari, T.U., Mohammad, M.: Cybersecurity and cyber forensics: machine learning approach systematic review. Semicond. Sci. Info. Dev. **2**(2), 25–29 (2020)
22. Goodfellow, I., Bengio, Y., Courville, A.: Deep Learning. MIT Press (2016)
23. Grajeda, C., Breitinger, F., Baggili, I.: Availability of datasets for digital forensics-and what is missing. Digit. Investig. **22**, S94–S105 (2017)
24. Hall, S.W., Sakzad, A., Choo, K.: Explainable artificial intelligence for digital forensics. Wiley Interdiscipl. Rev. Forensic Sci. **4**(2), e1434 (2022)
25. Hargreaves, C., Breitinger, F., Dowthwaite, L., Webb, H., Scanlon, M.: DFPulse: the 2024 digital forensic practitioner survey. Forensic Sci. Int. Digit. Investig. **51**, 301844 (2024)
26. Horsman, G.: Tool testing and reliability issues in the field of digital forensics. Digit. Investig. **28**, 163–175 (2019)
27. Horsman, G., Lyle, J.R.: Dataset construction challenges for digital forensics. Forensic Sci. Int. Digit. Investig. **38**, 301264 (2021)
28. Husain, M.I., Baggili, I., Sridhar, R.: A simple cost-effective framework for IPhone forensic analysis. In: Digital Forensics and Cyber Crime, pp. 27–37. Springer (2010)
29. Iqbal, S., Alharbi, S.A.: Advancing automation in digital forensic investigations using machine learning forensics. In: Digital Forensic Science. intechopen (2019)
30. Jigsaw: Toxic comment classification challenge (2018). https://www.kaggle.com/competitions/jigsaw-toxic-comment-classification-challenge/overview
31. Kadage, D.A.D., Meghya, D.B., Nayak, Sharad, D.V., Hingmire, Wanjale, D.K., Bogiri, N., Mandale, P.L.: AI-enhanced digital forensics: automated techniques for efficient investigation and evidence collection. J. Electric. Syst. (2024). https://doi.org/10.52783/jes.766
32. Kerr, O.S.: Searches and seizures in a digital world. Harv. L. Rev. **119**, 531 (2005)
33. Koroniotis, N., Moustafa, N., Sitnikova, E.: A new network forensic framework based on deep learning for internet of things networks: a particle deep framework. Futur. Gener. Comput. Syst. (2020). https://doi.org/10.1016/j.future.2020.03.042
34. Krizhevsky, A., Sutskever, I., Hinton, G.E.: Imagenet classification with deep convolutional neural networks. In: Advances in Neural Information Processing Systems (2012)
35. LeCun, Y., Bengio, Y., Hinton, G.: Deep learning. Nature **521**(7553) (2015)
36. Lovanshi, M., Bansal, P.: Comparative study of digital forensic tools. Data Eng. Appl. **2**, 195–204 (2019)
37. Mitchell, T.M.: Machine Learning. McGraw-Hill (1997)
38. Mokhonoana, P.M., Olivier, M.S.: Acquisition of a Symbian smart phone's content with an on-phone forensic tool. In: Proceedings of the Southern African Telecommunication Networks and Applications Conference, vol. 8. Citeseer (2007)
39. Mombelli, S., Lyle, J.R., Breitinger, F.: Fairness in digital forensics datasets' metadata-and how to improve it. Forensic Sci. Int. Digit. Investig. **48**, 301681 (2024)
40. Nayerifard, T., Amintoosi, H., Bafghi, A.G., Dehghantanha, A.: Machine learning in digital forensics: a systematic literature review. arXiv preprint arXiv:2306.04965 (2023)
41. Nazario, J.: Phishing Corpus. https://monkey.org/~jose/phishing/ (2004)

42. Oh, D.B., Kim, D., Kim, D., Kim, H.K.: VolGPT: evaluation on triaging ransomware process in memory forensics with large language model. Forensic Sci. Int. Digit. Investig. **49**, 301756 (2024). https://doi.org/10.1016/j.fsidi.2024.301756, https://www.sciencedirect.com/science/article/pii/S2666281724000751, dFRWS USA 2024 - Selected Papers from the 24th Annual Digital Forensics Research Conference USA
43. Oladipo, F., Ogbuju, E., Alayesanmi, F.S., Musa, A.E.: The state of the art in machine learning-based digital forensics. Available at SSRN 3668687 (2020)
44. Pan, L., Batten, L.M.: Robust performance testing for digital forensic tools. Digit. Investig. (2009). https://doi.org/10.1016/j.diin.2009.02.003
45. Qadir, A.M., Varol, A.: The role of machine learning in digital forensics. In: 2020 8th International Symposium on Digital Forensics and Security (ISDFS), pp. 1–5. IEEE (2020)
46. Reith, M., Carr, C., Gunsch, G.: An examination of digital forensic models. Int. J. Digit. Evidence **1**(3), 1–12 (2002)
47. Research Rabbit: research rabbit: literature mapping tool. https://www.researchrabbit.ai/ (2023). Accessed 01 April 2025
48. Ring, M., Wunderlich, S., Grüdl, D., Landes, D., Hotho, A.: Flow-based benchmark data sets for intrusion detection. Proceedings of the 16th European Conference on Cyber Warfare and Security, pp. 361–369 (2017)
49. Rogers, M.K., Goldman, J., Mislan, R., Wedge, T., Debrota, S.: Computer forensics field triage process model. J. Digit. Forensics Secur. Law **1**(2), 2 (2006)
50. Ruan, K., Carthy, J., Kechadi, T., Crosbie, M.: Cloud forensics. In: IFIP International Conference on Digital Forensics, pp. 35–46. Springer (2011)
51. Russell, S., Norvig, P.: Artificial Intelligence: A Modern Approach. Pearson, 4th EDN. (2021)
52. Sachdeva, S., Ali, A.: Machine learning with digital forensics for attack classification in cloud network environment. Int. J. Syst. Assur. Eng. Manag **13**(Suppl 1), 156–165 (2022)
53. Sanna, S.L., Regano, L., Maiorca, D., Giacinto, G.: Exploring the robustness of AI-driven tools in digital forensics: a preliminary study. arXiv preprint arXiv:2412.01363 (2024). https://doi.org/10.48550/arXiv.2412.01363
54. Scanlon, M., Breitinger, F., Hargreaves, C., Hilgert, J.N., Sheppard, J.: ChatGPT for digital forensic investigation: the good, the bad, and the unknown. Forensic Sci. Int. Digit. Investig. (2023). https://doi.org/10.48550/arxiv.2307.10195
55. Sharafaldin, I., Lashkari, A.H., Ghorbani, A.A.: Toward generating a new intrusion detection dataset and intrusion traffic characterization. In: Proceedings of the 4th International Conference on Information Systems Security and Privacy (ICISSP), pp. 108–116 (2018)
56. Solanke, A.A., Biasiotti, M.A.: Digital Forensics AI: evaluating, standardizing and optimizing digital evidence mining techniques. Ki - Künstliche Intell. (2022). https://doi.org/10.1007/s13218-022-00763-9
57. Stirparo, P., Kounelis, I.: The Mobileak Project: forensics methodology for mobile application privacy assessment. In: Internet Technology And Secured Transactions, 2012 International Conference for, pp. 297–303. IEEE (2012)
58. Stolfo, S.J., Fan, W., Lee, W., Prodromidis, A., Chan, P.K.: Cost-based modeling for fraud and intrusion detection: results from the jam project. In: Proceedings DARPA Information Survivability Conference and Exposition. DISCEX'00, vol. 2, pp. 130–144. IEEE (2000)
59. Sutton, R.S., Barto, A.G.: Reinforcement Learning: An Introduction. MIT Press, 2nd EDN. (2018)

60. Usman, N., et al.: Intelligent dynamic malware detection using machine learning in IP reputation for forensics data analytics. Futur. Gener. Comput. Syst. (2021). https://doi.org/10.1016/j.future.2021.01.004
61. Wang, A., Singh, A., Michael, J., Hill, F., Levy, O., Bowman, S.: GLUE: a multi-task benchmark and analysis platform for natural language understanding. Proceedings of the 2018 EMNLP Workshop BlackboxNLP: Analyzing and Interpreting Neural Networks for NLP, pp. 353–355 (2018)
62. Wickramasekara, A., Breitinger, F., Scanlon, M.: SOK: exploring the potential of large language models for improving digital forensic investigation efficiency. arXiv.org (2024). https://doi.org/10.48550/arxiv.2402.19366
63. Wilson-Kovacs, D.: Digital media investigators: challenges and opportunities in the use of digital forensics in police investigations in England and wales. Policing: An International Journal (2021). https://doi.org/10.1108/pijpsm-02-2021-0019
64. Xu, E., Zhang, W., Xu, W.: Transforming digital forensics with large language models: unlocking automation, insights, and justice. Int. Conf. Info. Knowl. Manag. (2024). https://doi.org/10.1145/3627673.3679091
65. Yates, M., Chi, H.: A framework for designing benchmarks of investigating digital forensics tools for mobile devices. ACM-SE'11 (2011). https://doi.org/10.1145/2016039.2016088
66. Zatyko, K.: Commentary: defining digital forensics. Forensic Mag. **20** (2007)

The Impact of Anti-forensic Techniques on Data-Driven Digital Forensics: Anomaly Detection Case Study

Zuzana Hennelová, Eva Marková(✉), and Pavol Sokol

Institute of Computer Science, Faculty of Science, Pavol Jozef Šafárik University in Košice, Jesenná 5, 040 01 Košice, Slovakia
{zuzana.hennelova,eva.markova,pavol.sokol}@upjs.sk
https://ics.science.upjs.sk/en/

Abstract. Digital forensics is vital in responding to cybersecurity threats and incidents by enabling investigators to identify, collect, and analyze digital evidence. As cyberattacks become increasingly sophisticated, adversaries leverage anti-forensic techniques to evade detection and hinder forensic investigations. These techniques aim to remove, obfuscate, or manipulate digital traces, thereby reducing the effectiveness of forensic analysis. Despite growing interest in anti-forensics, limited attention has been given to systematically evaluating their real-world impact. In this paper, we investigate the effects of selected anti-forensic techniques, such as file deletion, log deletion, data hiding in alternate data streams (ADS), encryption, fake evidence creation, and timestamp manipulation, on two critical aspects: the integrity and availability of digital traces, and the accuracy of algorithmic anomaly detection in data-driven forensic analysis. Our study is guided by two primary research questions: (1) How can the impact of anti-forensic techniques on specific digital artifacts and anomaly detection accuracy be quantified? (2) What is the measurable effect of selected anti-forensic techniques on the quality and reliability of forensic investigations? To address these questions, we propose a methodology based on impact levels and an impact matrix supported by quantitative evaluation using precision, recall, and F1 score. Experiments were conducted using a Windows operating system with an NTFS filesystem.

Keywords: Anti-forensics · data analysis · digital forensics

1 Introduction

With significant technological advancements, cyberspace has become a tool for societal development and an opportunity for attackers. For several years, there has been a continuous increase in both the number and sophistication of cyber threats. Attacks are executed faster, more precisely, and often with automated

E. Marková—Primary Author.

tools. In this context, the ability of organizations to respond quickly and appropriately to incidents has become essential for protecting their assets.

Responding to cyber incidents, including executing digital forensic analysis, has become a standard component of security operations in many organizations. Digital forensics, which relies on examining digital traces, enables investigators to understand what happened, how, and why the incident occurred.

However, adversaries also recognize these capabilities and frequently attempt to erase or otherwise conceal the digital traces they leave behind in compromised systems. This reduces the ability of organizations to effectively analyze security incidents. Attempts to alter, disrupt, negate, or interfere with scientifically valid forensic investigations in any way can be defined as **anti-forensics** [9]. Anti-forensic techniques encompass various methods that can be applied to digital data or the hardware on which the data resides. Their primary goals include avoiding detection of the event, disrupting the information-gathering process, prolonging the investigation time, and questioning the results of forensic analysis [2,16].

Another significant challenge in digital forensic analysis is the high proportion of manual work required to identify and interpret digital traces. Most current approaches depend on manual searching and evaluation [30]. In this regard, supervised and unsupervised machine learning methods offer promising potential to accelerate the forensic process—particularly in pattern recognition and anomaly detection [27]. Data-driven forensics, supported by such techniques, is a promising approach to addressing cybersecurity threats and resolving incidents more efficiently.

This paper presents a case study in data-driven forensics, focusing on automatically identifying unusual digital trace occurrences extracted from the file system. Most existing approaches rely on known patterns and assume prior input knowledge. As such, the forensic analyst is not informed whether a given record is anomalous, outlying, or relevant for investigation. This approach is more realistic, as annotated datasets are rarely available in real-world scenarios—and if they were, analysis would be largely redundant. Similar approaches can be found in [10,18].

Contemporary research on anti-forensic techniques primarily focuses on their description and demonstration, often using specific tools and, in some cases, offering mitigation strategies. However, according to our findings, there is a lack of systematic studies assessing the *impact* of anti-forensic techniques on digital forensic analysis. Most of the available literature concentrates on which artifacts a particular technique affects and how [2,3].

The decision on whether an anti-forensic technique is severe enough to be detected during an investigation is left to the forensic analyst. However, assessing the use of such techniques in a specific case is time-consuming and requires considerable effort. Some techniques are relatively easy to detect, while others require advanced analytical methods. A comprehensive understanding of the impact of various anti-forensic techniques can significantly support the decision-making and planning of forensic procedures.

The main objective of this paper is to understand and **quantify the impact of anti-forensic techniques** on digital forensic analysis. To achieve this goal, we define the following research sub-objectives:

- To propose a method for quantifying the impact of anti-forensic techniques on specific digital artifacts and the accuracy of anomaly detection algorithms within the forensic analysis.
- To evaluate the impact of selected anti-forensic techniques on the quality and effectiveness of forensic investigations.

To address these research questions, we focused on various anti-forensic techniques and analyzed their impact on digital artifacts and automated forensic analysis when detecting anomalies in the file system. Our approach is based on the categorization proposed in the papers [9,17], where the authors identify four and five main categories of anti-forensic techniques, respectively, and describe their underlying principles. In our paper, we focus on the categories that are relevant to data-driven digital forensics. We do not focus on attacks against the forensic process. We specifically examined the impact of the following techniques:

- file deletion,
- log deletion,
- hiding data in Alternate Data Streams (ADS),
- encryption,
- creation of false evidence,
- manipulation of timestamps (timestomping).

The impact quantification is implemented using defined approaches such as *impact levels* and *impact matrices*, which consider various factors, including detection difficulty and the degree of artifact degradation. Our case study focuses on anomaly detection within the file system under the **Windows operating system**, using the **NTFS file system**. The analyzed artifact is the **file inode**.

This paper offers an innovative perspective on anti-forensic techniques by going beyond their description and providing a *systematic evaluation of their impact* on specific digital traces and the accuracy of automated anomaly detection. A key contribution lies in developing a *quantification methodology* based on impact levels and matrices that consider detection complexity and artifact degradation. The paper's experimental focus on the Windows environment and NTFS file system also enhances the **practical applicability** of the findings.

This paper is divided into five sections. Section 2 discusses papers relevant to this research. Section 3 specifies the methodology employed in this paper, including the description of the dataset used. Section 4 outlines the evaluation of different anti-forensic techniques. Section 5 provides a summary, including our suggestions for future research.

2 Related Works

Research on anti-forensic techniques represents an important component of digital forensic analysis and investigation [4,24]. The relevance of this area is further emphasized by several papers providing systematic reviews of anti-forensic techniques, highlighting the increasing sophistication of attacks and the growing need to enhance analytical capabilities to detect and mitigate anti-forensic threats [5, 11, 13, 32].

Beyond general studies addressing digital forensics and its challenges, including anti-forensic methods, numerous papers focus on specific anti-forensic techniques, their nature, and approaches for identification and mitigation. Given the paper's focus on the Windows operating system and the NTFS file system, only publications related to these technologies are discussed. In the area of file deletion or artifact wiping an important study is presented in [14], where the authors analyzed traces in 13 Windows artifacts after executing 10 file-wiping tools. Another example involves hiding data in Alternate Data Streams (ADS). In paper [7, 12], authors describe various forensic techniques to detect and analyze hidden data in ADS or NTFS timestamps. An example of the creation of false evidence is discussed in paper [29], where the authors address the emerging threat of anti-forensic attacks using generative adversarial networks (GANs). They demonstrate how synthetic digital forensic traces can be created using GANs to evade detection.

A significant portion of the literature focuses on the manipulation of timestamps (timestomping), which can delay investigations or lead to the loss of crucial evidence [28]. Authors have examined manipulations within the USN journal, LNK files, prefetch files, and event logs [23], confirming that NTFS journal-based detection is among the most effective methods for identifying such manipulations [21]. Others explore the challenges of detecting tampering on live systems [31]. Another notable contribution is [8], where the authors analyze the impacts of multiple anti-forensic actions that users might perform deliberately or inadvertently.

Our research focuses on analyzing the impact of anti-forensic techniques on data-driven digital forensics. Several studies address similar themes, evaluating how anti-forensic techniques affect digital forensic investigations [1, 20, 22, 25, 26]. In paper [22], the authors tested various anti-forensic methods and assessed their effectiveness against forensic tools. Results showed that only a few techniques were highly effective, while many failed to hide or delete crucial data successfully. In paper [25], an overview of standard anti-forensic measures in media forensics is presented, with a qualitative evaluation of their trade-offs between usability and effectiveness. The same research group expanded their work in paper [26], providing a general summary and evaluating techniques for tampering with media stored on local devices such as images and videos.

Another interesting contribution is paper [1], which investigates the anti-forensic dilemma across multiple levels of the forensic process and assesses its impact on digital forensic research. Finally, paper [20] proposes an abstract framework to validate digital forensic models by factoring in the influence of anti-forensic techniques at various stages of the investigation.

Across the reviewed literature, we identified a significant gap in evaluating the impact of both existing and emerging anti-forensic techniques. Our work reflects the growing need to assess the resilience of forensic tools and processes under realistic investigative scenarios, providing a foundation for the analytical, experimental, and methodological evaluation of their effectiveness.

3 Methodology

In this section, we describe the dataset utilized and present approaches for determining the impact of anti-forensic techniques on specific artifacts and algorithmic anomaly detection results.

In the initial phase of this study, we describe selected anti-forensic techniques and evaluate them using the approaches delineated in 3.2. This allows us to formulate hypotheses regarding the anticipated impact in the following steps. We preprocess the selected dataset using the approach described in [18], then apply the anti-forensic techniques, and execute the anomaly detection algorithm. Employing the evaluation metrics described in 3.3, we can observe the alterations in the results and determine the most impactful techniques.

3.1 Dataset and Anomaly Detection

For this research, we have used an existing dataset to investigate the impact of anti-forensic techniques by searching for anomalies. The dataset originates from the DFIR Madness portal, specifically from the case *Case001 âĂŞ The Stolen Szechuan Sauce*. This case is well-documented and has even been utilized in several research papers.

Our analysis will be based on the paper [18], which explores Local Outlier Factor (LOF) anomaly detection algorithm in the case of The Stolen Szechuan Sauce, mainly using data obtained from a disk image of the server.

For this study, we selected Empirical-Cumulative-Distribution-based Outlier Detection (ECOD) considering the algorithm's complexity ($O(n*d)$, where n is the number of data rows and d is the number of dimensions) and input parameters. For purposes of this paper, we consider this method to be sufficient. In principle, any anomaly detection method may be employed; however, the efficacy of the method may vary.

During the program's execution, all combinations for seven contamination values, four aggregation functions, and all combinations of logical attribute groups are tested (i.e., not every program run uses all available attributes). The method also distinguishes between anomaly detection based on so-called inodes. The term *inode* refers to a number that serves as a unique identifier for a file in the NTFS file system [6].

As in the aforementioned paper, we will use preprocessed data extracted from the disk image, specifically data related to files, in which 15 anomalous inodes are identified. We performed ECOD on the data from the time of the attack and examined the summary results. The data is stored in CSV format; each row contains 60 attributes. The attributes used in the analysis are binary (e.g., if a record has an M timestamp, the M attribute is set to 1) and are grouped into eight logical groups.

3.2 Approaches to Determining Impact

We have defined two methods (impact levels and an impact matrix) to assess the level of impact of an anti-forensic technique on an artifact. While the first method does not consider any circumstances, the second one considers the difficulty of detecting the applied technique. Precision evaluation will be used to assess the impact of anomaly detection.

Impact Levels. The impact of an anti-forensic technique on the quality of an artifact, without considering other circumstances (such as detection difficulty or artifact importance), can be characterized by the following four impact levels:

- **No Impact**: The anti-forensic technique does not affect the artifact.
- **Low Impact**: The technique changes the artifact's location and/or creates fake artifacts.
- **Medium Impact**: The technique partially alters the content and/or modifies the artifact's metadata.
- **High Impact**: The technique hides the artifact's existence, deletes it (and any evidence), and/or irretrievably overwrites it.

Anti-forensic techniques may not be applicable to every type of forensic artifact, but their existence is relevant - the mere possibility of their use is a factor that must be taken into account in the analysis, regardless of whether they were actually implemented in a particular case.

Impact Matrix. One option for comparing the impact of different techniques on artifacts is the impact matrix of the anti-forensic technique on the artifact (Table 1). The matrix considers the difficulty of detecting the use of the anti-forensic technique and the artifact's state. The output consists of three levels of impact on the artifact:

- **Low Impact**: The anti-forensic technique targets artifacts that others can replace, or the artifacts are partially recoverable. Detection of the technique is trivial because it leaves obvious evidence in the system. A low impact also applies to a combination of a hard-to-detect technique with a replaceable artifact, as it suffices to replace the affected artifact once the technique is detected.
- **Medium Impact**: This level corresponds to either an almost impossible detection but a replaceable artifact, a partially recoverable artifact with difficult detection, or an unrecoverable artifact but trivial detection.
- **High Impact**: Techniques that invalidate entirely the artifact and are difficult or almost impossible to detect will have a high impact. Similarly, a nearly undetectable technique that affects a partially replaceable artifact will significantly impact it. Such techniques will be essential in automating forensic and manual analysis processes.

Table 1. Impact matrix of anti-forensic technique on artifact and detection difficulty.

Impact of anti-forensic technique on artifact		Replaceable	Partially recoverable	Unrecoverable
Detection	Almost impossible			High impact
	Difficult		Medium impact	
	Trivial	Low impact		

Table 1 does not include the scenario where the artifact is affected by the technique but is irrelevant for forensic analysis, as such artifacts will not be evaluated. We also do not consider the possibility of impossible detection since even theoretically undetectable techniques may have imperfect practical applications (human factor), which still leave evidence in the system.

3.3 Evaluation Techniques

We used metrics such as precision, recall, and F1 score to evaluate the impact of anti-forensic techniques on specific artifacts and algorithmic anomaly detection results. We provide their formal definitions in the following text.

Precision. Precision is used to evaluate the proportion of correctly identified anomalies (True Positives, denoted as TP) to all identified anomalies, including correctly identified and incorrectly identified ones (False Positives, denoted as FP).

$$\text{Precision} = \frac{TP}{TP + FP} \qquad (1)$$

Recall. Recall measures the number of correctly identified anomalies (TP) relative to all anomalies that should be correctly labeled. It is the ratio of TP to the sum of TP and incorrectly unidentified anomalies (False Negatives, denoted as FN).

$$\text{Recall} = \frac{TP}{TP + FN} \qquad (2)$$

F1-Score. The F1 score combines precision and recall, with the best possible value being 1. It is calculated using the following formula:

$$\text{F1-score} = 2 \times \frac{\text{Precision} \times \text{Recall}}{\text{Precision} + \text{Recall}} \qquad (3)$$

The maximum possible value for all these evaluations is 1 [15]. The F1-score will be given the most significant weight in determining impact, as it combines the previous two metrics. However, precision and recall are also important.

We will use the sum of the anomalies found across all program runs, their precision evaluation, and the average values for the five settings that yield the best results for the original data.

4 Results

In this section, we evaluate the impact of anti-forensic techniques on specific artifacts and algorithmic anomaly detection results.

4.1 Impact of File Deletion

Impact on Artifacts. We used two tools designed for file deletion: BitKiller version 2.0 and Eraser. BitKiller's author is Hasan N. Genc. According to the attached documentation, BitKiller first overwrites the selected file according to the chosen method, then reduces the file size to 0. The file is then renamed randomly 10 times and deleted. The method used by the Eraser tool is not described.

We repeated the same deletion process (for PDF files) with both tools and tried all five available methods in the case of BitKiller. We then created a disk image using Access Data FTK Imager version 7.4.1 and uploaded it to Autopsy version 4.19.3. In both cases, we found the link files of the deleted files with their original names and locations, as well as the record of the deletion tool execution, in the prefetch files.

No relevant records were found in the logs, and the deleted files were never successfully extracted from memory. The extraction of PDF files using Bulk Extractor version 5.1 and Scalpel 2.0 was unsuccessful.

Thus, file deletion only affects the data that cannot be recovered, and the technique has no impact on other artifacts. The impact level on file data is high, but considering the simplicity of detecting the technique, the impact on data according to the impact matrix is medium.

Impact on Anomaly Detection. In the preprocessed data, we simulated the deletion of the NoJerry.txt file in four different ways. The first two methods simulate simple file deletion by setting the file size (and its corresponding LNK file) to 0 and marking it as unallocated. This proved less effective than simulating a deletion application and will not be considered further.

Simulating complete deletion in the data resulted in removing relevant records from the data, i.e., the removal of the NoJerry.txt record (and also NoJerry.lnk) from the file system. We did not remove records related to the MFT and the journal, as the applications do not interfere with these records.

Table 2 shows the difference in the number of identified anomalies compared to the original results.

Identifying anomalies based on inode aggregation and only deleting the file decreased the number of correctly identified anomalies the least. When the file and its link were deleted, the number of incorrectly identified anomalies decreased, meaning the forensic analyst would have six fewer irrelevant records to investigate.

Table 2. Anomaly detection quality comparison (file deletion).

Comparison	Precision	Recall	F1 Score
Original	0.2830	0.0220	0.0409
File Deletion	0.2733	0.0229	0.0422
File and LNK Deletion	0.2819	0.0237	0.0438

When comparing file deletion with file deletion and its link, the first option achieves lower overall precision, probably because the undeleted LNK files without the corresponding file they reference may appear more anomalous.

For comparison, we also calculated the average of the five best settings for results in the original data. The average values are shown in Table 3. For anomaly detection by name, the worst F1 score is for deleting the file and its link. The results are less clear for inode-based detection, but even here, the deletion of the file and its link achieved the worst F1 score.

Table 3. Average of the five best settings (file deletion).

Comparison	TP	FP	Precision	Recall	F1 Score
Original	12.0	10.2	0.5513	0.8000	0.6483
File Deletion	11.6	10.2	0.5434	0.8286	0.6521
File & LNK Deletion	11.4	10.4	0.5354	0.8143	0.6419

4.2 Impact of Log Deletion

Impact on Artifacts. Deleting an entire EVTX file generates new logs with ID 1102 or 104. In the case of a running logging service, detecting log deletion is simple. While the impact on logs is high (assuming logs are not regularly backed up), considering the simplicity of detection, the impact according to the impact matrix is medium.

If we want to prevent logs from being generated by stopping the Windows Event Log service, a new log with ID 1100 is created (additionally, automatic service startup must be turned off). However, when the service is restarted, several error logs are generated.

We retrieved the process ID under which the logging service was running. We terminated this process without stopping the service itself, but the process was immediately restored (even though its automatic startup was disabled).

This method of manually stopping services proved ineffective, as the service started automatically after being disabled. To suspend the logging service, we tried the tools SuspendorResumeTid.exe and SuspendoerResumeTidEx.exe. The tools appeared to suspend the logging service threads, but new logs continued to be generated. We also tested the Phant0m tool for the same purpose. It was blocked by the built-in anti-malware solution Windows Defender, but even after deactivating it and running the program, we could not successfully stop logging. Moreover, all these tools required administrative privileges to run.

Impact on Anomaly Detection. In the dataset, we simulated the deletion of an entire category of logs by setting their size and related attributes to 0. Deleting application logs did not cause any significant changes in the observed values (precision, recall, F1 score). Some values differed only from the fifth decimal place. This applies to the summary results for all anomaly detection runs and the average results for the five best settings.

In this case, log deletion has no impact on anomaly detection. However, this detection only occurs over the file system and does not consider the content of EVTX files. If anomaly detection were performed directly on the content of EVTX logs, the impact of deletion might be more significant.

4.3 Impact of Hiding in ADS

We created a text file and inserted ADS (Alternate Data Streams) into it. The insertion updated the timestamps of the displayed file, and the changes were recorded in the journal (Fig. 14). The reason for the metadata update is listed as "StreamChange," indicating a data stream change. Opening the data stream creates a new link (also recorded in the journal). At the same time, all ADS can be quickly listed with a command.

According to Impact Levels, ADS highly impacts the data itself, as it hides it. However, ADS detection is relatively trivial and does not delete or modify the data, so according to the Impact Matrix, alternate data streams have a low impact on the data.

4.4 Impact of Encryption

We used the AES Crypt tool to encrypt a single file. The tool can be used via the command line and is an option when right-clicking a file. When run on a specific file, a new file with the same name and the .aes extension is created after entering the password, and the original file remains unchanged. The first problem with file encryption is the existence of the original file itself. It must be thoroughly deleted; otherwise, the encryption is meaningless.

The encrypted file cannot be opened directly without entering the correct password. The encryption algorithm's name and program are visible in the header when the text is displayed. The rest of the data is unreadable. Moreover, the program's installation is logged in the system.

The detection of file encryption is trivial, and the data can only be recovered if the original file is not properly deleted. Suppose we assume that the attacker can delete the data of the unencrypted file. In that case, encryption has a high impact level on the data, no impact on other artifacts according to Impact Levels, and a medium impact according to the Impact Matrix.

Again, detecting the technique for encrypting an entire partition or disk is very simple, as the data is unreadable. However, not only the data of specific files is affected, but everything that is stored on that partition, including MFT, journal, logs (if it is the partition where the operating system is stored), Recycle Bin content, prefetch files, links, etc.

According to the impact levels, encryption significantly impacts all encrypted partition/disk artifacts. However, considering the simplicity of detection, the impact matrix shows only a medium impact. In this case, the impact level evaluation is more accurate, as forensic analysis of an encrypted disk is usually unsuccessful.

4.5 Impact of Creating Fake Evidence

We tested the impact of creating new files that appeared during the attack on anomaly detection. We added modified records to the dataset, which are created for another file with the same extension (.txt, .exe). We changed the name, inode, and timestamps. Table 4 shows the resulting values for the sum of all ECOD function runs. There was a significant decrease in name-based aggregation, but inode-based aggregation also decreased in all evaluation techniques.

Table 4. Comparison of evaluation techniques (fake evidence).

Comparison	Precision	Recall	F1 Score
Original	0.2830	0.0220	0.0409
Fake .txt File	0.2527	0.0207	0.0382
Fake .exe File	0.2681	0.0215	0.0398

Table 5 shows the final values for the average of the five best settings. Again, all evaluation techniques saw a decrease. As a result, even creating a single misleading trace (file) can significantly worsen the results of automated anomaly detection.

Table 5. Average of the five best settings (fake evidence).

Comparison	TP	FP	Precision	Recall	F1 Score
Original	12.0	10.2	0.5513	0.8000	0.6483
Fake .txt File	7.2	13.2	0.3634	0.4800	0.4126
Fake .exe File	8.4	12.8	0.4067	0.5600	0.4672

4.6 Impact of Timestomping

Impact on Artifacts. We tested timestamp modification using the command line and the nTimestomp and Timestomp tools; however, these tools could only modify SI timestamps. Using the PowerShell command line proved to be the most effective method, and it also leaves no evidence of installation.

In PowerShell, timestamps can be changed by simply setting the timestamp of file $a to date $b, e.g., $a.CreationTime = $b. This allows setting the creation timestamp (B), last modification (M), and last access (A). This approach can be combined with file relocation.

Table 6 and Table 7 show the extracted timestamps. Procedure 1 represents only the timestamp change, and Procedure 2 includes relocation. It can be seen that the first procedure is not effective at all, but by the second method, it is possible to indirectly set even the system timestamps (FN, 0×30). That means that using PowerShell we are able to modify both SI and FN timestamps. Timestamps are not modified because the file was further manipulated. However, the Last Record Change timestamps are noteworthy as they indicate the last metadata update. Without context, it might appear that the file was only moved (which updates only the C timestamp) and opened (which changes only the A timestamp). Based on this data, it is not possible to definitively confirm timestomping.

Table 6. Timestamps from MFT (Part 1).

Attribute	1	2
Created 0×10	10.10.2022 13:14	15.10.2022 12:49
Created 0×30	06.03.2023 14:01	
Last Modified 0×10	11.11.2022 14:15	15.10.2022 12:49
Last Modified 0×30	06.03.2023 14:01	

Table 7. Timestamps from MFT (Part 2).

Attribute	1	2
Created 0×10	10.10.2022 13:14	15.10.2022 12:49
Created 0×30	06.03.2023 14:01	
Last Modified 0×10	11.11.2022 14:15	15.10.2022 12:49
Last Modified 0×30	06.03.2023 14:01	

Suppose file manipulation is still visible in the journal. In that case, it is not possible to determine what changes have been made, as all timestamp modifications are recorded with the same description (see Table 8). Therefore, it is also impossible to confirm timestomping based on the journal.

Table 8. Journal record for MACB update.

Name	UpdateTimestamp	UpdateReasons
timestomping.docx	06.03.2023 14:16	BasicInfoChange
timestomping.docx	06.03.2023 14:16	BasicInfoChange|Close

Another potential indicator of timestomping is the use of link files. We tested the hypothesis that opening a file during timestomping updates the timestamps of the corresponding link files based on the tampered file time, but this proved to be false. The timestamps of the link files are instead set according to the system time at the moment the file is opened. As a result, we manually modified the link files, but after moving them, it was no longer possible to return them to their original folder. Therefore, only the first timestomping method can be applied to link files, which creates a mismatch between the Standard Information (SI) and File Name (FN) timestamps and is thus ineffective. However, link files can be permanently deleted, which may indicate suspicious activity on the system.

Timestomping can achieve a high impact on MACB located in the MFT. To some extent, link files (whether system or Office recent files) can also be affected, making them medium impact. Other artifacts were not affected. The same impact evaluation on individual artifacts is obtained from the impact matrix, where timestomping is categorized as almost undetectable.

Impact on Anomaly Detection. In the CSV file, we simulated timestomping by changing the date and time attributes for the NoJerry.txt file, specifically all its data except for the journal records, as these records cannot be timestomped in the system. We set the date and time before the attack, specifically January 18, 2023. Anomalies were searched for based on inodes in this data. The anomaly detection ignored these modified records by changing the time to before the attack.

The evaluation techniques (Table 9) show that using timestomping reduced all values when searching by name. However, when searching by inodes, recall improved, and thus, the resulting F1-score is slightly higher.

Table 10 compares values for the five best settings relative to the original data. The worst detection of anomalies based on names was for the data with applied timestomping, which had the worst results in all parameters. Even for inode-based detection, timestomping significantly decreased precision, recall, and F1 score.

Timestomping can therefore significantly impact automated anomaly detection.

Table 9. Comparison of evaluation techniques (Timestomping).

Comparison	Precision	Recall	F1 Score
Original	0.2830	0.0220	0.0409
Timestomping	0.2657	0.0229	0.0421

Table 10. Average of the five best settings (timestomping).

Comparison	TP	FP	Precision	Recall	F1 Score
Original	12.0	10.2	0.5513	0.8000	0.6483
Timestomping	8.6	13.0	0.4141	0.6143	0.4902

5 Discussion and Conclusion

The resulting impacts of selected anti-forensic techniques on manual and automated forensic investigations are summarised and categorised according to the two proposed comparison approaches. The influence of each technique on specific artifacts during manual forensic analysis is presented in Table 11.

Table 11. Summary of the impact of selected Techniques.

Comparison Method	Anti-Forensic Technique	File Data	MACB	Logs
Impact Level	File Deletion	High	None	None
	ADS	High	None	None
	File Encryption	High	None	None
	Disk Encryption	High	High	High
	Log Deletion	None	None	High
	Timestomping	None	High	None
	Fake Evidence	Low	None	None
Impact Matrix	File Deletion	Medium	-	-
	ADS	Low	-	-
	File Encryption	Medium	-	-
	Disk Encryption	Medium	Medium	Medium
	Log Deletion	-	-	Medium
	Timestomping	-	High	-
	Fake Evidence	Low	-	-

Among all the tested techniques, disk encryption was the most significant, as it has a high to medium impact on all artifacts stored on the disk. The second most significant technique is timestomping, as it has a high impact, according to both evaluations. File encryption and file deletion have the same impact on file data and are ranked third. Following this is log deletion with a high or medium impact and hiding in ADS with a high or low impact. The least significant technique was creating fake evidence, which had a low impact.

It should be noted that these results are only indicative and may vary depending on specific circumstances. Some parameters for determining impact may be more important than others, so it may be worth considering alternative comparison methods that reflect the importance of specific assets for a given organization. The impact determination may also depend on whether the emphasis must be placed on the integrity, confidentiality, or availability of the given artifact, which stems from the organization's focus.

Table 12 summarises the resulting F1 scores for the average values of the five best parameter settings for ECOD (based on the unmodified dataset).

Table 12. Comparison of F1 Score for selected techniques.

Comparison	TP	FP	F1 Score
Fake File txt	7.2	13.2	0.4126
Fake File exe	8.4	12.8	0.4672
Timestomping	8.6	13.0	0.4902
Original	12.0	10.2	0.6483
EVTX Log Deletion	12.0	10.2	0.6483
Deleted File and Link	12.0	10.2	0.6483
Deleted File	11.6	10.2	0.6521

The creation of fake evidence, primarily text, and executable files has a significant impact on automated anomaly detection. These files were created during the attack and appear to be potentially malicious. They can blur the line between what is identified as an anomaly and what is not.

The technique of timestamp modification, known as timestomping, also showed a significant impact. On the other hand, log or file deletion did not cause significant changes, and these are negligible anti-forensic techniques in automated anomaly detection.

The creation of misleading files cannot be prevented in the system or easily detected. Therefore, it is desirable to investigate further the behavior of such fake files (i.e., whether they were opened, executed, or triggered by other processes) and propose a method for detecting them to filter them out during data preprocessing.

In the context of discussing anti-forensic techniques, it is also appropriate to mention possible approaches to their mitigation. For most anti-forensic techniques (such as file deletion, Alternate Data Streams (ADS), file encryption, disk encryption, log deletion, and creation of fake evidence), standard countermeasures can be applied. One deviation from standard practice could involve sending selected forensic artifacts to a remote server. Comparing current data with backed-up data should reveal specific changes, enabling the identification of the applied anti-forensic technique and the potential for data restoration or adjustment.

Another example is timestomping, which significantly affects data-driven analyses that rely on timestamps as attributes or aggregate data based on these timestamps. A possible solution is to disregard highly inaccurate timestamps. The timestamp should ideally fall within the range between the installation of the operating system and the acquisition of the digital image. The drawback of this approach is the potential loss of relevant information. Another possible solution for certain forensic artifacts is to compare the Standard Information and File Name entries in the Master File Table (MFT) or to compare timestamps with those of the corresponding link files. This preprocessing step can help identify incorrect timestamps and facilitate their correction.

Subsequent experimentation with various anomaly detection methods is recommended to assess their comparative efficacy and reliability. We anticipate that the results of employing different types of anomaly detection methods, such as proximity-based (e.g., Local Outlier Factor, LOF), outlier ensembles (e.g., Isolation Forest), or linear models (e.g., Principal Component Analysis), in place of the probabilistic approach utilized by ECOD, may vary.

From the perspective of further research, it is appropriate to consider the use of an expanded spectrum of datasets. In our contribution [19], we present several additional datasets that could serve as suitable environments for testing anti-forensic techniques. However, it is necessary to take into account that individual datasets differ in size, structure, and types of forensic artifacts contained, which can fundamentally affect the course and results of the analysis. Therefore, it is necessary to carefully evaluate which anti-forensic techniques are suitable and meaningful for a particular dataset.

It is also necessary to consider the limitations when testing the impact of automation. One such limitation is using a dataset consisting only of data obtained from the file system, over which not all techniques can be tested. Additionally, other methods for anomaly detection could be used in testing, which might yield different results.

Describing the impacts of anti-forensic techniques on forensic investigations could benefit both manual forensic analysis and its automation. Given the rise in anti-forensic techniques, it will also be necessary to include the identification and mitigation of anti-forensic techniques in procedures and processes, with attention to the impact of individual techniques, as it is not feasible to address all techniques.

This work described our testing of selected anti-forensic techniques (since not all tools and documented procedures may be functional or practical) and discussed the affected artifacts. We also explored the impact of these techniques on automation by applying anti-forensic techniques to already secured and preprocessed data, which can be used for automated anomaly detection (records in data that may be of interest from a forensic analysis perspective).

Acknowledgments. This research was funded by the EU NextGeberationEU through Recovery and Resilience Plan for Slovakia under project No. 09-I05-03-V02-00079 (Automatization of digital forensics and incident response - ADFIR).

Disclosure of Interests. The authors have no competing interests to declare that are relevant to the content of this paper.

References

1. Abdullahi, Z.H., Singh, S.K., Hasan, M.: The impact of anti-forensic techniques on forensic investigation challenges. In: Computer Science Engineering and Emerging Technologies, pp. 697–701. CRC Press (2024)
2. Adamu, B.Z., Karabatak, M., Ertam, F.: A conceptual framework for database anti-forensics impact mitigation. In: 8th International Symposium on Digital Forensics and Security (ISDFS 2020), pp. 1–6. IEEE (2020). https://doi.org/10.1109/ISDFS49300.2020.9116375
3. Alazab, M., Venkatraman, S., Watters, P.: Effective digital forensic analysis of the NTFS disk image. Ubiq. Comput. Commun. J. **4**(1), 551–558 (2009)
4. Breitinger, F., Hilgert, J.N., Hargreaves, C., Sheppard, J., Overdorf, R., Scanlon, M.: DFRWS EU 10-year review and future directions in digital forensic research. Forensic Sci. Int. Digit. Investig. **48**, 301685 (2024)
5. Breitinger, F., Studiawan, H., Hargreaves, C.: SOK: timeline based event reconstruction for digital forensics: terminology, methodology, and current challenges. arXiv preprint (2025)
6. Carrier, B.: File System Forensic Analysis. Addison-Wesley Professional (2005)
7. Cho, G.S.: Data hiding in NTFS timestamps for anti-forensics. Int. J. Internet Broadcasting Commun. **8**(3), 31–40 (2016)
8. Choi, J., Park, J., Lee, S.: Forensic exploration on windows file history. Forensic Sci. Int. Digit. Investig. **36** (2021). https://doi.org/10.1016/j.fsidi.2021.301134
9. Conlan, K., Baggili, I., Breitinger, F.: Anti-forensics: furthering digital forensic science through a new extended, granular taxonomy. Digit. Investig. **18**, S66–S75 (2016)
10. Du, X., Le, Q., Scanlon, M.: Automated artefact relevancy determination from artefact metadata and associated timeline events. In: 2020 International Conference on Cyber Security and Protection of Digital Services (Cyber Security), pp. 1–8. IEEE (2020). https://doi.org/10.1109/CyberSecurity49315.2020.9138874
11. González Arias, R., Bermejo Higuera, J., Rainer Granados, J.J., Bermejo Higuera, J.R., Sicilia Montalvo, J.A.: Systematic review: anti-forensic computer techniques. Appl. Sci. **14**(12), 5302 (2024)
12. Hermon, R., Singh, U., Singh, B.: Forensic techniques to detect hidden data in alternate data streams in NTFS. In: 2022 IEEE Bombay Section Signature Conference (IBSSC), pp. 1–6 (2022)
13. Javed, A.R., Ahmed, W., Alazab, M., Jalil, Z., Kifayat, K., Gadekallu, T.R.: A comprehensive survey on computer forensics: state-of-the-art, tools, techniques, challenges, and future directions. IEEE Access **10**, 11065–11089 (2022)
14. Joo, D., Lee, J., Jeong, D.: A reference database of windows artifacts for file-wiping tool execution analysis. J. Forensic Sci. **68**(3), 856–870 (2023)
15. Kanstrén, T.: A look at precision, recall, and f1-score (2020). https://towardsdatascience.com/a-look-at-precision-recall-and-f1-score-36b5fd0dd3ec

16. Liu, V., Brown, F.: Bleeding-edge anti-forensics. In: Infosec World Conference & Expo, MIS Training Institute (2006)
17. Majed, H., Noura, H.N., Chehab, A.: Overview of digital forensics and anti-forensics. In: 8th International Symposium on Digital Forensics and Security (ISDFS 2020), pp. 1–6. IEEE (2020). https://doi.org/10.1109/ISDFS49300.2020.9116367
18. Markova, E., Sokol, P., Kovacova, K.: Detection of relevant digital evidence in the forensic timelines. In: 2022 14th International Conference on Electronics, Computers and Artificial Intelligence (ECAI) (2022). https://doi.org/10.1109/ECAI54874.2022.9847438
19. Marková, E., Sokol, P., Krišáková, S.P., Kováčová, K.: Dataset of windows operating system forensics artefacts. Data Brief **55**, 110693 (2024)
20. Mothi, D., Janicke, H., Wagner, I.: A novel principle to validate digital forensic models. Forensic Sci. Int. Digit. Investig. **33**, 200904 (2020)
21. Oh, J., Lee, S., Hwang, H.: Forensic detection of timestamp manipulation for digital forensic investigation. IEEE Access **12** (2024)
22. Pajek, P., Pimenidis, E.: Computer anti-forensics methods and their impact on computer forensic investigation. In: Communications in Computer and Information Science, vol. 45, pp. 145–155 (2009). https://doi.org/10.1007/978-3-642-04062-7_16
23. Palmbach, D., Breitinger, F.: Artifacts for detecting timestamp manipulation in NTFS on windows and their reliability. Forensic Sci. Int. Digit. Investig. **32**, 300920 (2020)
24. Reedy, P.: Interpol review of digital evidence for 2019–2022. Forensic Sci. Int. Synergy **6**, 100313 (2023)
25. Schmitt, L., Kul, G.: Anti forensic measures and their impact on forensic investigations. In: Adversarial Multimedia Forensics, pp. 237–261. Springer Nature Switzerland (2023)
26. Schmitt, L., Kul, G.: Anti forensic measures and their impact on forensic investigations check for updates. Adversarial Multimedia Forensics **104**, 237 (2024)
27. Shahzad, F., Javed, A.R., Jalil, Z., Iqbal, F.: Cyber forensics with machine learning. In: Phung, D., Webb, G.I., Sammut, C. (eds.) Encyclopedia of Machine Learning and Data Science, pp. 1–6. Springer US, New York, NY (2020). https://doi.org/10.1007/978-1-4899-7502-7_987-1
28. Song, J.H., Lee, H.S.: A design of timestamp manipulation detection method using storage performance in NTFs. J. Internet Things Converg. **9**(6), 23–28 (2023)
29. Stamm, M.C., Zhao, X.: Anti-forensic attacks using generative adversarial networks. In: Multimedia Forensics, pp. 109–134. Springer (2022). https://doi.org/10.1007/978-981-16-6890-4_6
30. Studiawan, H., Sohel, F.: Anomaly detection in a forensic timeline with deep autoencoders. J. Info. Secur. Appl. **63**, 103002 (2021). https://doi.org/10.1016/j.jisa.2021.103002
31. Vanini, C., Gruber, J., Hargreaves, C., Benenson, Z., Freiling, F., Breitinger, F.: Understanding strategies and challenges of timestamp tampering for improved digital forensic event reconstruction. In: Proceedings of the Digital Forensics Doctoral Symposium, pp. 1–8 (2025)
32. Vanini, C., Hargreaves, C., Breitinger, F.: Evaluating tamper resistance of digital forensic artifacts during event reconstruction. arXiv preprint (2024)

Proceedings of the Fourteenth International Workshop on Cyber Crime (IWCC 2025)

IWCC 2025 Preface

The societies of today's world are becoming increasingly dependent on online services, where commercial activities, business transactions, government services, and biomedical diagnostics are realized. This tendency has been evident during the recent COVID-19 pandemic. These developments, along with the growing number of military conflicts worldwide (Ukraine, Israel, etc.), have led to the fast development of new cyber threats and numerous information security issues exploited by cybercriminals. The inability to provide trusted, secure services in contemporary computer network technologies has a tremendous socio-economic impact on global enterprises and individuals.

Moreover, the frequently occurring international frauds impose the necessity to conduct investigations spanning multiple domains and countries. Such examination is often subject to different jurisdictions and legal systems. A good illustration of the above is the Internet, which has made it easier to prepare and perpetrate traditional – but now cyber-enabled – crimes. It has acted as an alternate avenue for criminals to conduct their activities and launch attacks with relative anonymity, a high degree of deniability, and the opportunity to operate in a border-agnostic environment. Worrying developments in the abuse of artificial intelligence and machine learning technologies lead to the increased capabilities of malign actors who leverage these tools to design and propagate disinformation, which is especially dangerous (and effective) during emergencies and crises of all kinds. The developments in Generative Artificial Intelligence have also enabled the increase of criminal capabilities in the production, dissemination, and weaponization of high-quality, convincing fake content (text, audio, images, and videos), which translates not only to the truth and trust decay among the affected societies but also to the enhanced capabilities in orchestrating the sophisticated cyber crimes.

Furthermore, nowadays, the majority of life-science-based techniques and resulting data hinge on information technologies. Despite their considerable advantages, dependence on cyber technologies also exposes vulnerabilities. Various threats in the digital realm could target biomedical systems, leading to adverse consequences. The field of CyberBioSecurity was established to assist bio-related sciences in comprehending potential cyber threats and formulating defense approaches, recovery protocols, and resilience strategies.

The increased complexity of communications and the networking infrastructure is making the investigation of these new types of crimes difficult. Traces of illegal digital activities are difficult to analyze due to large volumes of data. Nowadays, the digital crime scene functions like any other network, with dedicated administrators functioning as the first responders. This poses new challenges for law enforcement and intelligence communities and forces computer societies to utilize digital forensics to combat the increasing number of cyber crimes. Forensic professionals must be fully prepared to provide court-admissible evidence. Forensic techniques should keep pace with new technologies to make these goals achievable. Prevention, mitigation, and interdiction of new and emerging threats necessitate an increasingly thorough and multidisciplinary approach. They also require the collaboration of all relevant actors and stakeholders in designing the technology regulation and cyber governance measures.

This year, our 14th International Workshop on Cyber Crime (IWCC 2025) received ten submissions, out of which we selected the five best ones. They cover various topics, starting from deep fake images: their generation and collection (papers: "Generating Deepfakes with Stable Diffusion, ControlNet and LoRA" and "Towards Creating a Darknet Image Database"), through protecting anonymity ("Hello, won't you tell me your name?: Investigating Anonymity Abuse in IPFS") and a paper on the analysis of malicious financial transactions ("Countering Financial Cyber Crime: New Method for Subsequent Steps Analysis in Large Complex Graphs of Financial Transactions"), ending with a review of darknet marketplaces ("From Sign-Up to Multi-Million Revenues: A Deep Dive into Vendors on Darknet Marketplaces"). The reviewing process was double-blind; each of the submissions was assessed by at least three experts. We would like to thank all the authors who contributed to our workshop and all the reviewers who helped with the selection process.

August 2025

Artur Janicki
Kacper Gradoń
Katarzyna Kamińska

IWCC 2025 Organization

Workshop Chairs

Artur Janicki — Warsaw University of Technology, Poland
Kacper Gradoń — Warsaw University of Technology, Poland
Katarzyna Kamińska — Warsaw University of Technology, Poland

Program Committee

Yulliwas Ameur — CNAM, France
Jędrzej Bieniasz — Warsaw University of Technology, Poland
Luca Caviglione — CNR - IMATI, Italy
Eric Chan-Tin — Loyola University Chicago, USA
Michał Choraś — Bydgoszcz University of Science and Technology, Poland
Jana Dittmann — Otto-von-Guericke-Universität Magdeburg, Germany
Stefan Katzenbeisser — University of Passau, Germany
Christian Kraetzer — Otto-von-Guericke-Universität Magdeburg, Germany
Roberto Magán-Carrión — University of Granada, Spain
Gerard Memmi — Telecom Paris, France
Mariusz Sepczuk — Warsaw University of Technology, Poland
Ewa Syta — Yale University, USA
Stefan Wendzel — University of Ulm, Germany

Generating Deepfakes with Stable Diffusion, ControlNet, and LoRA

Stefano Bistarelli[1], Francesco Santini[1(✉)], and Edoardo Toma Tavassi[2]

[1] Department of Mathematics and Computer Science, University of Perugia, Perugia, Italy
{stefano.bistarelli,francesco.santini}@unipg.it
[2] Perugia, Italy
edoardotavassi232@gmail.com

Abstract. We propose a different approach to generate deepfake videos based on *Stable Diffusion*, *ControlNet*, and *Low-Rank Adaptation* (*LoRA*). Stable Diffusion offers us greater control and fine-tuning options in the generation process. Compared to GANs, the proposed technique enables quick and easy modification of the obtained video by using a text prompt, adding or removing details, and altering the style and context of the deepfake. We describe the approach used and the generation pipeline, and then we show the application interface developed for the generation. Finally, we compare the quality of our deepfake generation framework with two other related approaches using two different tools that detect video/image manipulations.

Keywords: Deepfake · Stable Diffusion · Detection

1 Introduction

Deepfakes have become a popular subject of discussion in recent years. Creating convincing and high-quality deepfakes has proven challenging and requires advanced techniques and algorithms [15]. The term "deepfake" has been applied more broadly to any AI-generated video that impersonates a human. A general classification considers four types of deepfake according to media types [18], as "video with audio", "video without audio", "audio", and "image". In this work, we focus on "video without audio", as we focus only on video generation.

In this paper, we focus on face swapping using a novel approach to deepfake generation, combining *Stable Diffusion*, *ControlNet*, and *Low-Rank Adaptation* (LoRA). Stable Diffusion is a deep learning, text-to-image model released in 2022, based on diffusion methods. Although it can be used for various tasks, including the creation of image-to-image translations directed by text prompts, its primary application is to generate detailed images conditioned on text descriptions. Stable Diffusion is a *Latent Diffusion* model [19], and its code and model

---

E. T. Tavassi—Independent Researcher.

weights were made freely available to the public. ControlNet [24] is a neural network structure to control pre-trained large diffusion models to support additional input conditions. Finally, LoRA [8] is a technique that optimizes the fine-tuning of large-scale models by freezing the pre-trained model weights while significantly reducing the number of trainable parameters for downstream tasks.

In doing so, we propose a different approach to generate deepfakes, while the literature widely uses *Generative Artificial Neural Network (GAN)* [25] (Sect. 3).

The use of Stable Diffusion enables the rapid design and prototyping of deepfakes for several reasons. First, it allows users to provide a textual description of the deepfake to be generated, making it possible to modify it quickly and accurately. Moreover, due to its characteristics, it is also possible to easily change the style of the image (e.g., from summer to winter, or from realistic to cartoonish) or to add different details to the deepfake (e.g., some objects in the background). Indeed, Stable Diffusion models tend to be, in general, more computationally demanding than GANs due to their iterative nature, particularly when handling larger and more complex datasets. However, the training process is usually more stable than GANs, which can suffer from the *mode collapse* problem (characterized by focusing on only a few variations of the input distribution during training) [11], and it is more fine-grained.

In Sect. 2, we review the most important generative models used in the related work and our approach, for example, GANs and Stable Diffusion. Section 3 summarizes the related work by also providing technical details on how deepfakes are commonly generated in the literature. In Sect. 4, we show and describe the pipeline assembled to create a standalone application to generate deepfakes. Section 5 compares the deepfake quality of our approach with two related models (e.g., SAEHD and Quick96) by detecting video manipulations using the works in [2, 6]. Finally, Sect. 6 provides conclusions and possible future work.

2 Background

Stable Diffusion. Stable Diffusion [19] changes the architecture of the diffusion model making it *Latent Diffusion Model.* Training and sampling are performed in the *latent space*, a lower-dimensional representation of images, which gives the model a performance boost. Stable Diffusion also accepts textual prompts as a conditioning input, making it a *text-guided diffusion model.*

The Architecture. Figure 1 shows the architecture of the Stable Diffusion model. The first element is a VAE that transforms the pixel space of the input tensor into a latent space that is perceptually equivalent to the data space. The *universal autoencoding stage* is trained before the DM, making it reusable across multiple DM training sessions. A *Transformer language model* τ_θ is used as the language understanding component that takes the text prompt and produces *token embeddings.* τ_θ outputs 77 token embedding vectors, each in 768 dimensions. The text representation is concatenated to the input tensor for diffusion. At the same time, all the generated tokens are mapped into the U-Net via the *multi-head Attention* (Q, K, V) layers. The model still uses multiple *skip connections* and time step embeddings, as in the pure Diffusion model.

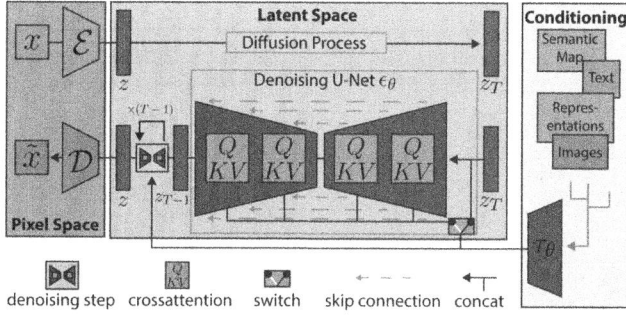

Fig. 1. The LDM architecture with the conditioning mechanism.

The *Transformer language model* used as the language understanding component within the LDM is *ClipText*, based on the OpenAI CLIP model.[1] CLIP stands for *Contrastive Language-Image Pretraining* and is an open-source, multimodal, zero-shot model. Given an image and text description, the model can predict the most relevant text description for that image without optimizing for a particular task. CLIP is trained on a 400 million image-text pairs dataset.

First, each image and caption is encoded with an image and a text encoder. Then, using *cosine similarity*, the two embeddings are compared to each other, yielding a score that is initially low. The two models are updated until the resulting embeddings are similar. After repeating these steps across the dataset with large batch sizes, the two encoders can produce similar embeddings for the correct image-text pairs.

Classifier-Free Guidance. During inference, instead of using a CLIP-guided diffusion method, Stable Diffusion uses *classifier-free guidance* [7] (*CFG*) that improves quality and decreases the sample diversity; this method also helps to emphasize prompt input during the diffusion process. The CFG scale controls how coherent the diffusion process is with the prompt. A lower CFG value will result in an image of higher quality, but less faithful to the original. In contrast, a higher value will result in a more coherent but distorted image.

Stable Diffusion can also generate an image from an initial image. This process, defined in multiple applications as *"img2img diffusion"*, is carried out by applying *forward diffusion* to the input image for a certain number of steps and then running the *backward diffusion* process on the noisy image until the model recovers a new one. A noise strength parameter from 0.0 to 1.0 corresponds to the percentage of each noise step added to the initial image. A higher parameter value causes the diffusion process to deviate more from the original image, resulting in an image with additional new details.

ControlNet. ControlNet [24] is a neural network architecture that can enhance pre-trained image diffusion models with task-specific conditions. The model

---

[1] OpenAI CLIP: https://openai.com/research/clip.

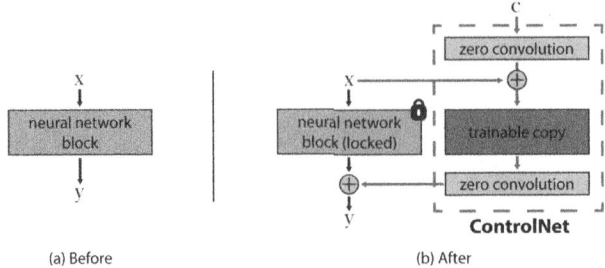

Fig. 2. Application of ControlNet to an arbitrary neural network block.

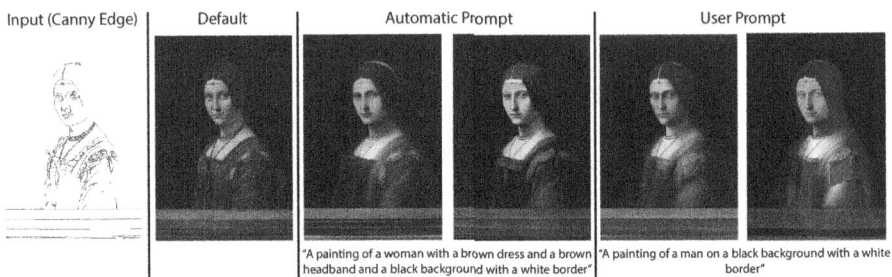

Fig. 3. Controlling Stable Diffusion with Canny edges.

manipulates the input conditions of the network blocks to control the overall behavior of an entire neural network.

Figure 2(a) shows an arbitrary *neural network block* $\mathcal{F}(\cdot;\Theta)$, with a set of parameters Θ, where, for example, a *feature map* $x \in \mathbb{R}^{h \times w \times c}$, with h, w, c being height, width, and channel numbers is transformed into another feature map y with $y = \mathcal{F}(x;\Theta)$. Figure 2(b) shows how a ControlNet is applied to a neural network block. All Θ parameters are locked and then cloned to a trainable copy Θ_c, which is trained with an external condition vector c. This copy is created to avoid overfitting when the training dataset is small and to preserve the quality of large models. The two blocks are then connected through a *zero convolution layer*, a 1×1 convolution layer with weight and bias initialized as zeros.

ControlNet controls each level of the Stable Diffusion U-Net in a computationally efficient way due to the locked weights of the diffusion model, so no gradient computation is needed on the original encoder for training. ControlNet generates a trainable copy of the 12 encoding blocks and the 1 middle block of Stable Diffusion. The 12 blocks are in 4 resolutions (64×64, 32×32, 16×16, 8×8) with each having 3 blocks. The outputs are added to the 12 skip connections and the 1 middle block of the U-net.

Figure 3 shows how *Canny Edge Conditioning* can control the diffusion process. This leads to the creation of novel images that retain the same underlying structure while exhibiting various styles and subjects. ControlNet enhances the preservation of critical structural features during diffusion, producing visually compelling and contextually rich variations that result in new images with the same structure but different styles and subjects.

LoRA (Low-Rank Adaptation). LoRA [8] is a method that was first developed to adapt *Large Language Models* (LLMs) to particular tasks or domains. "This method freezes the pre-trained model weights and injects *trainable rank decomposition matrices* into each layer of the Transformer architecture, greatly reducing the number of trainable parameters for downstream tasks" [8].

Some users started to use LoRA as an alternative to *Dreembooth* [20], and *textural inversion* [3] to fine-tune the Stable Diffusion model. LoRA has some advantages over the other two techniques, resulting in small model files (2–200 MBs), smaller than Dreembooth, while maintaining an optimal result during diffusion. A LoRA model must be used in conjunction with an SD model checkpoint file, such as for textual inversion. In this case, LoRA applies small changes to *cross-attention layers* by adding its weights to their weight matrices. LoRA achieves a smaller file size by breaking its weight matrix into two low-rank matrices.

2.1 MediaPipe

MediaPipe[2] is an open-source framework to build pipelines to perform computer vision inference on arbitrary sensory data, such as video or audio. This paper focuses on its solutions for *Face Detection* and *Face Mesh*.

Face Detection is a MediaPipe solution that detects human faces in an image or a video, with six landmarks and multi-face support. It is based on *BlazeFace* [1], a lightweight and well-performing face detector tailored for mobile GPU inference. In Fig. 4, we can see how the BlazeFace pipeline can detect a face, defined by the red bounding box, while the six green dots represent the detected landmarks. *Face Mesh* is a MediaPipe solution that estimates 468 3D face landmarks in an image or a video using machine learning to infer the 3D facial surface without the need for a dedicated depth sensor. This pipeline consists of two real-time deep neural networks that work in tandem. The first is a *detector* based on *BlazeFace* that computes face locations on the full image. The second is a *3D face landmark model* [9] that operates in those locations and predicts the approximate 3D surface by regression (see Fig. 4 for an example).

3 Related Work

Even if it has only emerged as a recent cybersecurity threat (since 2017), the high interest in video deepfake generation and detection is also evident in the large number of references in the scientific literature. For example, only some of the most recent detection surveys are [5, 18, 23].

Some pre-"Deep Learning boom" proposals for face-swapping, more strictly related to this paper, were generally based on three steps (e.g., [21]). These

---

[2] MediaPipe Web page: https://mediapipe.dev/.

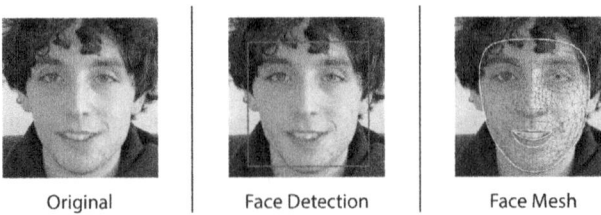

Fig. 4. Example of Face Detection and Face Mesh.

methods first identify faces in the source photos; then, they choose a candidate face image from the facial library that closely resembles the input facial positions and aspects. Second, the approach replaces the face's eyes, nose, and mouth, and further modifies the candidate face image's lighting and color to match the appearance of the input photographs. Finally, the method flawlessly combines the two faces. The third stage then computes the distance between the matches in the overlap region to classify the blended candidate replacement. In some cases, these methods can present significant drawbacks: *i)* the expressions of the input face image are lost when they first completely replace the input face with the target face, and *ii)* the artificial result is highly rigid. The substituted face appears unnatural: it must be in a similar position to produce effective results.

Due to their realistic outcomes, Deep Learning-based techniques have gained popularity for producing synthetic media. The first 2017 approach used a neural network to morph a victim's face into someone else's features while preserving the original expressions [15]. Successive approaches used two encoder-decoder pairs, such as the FakeApp and FaceSwap applications. Typically, a decoder is used to reconstruct a face after an encoder extracts the latent features of a face from an image. Two pairs of encoders and decoders, each trained on the source and target images separately, are needed to swap the faces between the source and target images. After training is complete, the decoders are switched, allowing the target picture to be recreated using the features of the source image with the original encoder of the source image and the decoder of the target image.

Most of the research focused on advances in face-swapping technology, either using a reconstructed *3D morphable model (3DMM)* [10], or a GAN-based model [16]. The work in [10] proposed a *Convolutional Neural Network (CNN)* to transfer the semantic content, such as facial posture, facial expression, and illumination conditions, of the input image, thereby creating the same style in a different image. They introduced a loss function composed of a weighted combination of style loss, content loss, light loss, and variation regularization.

FSGAN [16] allows face swapping and reenactment in real time. Pose, expression, and identity are manipulated simultaneously, achieving excellent and temporally cohesive outcomes. GAN-based methods outperform several current autoencoder-decoder techniques (e.g., FakeApp and FaceSwap) since they do not require explicit training on subject-specific images. They are also well-suited for face alteration jobs, such as creating lifelike images of artificial faces, due to

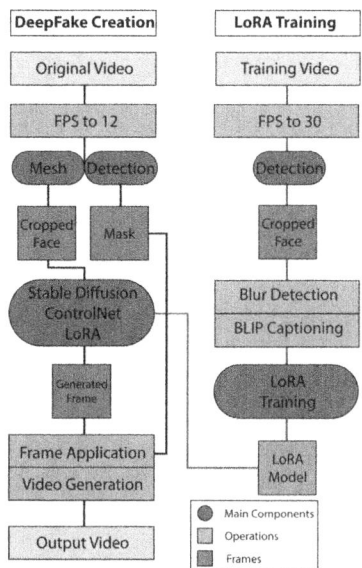

Fig. 5. Pipeline of the deepfake generation procedure.

their iterative nature. *FSNet* [13] provides a framework for face-swapping using a latent space, which allows the source identity's face area and the target identity's landmarks to be independently encoded and then combined to produce the swapped face. For both approaches in [13,14], it is difficult to maintain target characteristics such as target occlusion and lighting conditions. Face-swapping techniques can be complicated to manage when facial occlusions occur, as hair, spectacles, a hand, or another object partially obscures the source's or target's face.

4 Our Approach

In this section, we will explore how the technologies presented in the previous section can be used to create an application that generates deepfakes using Stable Diffusion. We developed our project code in Python; the repository is freely available online.[3] The created deepfake aims to replace the face of one author of this paper (an author of this paper, Edoardo Tavassi in Fig. 4) with the face of another author (another author of this paper, Francesco Santini in Fig. 8a).

In Fig. 5, we can see the entire pipeline used to create deepfakes from a video source. First, the input video is decreased to 12 frames per second. Then, for every frame, by using *MediaPipe*, we can extrapolate face locations and their structure. Next, the structure created with *Face Mesh* is processed to generate a

---

[3] The GitHub repository of our implementation: https://github.com/edoardotavassi/SCL_deepfake.

mask for the latter application of the diffused image, while the locations detected by *Face Detection* are used to extract just the face. After this, every cropped image is processed through *Stable Diffusion* with *ControlNet* and *LoRA*.

This LoRA model was previously trained on the target face in a process that will be further explained in Sect. 4.3. Finally, every diffused image gets applied to the corresponding input frame and then exported as a video.

4.1 Video Preprocessing

We need to optimally prepare a video to improve processing efficiency and ensure almost smooth video playback, and this process involves frame rate reduction We will focus on automating face cropping to maintain consistency during subsequent processing tasks and minimize computational requirements. Additionally, we will generate a face mask using a face landmark detection algorithm, followed by operations to smooth the mask's boundaries and ensure seamless integration with the processed frames.

Decreasing Frame Rate. The first step of the preprocessing pipeline is to decrease the frame rate to 12 FPS (see Fig. 5). This processing saves time later during the diffusion phase, as it allows for fewer frames to be processed. Twelve frames per second, also known as *animating on twos* [22], is the frame rate used in all major animation studios to ensure the minimum number of frames while maintaining fluidity in a video. The Python interface to *OpenCV*[4] was used to achieve this goal. First, a function called "*get-saving-frames-durations*" returns the list of durations at which to save the frames, achieved by creating a list of evenly spaced time-points from $t = 0$ to the end of the video (with a step size of $1/12$).

After this, the primary function extracts the earliest saving time from the list of durations. If this is less than or equal to the current frame duration, calculated by dividing the frame counter by the original frame rate (FPS), then the current frame is saved, and the frame counter is incremented. This iterative process stops when the list of durations is empty, resulting in the desired frame rate. In Fig. 6a, we can see an example of a frame from the input video. This frame will be used as the basis for the following examples.

Face Detection and Face Mesh. The next step is to crop only the face. This decision aims to maintain consistency throughout every frame during diffusion, as the added noise remains constant, resulting in a similar output for each frame (the seed is locked). Additionally, the decrease in image size also helps reduce the time required for diffusion. To achieve this result, in Fig. 5 we use *MediaPipe Face Detection* which, given an input frame, returns a *proto message* that contains a bounding box and *six key points* (right eye, left eye, nose tip, mouth center, right ear tragion, and left ear tragion). The bounding box is composed of $xmin$

---

[4] OpenCV website: https://opencv.org/.

(a) Example of an input frame.   (b) Cropped frame.

Fig. 6. Outputs from MediaPipe preprocessing.

and *width* by *ymin* and *height*, all normalized to $[0.0, 1.0]$. At the same time, each key point comprises x and y, which are also normalized to $[0.0, 1.0]$ by the width and height of the image, respectively.

Since the bounding box is located on the face, a padding of 30 pixels was added to ensure full face capture. Then, all the bounding box points get saved as a *PKL file* for later use. Figure 6b shows an example of a cropped frame. After cropping, all images are resized to 512×512 to ensure further coherence during diffusion. The next step is to compute the face mask. In Fig. 5, this is done through *MediaPipe Face Mesh* which, given an input frame, returns a list of 468 face landmarks where each landmark is composed of x, y, and z, all normalized to $[0.0, 1.0]$. Next, we must find the *convex hull* of all the returned landmarks to locate the face mask points, considering only the x and y coordinates. This was done with *Graham's scan algorithm* [4] that works in $O(n \log n)$ time. Consider an array of n points:

1. Find the point with the lowest y coordinate, breaking the tie by choosing the point with the lowest x coordinate. Let this point be P_0. Place P_0 at the first position in the output hull.
2. Consider the remaining $n-1$ points and sort them by polar angle in counter-clockwise order around P_0.
3. Check if two or more points have the same polar angle. If so, remove all except the one farthest from P_0. Let the size of the remaining set of points be m.
4. If $m \leq 2$, the algorithm terminates; the convex hull is not possible.
5. Create an empty stack S and push P_0, P_1, and P_2 to it.
6. Process the remaining $m-3$ points one at a time, starting from P_3. by doing:
   (a) Keep removing points from S while the orientation of the topmost point, next-to-top point, and current point is not counter-clockwise.
   (b) Push the current point to S.
7. The points in S are the output convex hull.

After finding the convex hull, we can draw a white polygon on a black background corresponding to the face mask, and an example can be seen in Fig. 7a. This image can be used to do *soft masking* of the diffused image by making all

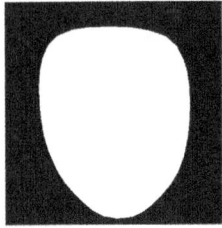  

(a) Mask without processing. (b) Output with mask in a. (c) Face mask.

Fig. 7. Mask and its application without processing.

pixels corresponding to a black pixel on the mask transparent. Applying this mask would result in a *detectable compositing* due to the straight borders, as shown in Fig. 7b. To solve this problem, we need to smooth all the borders of the mask. This was carried out through multiple steps of *erosion* and *Gaussian blur*, resulting in a mask with smooth borders that can be seen in Fig. 7c.

4.2 Stable Diffusion WebUI

A browser interface based on *Gradio library*[5] created by AUTOMATIC1111[6] was used to operate Stable Diffusion. This interface offers Stable Diffusion modules optimized for lower VRAM usage, down to 2 GB. The software creates a local server on port 7860 and, using the *Xformers library*[7] further speeds up the image generation process on an Nvidia RTX 3070 Ti with 8 GB of VRAM.

One of the most interesting features of this software is that it offers an extension module to implement ControlNet and LoRa models with just a single click. To call a LoRA model for diffusion, we need to write "$<lora : ModelName : \alpha>$" in the prompt, where ModelName is the name of the model file without the extension, and α is the weight applied to the LoRA model that goes from 0 to 1 (with 0 the model is disabled).

The JSON payload used for diffusion comprises several elements. First, we have an array of images to diffuse (in our case, just one image), where each image is encoded to Base64. Then, we have the conditioning parameters, *prompt* and *negative prompt*, which instruct Stable Diffusion on what to generate and what not to generate during the diffusion process. The steps represent the number of diffusion steps needed, while the width and height are the dimensions of the output image. The seed parameter is used for generating Gaussian noise and is typically set to a fixed value. The *CFG scale* is used for *Classifier-free guidance* during diffusion, and the denoising strength tells Stable Diffusion how much noise to put on the input image. The sampler index indicated which sampler to use;

---

[5] Gradio website: https://gradio.app/.
[6] Stable Diffusion WebUI Github: https://github.com/AUTOMATIC1111/stable-diffusion-webui.
[7] Xformers GitHub: https://github.com/facebookresearch/xformers.

(a) Sample from the training dataset. (b) Example of an output frame.

Fig. 8. Training sample and final output frame.

in our case, "Euler a", which is the one that yielded better results during testing. Ultimately, the *controlnet units* represent which pre-processing module and model to use with ControlNet. This payload is then sent to "*127.0.0.1:7860/controlnet/img2img*" for processing. The response comprises two images: the image generated with Stable Diffusion and the image resulting from the ControlNet Canny pre-processing of the input.

4.3 LoRA Training WebUI

To train a LoRA model (right side of Fig. 5), a *Windows-focused Gradio GUI*[8] for *Kohya's Stable Diffusion trainers*[9] was used. The GUI enables us to set the training parameters and execute the necessary CLI commands to train the model with only 7GB of VRAM. The first step is to prepare the dataset. For this purpose, a video of the target subject displaying multiple facial expressions in various lighting conditions is required. In our case, a 2-minute video of Francesco Santini was recorded on a mobile phone. The 60 FPS video was then reduced to 30 FPS to reduce the number of practically identical frames. Given that many images were not necessary to train the model, 30 FPS was arbitrarily chosen to achieve this reduction and optimize the training process. The face was extracted from all frames by using *MediaPipe Face Detection*. Having the model trained on a dataset of 512×512 images similar to the input images of the diffusion process helps us to achieve a more consistent result. Then, we need to remove all the blurred images from the dataset. To perform *blur detection*, we can use the *variance of the Laplacian* [17]. This method can be implemented with the help of OpenCV. First, we convolve a single channel of the input image with the *Laplacian kernel* with matrix rows $\{0, 1, 0\}$, $\{1, -4, 1\}$, $\{0, 1, 0\}$.

Furthermore, we take the response's variance (i.e., standard deviation squared) and compare it to a predefined threshold; if it falls below, the image is blurry; otherwise, it is not. The Laplacian operator is typically used to calculate the second derivative of an image, highlighting regions with rapid intensity changes. We can confirm that if the image contains a high variance, it will exhibit

---

[8] Kohya WebUI Github: https://github.com/bmaltais/kohya_ss.
[9] Kohya ss scripts Github: https://github.com/kohya-ss/sd-scripts.

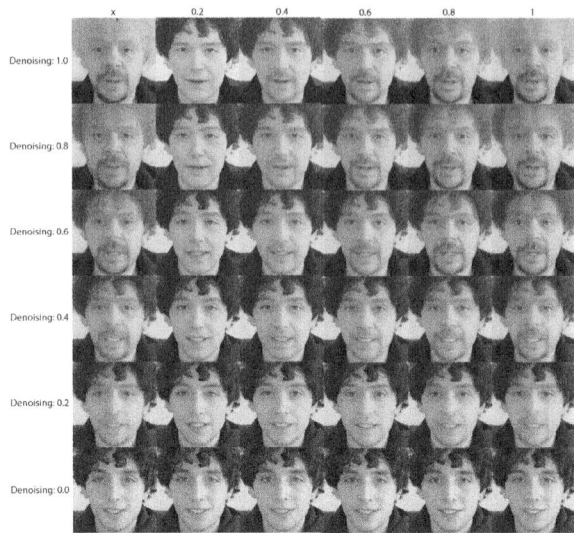

Fig. 9. Effects of Denoising and weight of a LoRA model on diffusion.

widespread responses, indicating an in-focus image. On the other hand, a low variance represents a small spread of answers, indicating few and small edges, a clear sign of blur. Now that we have eliminated all the blurry images, we must pair each frame with a textual description before training. As we do not want to perform this process manually, we utilize *Bootstrapping Language-Image Pre-training (BLIP)* captioning [12] to generate all the captions for us automatically.

We use Fig. 8a as an example: BLIP captioning generates the following caption, where we add the name of our target subject as an identifier at the start: "Francesco Santini, a bald man with a beard and a black shirt".

We are now ready to start the training process. First, all training parameters are set with a JSON file generated by the main application, so we need to press a button. The training step, for a small dataset of around a thousand images, takes about 4 h on a machine with an Nvidia RTX 3070 Ti with 8 GB of VRAM. The result is a 200 Mb *SafeTensors file* (our model) that needs to be added to the Stable Diffusion web UI and is now ready for diffusion.

4.4 Image Generation

As seen in Sect. 4.2, the image generation process is performed through a local server running Stable Diffusion. It takes about 15 s for each 512×512 image. The main software offers the possibility of testing different parameters on a single image and, when ready, applying them to all the images. These parameters define how the process will occur. First, we have the prompt to describe what face we want, or in the case of LoRA, which model to use. Then, a negative prompt

Fig. 10. How the CFG scale affects the image generation (towards Hollywood movie actor Leonardo DiCaprio).

(a) Correct canny.   (b) Incorrect Canny.

Fig. 11. Examples of Canny pre-processing.

describes what we do not want to see in the final image to further condition the diffusion.

For example, the negative prompt in our case was: "Distorted eyes, distorted mouth, distorted face, blue eyes, distorted teeth". The number of *diffusion steps* will result in a less detailed image with lower values and a more detailed image with higher values. It is essential to note that many steps can result in the model "hallucinating" too many details, distorting the final image. In Fig. 9, we can see how the *denoising strength* (on the left) and the α *parameter* (on top) of the LoRA model affect the diffusion. The denoising strength describes how closely the final image resembles the original, while α indicates the weight of the LoRA model. Through testing, a denoising strength of 0.4 and $\alpha = 1$ were found to be optimal for deepfake generation.

If we did not use a LoRA model and instead a pure Stable Diffusion model, it was crucial to consider the CFG scale. This parameter indicates how much the diffusion process will adhere to the prompt. For example, in Fig. 10, we can see how it affects the final image. Like the number of steps, a higher value will result in a distorted output. However, a lower value will not affect the original image, resulting in an output that is almost identical. Through testing, the optimal CFG scale value was around 7.

The last thing to consider is *ControlNet canny pre-processing*. The canny pre-processing is controlled through a low threshold and a high threshold. Unfortunately, when writing this paper, there is no way of managing these two through the API. In this case, our objective is to obtain an image similar to Fig. 11a, where essential parts, such as the mouth, nose shape, and eyes, are highlighted without including too many details. Furthermore, this image will produce an optimal and consistent generation through each frame, further helping to resolve

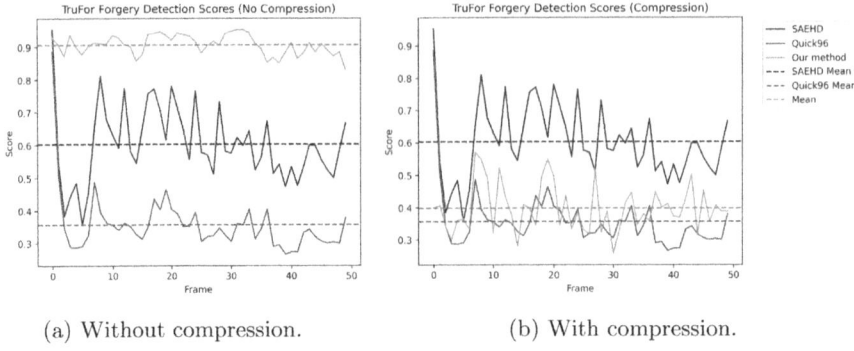

(a) Without compression. (b) With compression.

Fig. 12. TruFor detection scores with and without compression.

the non-deterministic behavior of Stable Diffusion. In contrast, an image similar to Fig. 11b will result in a distorted output due to many details.

The final step of this process is to apply the diffused images to the initial frames and then create the final video. To complete this process, the software cycles through all the diffused images and finds the corresponding initial frame and mask for each one. Then, to determine where to apply them, the software utilizes the *PKL file*, which contains all the original box sizes and locations. The image is resized to its original size and then pasted to its correct position on the initial frame with its mask. Figure 8b shows an example of a final frame. Finally, all the frames are combined into a single 12 FPS AVI file using OpenCV.[10]

5 Tests and Comparison

To evaluate the presented approach, we trained two deepfake models, *SAEHD* (*Self-Attention Encoder-Decoder with Hierarchical Discriminators*) and *Quick96*, both by *DeepFaceLab*[11], with the same dataset and target video. DeepFaceLab is a popular open-source software for creating deepfakes, maintained by a community of developers. Within DeepFaceLab, SAEHD and Quick96 are two models used for training deepfake videos. The Quick96 uses fewer resources (e.g., less VRAM) and requires fewer iterations to create a deepfake, albeit at the expense of picture quality. SAEHD generally produces higher-quality deepfakes due to its advanced architecture and customization options. We used two models to assess the deepfake quality: *TruFor* [6] and a deepfake detection model in [2].

5.1 Comparison Using TruFor

TruFor is a forensic framework designed to detect and localize image manipulations, ranging from traditional *cheapfakes* to advanced *deep learning-based*

---

[10] A video showing the initial frames, the result of Stable Diffusion, the application of the mask on the face, and the final result: https://www.youtube.com/shorts/OcuALrcSxfc.

[11] DeepFaceLab: https://github.com/iperov/DeepFaceLab.

alterations. The system utilizes a *transformer-based fusion architecture* that integrates high-level and low-level traces from the image. This fusion is achieved by combining the *RGB image* with a learned noise-sensitive fingerprint known as *Noiseprint++*. This fingerprint is trained to embed artifacts related to the camera's internal and external processing.

TruFor lies can detect anomalies by identifying deviations from the regular patterns found in pristine images. The model outputs a *pixel-level localization map*, a whole-image integrity score, and a reliability map that highlights areas prone to errors. This multi-faceted approach enables TruFor to detect local manipulations and robustly generalize across different image forgeries. The integrity score indicates the likelihood of an image being manipulated, with higher scores suggesting a higher probability of tampering.

Our initial test involved using the video produced directly from the current version of our deepfake generation system. As shown in Fig. 12a, our system performed poorly according to the TruFor forgery detection scores (in this and subsequent figures, 1 point indicates a higher probability of being a deepfake image). To address this, we applied a strong compression of around 70% to each frame, resulting in the graph shown in Fig. 12b.

The application of compression enhanced the system's ability to generate less detectable deepfakes. This improvement is likely due to the compression process smoothing out high-frequency noise and artifacts, which the detection model, TruFor, might have targeted. By maintaining essential image quality and eliminating extraneous details, the compressed frames made it more challenging to identify manipulations, thereby increasing the perceived authenticity of the deepfakes. The anomaly maps in Fig. 13 further illustrate this effect. Figure 13a shows the *TruFor anomaly map* without compression, where the model identifies significant inconsistencies in the manipulated regions, particularly around the face and head. In contrast, Fig. 13b presents the TruFor anomaly map with compression, where these inconsistencies are significantly reduced. The compression appears to have blurred the telltale signs of manipulation, making the deepfake seem more authentic and more challenging for the detection model. The analysis of these anomaly maps shows that compression effectively masks the artifacts introduced during deepfake generation. This masking effect explains why the TruFor model scored compressed deepfakes as more authentic.

5.2 Comparison Using the Approach in [2]

The approach proposed in [2] leverages an ensemble of *Convolutional Neural Networks (CNNs)*, specifically using *EfficientNetB4*, enhanced with *attention layers* and *siamese training strategies*.

The detection model operates by analyzing frames extracted from videos, targeting modern facial manipulation techniques such as deepfakes, *FaceSwap*[12], and *NeuralTextures*. The attention mechanism allows the model to focus on the most informative regions of the face, enhancing its ability to detect subtle

---

[12] FaceSwap: https://faceswap.dev.

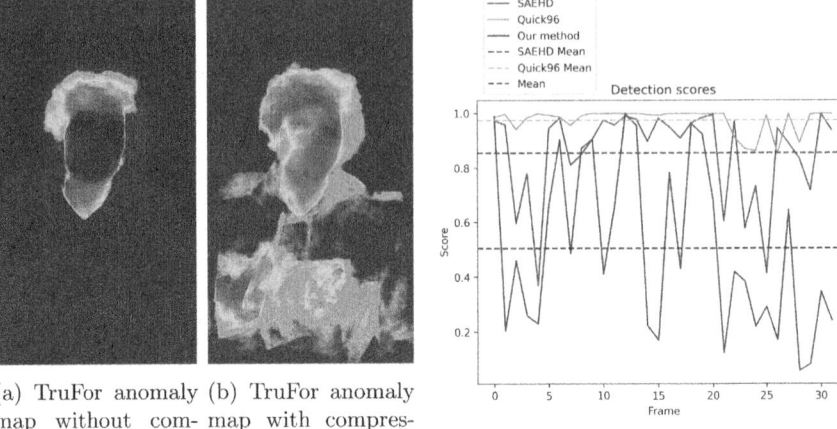

(a) TruFor anomaly map without compression. (b) TruFor anomaly map with compression. (c) The detection scores obtained with [2].

Fig. 13. An example of TruFor anomaly maps and detection scores with [2].

forgeries. The siamese training strategy also improves the model's ability to learn robust feature representations, further enhancing its detection precision.

The model provides a detection score for each analyzed frame, indicating the likelihood of manipulation. Higher detection scores suggest a higher probability of manipulation. Using these detection scores, we can rigorously assess the detectability of the deepfakes generated by our system. In Fig. 13c, we observe the detection scores generated by [2] for the three different deepfake generation methods. Overall, the results indicate that while that model effectively detects manipulations of *SAEHD* and *Quick96*, the approach described in this paper produces deepfakes that are less identifiable. The detection scores for *SAEHD* and *Quick96* are relatively high and stable, suggesting that the detection model more easily recognizes these methods.

In contrast, our method shows more variability in the detection scores, suggesting that our deepfakes can sometimes evade the detection mechanisms more effectively. This variability highlights the potential of our approach to generate deepfakes that are less detectable in certain frames, emphasizing the need for continuous advancements in detection models to address these challenges.

6 Conclusion

We propose a novel approach to creating deepfakes using Stable Diffusion, ControlNet, and LoRA. This approach enables quick and easy modification of the obtained video by using a text prompt, adding or removing details, and altering the style and context of the deepfake. With Stable Diffusion, it is also possible to have more control over the fine-tuning of the result and to avoid some training problems that may occur in GANs (e.g., the mode collapse problem [11]).

The use of Stable Diffusion easily allows for the inpainting of objects (e.g., glasses or hats) in deepfakes or the complete change of style. Furthermore, we have demonstrated how to fine-tune a Stable Diffusion model through LoRA, allowing us to generate new faces not present in the original datasets. This may be an advantage for GAN-based models, which rely more heavily on the training set in this specific case.

Since MediaPipe supports multi-face detection, future versions of this software could expand the possibilities to a multi-face deepfake solution. Given that this solution could be slow with the current pipeline, an option is to distribute the diffusion process on multiple machines. The current software does not replicate the original audio to the output video. To solve this problem, we could copy the original audio to the final video or implement an ML-based solution to generate the audio with the target subject's voice. Finally, the last improvement could be an ML-based frame interpolation strategy, which results in a 24 FPS or even a 60 FPS output video.

Acknowledgements. This work is partially supported by MUR PNRR project SERICS (PE00000014 AQuSDIT: CUP_H73C22000880001 and COVERT: CUP_J93C23-002310006), funded by Next Generation EU; University of Perugia - Fondo Ricerca di Ateneo (2020, 2022) - Projects FICO and RATIONALISTS.

References

1. Bazarevsky, V., Kartynnik, Y., Vakunov, A., Raveendran, K., Grundmann, M.: Blazeface: sub-millisecond neural face detection on mobile GPUs. CoRR abs/1907.05047 (2019)
2. Bonettini, N., Cannas, E.D., Mandelli, S., Bondi, L., Bestagini, P., Tubaro, S.: Video face manipulation detection through ensemble of CNNs (2020). https://arxiv.org/abs/2004.07676
3. Gal, R., et al.: An image is worth one word: Personalizing text-to-image generation using textual inversion. In: ICLR. OpenReview.net, Kigali, Rwanda (2023)
4. Graham, R.L.: An efficient algorithm for determining the convex hull of a finite planar set. Inf. Process. Lett. **1**(4), 132–133 (1972)
5. Güera, D., Delp, E.J.: Deepfake video detection using recurrent neural networks. In: International Conference on Advanced Video and Signal Based Surveillance, pp. 1–6. IEEE (2018)
6. Guillaro, F., Cozzolino, D., Sud, A., Dufour, N., Verdoliva, L.: Trufor: leveraging all-round clues for trustworthy image forgery detection and localization (2023). https://arxiv.org/abs/2212.10957
7. Ho, J., Salimans, T.: Classifier-free diffusion guidance. CoRR abs/2207.12598 (2022)
8. Hu, E.J., et al.: LoRA: low-rank adaptation of large language models. In: ICLR, OpenReview.net, Virtual event (2022)
9. Kartynnik, Y., Ablavatski, A., Grishchenko, I., Grundmann, M.: Real-time facial surface geometry from monocular video on mobile GPUs. CoRR abs/1907.06724 (2019)

10. Korshunova, I., Shi, W., Dambre, J., Theis, L.: Fast face-swap using convolutional neural networks. In: IEEE International Conference on Computer Vision, ICCV, pp. 3697–3705. IEEE Computer Society (2017)
11. Kushwaha, V., Nandi, G.: Study of prevention of mode collapse in generative adversarial network (GAN). In: 2020 IEEE 4th Conference on Information and Communication Technology (CICT), pp. 1–6. IEEE (2020)
12. Li, J., Li, D., Xiong, C., Hoi, S.C.H.: BLIP: bootstrapping language-image pre-training for unified vision-language understanding and generation. In: ICML. Proceedings of Machine Learning Research, vol. 162, pp. 12888–12900. PMLR (2022)
13. Natsume, R., Yatagawa, T., Morishima, S.: FSnet: an identity-aware generative model for image-based face swapping. In: ACCV (6). LNCS, vol. 11366, pp. 117–132. Springer, Cham (2018)
14. Natsume, R., Yatagawa, T., Morishima, S.: RSGAN: face swapping and editing using face and hair representation in latent spaces. In: SIGGRAPH Posters, pp. 69:1–69:2. ACM (2018)
15. Nguyen, T.T., et al.: Deep learning for deepfakes creation and detection: a survey. Comp. Vision Image Underst. **223** (2022)
16. Nirkin, Y., Keller, Y., Hassner, T.: FSGAN: subject agnostic face swapping and reenactment. In: ICCV, pp. 7183–7192. IEEE (2019)
17. Pech-Pacheco, J.L., Cristobal, G., Chamorro-Martinez, J., Fernandez-Valdivia, J.: Diatom autofocusing in brightfield microscopy: a comparative study. In: Proceedings of ICPR, vol. 3, pp. 314–317 (2000)
18. Rana, M.S., Nobi, M.N., Murali, B., Sung, A.H.: Deepfake detection: a systematic literature review. IEEE Access **10**, 25494–25513 (2022)
19. Rombach, R., Blattmann, A., Lorenz, D., Esser, P., Ommer, B.: High-resolution image synthesis with latent diffusion models. In: CVPR, pp. 10674–10685. IEEE (2022)
20. Ruiz, N., Li, Y., Jampani, V., Pritch, Y., Rubinstein, M., Aberman, K.: Dreambooth: fine tuning text-to-image diffusion models for subject-driven generation. In: CVPR, pp. 22500–22510. IEEE (2023)
21. Smith, B.M., Zhang, L.: Joint face alignment with non-parametric shape models. In: Fitzgibbon, A., Lazebnik, S., Perona, P., Sato, Y., Schmid, C. (eds.) ECCV 2012. LNCS, vol. 7574, pp. 43–56. Springer, Heidelberg (2012). https://doi.org/10.1007/978-3-642-33712-3_4
22. Teh, S., Perumal, V., Hamid, H.: Investigating how frame rates in different styles of animation affect the psychology of the audience. Int. J. Creative Multimedia **4**, 10–31 (2023)
23. Yu, P., Xia, Z., Fei, J., Lu, Y.: A survey on deepfake video detection. IET Biom. **10**(6), 607–624 (2021)
24. Zhang, L., Agrawala, M.: Adding conditional control to text-to-image diffusion models. CoRR abs/2302.05543 (2023)
25. Zhang, T.: Deepfake generation and detection, a survey. Multimedia Tools Appl. **81**(5), 6259–6276 (2022)

Towards Creating a Darknet Image Database

York Yannikos[(✉)], Marc Leon Agel, Julian Heeger, Lukas Graner, and Martin Steinebach

Fraunhofer Institute for Secure Information Technology (SIT), National Research Center for Applied Cybersecurity (ATHENE), Rheinstr. 75, 64295 Darmstadt, Germany
{york.yannikos,marc.agel,julian.heeger,lukas.graner, martin.steinebach}@sit.fraunhofer.de

Abstract. With the increasing popularity of the darknet, especially the Tor network, all kinds of multimedia data are shared anonymously, most of them being images. While several reverse image search engines are available for the clearnet, no suitable solutions exist for the darknet. Uncertainty about the image content that can be found on the darknet and the legal implications of collecting such images probably contribute to the fact that image databases typically do not include content from the darknet. However, a darknet image database could be helpful for researchers or law enforcement, e.g. to search for identical or similar images on the darknet and the clearnet in order to derive information about their creators.

In this paper we present a conceptual design, implementation details and first evaluations of a darknet image database, that indexes and securely stores images automatically scraped from the Tor network. We apply cryptographic and robust hashing, deduplication, and threshold encryption to implement a fast reverse image search while enforcing strict access controls for the collected image data. With integrated functionality from MAMPF, a self-developed distributed scraping framework, we provide promising results towards an efficient automated collection of images.

Keywords: Darknet crawling · Image database · Robust hashing · Reverse image search · Threshold encryption

1 Introduction

The darknet has become a critical domain for both cybercriminal activity and investigative research. While originally developed to ensure privacy and anonymity – especially for individuals living under repressive regimes – the darknet is now also exploited for illicit purposes including drug trafficking, cybercrime services, and the distribution of exploitative multimedia content. Its anonymous and decentralized nature presents challenges to law enforcement and require the development of specialized methods to monitor, analyze, and investigate activities within this domain.

Recent advances in open-source intelligence, web scraping, and machine learning have enabled researchers to extract relevant data from the darknet. Especially a systematic collection and analysis of multimedia data can provide valuable insights for further investigations. The large number of images shared on darknet forums or marketplaces may carry metadata that can be used to uncover critical information or the visual content may reveal geographic clues or environmental features.

In this paper, we present the conceptual design and a first evaluation of a darknet image database that securely stores images found on the darknet by the use of continuous and distributed web scraping. The aim of the database is to provide a service that can be queried to determine if specific images have previously been found on the darknet. This capability would be particularly valuable for law enforcement agencies, as it allows them to trace the distribution path of relevant content from hidden services on the darknet to more publicly accessible websites on the clearnet. By identifying instances where darknet images appear in open forums, social media, or publicly indexed websites, investigators can uncover leads about the individuals disseminating the content or participating in the underlying illegal activities.

2 Images on the Darknet

When we use the term *darknet* in this paper, we refer to the Tor network as it is the largest and most popular darknet. In Tor, a wide range of multimedia content is hosted via onion services. Common content types include images, audio files, documents, and video content. Such media appears on various platforms ranging from anonymous forums, whistleblowing and leak sites to illicit marketplaces. However, due to anonymity concerns, the delivery and reference of this content differ significantly from the clearnet. In the following, we describe in more detail how images are hosted in Tor.

2.1 Hosting

Images are usually hosted locally from the onion service itself. This design ensures user and server anonymity by avoiding connections to third-party infrastructure outside of Tor, especially clearnet-based content delivery networks (CDNs): When a user accesses a website with an image hosted on a clearnet domain, e.g. a conventional CDN, the browser initiates a direct request to that server to download the image, which may log IP addresses, timestamps, and requested resources. Even when the user accesses clearnet domains through Tor, such external requests can be used as tracking beacons or for traffic correlation attacks. Therefore, images hosted on onion services in Tor are typically referenced by their relative path in HTML documents. In some cases images are embedded base64-encoded directly within HTML documents. This enhances portability and offline usability but increases file sizes and website rendering times.

Even when images are hosted within the Tor network, the anonymity of the hoster can still be compromised if identical copies of these files are also accessible on the clearnet: In such cases law enforcement agencies can use standard investigation techniques to identify the person responsible for the clearnet upload and can then try find out whether it is the same person who uploaded the darknet content. Technical methods to measure image similarity, such as cryptographic and robust hashing, are typically used to identify identical or slightly modified images within both domains.

2.2 Content

The content of images hosted in Tor differs drastically, from harmless favicons and avatar images in forums, through product pictures of pharmaceuticals on darknet marketplaces, to images on platforms sharing child sexual abuse material (CSAM). Users visiting one website on the darknet may encounter illicit image content while they can safely visit another without encountering such material. This unpredictability can pose significant legal and psychological risks.

In order to collect, process and store images found on the darknet, suitable methods for filtering unwanted material are required. Especially the processing and storage of CSAM is illegal in many countries for entities that are not authorized law enforcement or designated child protection agencies. While methods for automatic image content classification exist, these are often error-prone with high false positive or negative rates. For example, methods for automatic classification of CSAM often struggle with edge cases where features overlap. Existing tools are also often based on convolutional neural networks (CNNs) or vision transformers (ViTs) that require training data. Such training data is mostly not sufficiently available.

3 Reverse Image Search

Reverse image search is a valuable tool for researchers, investigators, or journalists who collect images from various sources and want to trace the origin or association of images within a specific domain. While various reverse image search engines exist for the clearnet, we are not aware of any suitable search engine for images found on the darknet. With the development of our darknet image database that we describe in Sect. 5, we take a step into that direction.

3.1 Search Engines

Utilizing reverse image search is an important step in order to identify a person who published an image in a darknet forum. Several publicly available platforms exist that provide services for identifying similar images on the Internet. Examples of reverse image search platforms are Google Images[1], Bing Visual Search[2], TinEye[3], or Yandex Image Search[4]. Such platforms usually employ proprietary technology and require uploading an image or providing an image URL in order to search for similar images. Some provide specialized APIs but do not provide information or tools to allow searching for images without providing the actual image, e.g. by using robust hashes of images instead. Therefore, applying a reverse search for images with unclear origin or showing critical content can be very problematic, as described in Subsect. 2.2.

3.2 Robust Hashing

Robust hashing algorithms are designed to preserve similarity under nonsemantic transformations like compression or scaling. Therefore, they are widely applied in fields such as image retrieval, duplicate detection, and image authentication. Traditional robust hashing methods utilize perceptual features to achieve this, while modern approaches use deep learning to develop hash codes that remain invariant under transformations and maintain content integrity.

In our darknet image database we use three traditional robust hashing approaches that are commonly referenced in literature or used in digital forensics:

- **rHash** is a robust hashing algorithm introduced by Steinebach et al. in 2012 [16]. Based on block-based robust hashing, the hash is calculated by converting an image into grayscale, downscaling it to 16×16 pixels and then dividing it into four subsections, where each pixel value is compared to median of the subsection to set the hash bits.
- **PhotoDNA** is a robust hashing algorithm developed by Microsoft in collaboration with Hany Farid (then from Dartmouth College) in 2009 [12]. Here, the image is downscaled and divided into overlapping blocks on which edge detection is applied. The result is a list of bytes describing positive and negative edge strength in vertical and horizontal direction.
- The **ISCC Content-Code Image**[5] is a widely used part of ISCC codes[6]. It aims to preserve the similarity of image objects by converting the input image to a grayscale representation, downscaling it to a fixed 32×32 pixels resolution and applying a discrete cosine transform (DCT). Then the values from the top left of the DCT matrix are compared with their median values to set the hash bits.

---

[1] Google Images: https://images.google.com.
[2] Bing Visual Search: https://www.bing.com/visualsearch.
[3] TinEye: https://www.tineye.com.
[4] Yandex Image Search: https://yandex.com/images.
[5] The ISCC Content-Code Image: https://core.iscc.codes/units/content/code_content_image/.
[6] ISCC codes: https://iscc.codes/.

We focus on these traditional approaches because they are widely accepted, easy to implement, require less resources, and provide fully explainable results compared to deep learning approaches. Moreover, some deep learning approaches carry the risk that their hashes may be partially invertible.

4 Related Work

In this section, we will explore related work that is relevant to the topics discussed in the paper.

4.1 Tor Crawling

Crawling Tor websites poses distinct challenges for content extraction. Websites within the Tor network are not indexed by conventional search engines, which makes them harder to find. The network is also prone to unreliability, meaning websites cannot always be accessed.

De Pascale et al. [4] outline their architecture named CRATOR, which is designed for page content extraction and mitigating anti-bot measures such as CAPTCHAs. They assess their crawler's performance compared to the existing ACHE crawler[7] and demonstrate that CRATOR surpasses ACHE in terms of coverage, performance, and robustness.

David et al. [3] introduce a novel approach for identifying crawler traps by proposing a new distance metric that evaluates the similarity between two websites. Their dynamic classification model is generated in real-time for each website and determines whether the crawled site aims to trap the crawler.

Hartel et al. [8] present a new explainable near-duplicate detection algorithm for the dark web. In contrast to the state of the art, their algorithm provides an explanation why two websites are considered near-duplicates, using regular expressions applied to the output of the diff-match-path of the two websites.

4.2 Tor Search Engines

The current landscape of search engines for the Tor network shows several technical challenges inherent to the network's design and approaches for solutions.

Ahmia[8] is an example of a search engine for Tor's onion services. It operates as a clearnet-accessible platform that indexes onion sites, employing a crawler based on Scrapy, Elasticsearch, and a Django web interface. Ahmia's architecture incorporates a strict filtering policy to exclude illicit content like CSAM. The search engine tries to keep a balance between accessibility and compliance with legal regulations for online content.

Nurmi et al. [13] analyzed a list of all search queries from Ahmia from February 2018 to February 2023. They identified 176,683 onion domains, with one-fifth

---

[7] ACHE Focused Crawler: https://github.com/VIDA-NYU/ache/.
[8] Ahmia: https://ahmia.fi.

containing CSAM. In their analysis of 110,133,715 search sessions, they found that 11.1% of users were searching for CSAM.

Advancements in machine learning have also been utilized for classifying and identifying Tor onion services. For instance, the Frequency-Dominant Neighborhood Structure (F-DNS) method leverages perceptual hashing to categorize onion services based on visual content, achieving high accuracy rates [2]. This approach addresses the challenge of identifying and classifying the vast array of content hosted on the darknet, which often lacks standardized metadata.

4.3 CSAM

The article "Child Sexual Abuse Material on the Darknet" by Gannon et al. [6] explores the structural and behavioral dynamics of CSAM distribution within forums in the Tor network. The authors describe how these forums operate as tightly controlled online communities, where access and status are depend on active participation, including the sharing of illicit material.

The study by Koebe et al. [11] investigates the spatial distribution of CSAM consumption in France by analyzing mobile traffic data associated with the Tor network. Focusing on 1,341 communes across 20 metropolitan regions during March to May 2019, the researchers estimate that approximately 0.08% of Tor mobile download traffic in France is linked to CSAM, compared to a global estimate of 0.19%. These estimates are derived by correlating temporal patterns of general pornography consumption with Tor traffic, under the assumption that consumption behaviors exhibit similar temporal characteristics.

An IWF study [9] from 2023 describes a forum in the darknet where synthetic CSAM is discussed and shared.

Wang et al. [17] compiled keywords which allowed them to search darknet markets for CSAM and create a new text-based dataset for further analysis, based on the content of the websites. Over a 44-week observation period, they recorded 3,449 sales of CSAM, all of which occurred in Chinese markets, with no sales reported in English-speaking markets. The authors note that clearnet cloud-based data storage services (Baidu Web Drive, Microsoft OneDrive, etc.) were used for the distribution and sharing of CSAM.

Guerra et al. [7] suggest a method for the automatic detection of child sexual abuse images based on patterns observed in folder and file naming conventions used by websites. Their findings indicate that websites make little to no effort to conceal the nature of their content, as 61% of 82 examined websites displayed CSAM in their root folders. Only 16% showed minimal attempts to conceal the content by utilizing multiple sub-folders ($n > 4$), which likely served more as content organization. 20% of the websites hosted and displayed CSAM.

4.4 Reverse Image Search

Jones et al. [10] examined the reverse image search capabilities of major search engines, focusing on their effectiveness in discovering abstract images such as charts and diagrams. They found that Yandex outperformed all the other engines tested across various categories, while Google and Yandex showed comparable performance when the first page of results was evaluated. Both search engines achieve a higher detection rate with natural images compared to abstract images, with a difference of up to 54%.

5 Darknet Image Database

In the following we describe the conceptual design of the darknet image database (DIDB), an architecture to collect, process and store images from the darknet. The architecture is divided into two parts: one for data acquisition and processing of images on the darknet (i.e. the Tor network) and the other for secure data storage and access control.

Figure 1 provides an overview of the architecture. The individual parts of the DIDB are described in the following subsections.

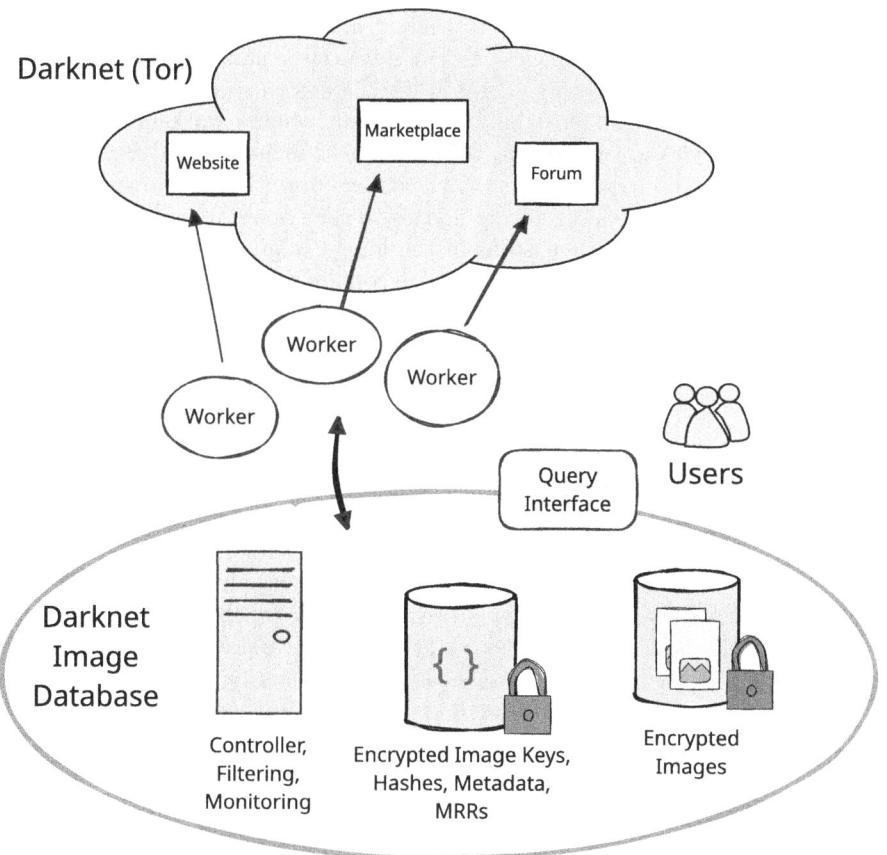

Fig. 1. Overview of the DIDB architecture.

5.1 Data Acquisition and Processing

The data acquisition and processing is done in a pipeline that consists of four phases:

1. Automated collection of images from various sources on the darknet
2. Filtering of content that should not be processed and stored
3. Calculation of common cryptographic and robust hashes for each image
4. Creation of a minimal robust representation of each image suitable for reverse image search

Image Collection. The collection of images is carried out through the recursive scraping of various darknet websites. The general process is as follows: A web request is made for a given onion service URL, the returned web content is parsed, and links to internal and external pages, i.e. contained in HTML anchor elements or image resources, are extracted. The images are then downloaded and securely stored as described in Subsect. 5.2. For the gathered hyperlinks, the process is then repeated to recursively crawl subpages and to extend the image collection to external pages. To facilitate this recursive image collection, we use our crawling framework MAMPF [18], a system consisting of a central component that controls a scalable number of distributed workers. The central component provides a task queue, which stores the image and website links and distributes them to the workers. The workers download the images, process new websites, and send the resulting images to the central component, which is responsible for the subsequent steps in the image acquisition pipeline outlined above. During this crawling step, we perform content deduplication and also filter out unwanted content that is not subject to our research. The applied content filters are outlined in the following subsection. Any image collection task has to be seeded with initial web pages to begin crawling from.

Content Filtering. When collecting images from the darknet, filtering out unwanted content is a critical processing step before storing images in a database. Often illicit content is interlinked with pornographic content, e.g. non-consensual, CSAM or other exploitative material. Therefore, we apply filters to all downloaded images to detect and remove pornographic images or images containing nudity from any further processing in our pipeline. Based on results published in [1] we are currently experimenting with the NudeNet[9] and LSPD [14] datasets and several models. We believe that by filtering out such content, we can avoid processing and storing the majority of critical images on the darknet.

Cryptographic and Robust Hashing. After images have been collected, cryptographic hashes are calculated, e.g. SHA-2/3 and BLAKE2/3 (and also

---

[9] NudeNet: https://academictorrents.com/details/1cda9427784a6b77809f657e772814dc766b69f5.

deprecated MD5 and SHA-1 hashes, because many tools still rely on those per default). Additionally, the robust hashes rHash, ISCC Content-Code Image and PhotoDNA are calculated for each image. All cryptographic and robust hashes are stored in the database to allow queries for identical or similar images.

Minimal Robust Representation. In Subsect. 2.2 we already raised concerns regarding reverse image searches of unknown image material found on the darknet. Unfortunately, we are currently not aware of any large image database that provides a suitable API to search for images using commonly used robust hashing approaches. In order to still be able to use reverse image search engines in the clearnet, we propose to create *minimal robust representations* (MRRs) of each image (one per search engine) that we store in our database.

We define an MRR as a version of the original image that is modified in such a way, that the information a human can derive from the image is reduced drastically, i.e. illicit and generally unwanted content is not recognizable as such anymore. This could be done e.g. through reducing color information, decreasing resolution, (repeatedly) applying filters, or presenting only relevant features. However, the representation must still provide a significant number of suitable matches when used as input for a reverse image search.

Because available reverse image search engines typically each use their own proprietary technology, an MRR of an image is always tied to a specific platform: For example, an MRR for Google Images would be different from one for TinEye or one for Yandex Image Search. Since it is quite difficult to find an

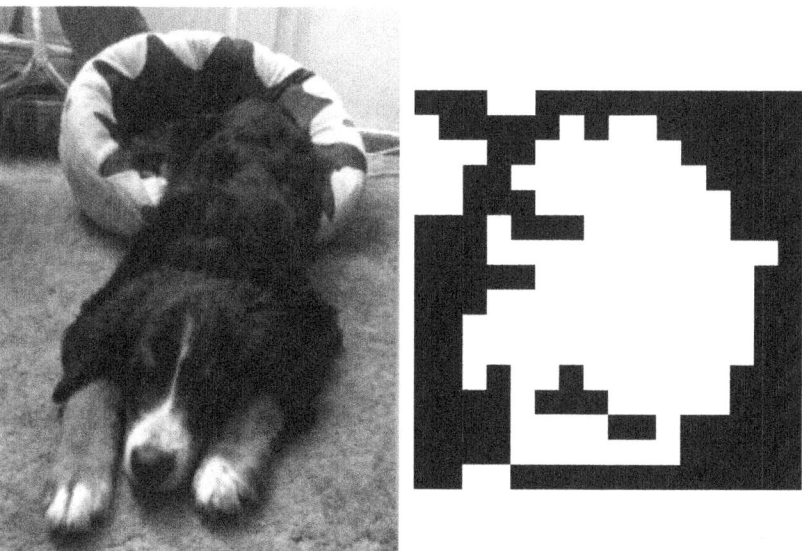

Fig. 2. Example of a possible MRR (right) of an image (left) for reverse image search engines that use the rHash robust hashing algorithm [19].

MRR for a reverse image search engine through only black-box testing, we are currently experimenting with different approaches. In contrast, when the used robust hashing algorithm of a search engine is publicly known, it is easy to provide a suitable MRR using that algorithm. Figure 2 shows an example of a possible MRR for search engines using the rHash robust hashing algorithm.

5.2 Secure Storage and Access Control

After collecting and processing images, we store them in our database. One core aspect of the DIDB is to secure any collected images against unprivileged access, even from a database administrator with maximum privileges. Since we can never be certain that 100% of unwanted image content will be filtered out, we enforce a strict access control using encryption and mandatory involvement of multiple parties.

The collected images are stored in the file system and referenced in the database. In the first step, we calculate the SHA-256 cryptographic hash of an image file content to deduplicate any already-known content: If we already downloaded a file with the same hash we do not store it a second time. We then encrypt the image file a using a symmetric cipher like AES, using a unique key per image file, as shown in Fig. 3. This ensures that access to any image file is not possible without possession of its corresponding image key. The encrypted image is then stored in the file system, using the calculated SHA-256 hash of its decrypted content as filename.

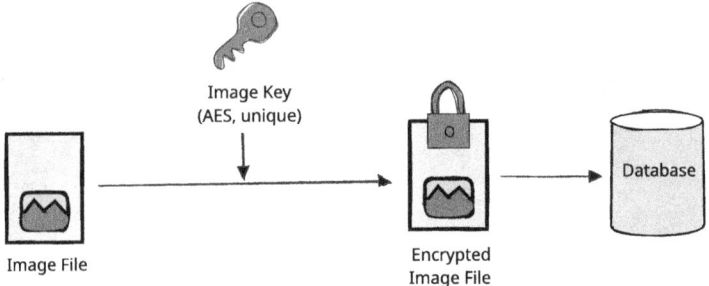

Fig. 3. Encryption of an image file using a unique, file-specific AES key.

In order to protect the images keys and to implement strong access control for the database, we propose using a secure threshold encryption scheme like Threshold ElGamal [5]. It applies Shamir's Secret Sharing [15] to ensure that n different participants hold shares of a secret s (private key) and $i \leq n$ participants are needed to perform any decryption tasks with it. The distribution of the secret shares is depicted in Fig. 4.

All image keys are individually encrypted using the global public key in the threshold encryption scheme, as shown in Fig. 5. The result is a tuple of

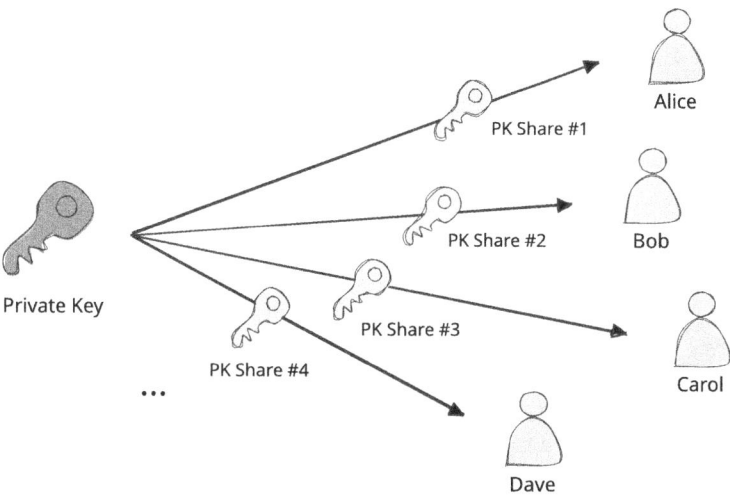

Fig. 4. Distribution of private key shares to $n = 4$ participants.

two components that is stored in the database together with the corresponding image metadata. For the decryption of an image, all participants have to perform a partial decryption on their own using their share of s. The image key can then be reconstructed by combining the decrypted parts, without revealing any information about s or its shares. Figure 6 shows the abstract decryption process of an image key (as an example with $i = 3$ of $n = 4$ participants required).

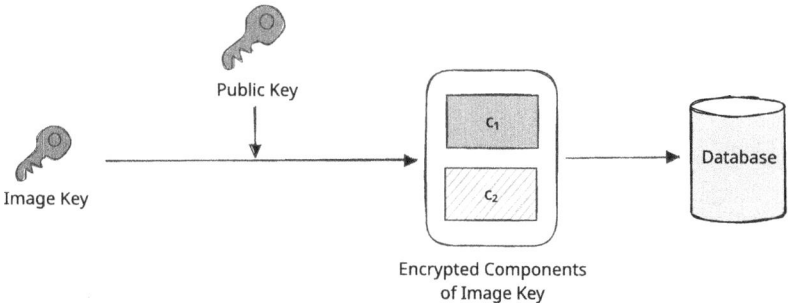

Fig. 5. Encryption of an image key using the global public key.

Using this encryption scheme enables scenarios where the involvement of law enforcement agents or prosecutors is mandatory when image data from the database should be decrypted. At the same time, a single participant cannot gain access to any decrypted image data without collaborating with $i - 1$ other participants holding shares of s. Even a database server administrator eaves-

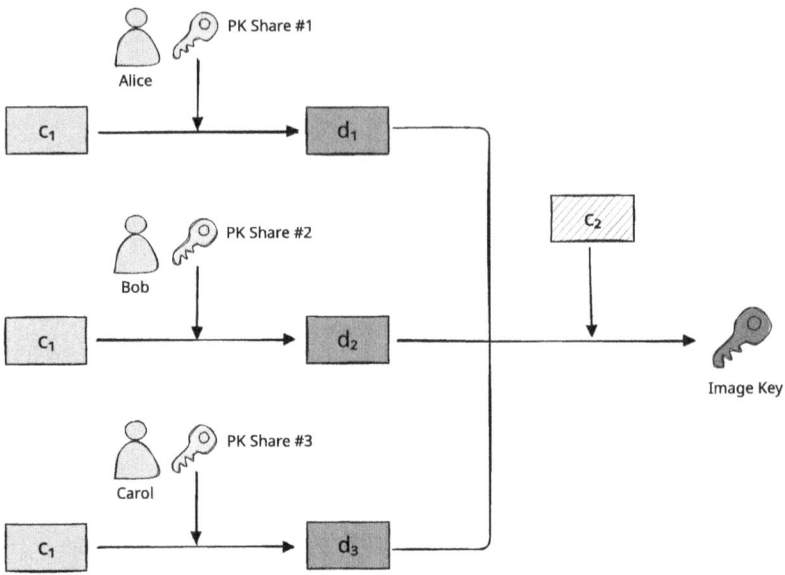

Fig. 6. Decryption of an image key by combining $i = 3$ partial results decrypted from participants holding a share of the private key.

dropping any collaborative decryption tasks with maximum system privileges cannot learn s (or any shares of it).

The metadata associated with the images are stored in a PostgreSQL database along with the cryptographic and robust hashes of the image, the originating URL in the darknet and a timestamp of the image download. The MRRs of each image (one for each supported reverse image search engine) are also stored in the file system with their references stored in the database.

6 Discussion

In the following we discuss first evaluation results of an automated image collection in the darknet as well as several technical aspects of the DIDB.

6.1 First Evaluations

The usefulness of a darknet image database for law enforcement purposes is trivially dependent on the number of images stored. As such, it is desirable to crawl link aggregators or darknet search engines (see Subsect. 4.2) to gain access to multiple darknet website networks. Since another image collection task can be started at any time using additional websites as seed, isolated darknet website networks that have been found at a later time can be indexed as well.

To assess the performance and the scalability of our distributed crawling system MAMPF, we set up a test crawl of the front page of the Hidden Wiki[10] using 4, 8, 16 and 32 parallel workers on a server appliance with an AMD EPYC 7702P CPU. The crawl entailed the download and processing of all image resources linked from the Hidden Wiki main page and from all secondary web pages linked therein. At the time of the test, we found 721 web pages linked on the Hidden Wiki main page. A total of 3,180 images were fetched from 722 web pages, of which 2,069 were unique. Due to the nature of the Tor protocol, requests to resources on the darknet are inherently subject to timing fluctuations and high variability, as Tor routes traffic through randomly selected relays with differing performance characteristics. Furthermore, circuit rebuilding, varying network congestion, and transient relay issues can significantly affect individual request times. To account for these sources of variability and to ensure statistically meaningful results, each test was carried out five times.

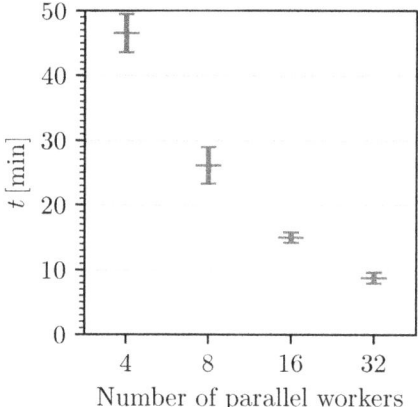

Fig. 7. Total crawl time in minutes for the Hidden Wiki test crawl using 4, 8, 16, and 32 parallel workers. Each measurement represents the average of five runs, with standard deviation included as error bars.

In Fig. 7, the total crawl time is shown in relation to the number of parallel workers (exact numbers are given in Table 1). The figure demonstrates that the system scales efficiently: doubling the number of workers (e.g., from 4 to 8 or 8 to 16) results in a near-halving of the crawl time, indicating effective parallelization of the workload. While the performance gains become slightly less pronounced at higher worker counts, this is expected and can be attributed to moderate effects from Tor network characteristics such as relay variability and background load. Each test was averaged over five runs to smooth out these fluctuations. Overall, the system shows robust and reliable scalability, making it well-suited for large-scale darknet image crawling and processing.

---

[10] Hidden Wiki: http://zqktlwiuavvvqqt4ybvgvi7tyo4hjl5xgfuvpdf6otjiycgwqbym2qad.onion/wiki/index.php/Main_Page.

Table 1. Crawl time of our test run using a different number of parallel workers.

Parallel workers	Time in minutes
4	46.5 ± 2.9
8	26.1 ± 2.8
16	15.0 ± 0.8
32	8.8 ± 0.8

6.2 Challenges in Image Collection

Scraping images from darknet websites poses unique challenges that differ substantially from those encountered when scraping clearnet resources. While clearnet web services typically benefit from robust, professionally maintained infrastructures, darknet sites often rely on limited or volunteer-driven hosting. As a result, requests to darknet servers are generally more error-prone, with higher rates of timeouts, broken connections and unresponsive endpoints. The design of our crawling system based on MAMPF keeps these instabilities in mind: By implementing mechanisms to requeue failed requests at a later time we can respect rate limits and maximize the likelihood of a successful data collection.

Furthermore, websites associated with illicit activities frequently employ additional mechanisms to preserve exclusivity and ensure anonymity. These include CAPTCHAS, rate limiting and bot detection systems that are more aggressive and less standardized than those found on the clearnet. These defenses are intentionally designed to hinder automated access, which poses a significant barrier to data collection for researchers attempting to analyze content associated with criminal activities. Even though our crawling system already accounts for duplicate websites by comparing the exact cryptographic hashes of request response bodies, bot traps that operate by showing many versions of the same web page with small differences in the source code and linking between them are not reliably detected and filtered. In the future, we aim to integrate automated CAPTCHA solving and duplicate detection mechanisms such as the ones outlined in Subsect. 4.1 into the crawling. For the detection of near-duplicate web pages, we are also planning to propose and evaluate an algorithm based on the robust hashing of the visual website representation.

6.3 Challenges in Reverse Image Search

Available reverse image search engines typically require uploading a full image file to search for similar or identical matches. Since the search engines use proprietary algorithms or models for robust hashing to find suitable matches, it would be advisable to provide corresponding APIs that allow queries based on robust hashes and similar feature vectors.

While these APIs are not available, we are experimenting with our proposed approach to build an MRR per image and search engine. This takes a considerable amount of time – and we cannot be certain if a specific approach or algorithm for creating an MRR for one image is still suitable for another, even when using the same search engine. For example, if we believe to have found an MRR of an image containing a group of people, that we can use with Google Images, we cannot be certain that the same algorithm to create the MRR works for another image showing a number of cars. Therefore, we may have to consider other approaches for reverse image search without providing the original images.

7 Conclusion and Future Work

In this paper we presented the conceptual design and implementation of a darknet image database that can be used for reverse image search with strong security against unprivileged access to the collected data. We integrated functionality of our distributed scraping framework MAMPF to automatically collect and filter images from the Tor network. We argue that the design of the DIDB is suitable to deal with potential (legal) implications when collecting unknown images from the darknet and the uncertainty that comes with it.

Currently we are experimenting with minimal robust representations (MRRs) of collected images for several popular reverse image search engines to work around the fact that these typically do not offer a query interface for robust hashes of images instead of actual image data. With our MRRs we hope to find solutions for clearnet search engines that provide sufficient results without requiring an upload of the original image data. We are also planning to further work on the effectiveness and efficiency of MAMPF to increase the number of images we can collect and to work around anti-scraping mechanisms we encounter.

Acknowledgments. This research work was supported by the National Research Center for Applied Cybersecurity ATHENE. ATHENE is funded jointly by the German Federal Ministry of Research, Technology and Space and the Hessian Ministry of Science and Research, Arts and Culture.

References

1. Akyon, F.C., Temizel, A.: State-of-the-art in nudity classification: a comparative analysis. In: 2023 IEEE International Conference on Acoustics, Speech, and Signal Processing Workshops (ICASSPW), pp. 1–5 (2023). https://doi.org/10.1109/ICASSPW59220.2023.10193621
2. Biswas, R., Vasco-Carofilis, R.A., Fidalgo, E., Martino, F.J., Medina, P.B.: Perceptual hashing applied to tor domains recognition. arXiv preprint arXiv:2005.10090 (2020)
3. David, B., Delong, M., Filiol, E.: Detection of crawler traps: formalization and implementation—defeating protection on internet and on the TOR network. J. Comput. Virol. Hack. Tech. **17**(3), 185–198 (2021). https://doi.org/10.1007/s11416-021-00380-4
4. De Pascale, D., Cascavilla, G., Tamburri, D.A., Van Den Heuvel, W.J.: CRATOR a CRAwler for TOR: turning dark web pages into open source INTelligence. In: Garcia-Alfaro, J., Kozik, R., Choraś, M., Katsikas, S. (eds.) Computer Security - ESORICS 2024, pp. 144–161. Springer, Cham (2024)

5. Desmedt, Y., Frankel, Y.: Threshold cryptosystems. In: Brassard, G. (ed.) Advances in Cryptology - CRYPTO' 89 Proceedings, pp. 307–315. Springer, New York (1990)
6. Gannon, C., Blokland, A.A., Huikuri, S., Babchishin, K.M., Lehmann, R.J.: Child sexual abuse material on the darknet. Forensische Psychiatrie, Psychologie, Kriminologie **17**(4), 353–365 (2023)
7. Guerra, E., Westlake, B.G.: Detecting child sexual abuse images: traits of child sexual exploitation hosting and displaying websites. Child Abuse Neglect **122**, 105336 (2021). https://doi.org/10.1016/j.chiabu.2021.105336
8. Hartel, P., Haspels, E., van Staalduinen, M., Texeira, O.: DarkDiff: Explainable Web Page Similarity of TOR Onion Sites (2023). https://doi.org/10.48550/arXiv.2308.12134
9. IWF: How AI is being abused to create child sexual abuse imagery (2023). https://www.iwf.org.uk/media/q4zll2ya/iwf-ai-csam-report_public-oct23v1.pdf
10. Jones, S.M., Oyen, D.: Abstract images have different levels of retrievability per reverse image search engine. In: Karlinsky, L., Michaeli, T., Nishino, K. (eds.) Computer Vision - ECCV 2022 Workshops, pp. 203–222. Springer, Cham (2023)
11. Koebe, T., del Villar, Z., Nutakki, B., Sagimbayeva, N., Weber, I.: Unveiling local patterns of child pornography consumption in France using Tor. Human. Soc. Sci. Commun. **11**(1), 1–11 (2024)
12. Microsoft: Microsoft and National Center for Missing & Exploited Children Push for Action to Fight Child Pornography (2009). https://news.microsoft.com/source/2009/12/15/microsoft-and-national-center-for-missing-exploited-children-push-for-action-to-fight-child-pornography/
13. Nurmi, J., et al.: Investigating child sexual abuse material availability, searches, and users on the anonymous tor network for a public health intervention strategy. Sci. Rep. **14**(1), 7849 (2024). https://doi.org/10.1038/s41598-024-58346-7
14. Phan, D.D., Nguyen, T.T., Nguyen, Q.H., Tran, H.L., Nguyen, K.N.K., Vu, D.L.: LSPD: a large-scale pornographic dataset for detection and classification. Int. J. Intell. Eng. Syst. **15**(1) (2022)
15. Shamir, A.: How to share a secret. Commun. ACM **22**(11), 612–613 (1979)
16. Steinebach, M., Liu, H., Yannikos, Y.: ForBild: efficient robust image hashing. In: Memon, N.D., Alattar, A.M., Delp III, E.J. (eds.) Media Watermarking, Security, and Forensics 2012. Proceeding of SPIE, vol. 8303, pp. 8303 0O–1–8 (2012)
17. Wang, Y., Arief, B., Franqueira, V.N.L., Coates, A.G., Ciardha, C.Ó.: Investigating the availability of child sexual abuse materials in dark web markets: evidence gathered and lessons learned. In: European Interdisciplinary Cybersecurity Conference, pp. 59–64. ACM, Stavanger Norway (2023). https://doi.org/10.1145/3590777.3590812
18. Yannikos, Y., Agel, M.L., Heeger, J., Bugert, S.: Cooking spiders: efficient OSINT with chefs and recipes. Electron. Imaging **37**(4), 302–1–302–1 (2025). https://doi.org/10.2352/EI.2025.37.4.MWSF-302
19. Yannikos, Y., Steinebach, M., Rettig, M.: Benefits of combining forensic image creation and file carving. Electron. Imaging **29**(7), 22–22 (2017). https://doi.org/10.2352/ISSN.2470-1173.2017.7.MWSF-321

Hello, Won't You Tell Me Your Name?: Investigating Anonymity Abuse in IPFS

Christos Karapapas[1]([✉])[iD], Iakovos Pittaras[1][iD], George C. Polyzos[1,2][iD], and Constantinos Patsakis[3,4][iD]

[1] Athens University of Economics and Business, Athens, Greece
{karapapas,pittaras}@aueb.gr, polyzos@acm.org
[2] School of Data Science, The Chinese University of Hong Kong, Shenzhen, China
[3] University of Piraeus, Piraeus, Greece
[4] Athena Research Center, Marousi, Greece
kpatsak@unipi.gr

Abstract. The InterPlanetary File System (IPFS) offers a decentralized approach to file storage and sharing, promising resilience and efficiency, while also realizing the Web3 paradigm. Simultaneously, the offered anonymity raises significant questions about potential misuse. In this study, we explore methods that malicious actors can exploit IPFS to upload and disseminate harmful content while remaining anonymous. We evaluate the role of pinning services and public gateways, identifying their capabilities and limitations in maintaining content availability. Using scripts, we systematically test the behavior of these services by uploading malicious files. Our analysis reveals that pinning services and public gateways lack mechanisms to assess or restrict the propagation of malicious content. Our findings demonstrate that attackers can exploit the decentralized nature of IPFS and its ecosystem to ensure persistent availability of malicious content while masking their identities. Moreover, we observed instances of this exploitation occurring in practice, further validating the real-world applicability of such attacks.

1 Introduction

Web3, often referred to as the *read-write-own* Web, has recently surged in popularity among users and researchers. Although initially presented as a new phase of the World Wide Web, it primarily represents an ideological shift rather than a technological breakthrough. Its main pillars are decentralization, returning data control to users, and the absence of a central authority, treating all users as peers. To achieve this goal, Web3 engulfs technologies such as blockchains, digital currencies, and decentralized identities, all of which have seen rapid growth.

In terms of security, Web3 seeks to mitigate single points of failure, which, in the recent past, have caused substantial disruptions across various technology sectors, including outages of well-known services, leading to widespread paralysis in different technological domains [18]. As with all things in life, Web3 has its dark aspects. The growing interest of users has also drawn the attention of malicious actors toward Web3. Lack of oversight and regulatory authority has led to significant financial losses due to various scams [8,28]. On the other hand, as the technologies that comprise Web3 are still in their infancy, they suffer from software vulnerabilities, which are exploited by various actors [10]. Another perspective from which Web3 undeniably faces challenges is that of privacy and anonymity, primarily due to its Peer-to-Peer (P2P) nature. While decentralization is a key advantage of Web3, the inherent transparency and traceability of P2P networks often conflict with users' privacy expectations [34].

Web3 consists of multiple stacks, each with various protocols that interoperate to deliver user services. These services range from data storage, domain name resolution, and decentralized identities to applications like social media, gaming, and marketplaces. As these protocols and their interconnections evolve, they present potential vulnerabilities that attackers can exploit or leverage. In data storage, there are various protocols, such as InterPlanetary File System (IPFS), Filecoin, Storj, SIA, and others. However, IPFS is widely recognized as one of the most prominent and broadly adopted solutions [11,38]. Its open-source nature, content-addressable design, and integration with technologies like Filecoin and public gateways have contributed to its popularity across Web3 applications. Developed by Protocol Labs [31] as an open-source project, it has gained considerable attention in recent years. Notably, companies such as Lockheed Martin have shown interest, even launching an IPFS node into orbit [25]. Furthermore, the growing number of research papers with 'IPFS' in their titles highlights its increasing prominence among researchers, with Semantic Scholar returning more than 800 results for such publications over the past two years. Among the tools that enhance the functionality of IPFS are pinning services, which play a crucial role in maintaining file availability across the network. These services allow users to ensure that specific files remain accessible by hosting them on dedicated nodes, even if the original uploader goes offline. Over time, IPFS has drawn the attention of both malicious actors and security researchers. One study [30] revealed that a notorious botnet exploited its network, while another highlighted that a significant proportion of its nodes are operated by malicious actors [22].

Recent works have shown that malware increasingly leverages benign Internet services to distribute payloads and evade detection. This includes both centralized platforms such as GitHub and Dropbox [40], and large-scale abuse of cloud services like Discord, Mediafire, and Google Drive [5]. Our work extends this threat model to decentralized infrastructures like IPFS, where anonymity, content immutability, and the absence of centralized moderation create an even more permissive environment for abuse. In this paper, we investigate how malicious actors can exploit existing technologies within the IPFS ecosystem to anonymously upload and distribute content. We begin by mapping the current landscape of tools and protocols used to add and access content on IPFS, including pinning services and public gateways. We then design and evaluate practical attacks that leverage these mechanisms to achieve anonymity and persistence within the network. Finally, we explore potential countermeasures to mitigate such exploits. As a result, our main research questions are the following.

RQ1: Do pinning services apply the best know your customer (KYC) practices to allow attribution when malicious content is pinned? (Answered in §4.1)
RQ2: Do pinning services apply any content scanning mechanism to prevent malicious content sharing? (Answered in §4.1)
RQ3: How could an adversary abuse these gaps to share malicious content anonymously? (Answered in §4.1)
RQ4: Is there evidence showing this abuse?(Answered in §4.4)
RQ5: How could an adversary abuse gateways' caching to anonymously share and preserve malicious content online?(Answered in §4.2).

As a result, our research reveals several ways in which IPFS can be abused without providing the necessary tracking mechanisms for perpetrator attribution.

Ethical considerations. While working with live systems, we have taken the necessary measures to ensure that no malware would propagate through the systems and cause any harm. First, any malicious file submitted to IPFS is not executed by any system. However, we acknowledge that once published on IPFS, files may be accessed by third-party systems—including automated scanners or research tools—that might perform dynamic analysis or sandbox execution. To mitigate this risk, all uploaded files either contained benign code flagged as malicious due to simulated behaviors, or were legacy malware samples that no longer pose realistic threats. Secondly, for someone to collect and execute our samples, they must know the CID or monitor all nodes to collect and execute each file. Since the CIDs have not been publicly promoted, the chances of someone collecting all uploaded files and executing them in an unprotected environment are very low. Even in this unlikely scenario, the malicious samples we created just trigger an antivirus without causing actual damage to the system. Finally, the malware we have used from the real world is very well known, and the corresponding URLs have been siphoned, further diminishing the chances of our work impacting any system. We acknowledge that detailing these attack vectors may inadvertently provide insights to malicious actors. However, we believe that openly discussing these issues is necessary to drive improvements in content moderation and security mechanisms within IPFS. Moreover, existing studies have already shown abuse of the IPFS ecosystem. Although no vulnerabilities were directly exploited, we recommend stakeholders in the IPFS ecosystem consider these findings to enhance security measures.

2 Background

The *InterPlanetary File System* (IPFS) [9] is a decentralized file-sharing system focusing on distributed data storage and quick file distribution. IPFS was created and is maintained by Protocol Labs as an open-source project [31]. Unlike traditional file systems, IPFS uniquely identifies files based on their content, assigning each file a distinct *Content IDentifier* (CID). A key IPFS component is *libp2p*, an open-source library of network protocols that includes KAD-DHT, a scalable variant of Kademlia *Distributed Hash Table* (DHT). The KAD-DHT manages three types of mappings, including *Provider Records*, which indicate who hosts specific content; *Peer Records*, which contain information about a specific peer; and *IPNS records*, which link a static address to dynamic data. IPNS names are essentially pointers (IPNS names) to pointers (IPFS CIDs), whereas IPFS CIDs are immutable (because they are derived from the content) pointers to content, Moreover, IPNS names are self-certifying. *Bitswap*, a key component of IPFS, acts as the data exchange and occasionally as a content discovery protocol, using "want-have" and "have" messages for efficient data transfer. IPFS employs Merkle DAGs, a combination of Merkle Trees and *Directed Acyclic Graph* (DAG), to certify the uniqueness of the exchanged data, ensuring that no duplicates are stored. A recent addition to the IPFS ecosystem is the InterPlanetary Network Indexers (IPNI), a centralized version of the DHT designed to efficiently index provider records. It serves primarily large content providers and complements the existing DHT by focusing solely on provider record management. Additionally, Protocol Labs and other companies offer services that offer public gateways, allowing users to access the content of the IPFS network without maintaining a node.

In IPFS, each peer manages a network of active connections, known as the *swarm*, which typically ranges from 600 connections (the *low water mark*) to 900 (the *high water mark*). When a user requests a file from the IPFS network, the Bitswap protocol is triggered. It sends a message to the user's swarm peers in the format `want-have <root CID>` [33]. Peers in the swarm individually check whether they have the specified CID locally. If a peer possesses the requested content, it responds with a `have` message. If no response is received within 1 s, the process is handed over to the DHT, which operates in two stages. Initially, the process searches for the Provider Record, which contains the Peer ID, which stores the content for the requested CID. Subsequently, it searches for the Peer Record, which shows how the Peer ID is linked to a network address. Once this process is finalized, Bitswap is reactivated to facilitate data exchange with the peer hosting the content [38].

3 Adding a File to IPFS

There are several ways to add a file to IPFS. In this section, we explore different methods and their respective modi operandi. Additionally, we examine the information about the original uploader that can be retrieved for each method and the duration that the files remain online.

IPFS Node. For the average user, the primary option for connecting to the IPFS network is the IPFS Desktop application, which supports the most operating systems and includes the functionality of an IPFS node within a user-friendly graphical interface. There is also a command-line version available called Kubo. When a new node connects to the network, if it has a public IP, it is characterized as a DHT Server. Otherwise, e.g., being behind NAT, it defaults to a DHT Client. This is managed by a mechanism called *Autonat*. This distinction ensures that DHT Servers store and provide data, while DHT Clients only request it, optimizing the network's efficiency [38]. When a user wishes to publish a file to IPFS, the process involves splitting the original file into smaller chunks, typically 256 KB. Each chunk is assigned a unique CID and organized into a Merkle DAG added to IPFS. Consequently, two types of records are created in the DHT, with one record stored across a set of 20 specific nodes and the other stored across a different set of 20 nodes. The first type, the Provider Record, indicates who is hosting the file and includes two additional parameters: the republish interval (12 h by default), which assigns new peers if the original 20 nodes go offline, and the expiration interval (24 h by default), which verifies that the publisher is still online. The second type is the Peer Record, which maps the peer to its physical address. From the above, it is clear that when a file is added to IPFS, the file itself is not replicated, instead only links pointing to the uploader are created. Upon file addition, the IPFS node automatically pins the file to the original uploader's node, ensuring its availability while the uploader remains online. Replication occurs only if another user requests the file, resulting in it being stored in their cache. Should the original uploader disconnect from the network, the file's availability relies entirely on the cache of interested users. The aforementioned process is depicted in Fig. 1. It is also worth mentioning that the Brave Browser natively supports the use of IPFS in conjunction with a local node [14], yet earlier versions provided the ability to add files via Public Gateways.

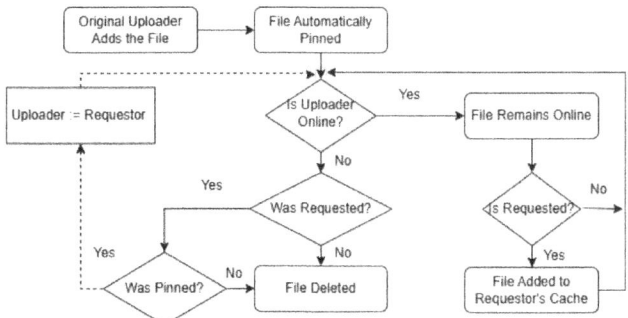

Fig. 1. The File Lifecycle In IPFS.

Pinning Services. IPFS, according to its design principles, does not provide a mechanism to ensure that files added to the network remain online if the original uploader deletes them or disconnects from the network. Files are primarily cached by requesters to ensure their availability to other nodes. The more popular a file is, the higher its chances of staying online for an extended period. Additionally, every IPFS node runs a garbage collector to free up storage space. As a result, cached files are periodically removed, leading some files to disappear from the network over time [11]. To prevent the garbage collector from removing a file, the user must pin it. Pinning can be categorized into two types: local pinning, where the user configures their node to retain the file, though it will fade once the node disconnects from the network; and remote pinning, where an external provider takes the responsibility to ensure that the file remains pinned [17].

A plethora of pinning services is available, with Pinata, Filebase, Fleek, and 4EVERLAND being among the most popular. These platforms offer user-friendly graphical interfaces for adding files to the IPFS network, simplifying the process for the average user. Moreover, they provide free storage space for uploading and pinning files, making them accessible to a wide range of users. Once added, the files can be retrieved through public gateways, which act as HTTP access points to the IPFS network.

Although Web3.Storage and NFT.Storage [27] are not strictly classified as pinning services, their functionality closely resembles traditional pinning solutions, so we include them in this section for completeness. These open-source services, developed by Protocol Labs, are designed to store general and NFT-related data, respectively, in the Web3 era. Both services operate decentralized, leveraging IPFS for content addressing and Filecoin for long-term data preservation rather than offering a pinning service. Web3.Storage is notably free for the community, while NFT.Storage operates under a paid model. NFT.Storage was excluded from further experiments, as it specializes exclusively in NFT metadata storage, which falls outside the scope of our analysis focusing on general-purpose file uploads.

3.1 Public Gateways

Public gateways act as HTTP entry points to the IPFS network, bridging the Web2 and Web3 ecosystems. They process HTTP requests containing CIDs and relay them to an IPFS node, enabling broader access to the network through conventional Web protocols. Although users cannot directly upload files through a gateway, indirect methods enable this functionality, justifying their classification in this section. Furthermore, the HTTP servers underpinning these gateways leverage caching mechanisms, most commonly the Least Recently Used (LRU) strategy which optimizes performance and user experience by evicting the least recently accessed content when the cache reaches its capacity [38]. Based on the above, it is evident that even if the original uploader disconnects from the IPFS network, the file may remain accessible, cached by gateways, with its persistence primarily influenced by its popularity. During the preparation of this study, we identified 10 online gateways [4]. Using the fingerprinting tool WhatWeb [20], we found that nine gateways utilize either Nginx software or Cloudflare proxies, which employ the LRU caching strategy to manage content efficiently.

The fact that public gateways serve as a bridge between the traditional Web and the P2P ecosystem of IPFS makes them very crucial for launching and countering several attacks. For instance, an adversary may host a phishing page on IPFS; however, the content must be rendered from the victim's browser. Thus, the bridge fetches the content from IPFS and brings it to the Web. It must be noted that while there is no official deletion mechanism for IPFS [29], some public gateways follow blocking mechanisms to prevent specific content from reaching the Web [35]. Nevertheless, not all gateways follow the same blocking mechanism and, of course, this does not remove the content from IPFS.

4 Exploiting IPFS for Anonymity: Attack Scenarios

The anonymity offered by IPFS can be exploited by malicious actors. In this section, we analyze how attackers leverage methods discussed in Sect. 3 to achieve anonymity, presenting and evaluating two distinct attack scenarios. The code is available at https://github.com/mmlab-aueb/ipfs-anonymity for reproducing the experiments.

4.1 The Pinning Service Attack

Pinning services ensure that a file remains online. Therefore, it is logical to consider that an attacker could exploit these services to upload a file and guarantee its availability. However, since our focus is on evaluating the level of anonymity, we first examine the information each pinning service requires from users to allow file uploads, i.e., the Know Your Customer (KYC) procedure. We selected Pinata, Filebase, Fleek, Web3.Storage, and 4EVERLAND based on a systematic Internet search. Specifically, we performed Google queries such as "top IPFS pinning services" and "most popular IPFS pinning services," identifying the services most frequently mentioned in developer documentation, technical articles, and community discussions. Academic literature specifically evaluating IPFS pinning services remains limited, further justifying the need to consult current developer ecosystems and real-world service availability. Besides the selected providers, our search also highlighted Infura and Temporal. However, Infura currently restricts access to pre-qualified customers [26], and Temporal appears to have discontinued operations. Thus, our study focuses exclusively on active and publicly available services, realistically representing the infrastructure accessible to potential anonymous attackers.

The Pinata, Fleek, and Filebase services require an email address for user registration. To achieve higher levels of anonymity, we attempted to use a temporary email service. A temporary email is a disposable email address that allows users to receive emails for a short period, often used to maintain anonymity or avoid spam during registration processes. During December 2024 and January 2025, we tested the registration process on Pinata, Fleek, and Filebase using email addresses generated by the service TempMail (https://temp-mail.org). Both Pinata and Fleek accepted the first temporary email we generated, allowing us to create accounts successfully. After four attempts with different temporary email addresses, Filebase accepted the registration, suggesting that its filtering against disposable emails may be incomplete. In all three cases, the platforms required us to verify the email address using a one-time password (OTP). 4EVERLAND, on the other hand, does not use email-based registration

Table 1. Registration Requirements & Free Storage for Pinning Services.

Pinning Pinning Service	URL	KYC	Temp Mail Accepted	Free Storage	Registered Country	DMCA Compliant
Pinata	https://pinata.cloud	E-mail	✓	1 GB	USA	✓
Filebase	https://filebase.com	E-mail	✓	5 GB	USA	✓
Fleek	https://fleek.co	E-mail	✓	5 GB	USA	✓
Web3.Storage	https://web3.storage	Credit Card	✓	5 GB	USA	-
4EVERLAND	https://4everland.org	Crypto Wallet	N/A	5 GB	AUS	✓

but instead requires a cryptocurrency wallet. Using Metamask, we successfully created an account on the platform, noting that even for creating the Metamask wallet, no email was needed. Finally, while Web3.storage accepted the temporary registration email, uploading files required linking a payment account, even though the platform also offers a free plan. This suggests that, although temporary emails are allowed, the payment account requirement serves as an additional verification step for users, limiting its suitability for fully anonymous abuse scenarios. Table 1 presents a summary of these findings.

To simulate malicious behavior, we developed a Python script packaged into a Windows executable using PyInstaller [1]. It mimicked keylogging, dummy process injection, basic file manipulation, and failed network connections. The file was safe by design, yet flagged by multiple antivirus engines on VirusTotal [2] due to behavioral heuristics. No harmful payload or external communication was included. To ensure unique Content Identifiers (CIDs), we created a distinct version of each script for each pinning service under evaluation. One of the key questions explored in this section is how pinning services handle files clearly marked as malicious, aiming to better replicate the perspective and actions of a potential attacker. In addition to the simulated malware, we also tested uploading known deprecated malware, specifically the WannaCry ransomware, to the pinning services. The result was identical: the file was successfully uploaded, and its CID was generated. Furthermore, we confirmed its accessibility through the public gateways. Notably, all files, including WannaCry, were immediately accessible, highlighting the absence of mechanisms in public gateways to evaluate the maliciousness of uploaded content. This raises significant concerns about the potential misuse of the IPFS network.

As previously discussed, in IPFS, the physical address of the node hosting a file can be identified. However, when files are hosted by pinning services, attackers are not concerned about their own address being exposed. The only potential exposure point is during the interaction with the pinning service's website for registration and file upload. To mitigate this risk, an attacker could use a public network or leverage the Tor [13] network to enhance their anonymity prior to registering and uploading files to the pinning services. Since many services implement protections that restrict access via Tor, we conducted a series of tests to verify the feasibility of using Tor to access these services. Our tests confirmed

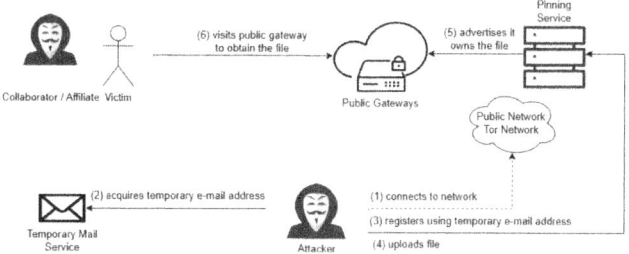

Fig. 2. Design of the "Pinning Service Attack".

that files could be successfully uploaded, and the recorded IP address differed from our actual address, ensuring the attacker's anonymity.

It is important to note that visitors to these files, once uploaded by the attacker, may include either unsuspecting users who were targeted by phishing [35] or malware campaigns, or, in CyberCrime-as-a-Service scenarios [21], collaborators of the attacker, such as affiliates. Even in the latter case, leveraging the Tor network can effectively mitigate the risk of exposing their identities or the nature of their activities. Figure 2 presents the steps that a malicious actor must follow to execute the "Pinning Service Attack". It allows the attacker to leverage the Tor network for anonymity and anonymously upload files to IPFS. By utilizing pinning services, the attacker ensures that uploaded files remain persistently online.

4.2 The Public Gateway Attack

As mentioned, Public Gateways of IPFS do not provide a direct method for uploading a file to the network. However, their caching might indirectly serve as a pinning service, providing file availability. In this section, we initially examine whether and for how long a file remains cached.

To better understand this phenomenon, we conducted a systematic experiment focusing on caching behavior across multiple gateways. The methodology we adopted is as follows. From the 10 gateways identified in Sect. 3.1, we selected five based on their strong association with well-known Web companies (e.g., Pinata, Infura), official status within the IPFS ecosystem, reputation, and service quality. Specifically, we chose (a) ipfs.io (the official gateway maintained by Protocol Labs), (b) gateway.pinata.cloud, (c) infura-ipfs.io, (d) flk-ipfs.xyz and (e) 4everland.io. For each selected gateway, we created four different files, resulting in 20 different files. First, we wanted each gateway to have different files to avoid cross-caching scenarios. Second, for each of these, we created four different files corresponding to the four time scenarios we are studying: 1 h, 6 h, 12 h, and 24 h. We use these intervals to request the respective files from the gateways to understand how popular a file needs to be to remain cached. Subsequently, we used an IPFS node to add the files, ensuring our node ran as a DHT server. Then, to confirm that all the gateways cached all files, we sent up to four requests per file to verify their caching status. The four requests were performed in a negligible amount of time, less than five minutes, and the files became available. After successfully ensuring that all files were cached across the gateways, we disconnected the node from the network, leaving the gateways as the sole source of file hosting. The latter allows us to isolate the role of gateway caching in maintaining file availability independent of the original node. By doing so, we could analyze how the caching mechanisms of public gateways sustain file accessibility over time.

We automated the process of sending requests to the gateways based on the aforementioned periods and recorded the responses for more than three days. The results indicate that caching duration varies significantly between gateways, with some maintaining availability longer than others, which could be attributed to differences in caching strategies or the relative popularity of each gateway. Figure 3 illustrates the ratio $\frac{\nu}{5}$ per hour, where ν represents the number of gateways caching our files at a given time across the different time scenarios. As depicted, two out of the five gateways removed our files from their cache shortly after 16 h, while the remaining three continued to retain them online. For ethical reasons, we refrain from disclosing which ones retained or removed the files.

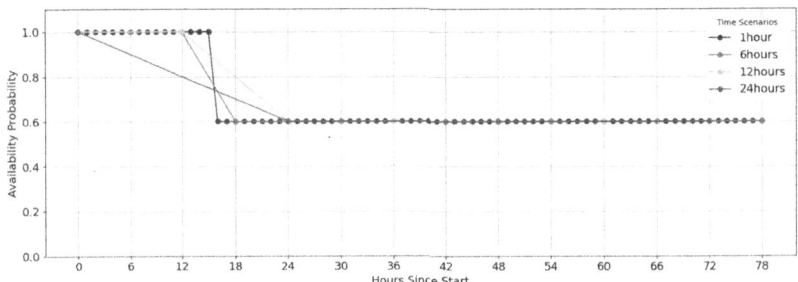

Fig. 3. Time-Dependent File Availability Analysis.

In conclusion, we have demonstrated that a malicious actor could potentially exploit Public Gateways to maintain files on the IPFS network anonymously. The process involves first uploading the files to the IPFS network and generating artificial traffic by repeatedly requesting these files. This ensures that the Public Gateways cache the files. Once the files are cached, the actor can sustain their availability by periodically sending requests for the files, preventing them from being removed from the cache due to inactivity. This approach allows the actor to leverage the distributed infrastructure of Public Gateways to maintain file availability while preserving anonymity, eliminating the need for a dedicated pinning service.

At this point, it should be noted that during the attack, the attacker only risks revealing their physical address while uploading the files via the local node. As

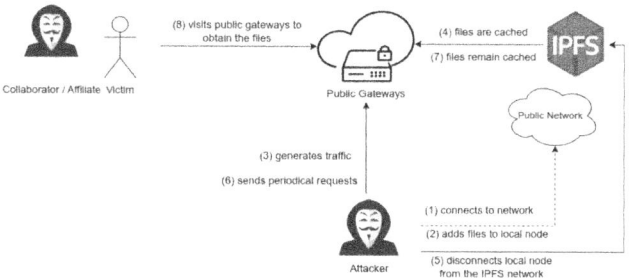

Fig. 4. Design of the "Public Gateway Attack".

previously mentioned, this process requires minimal time, significantly reducing the exposure window for the attacker. Additionally, the attacker could perform this step through a public network to further obscure their physical location. The subsequent periodic requests to the public gateways can also be accomplished through a public network or Tor. Additionally, the attacker could utilize a botnet under their control to generate artificial traffic towards the files without revealing their identity. By distributing requests across multiple geographically dispersed nodes, the botnet obscures the origin of the traffic, making it significantly harder to trace back to the attacker. Note that in the past, the IPFS network has been a victim of such botnet activity [30]. A step-by-step implementation of the attack is illustrated in Fig. 4.

4.3 Double Extortion Attack

Typically, ransomware attacks encrypt the victim's files and demand a ransom to be paid to hand over the decryption key. Nevertheless, modern organizations have invested in backup systems that limit the damages of a potential ransomware attack, significantly decreasing the amount of ransom they would be willing to pay. As a countermeasure, ransomware gangs siphon sensitive data to their premises, threatening their victims by leaking the data and creating what is often called a "double extortion".

The siphoning of the data can be performed in multiple ways, however, methods like DNS tunneling, while effective, can be very slow. Therefore, ransomware gangs tend to abuse cloud service providers to upload their "loot". For example, the notorious Conti group used RClone to upload data to multiple cloud storage providers [19]. With IPFS and the poor KYC practices of pinning services, ransomware gangs can have another more robust option. They may harvest sensitive information from the infected hosts and upload them to IPFS through pinning services. Beyond exploiting KYC to gain the necessary storage, ransomware gangs may also exploit whitelisted domains and the lack of content takedown mechanisms. Note that cloud service providers respond to takedown notices, e.g., the victim notifies the cloud service provider that leaked sensitive data are hosted and must be taken down. However, pinning services cannot remove content from the IPFS once it has been uploaded. Although pinning services comply with DMCA policies and can remove a pinned file from their hosted storage, this does not translate into the deletion of the file from the IPFS network. The decentralized nature of IPFS makes this nearly impossible, while the existence of public gateways, many of which do not adhere to the badbits list (as mentioned in 4.4), further complicates takedown efforts. Figure 5 illustrates this abuse scenario.

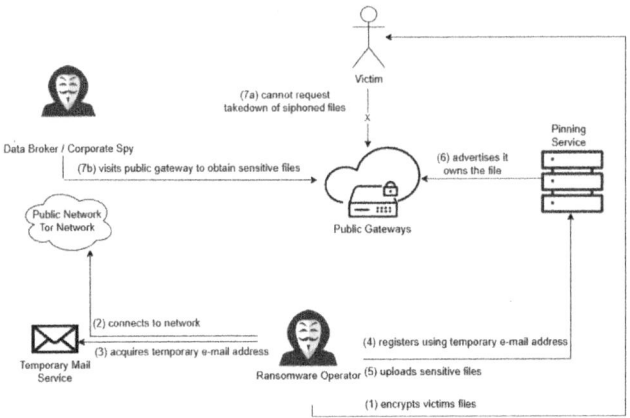

Fig. 5. Design of the "Double Extortion Attack".

4.4 Real-Life Evidence of Malicious Exploitation

While previous work such as [35] investigated the presence of malicious or illegal content across the IPFS network, our approach specifically targets pinning services, i.e., entities that intentionally maintain long-term availability of hosted content. By focusing on CIDs advertised by major pinning providers, our analysis offers a more precise view into deliberate, persistent misuse of the IPFS ecosystem and links it directly to infrastructures that facilitate anonymity and permanence.

We utilized `ipni-cli` [3] to monitor CIDs advertised by Pinata, Filebase, and Fleek pinning services on the `cid.contact` indexer for 24 h. For all providers, we repeatedly executed the following command:

`ipni ads get --ai=<provider addr> --head`

This command retrieves information about the latest advertisement from the specified provider, including the number of CIDs it contains. Once we obtained this information, we proceeded to extract the actual CIDs using:

`ipni random <provider addr>`

With the parameter n, this command returns m CIDs from a random selection of the most recent n advertisements. By setting n=1, we ensured that the selection always targeted the most recent advertisement. Since the previous command had already provided us with the exact number of CIDs, we could request all of them at once. This approach enabled us to systematically retrieve all hashes from every advertisement recorded since the beginning of the experiment. By continuously executing these queries and storing the results, we effectively built a historical record of all advertisements and their associated CIDs from each provider. During the 24-hour interval, we collected (i) 1,124,780 CIDs from Pinata, (ii) 718,578 from Filebase, and (iii) 339,684 from Fleek. For each of these, we standardized the format of the CIDs to match the entries in the Bad Bits Denylist [32], ensuring compatibility for an accurate comparison. The Bad Bits Denylist is a list maintained by Protocol Labs, updated upon email recommendations to filter undesirable files, such as malware, phishing content, or copyright-infringing materials. Note that the list is enforced on the public gateways operated by Protocol Labs but is advisory for all other nodes within the IPFS network. By matching the monitored CIDs against the entries in the denylist, we discovered that within 24 h, the pinning services advertised five CIDs included in the Bad Bits Denylist. It is worth mentioning that one of these CIDs was advertised by all three services, while two were common to two services. We consider the presence of these blocked CIDs –and even more so their simultaneous advertisement on the same day by multiple pinning services– a strong indication of malicious actors' organized exploitation of the anonymity provided by pinning services. Finally, we managed to retrieve three of them, discovering that one was a JavaScript file involved in a Bank of America phishing scam, the second was a login phishing webpage targeting a Korean webmail service, and the third was an image, likely used for malicious purposes.

5 Related Work

Research has shown that malware increasingly abuses centralized Web and cloud platforms for infrastructure, persistence, and evasion. Yao et al. [40] propose Marsea, a concolic execution engine that detects malware interaction with benign Web applications such as GitHub and Dropbox, revealing how these services are repurposed for malicious use. At a broader scale, Allegretta et al. [5] analyze threat intelligence from 36 vendors and identify over 22,000 abused benign domains, including services like Discord and Google Drive, used to distribute malware. These works demonstrate that even trusted, centrally managed services are vulnerable to abuse. In this work, we show that decentralized infrastructures like IPFS introduce new and arguably more permissive abuse surfaces, due to their inherent anonymity, lack of content moderation, and resistance to takedown.

In recent years, Web3 has emerged as a new paradigm for the Internet, prioritizing user anonymity and privacy. These features are especially significant as concerns about user privacy and tracking escalate. However, numerous studies indicate that these features are often compromised. Kshetri [24] highlights several vulnerabilities within Web3 and the metaverse, particularly the extensive data collection and exposure of personal and sensitive data due to numerous security breaches on Web3. Furthermore, the author points out that anonymity can be compromised via the traceability of blockchain transactions on Web3 platforms, potentially linking personal identities and actions to public transaction records.

On the other hand, other studies focus on how anonymity and privacy are compromised on Web3. Wang et al. [39] explore how Web3 social platforms, such as friend.tech [16], impact user privacy and anonymity. In particular, they identified that the integration between Web3 and legacy Web2 platforms could significantly undermine Web3 anonymity and lead to privacy leakage. This occurs because user actions on Web2 platforms can be associated with accounts on Web3 platforms since these actions are immutably written on blockchains. Then, the recorded actions can be linked and traced back to the users. To address these problems, the authors argue that a balanced approach between transparency and privacy in Web3 is needed. Additionally, Torres et al. [37] focus on how wallets and Decentralized Applications (DApps) manage user data. The authors conclude that current privacy measures are insufficient, highlighting that Web3 applications, particularly wallets, often expose sensitive user data, such as wallet addresses. This exposure directly contradicts the foundational privacy promises of Web3 by compromising user anonymity and privacy.

A central element of Web3 and a core focus of our study are distributed file systems, with IPFS being the most prominent. Previous research has demonstrated that IPFS can be exploited by malicious actors in various domains. For example, studies have shown its use in Malware as a Service systems [21], while others have reported the presence of phishing files or copyright violations within the IPFS network [35]. Moreover, IPFS also has some privacy violations. In particular, Balduf et al. [7] showcase a privacy attack on the IPFS network by leveraging the Bitswap protocol and introducing a set of attack vectors. The authors state that every IPFS node is susceptible to each of the introduced attacks, and moreover, they succeed in exploiting it by deploying a number of nodes with extended connectivity to passively monitor the Bitswap channel and demonstrate their attack methodology by discovering the PeerId of the public IPFS HTTP gateways.

In addition to attackers, security analysts can leverage Bitswap's privacy shortcomings. Son et al. [36] propose *IF-DSS*, a digital forensics investigation framework for Decentralized Storage Services (DSSs). They analyze the most critical DSSs from the point of view of digital forensics and apply the proposed framework to IPFS. To collect appropriate and sufficient data, they separate them into those that exist on the local side as well as remotely. Finally, they suggest tackling the dissemination of illegal material in three steps: (i) Content filtering, i.e., blacklisting of the inappropriate content, (ii) stop content sharing, i.e., turn the node from server to client, and finally, (iii) shutting down the node.

On the other hand, some works try to enhance IPFS privacy. Katsantas et al. [23] focus on hiding the identity of content on IPFS by using only hash functions. The authors aim to prevent intermediaries from detecting the retrieved contents without relying on trusted third parties. Furthermore, Daniel et al. [12] point out that as IPFS follows the ICN paradigm, a client requests content directly rather than visiting an address. Thus, Bitswap queries all the client's neighbors for content, resulting in the client's interest leaking. Aiming to reduce interest leakage, the authors propose three privacy-enhanced standards for content discovery. By using these protocols, on the one hand, the level of privacy of the client is improved, but that of the provider is reduced. More specifically, they propose a solution using bloom filters and `Bloom-Swap`, a solution using bloom filters in which the provider sends its inventory to the client, and he, in turn, checks locally whether the requested content is a Bloom Filter member to ask the block directly. `PSI-Swap`, which uses Private Set Intersection (PSI), reduces and improves privacy levels on the provider's side as well. Finally, the `BEPSI-Swap`, which combines the two previous ones, improves the efficiency of PSI-Swap, at the cost of making PSI probabilistic. The authors then implement a proof of concept of the proposed protocols and study them from the security and efficiency perspectives.

6 Countermeasures and Conclusions

The decentralized nature of the technologies we study, combined with the fact that the majority of the software is open-source, makes enforcing rules for implementing countermeasures challenging. From the perspective of pinning services, KYC practices must become stricter. Measures such as filtering temporary emails, implementing blockchain-based identity systems, e.g., cryptocurrency wallets with benign transaction history, applying stricter criteria for users operating through Tor networks, enabling content scanning mechanisms, and adhering to a centralized deny list like Bad Bits should be enforced. Public gateways act as bridges for Web2 users to access the Web3 ecosystem. For the average user, requiring a blockchain-based identity would deter them from utilizing these gateways. However, all gateways could be required to comply with the Bad Bits, a policy currently enforced only on gateways managed by Protocol Labs. Moreover, even if a CID is listed on the Bad Bits Denylist, a malicious actor can circumvent it by simply choosing an alternative chunking size when adding the file to IPFS (**RQ5**). This approach generates a different CID that is not associated with the blacklisted one [35], making content filtering on gateways significantly more challenging. In this study, we examined the vulnerabilities of IPFS pinning services and public gateways, highlighting how malicious actors can exploit their anonymity features or lack of proper KYC policies to share undesirable content. By implementing and testing two distinct attack methodologies, we demonstrated not only their feasibility (**RQ3**) but also observed instances of malicious activity occurring within the IPFS ecosystem (**RQ4**). Our findings reveal critical issues, including the lack of robust KYC practices in pinning services (**RQ1**), insufficient content filtering mechanisms (**RQ2**), and the challenges posed by the decentralized and open-source nature of the IPFS ecosystem. These gaps enable attackers to take advantage of the anonymity features of the system while avoiding accountability. Since current KYC practices in pinning services can be easily bypassed, the use of stricter measures, of even the consideration of blockchain-based identity verification methods, such as zero-knowledge proofs (ZKPs), e.g., zkLogin [6], would allow users to verify their legitimacy without exposing their full identity.

It should be stressed that the decentralized nature of IPFS raises significant legal and regulatory challenges, particularly in the enforcement of content moderation and compliance with existing digital laws. While platforms operating in centralized environments are bound by regulations such as the Digital Services Act (DSA) [15], decentralized systems like IPFS lack clear accountability structures. This creates a regulatory gap that malicious actors can exploit to distribute illicit content while avoiding legal repercussions. One of the main concerns is jurisdictional ambiguity. Since IPFS content is hosted on a distributed network of peers, it is often unclear which jurisdiction has the authority to enforce takedown requests or prosecute offenders. This is especially true on platforms like IPFS, where there is no deletion mechanism and data ownership is not always known. Pinning services, many of which operate in different countries with varying legal requirements, further complicate the enforcement process.

However, this sparks the debate surrounding IPFS security and other such platforms regarding the trade-off between privacy and censorship resistance. While decentralization offers increased resilience against state-sponsored censorship, it also enables unmoderated content proliferation, including, but not limited to, extremist propaganda, child sexual abuse material, and malware distribution. The ability of malicious actors to exploit anonymity for illegal activities creates a dilemma where content moderation mechanisms must be introduced without undermining the fundamental principles of decentralized storage. Strengthening the security of IPFS and the surrounding ecosystem is essential not only to prevent its misuse but also to promote its adoption as a reliable and privacy-preserving tool for decentralized file sharing, which is fundamental to the Web3 paradigm. Thus, future research could focus on the development of automated tools to detect malicious CIDs in a decentralized and scalable way. Another approach would be decentralized content moderation, where community-driven flagging mechanisms allow for voluntary filtering rather than direct deletion. Likewise, user-driven reputation systems for pinning services and nodes could help differentiate legitimate operators from malicious ones. By assigning trust scores to nodes based on their activity and compliance with community standards, users could make informed choices about which nodes to trust for content retrieval and caching.

Acknowledgements. This work was supported in part by the European Commission under the Horizon Europe Programme, as part of the project SafeHorizon (Grant Agreement no. 101168562). The content of this article does not reflect the official opinion of the European Union. Responsibility for the information and views expressed therein lies entirely with the authors.

References

1. https://pyinstaller.org/
2. https://www.virustotal.com/
3. ipni-cli. https://github.com/ipni/ipni-cli
4. Public gateway checker. https://ipfs.github.io/public-gateway-checker/
5. Allegretta, M., Siracusano, G., González, R., Gramaglia, M., Caballero, J.: Web of shadows: investigating malware abuse of internet services. Comput. Secur. **149**, 104182 (2025)
6. Baldimtsi, F., et al.: zklogin: Privacy-preserving blockchain authentication with existing credentials. In: Proceedings of the 2024 on ACM SIGSAC Conference on Computer and Communications Security. CCS '24, pp. 3182–3196. ACM, New York, NY, USA (2024). https://doi.org/10.1145/3658644.3690356
7. Balduf, L., Henningsen, S., Florian, M., Rust, S., Scheuermann, B.: Monitoring data requests in decentralized data storage systems: a case study of IPFS. In: 2022 IEEE 42nd International Conference on Distributed Computing Systems (ICDCS), pp. 658–668. IEEE (2022)
8. Bartoletti, M., Lande, S., Loddo, A., Pompianu, L., Serusi, S.: Cryptocurrency scams: analysis and perspectives. IEEE Access **9**, 148353–148373 (2021)
9. Benet, J.: IPFS-content Addressed, Versioned, P2P File System. arXiv preprint arXiv:1407.3561 (2014)
10. Carpentier-Desjardins, C., Paquet-Clouston, M., Kitzler, S., Haslhofer, B.: Mapping the defi crime landscape: an evidence-based picture. arXiv preprint arXiv:2310.04356 (2023)
11. Daniel, E., Tschorsch, F.: IPFS and friends: a qualitative comparison of next generation peer-to-peer data networks. IEEE Commun. Surv. Tutor. **24**(1), 31–52 (2022)
12. Daniel, E., Tschorsch, F.: Privacy-enhanced content discovery for Bitswap. In: 2023 IFIP Networking Conference, pp. 1–9 (2023)
13. Dingledine, R., Mathewson, N., Syverson, P.F., et al.: Tor: the second-generation onion router. In: USENIX Security Symposium, vol. 4, pp. 303–320 (2004)
14. Doan, T.V., Psaras, Y., Ott, J., Bajpai, V.: Toward decentralized cloud storage with IPFS: opportunities, challenges, and future considerations. IEEE Internet Comput. **26**(6), 7–15 (2022)
15. European Union: Regulation (EU) 2022/2065 of the European Parliament and of the Council of 19 October 2022 on a Single Market For Digital Services and amending Directive 2000/31/EC (Digital Services Act) (2022). https://eur-lex.europa.eu/eli/reg/2022/2065/oj/eng
16. friend.tech/: https://www.friend.tech/
17. Guidi, B., Michienzi, A., Ricci, L.: Data persistence in decentralized social applications: the IPFS approach. In: 2021 IEEE 18th Annual Consumer Communications and Networking Conference (CCNC), pp. 1–4. IEEE (2021)
18. Hatchimonji, G. (2024). www.techtarget.com/whatis/feature/8-largest-IT-outages-in-history
19. Heller, M.: A conti ransomware attack day-by-day (2021). https://news.sophos.com/en-us/2021/02/16/conti-ransomware-attack-day-by-day/
20. Horton, A.: Whatweb. https://github.com/urbanadventurer/whatweb
21. Karapapas, C., Pittaras, I., Fotiou, N., Polyzos, G.C.: Ransomware as a service using smart contracts and IPFS. In: 2020 IEEE International Conference on Blockchain and Cryptocurrency (ICBC), pp. 1–5. IEEE (2020)

22. Karapapas, C., Polyzos, G.C., Patsakis, C.: What's inside a node? Malicious IPFS nodes under the magnifying glass. In: Meyer, N., Grocholewska-Czuryło, A. (eds.) ICT Systems Security and Privacy Protection, pp. 149–162. Springer, Cham (2024)
23. Katsantas, T., Thomas, Y., Karapapas, C., Xylomenos, G.: Enhancing IPFS privacy through triple hashing. In: 2024 IEEE Symposium on Computers and Communications (ISCC), pp. 1–6 (2024)
24. Kshetri, N.: Privacy violations, security breaches and other threats of Web3 and the metaverse. In: 32nd European Regional ITS Conference, Madrid 2023: Realising the Digital Decade in the European Union – Easier said than done? 277993, International Telecommunications Society (ITS) (2023)
25. Lockheed Martin (2024). https://www.lockheedmartin.com/en-us/news/features/2024/smartsat-equipped-satellite-uploads-new-mission-on-orbit.html
26. MetaMask. https://docs.metamask.io/services/reference/ipfs/
27. NFT.Storage.https://nft.storage/
28. Patsakis, C., Casino, F., Lykousas, N., Katos, V.: Unravelling ariadne's thread: exploring the threats of decentralised DNS. IEEE Access **8**, 118559–118571 (2020)
29. Politou, E., Alepis, E., Patsakis, C., Casino, F., Alazab, M.: Delegated content erasure in IPFS. Futur. Gener. Comput. Syst. **112**, 956–964 (2020)
30. Pripoae, S.: Looking Into the eye of the interplanetary storm (2020). https://www.bitdefender.com/files/News/CaseStudies/study/376/Bitdefender-Whitepaper-IPStorm.pdf
31. Protocol Labs. https://www.protocol.ai/
32. Protocol Labs: Bad Bits Denylist. https://badbits.dwebops.pub/
33. De la Rocha, A., Dias, D., Psaras, Y.: Accelerating Content Routing with Bitswap: a multi-path file transfer protocol in IPFS and Filecoin (2021)
34. Sheridan, D., Harris, J., Wear, F., Cowell Jr., J., Wong, E., Yazdinejad, A.: Web3 challenges and opportunities for the market. arXiv preprint arXiv:2209.02446 (2022)
35. Sokoto, S., et al.: Guardians of the galaxy: content moderation in the interplanetary file system. In: Balzarotti, D., Xu, W. (eds.) 33rd USENIX Security Symposium, USENIX Security 2024, Philadelphia, PA, USA, 14–16 August 2024. USENIX Association (2024)
36. Son, J., Kim, G., Jung, H., Bang, J., Park, J.: IF-DSS: a forensic investigation framework for decentralized storage services. Forensic Sci. Int. Digit. Invest. **46**, 301611 (2023)
37. Torres, C.F., Willi, F., Shinde, S.: Is your wallet snitching on you? An analysis on the privacy implications of web3. In: Proceedings of the 32nd USENIX Conference on Security Symposium. SEC '23, USENIX Association, USA (2023)
38. Trautwein, D., et al.: Design and evaluation of IPFS: a storage layer for the decentralized web. In: Proceedings of the ACM SIGCOMM 2022 Conference, pp. 739–752 (2022)
39. Wang, B., et al.: The Illusion of Anonymity: Uncovering the Impact of User Actions on Privacy in Web3 Social Ecosystems (2024). https://arxiv.org/abs/2405.13380
40. Yao, M., Fuller, J., Kasturi, R.P., Agarwal, S., Sikder, A.K., Saltaformaggio, B.: Hiding in plain sight: an empirical study of web application abuse in malware. In: 32nd USENIX Security Symposium (USENIX Security 23), pp. 6115–6132 (2023)

Countering Financial Cyber Crime: New Method for Subsequent Steps Analysis in Large Complex Graphs of Financial Transactions

Rafał Kozik[1], Piotr Gocał[2], and Michał Choraś[1(✉)]

[1] Bydgoszcz University of Science and Technology, Bydgoszcz, Poland
chorasm@pbs.edu.pl
[2] Matic SA, Warsaw, Poland

Abstract. In this paper, we focus on the proposition of new computational mechanisms for the individual and subsequent steps detection in the financial flows analysis. In other words, for selected starting points (e.g. bank account, date, value, etc.), the analysis aimed to identify further actions taken by the perpetrators. Such solution is much needed for the police, forensic experts and analysts of financial crimes and transactions, who need to manually analyze big complex data. In this paper, we show the application of our proposed method and solution for two financial Internet-related crimes, namely financial pyramid and on-line shopping fraud.

Keywords: Cyber crime · Online shopping frauds · Graphs analysis · Complex data analysis · Financial transactions and crimes

1 Introduction

1.1 Context and Rationale

Crimes targeting both individuals and businesses to steal funds or to legitimize other illegal activities are a significant part of the broader landscape of crime, and these types of offences constitute a large part of total criminal cases initiated by law enforcement and courts.

While financial and economic crimes may not involve physical violence against the victim, they still have real victims. These offences can seriously harm people, businesses, governments and international organizations.

Large part of financial crimes are conducted within and with the use of Internet, exactly like the cases we discuss in this paper: online shopping fraud and financial pyramid.

The problem is becoming more and more serious and the number of financial crime cases is rising because of two factors – growing economies and financial instruments that can be targeted (e.g. the rise of cryptocurrencies), as well as the growing sophistication of criminals – linked to the latest technological advancements (e.g. AI-assisted attacks as an example of this trend).

According to Occupational Fraud 2024: A Report to the Nations – 13th edition of the largest global study on occupational fraud prepared based on almost 2000 real cases from 138 countries, organizations estimate losses at level 5% of their revenues each year resulting from occupational fraud, with the median loss of $145,000.

Key findings from the report include the fact that almost half of all reported cases included corruption, that a significant part of fraud crimes constitute non-cash cases (theft of organization assets) and that a typical fraud case lasts 12 months before detection.

The major problem is the scale of the analyzed data, some financial crimes are being manually analyzed for decades. Also, there are not many tools that can support such forensic analysis and experts demand new tools and solutions to support their struggle to counter financial crimes.

1.2 Our Contribution

In this work we considered the variability of cyber criminals' modus operandi in the cyberspasce and the range of methods employed. One of the research challenges was the complexity of the data analysis due to the variety of contexts and situations in which the crimes may have occurred.

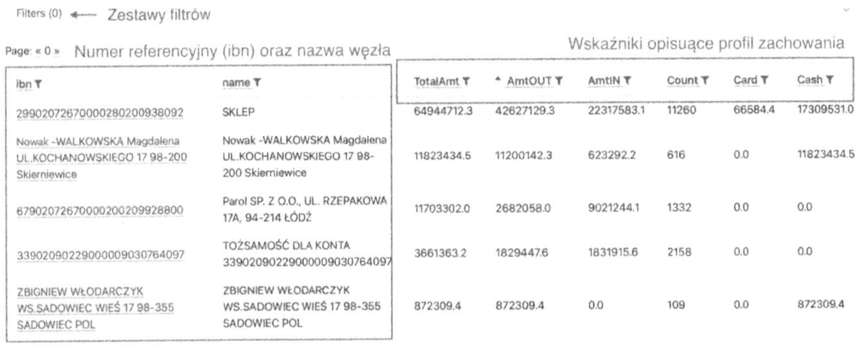

ibn	name	TotalAmt	AmtOUT	AmtIN	Count	Card	Cash
29902072670000280200938092	SKLEP	64944712.3	42627129.3	22317583.1	11260	66584.4	17309531.0
Nowak -WALKOWSKA Magdalena UL.KOCHANOWSKIEGO 17 98-200 Skierniewice	Nowak -WALKOWSKA Magdalena UL.KOCHANOWSKIEGO 17 98-200 Skierniewice	11823434.5	11200142.3	623292.2	616	0.0	11823434.5
67902072670000200209928800	Parol SP. Z O.O., UL. RZEPAKOWA 17A, 94-214 ŁÓDŹ	11703302.0	2682058.0	9021244.1	1332	0.0	0.0
33902090229000009030764097	TOŻSAMOŚĆ DLA KONTA 33902090229000009030764097	3661363.2	1829447.6	1831915.6	2158	0.0	0.0
ZBIGNIEW WŁODARCZYK WS.SADOWIEC WIEŚ 17 98-355 SADOWIEC POL	ZBIGNIEW WŁODARCZYK WS.SADOWIEC WIEŚ 17 98-355 SADOWIEC POL	872309.4	872309.4	0.0	109	0.0	872309.4

Fig. 1. Screen for selecting the path start node. Key elements are highlighted in the image to narrow down the search area.

In this paper, we developed a set of new algorithms and mechanisms to enable intelligent mapping of the cause-and-effect sequence of a crime. The data used in this work came from real crimes (anonymised data) and from algorithms generating synthetic financial cases.

As a result, the developed solution enabled an understanding of the logic of the individual steps of the financial flows.

In particular, the mechanisms developed search the network of financial flows and assess what may have happened, i.e. in what quantity and to what identities the funds may have gone.

We provided the results and examples basing on the real use-cases of financial cyber crime, namely online shopping and financial pyramid.

1.3 Structure of the Paper

The remainder of this paper is structured as follows. In Sect. 2 we provide the overview of the related work.

In Sect. 3 we present in detail our own original proposition of the new method for calculating the subsequent steps of financial crimes. We present the method for selecting the starting point of the analyzed graph with financial transactions, and then the method to analyze selected node.

In Sect. 4 we discuss the real data used in the study (financial crime datasets). Section 5 presents real use-cases of cyber financial crimes, namely financial pyramid and online shopping fraud. We show how our proposed algorithm can help in large graph analysis. Conclusions are given thereafter.

2 Related Work

Detecting and understanding financial crime has become an increasingly relevant topic in the field of forensics and data-driven financial analysis. Numerous approaches have been proposed to detect various types of financial fraud, ranging from purely symbolic approaches (e.g., rule-based systems) to machine learning and graph-based models.

The foundation for modern fraud detection using statistical and data mining techniques has been laid by Bolton et al. in [2]. In their work they focused on static indicators of financial fraud. Similarly, in [9] focused on data mining techniques to address the problem of the finance fraud detection. However, the temporal or sequential nature of financial aspects was not extensively modeled at that time.

The analysis of the literature shows that further research [1] has focused on the role of transaction networks. Often the graph-based methods are used where accounts are modeled as nodes and transfers as edges. Such approaches are still particularly useful for detecting anomalies or communities that exhibit fraudulent behavior. Recent research [3,8] seeks to adopt the latest advancements in artificial intelligence and machine learning.

From the graph structure, various techniques leveraging graph theory are often extrapolated. Such an approach was explored in [5], where the authors highlighted that several features of network flows, such as the constancy of flow across a network, have proven particularly useful in this field of finance.

While many researchers have considered money laundering, fewer works have focused on modeling financial pyramids or online purchase fraud in detail [10]. In order to approach this issue, the authors of [7] used dedicated training procedure to achieve better detection of fraudulent financial behaviors.

However, still most of the existing methods aim at classification or anomaly scoring at the transaction level [4,6], without explicitly reconstructing the likely next steps of the financial crime. Furthermore, the evaluation is often performed using standard benchmark datasets (e.g., PaySim), which may not reflect the characteristics of specific real-world fraud scenarios.

In contrast to existing approaches, our method focuses on reconstructing the sequential actions taken by fraudsters. We begin with known evidence (such as an initial account, date, or transaction) and then pivot through various scenarios to mimic the behavior of human experts in real crime investigations. This perspective complements prior work by focusing on the interpretability and progression of fraudulent activity, rather than solely its detection.

3 Data Used in the Study

In this work we used 10 datasets, representing different types of financial crime that leave traces in financial flows, particularly in bank transfers.

The data was compiled in collaboration with analysts, who provided historical, anonymised data on the one hand and provided valuable guidance in the creation of additional synthetic data to enrich the test scenarios on the other. The Table 1 shows the general characteristics of the data sets used. It includes a description of crime scenarios and the volume of data.

Table 1. General characteristics of the datasets used and types of crimes analyzed.

No.	Code/symbol	Type of crime	Number of transactions
1	WP	Withdrawal of funds from the company	1'229'221
2	WH	Gambling	1'477'094
3	NS	Turnover of illegal funds	1'088'173
4	OB	Fraud in the construction industry	1'106'777
5	PP	Money laundering	1'107'319
6	KV	VAT carousel	1'068'892
7	ZO	Money extortion	1'083'094
8	PF	Financial pyramid	1'061'118
9	KK	Credit card fraud	1'066'293
10	FF	Fraud related to false invoices	1'353'090

The sizes of the datasets in the table above range from 1 to 1.5 million transactions. All datasets were enriched with so-called on-board transactions in order to generally balance the number of transactions to over 1 million. Such transactions are not related to crime and represent typical financial transactions of individuals (e.g. systematic credits, tax payments, card purchases, etc.).

However, an example of the volume of information in such a dataset is provided by the identity relationship diagram shown in the Fig. 2. This number of translations makes it significantly more difficult to place vertices on the plane and generally requires several minutes of graphics card operation.

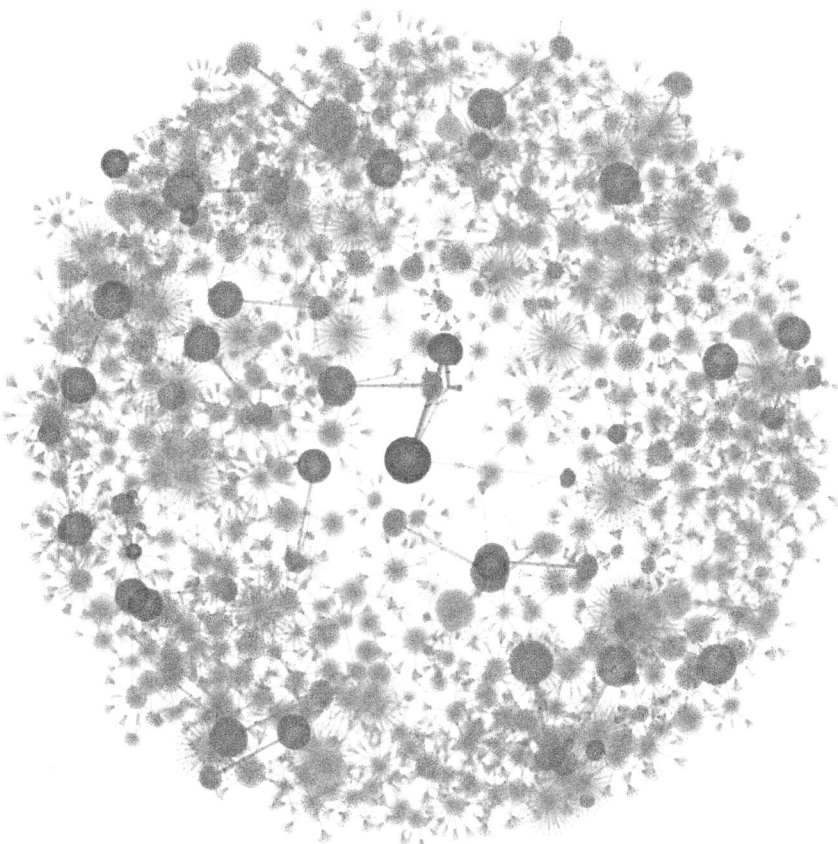

Fig. 2. Relationship graph between identities generated from over one million financial transactions.

4 Proposition of the New Method for Calculating the Subsequent Steps of Financial Crimes

The next-step analysis algorithm for financial flows is based on iteratively traversing a graph of financial flows in which the vertices represent accounts or entities and the edges represent financial transfers.

Key elements of the algorithm include selecting a starting point, iteratively traversing paths, analysing nodes and edges, identifying anomalies (within a node) and (most importantly) proposing the next jams (nodes) that should be checked.

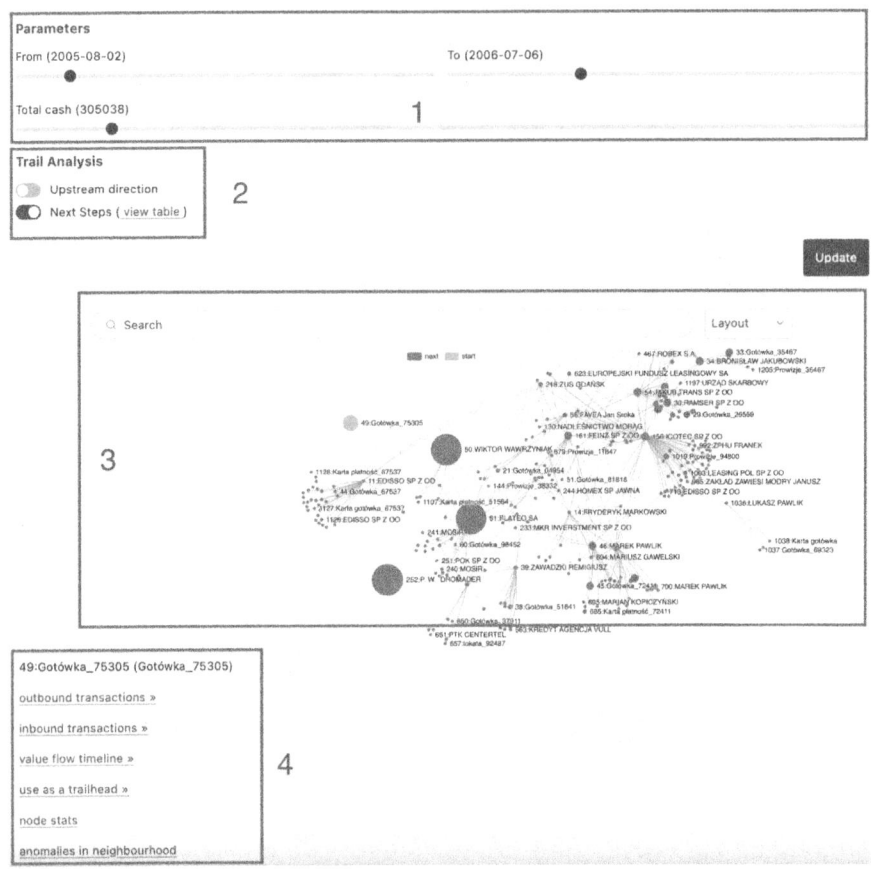

Fig. 3. Screen for analysing the next steps (nodes) in the path.

4.1 Selection of Starting Point in Graph

The first step is to select a starting point, i.e. a node (identity) in the graph.

To this end, a dedicated screen has been developed to support the selection of a starting point in the financial flow analysis. It allows the user to identify a starting node based on defined indicators and criteria.

This is a key stage of the analysis that significantly affects the efficiency and relevance of the results. The user selects a vertex in the network (e.g. a bank account or entity) as the starting point for the analysis. Selection can be based on known suspicious accounts or transactions, nodes with the highest financial flow, or nodes showing unusual characteristics (e.g. a high number of related edges). An overview of the user screen is shown in the Fig. 1.

Based on good practice in combating financial crime, key statistics describing the behavioural profile of individual nodes (i.e. identities) in the financial flow network were defined.

These features make it possible to quantitatively describe certain node behaviours and support flow analysis in the context of identifying suspicious activity. Key features include:

- The sum of all funds passing through the node, both incoming and outgoing. Indication of the overall scale of the node's financial activity.
- Total incoming payments per node.
- Total funds paid from the node.
- Total number of transactions associated with the node.
- Analysis of flows taking into account the way in which transactions are carried out (card transactions. cash or transfers). This helps to indicate the node's preference for payment instruments.
- Analysis of funds related to tax operations (in particular the amount of tax refunds in the context of extortion).
- Statistics on node activity (number of transactions and flows) over the selected period (regularity of activity indicator).
- Classification of the node based on its function in the network into accumulating account (accepts funds but sends them within a limited scope), introducing account (introduces funds into the system, e.g., in the form of cash), intermediary account (receives funds and transfers them further in a short period of time).
- Links to other accounts counted as variety of accounts: number of unique accounts with which the node had transactions, number of source accounts (accounts indicating the sources of income of the given node), number of target accounts (accounts to which funds were transferred)
- Sudden increases in node activity over a short period of time. It can indicate potentially suspicious activity, such as 'cleaning up' an account before closing it or executing larger financial schemes.

4.2 Analysis of the Selected Node

In the next step of the algorithm, once the starting point has been selected, we proceed to the analyse of the surroundings of the node in question.

This step allows for a detailed examination of where money of a certain total value may have been transferred, as well as for the identification of potential anomalies and a detailed analysis of the transactions.

The most important element of this stage is to suggest to the user the next steps, i.e. the nodes to jump to with the analysis. A general overview of is shown in the Fig. 3.

The key elements are:

1. analysis parameters (allow narrowing down the time and total value of the amount analysed).
2. launch of an algorithm proposing the next steps (in the desired direction from or to the selected node)
3. graph indicating the beginning of the path (yellow vertex) and the likely next steps (indicated as node size)
4. menu for detailed analysis

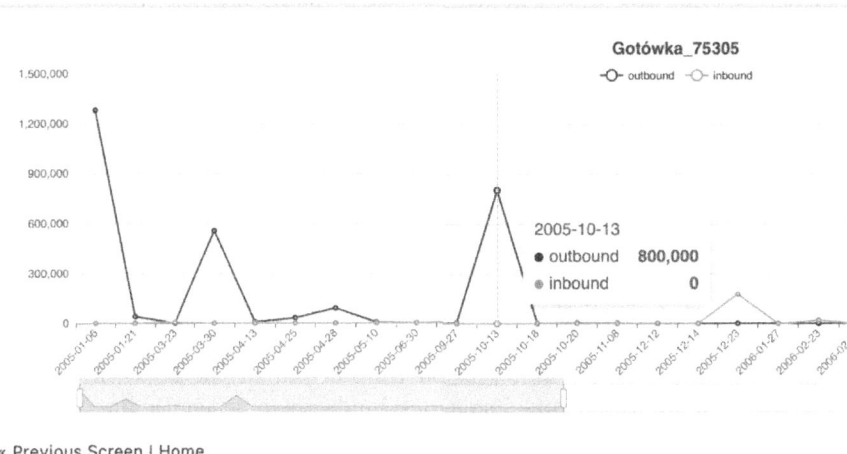

Fig. 4. Flow of incoming and outgoing transactions on the timeline (the Polish word 'gotówka' means cash).

The graph is intended to play a supporting role in analytics. It allows the perspective to be broadened by reviewing all neighbouring nodes (immediate and possibly further away) connected to a given node by edges representing transactions. It is also a tool for identifying the directions of flows: the accounts to which funds were transferred and the accounts from which they were received.

In contrast, the next step proposal algorithm is designed to identify those nodes that will be relevant from the point of view of flows. Through the use of the maximum flow mechanism, the algorithm can potentially identify aggregations of transfers that were previously broken down into multiple intermediary accounts.

The panel marked 4 (detailed analysis menu) allows to switch from a graph view to a detailed transaction table, or to a time chart of outgoing and incoming transfers Fig. 4.

In addition, an anomaly detection mechanism was built based on the OSVM algorithm and Isolation Forest. It allows analysis of the behavioural profiles (based on the aforementioned statistics) of the nearest neighbourhood of the node under analysis. It further feeds the analysis toolkit to identify potential outliers (e.g. an increase in the number of transactions or values over a short period of time, unusual recipients or senders of funds, etc.).

5 Detailed Algorithm Presentation, Experiments and Results

In this section we focus on selected financial crimes that leave traces in financial flows chosen out of the 10 datasets presented above.

We chosen Internet related cyber crimes, namely financial pyramid and online shopping fraud. Those two crimes recently became more common due to the ease of targeting potential victims using social media and Internet based services.

5.1 Results for the Financial Pyramid Crime (PF Dataset)

The data set labelled as PF refers to a financial pyramid scheme. In the data set analysed, there are organisers who set up a so-called financial pyramid scheme and investors who, encouraged by the organisers, deposit certain amounts into their accounts.

In order to keep investors interested and to get them to continue depositing, the organisers pay out part of their funds with a certain probability or at certain intervals. Such a mechanism is designed to inspire trust and encourage investors to increase their deposits, which in turn fuels the functioning of the entire financial pyramid.

A visualisation of the entire network of financial flows is shown in Fig. 5.

A node in a financial flow network that is an organiser of a financial pyramid is characterised by a number of features that distinguish it from other nodes. One of the key features is high centrality. The organiser is close to many other nodes in the network.

Another characteristic is the unusual asymmetry of financial flows. The organiser receives significantly more money than it spends, indicating an accumulation of capital from new participants in the pyramid.

In addition, organisers of the financial pyramid often have a large number of connections to other nodes, which means a high node degree. The organiser usually maintains direct links to multiple accounts of participants depositing funds into the system.

Our attention was paid to the key elements that characterise the nodes of the financial pyramid organisers when selecting the anchor point. Particular attention was focused on vertices with relatively high inflows, which at the same time showed a significant disparity between inflows and outflows, as can be seen in the first two columns of the data.

In addition, a diversity indicator was included, which describes the high diversity of links, both incoming and outgoing. Diversity was assessed in terms of the number of unique edges, indicating nodes connected to many different entities.

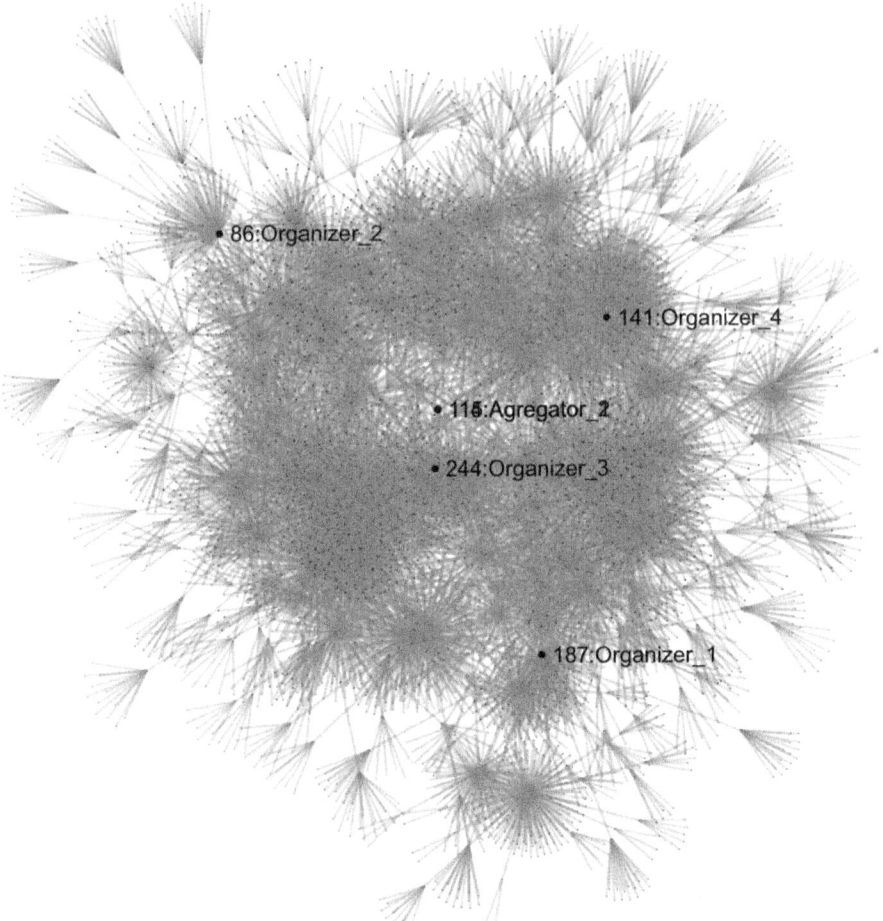

Fig. 5. A visualization of the entire network of financial flows in the pyramid scheme. Red nodes indicate the organizers and aggregators. (Color figure online)

Fig. 6. The nodes representing the organizesrs of the financial pyramid crime.

For the identified vertices selected as starting points, we select the first one in the list and analyse the downward stream of financial flows to identify the directions, to which the funds accumulated by vertex No. 135 may have been transferred.

As shown in the Fig. 7 a significant proportion of the flows lead to vertex No. 91.

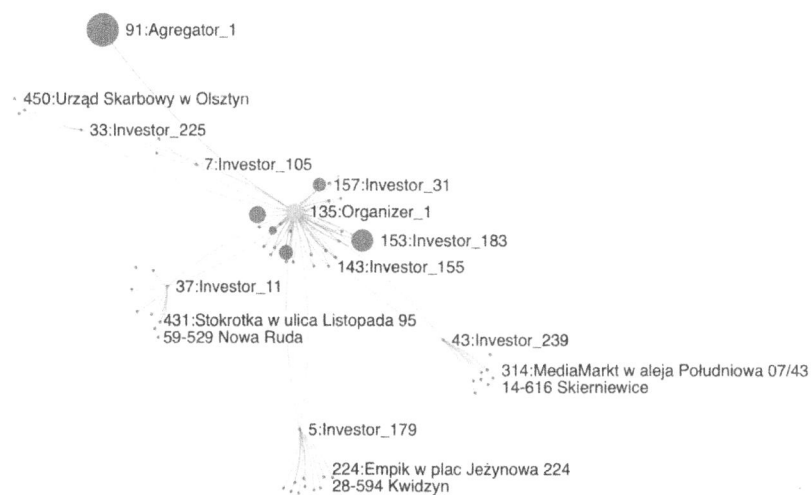

Fig. 7. Cash flow path grouping the payments from the source (investors), through the pyramid organizer, and down to the aggregator node.

The vertex No. 91 turns out to be the terminal end vertex, which means that the flow path ends at this point. However, in order to better understand the role of this node, we conduct an financial upstream analysis, examining the sources of funds that have flowed into this account.

The upstream analysis run (Fig. 8) identifies potential other financial pyramid organisers who may have paid funds into vertex No. 91.

The algorithm indicates significant flows from other nodes, which may confirm that this vertex plays a central role in the pyramid structure, receiving funds from different organisers.

Final Analysis of Financial Pyramid. To summarise the scenario, the algorithm was successful in identifying the entire financial funds flow pattern, identifying key vertices and intermediary layers.

In the second step, besides 91 nodes, several investors were also highlighted. This is because they also received a partial return of the funds invested in the pyramid. However, if they are considered as false detections, in relation to the total number of nodes, the FPR rate still remains low.

Therefore, from the point of view of the effectiveness of detecting the next step, the error values are shown in Table 2:

5.2 Results for the On-Line Shopping Fraud (ZO Dataset)

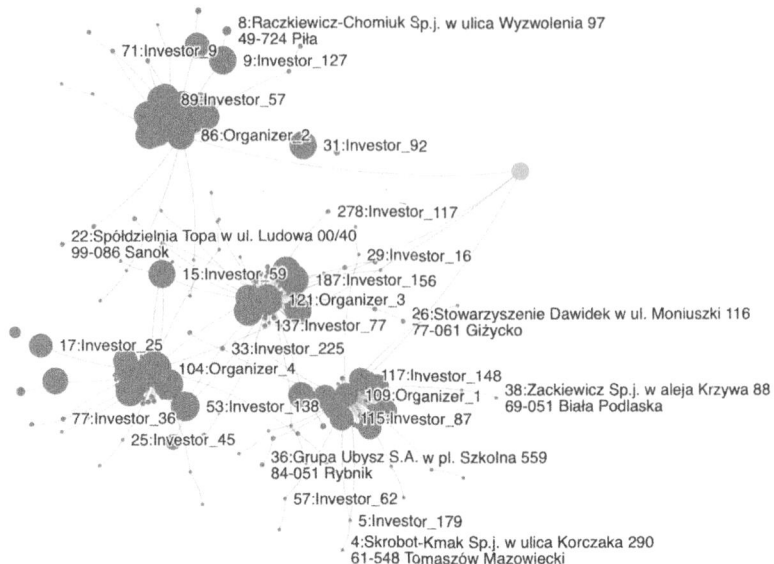

Fig. 8. The upstream analysis run identifying vertex No. 91 (yellow node). (Color figure online)

The data set marked ZO relates to a scheme of extortion in on-line shopping. In the case under review, we are dealing with a typical fraud in which the seller offers goods at attractive prices on shopping platforms or on-line shops, which attracts many customers. Customers make payments for the ordered goods but never receive them.

Table 2. Results for financial pyramid crime.

Step detection efficiency	FP (false positives)	FN (false negatives)
100%	<1%	0%

The funds are credited to the seller's account. The seller, instead of fulfilling orders, transfers the proceeds further to make them more difficult to detect. Money is channelled through different layers of financial nodes. Ultimately, the funds are paid out as cash, effectively breaking the trail of the transaction and hiding its ultimate origin.

Path. The pathway assumes a transition from the node, in which money is brought out as cash. Going up the stream of financial flows, we reach the intermediary layer, then the seller, and finally the customers who have been defrauded.

Fig. 9. Detection of nodes that withdrew money as cash.

Course of Operation of the Algorithm. As intended, we start the analysis by identifying the vertices that accumulate funds. To do this, we apply filters to the Inflow column, setting the probability threshold above 60%.

In addition, we sort the data by volume of inflows to focus on the vertices, through which the largest amounts flow. In the Fig. 10, you can see that a vertex named "'Bankomat" has been identified (the names were deliberately changed during the preparation of the data set to make it easier to present).

The launch of the path tracking algorithm distinctly identifies the scheme. In the first step, we see that all funds originate from the vertex No. 151. Vertex No. 151 obtains funds from a certain group of nodes, which presumably form an intermediary layer (funds are accumulated by the vertex No. 151). This layer is located between vertex No. 1, labelled "Tammy Greer", and "Nancy Martin" (node No. 151).

Vertex No.1 acquires funds from a large group of people who are probably customers paying money in exchange for purchased goods.

Summary of the Crime. To summarise the scenario, the algorithm successfully identified the entire scheme and path of the flow of funds, identifying the key vertices and intermediary layers involved in the process.

From the point of view of the effectiveness of detecting the next step, the results are shown in the Table 3.

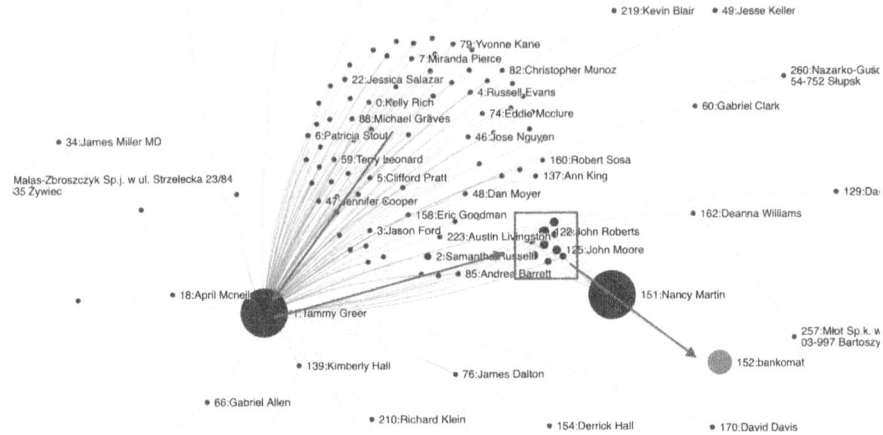

Fig. 10. Cash flow path from the source through the distribution network down to ATM withdrawal.

Table 3. Results for financial pyramid crime.

Step detection efficiency	FP (false positives)	FN (false negatives)
100%	0%	0%

6 Conclusions

In this paper, the mechanism to support the analysis of financial flow paths (in particular, the algorithm suggests which vertex to move to when tracking financial flows) has been developed and proposed.

The proposed approach includes original solutions to navigate the flow graph to analyse a variety of financial and economic crime scenarios. An element of the developed solution is a mechanism for selecting the starting path or starting vertex. For this purpose, an original method was proposed, suggesting from which vertex it is worth starting the analysis.

This method is flexible, allowing the analyst to configure the search criteria, allowing the algorithm to be tailored to the specific needs of the analysis.

During the development of the algorithm, a method was also developed to prompt subsequent paths. It is based on the analysis of maximum flows in financial graphs. Thanks to this solution, it is possible to identify long paths and dependencies between nodes, which allows us to understand the complex patterns of criminal activity.

Ten crime scenarios were analyzed by our method, and in this paper we selected and presented the flow and results for cyber crimes related financial pyramid and online shopping fraud use cases.

We presented examples on how the algorithm works, showing the key elements of the algorithm, the graphs, the results, and the output for end-users. The example shows that the algorithm can effectively identify the vertices responsible for splitting transactions into smaller amounts and their subsequent consolidation into a single vertex.

In summary, the algorithm has shown high efficiency in identifying relevant nodes and paths in financial flow graphs, which allows for effective recognition of criminal schemes.

It is worth noting that the developed solution is both flexible and precise, thus supporting analysts in even the most demanding tasks of analysing complex financial flow graphs with millions of transactions.

Acknowledgement. This publication is partially funded by the National Center for Research and Development within FENG program, number of application for funding: FENG.01.01-IP.02-0777/23.

We would also like to thank the anonymous experts in financial crime for providing the datasets and for their feedback and support.

References

1. Akoglu, L., Tong, H., Koutra, D.: Graph-based anomaly detection and description: a survey (2014). https://arxiv.org/abs/1404.4679
2. Bolton, R., Hand, D.: Statistical fraud detection: a review. Stat. Sci. **17** (2002). https://doi.org/10.1214/ss/1042727940
3. Chakraborty, S., Sharov, S.: Chapter 3 - graph based approach on financial fraudulent detection and prediction. In: Raj, P., Dutta, P.K., Chong, P.H.J., Song, H.H., Zaitsev, D.A. (eds.) Applied Graph Data Science, pp. 25–37. Morgan Kaufmann (2025). https://doi.org/10.1016/B978-0-443-29654-3.00019-3, https://www.sciencedirect.com/science/article/pii/B9780443296543000193
4. Desai, A., Kosse, A., Sharples, J.: Finding a needle in a haystack: a machine learning framework for anomaly detection in payment systems. J. Finance Data Sci., 100163 (2025). https://doi.org/10.1016/j.jfds.2025.100163, https://www.sciencedirect.com/science/article/pii/S2405918825000157
5. Eboli, M.: Financial Applications of Flow Network Theory, pp. 21–29 (2013). https://doi.org/10.1007/978-3-642-32903-6_3
6. Herreros-Martínez, A., Magdalena-Benedicto, R., Vila-Francés, J., Serrano-López, A.J., Pérez-Díaz, S.: Applied machine learning to anomaly detection in enterprise purchase processes (2024). https://arxiv.org/abs/2405.14754
7. Jullum, M., Løland, A., Huseby, R., Ånonsen, G., Lorentzen, J.: Detecting money laundering transactions with machine learning. J. Money Laundering Control ahead-of-print (2020). https://doi.org/10.1108/JMLC-07-2019-0055
8. Motie, S., Raahemi, B.: Financial fraud detection using graph neural networks: a systematic review. Expert Syst. Appl. **240**, 122156 (2024). https://doi.org/10.1016/j.eswa.2023.122156, https://www.sciencedirect.com/science/article/pii/S0957417423026581
9. Ngai, E., Hu, Y., Wong, Y., Chen, Y., Sun, X.: The application of data mining techniques in financial fraud detection: a classification framework and an academic review of literature. Decis. Support Syst. **50**(3), 559–569 (2011). https://doi.org/https://doi.org/10.1016/j.dss.2010.08.006, https://www.sciencedirect.com/science/article/pii/S0167923610001302, on quantitative methods for detection of financial fraud

10. Ślusarek, N.: The fraudulent phenomenon of the financial pyramids in the financial industry. Finanse i Prawo Finansowe, 87–107 (2022). https://doi.org/10.18778/2391-6478.S2.2022.06

From Sign-Up to Multi-million Revenues: A Deep Dive Into Vendors on Darknet Marketplaces

Julia Kramer[✉] [ID], Anne Streicher [ID], and Marcus Niemietz [ID]

Clavis - Institut für Informationssicherheit, University of Applied Sciences
Niederrhein, Krefeld, Germany
clavis@hs-niederrhein.de
https://www.hs-niederrhein.de/clavis/

Abstract. Darknet marketplaces promote cybercrime as these platforms enable and facilitate the trade of illegal goods and services as well as malware, exploits and stolen data through a high degree of anonymity. This is increasingly becoming a problem as it poses major challenges to law enforcement efforts and maintaining cyber security. The combination of user anonymity and the use of cryptocurrencies enables cybercriminals to carry out illegal transactions efficiently and with a low risk of detection. As a result, a dynamic ecosystem has emerged that benefits both buyers and vendors, while systematic insights into vendor behavior and the correlated market structures remain scarce. This paper analyzes the process of becoming a vendor, focusing on its complexity, the insights into sales conditions as well as their success measured in turnover, with the aim of gaining a better understanding and counteracting illicit online activities. We compare entry requirements for buyers and vendors, highlighting common features such as security measures, vendor-specific rules and the revenue model shedding light on commission structures within darknet marketplaces. Our findings also show that vendors across all product categories are able to generate multi-million dollar revenues across the marketplaces they operate as well as operated on.

Keywords: Darknet Marketplaces · Vendor · Digital Goods

1 Introduction

Darknet Market Places (DNMs) have become a persistent element of the digital underground economy, offering a broad range of illegal goods and services through anonymized platforms. Vendors use them to bypass geographic boundaries, customs regulations, and legal oversight, often selling high-risk commodities with global reach. At the same time, the highly competitive environment of these markets incentivizes vendors to refine their offerings, logistics, and reputation management strategies [15]. In response to law enforcement operations, such as the takedowns of Hydra in 2022 and Genesis Market in 2023 [1, 12], new marketplaces continue to emerge, often with enhanced security features and stricter internal regulations. While various aspects of vendor behavior, such as career

© The Author(s), under exclusive license to Springer Nature Switzerland AG 2025
B. Coppens et al. (Eds.): ARES 2025 Workshops, LNCS 15996, pp. 221–238, 2025.
https://doi.org/10.1007/978-3-032-00635-6_13

trajectories and reputation systems, have been studied in detail [9,25], other foundational elements of vendor activity remain underexplored. In particular, the initial steps vendors must take to begin operating on DNMs, the rules they must comply with, and the transparency of their marketplace presence have not yet been systematically examined across multiple platforms. Furthermore, while previous work has estimated vendor profitability based on listings and feedback, a fact-based, cross-market quantification of vendor revenue is still missing. To address these gaps, we pose the following research questions:

RQ1 *What entry requirements must be met to become a vendor on currently active darknet marketplaces (DNMs), and how do they differ in comparison to buyers?*

RQ2 *What types of vendor-related information can be extracted from DNMs?*

RQ3 *Which vendors have generated the highest cumulative revenue across all DNMs in which they have ever been active?*

Answering these questions is non-trivial due to the volatile and adversarial nature of DNMs. Platforms are often protected by anti-scraping technologies, access restrictions, and deliberate obfuscation mechanisms [22,23]. Despite these challenges, we make the following contributions:

- We conduct a cross-market analysis of vendor onboarding processes, documenting registration mechanisms, vendor fees and internal rulebooks from active DNMs (Sect. 4).
- We systematically identify and categorize extractable vendor-related data, including metadata from product listings, feedback systems, public vendor profiles and turnover mechanisms (Sect. 5).
- We introduce a novel, data-grounded method for calculating cross-market vendor revenue. Leveraging a unique data feature found on the Nexus marketplace, we reconstruct vendor earnings across platforms—including defunct ones—based on current and historic sales data (Sect. 6).

These findings offer a deeper empirical understanding of how vendors operate across DNMs and provide valuable insights for researchers and law enforcement agencies (LEAs) aiming to monitor or disrupt illicit online trade.

Artifact Availability. In line with responsible disclosure practices, we do not reveal onion URLs or any information that could facilitate access to illegal content. The set of snapshots is provided to the reviewers as supplementary material. This is due to ethical considerations because these pages reveal the usernames of both - buyers and sellers. All steps of data collection were performed without active market participation or transactions.

2 Methodology

Selection of Darknet Marketplaces. We conducted a multi-platform analysis of all active English-speaking DNMs. The website *Darknet Prime* provides detailed information about DNMs that are available and active, or offline and defunct. In our study, we excluded marketplaces that only offer physical products such as drugs. In our research we aim to shed a light on the variety of possible cybercrime that can both be conducted and sold via DNMs. At the time we did research on *Darknet Prime*, 16 anonymous markets were accessible via the TOR network. As a second criteria we focused on DNMs that contribute mainly to cybercrime by selling the most digital goods and offer therefore a platform for the main vendors in that field. Therefore, we observed only those DNMs that offer more than 500 digital goods to focus on only relevant marketplaces (measured on November 01, 2024). In descending order of the amount of digital goods those eight DNMs are included in our study: Nexus (Nx) (19,207), Ares (Ar) (7,589), DarkDock (DD) (5,112), Abacus (Ab) (4,263), Dark Matter (DM) (2,528), MGM Grand (MGM) (2,300), TorZon (TZ) (1,139), and WeTheNorth (WTN) (518) (Fig. 1).

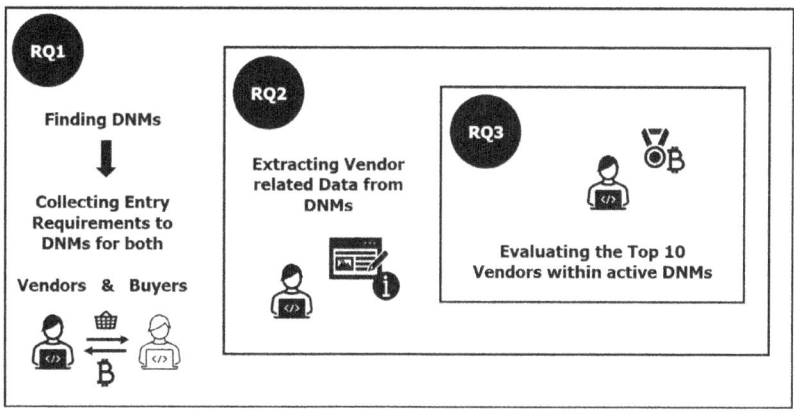

Fig. 1. Layered representation of the research methodology.

Study Time Frame and Research Approach. We first aggregated relevant papers in the context of sellers and general dynamics of DNMs and embedded them accordingly in the context of our research in Sect. 3. Afterwards we observed the selected DNMs from November 2024 to January 2025 to answer our research questions. The selection of this time frame was based on the availability of essential research resources, including market availability and data sets, as well as the alignment with key collaborations, ensuring an optimal and focused research process. To gain a comprehensive and firsthand understanding of how to become a vendor, we manually collected all relevant information. We systematically documented the entire vendor onboarding process and additionally collected platform metadata, vendor profiles, and regulatory guidelines. Other works, such as those by Wang et al., demonstrate that relevant information can also be automatically extracted [26]. We also encountered data outside the scope of our research questions, such as shipping routes and linguistic patterns in marketplace texts. While excluded from our analysis, these offered insights into vendors' and operators' potential geographic or linguistic backgrounds. In order to prove our results provided in Sects. 4, 5, 6 did snapshots from the websites in an semi-automated process. All amounts are expressed in US dollars ($).

3 Related Work

Table 1. This table presents three categories relevant to answering our research questions. Publications marked with the symbol ⊕ served as the foundation for further analysis and form the basis of our contributions.

Authors	Reference	Description
Mechanisms of DNMs		
Gomez et al.	ISSP 2023 [14]	Typization of market closures and early warning signals.
Ursani et al.	EuroS&PW 2021 [23]	Detecting anomalies in DNMs, to understand illegal activities.
Turk et al.	EuroS&PW 2020 [22]	Methods to collect data from sites with anti-scraping defenses.
Bradley et al.	EuroS&PW 2019 [5]	Investigates how cybercriminals can be disrupted in DNMs.
Lusthaus	EuroS&PW 2019 [18]	Outlines cybercrime layers.
Van Wegberg et al.	Usenix 2018 [24]	Analyzing the commoditization and B2B-area in cybercrime.
Wang et al.	EICC 2024 [28]	Analysis of Security Mechanisms of Dark Web Markets.
⊕ Soska and Christin	Usenix 2015 [20]	Tracks 16 DNMs over two years.
⊕ Christin	WWW 2013 [7]	Analysis of Silk Road (revenue, products, community growth).
Vendor Appearance		
Cuevas and Christin	Usenix 2024 [9]	Correlation between reputation signals and vendor success.
Labrador et al.	EuroS&PW 2022 [17]	6 DNMs (shipping routes, sales by location, vendor behavior).
⊕ Ouellet et al.	2022 [19]	Vendor movement between different DNMs.
⊕ Booij et al.	EuroS&PW 2021 [3]	Vendor careers (average duration of 4 months and low sales).
Tai et al.	SIGKDD 2019 [21]	Connections between disparate vendor accounts on DNMs.
Wang et al.	ASIACCS 2018 [25]	Linking multiple vendor accounts through photo analytics.
Yuan et al.	Usenix 2018 [31]	Analyzing criminal communication patterns.

Table 1 summarizes core research areas on the Darknet, including DNM mechanisms, vendor behaviour, and revenue analysis. These topics have been widely studied in academic literature, highlighting their relevance. Our work extends this research by incorporating recent developments to provide a current, ecosystem-level perspective on vendor dynamics across DNMs.

Mechanisms of DNMs. Silk Road, one of the first major DNMs, launched in 2011 [11,20]. Christin's foundational study analyzed its product range, sales volumes, and vendor behavior [7]. Building on this, Soska and Christin tracked 16 marketplaces over two years, revealing that vendors often migrate between platforms to remain resilient after takedowns [20]. They found that around 70% of listings were drug-related, a result supported by Van Wegberg et al. (81%) and Labrador et al., who also examined geographic patterns [6,17,24]. According to Europol, the average lifespan of a DNM is just over eight months [11]. Gomez et al. identified shutdown causes including law enforcement interventions, voluntary closures, and exit scams [5,14]. Wang et al. recently categorized DNM protections into web security (e.g., anti-phishing) and account security (e.g., multi-factor authentication) [28]. Ursani et al. used anomaly detection to assess the impact of DDoS attacks on DNM activity [23]. To prevent data collection, DNMs implement CAPTCHAs and IP blocking [13], requiring researchers to adapt with manual or semi-automated tools [22]. Nonetheless, Labrador and Pastrana were able to analyze DNM trends using a custom crawler [17].

Payment Mechanisms. DNMs employ escrow services to enable transactions in low-trust environments. Here, a third party—typically the marketplace—holds the payment until order completion, reducing fraud risk. However, markets have exploited this mechanism via "exit scams", such as Wall Street Market in 2018, which vanished with over $11 million in Bitcoin [8,27]. To counteract this, many DNMs use multisignature (2/3 multisig) transactions, requiring two of three parties (buyer, vendor, market admin) to release funds [27]. This prevents unilateral fund access and enhances trust [16]. Some markets offer a "finalize early" (FE) option, where funds go directly to the vendor. While limited to trusted vendors to expedite transactions, this exposes buyers to fraud if sellers fail to deliver [27].

Vendor Appearance. Vendor reputation is a key factor shaping buyer trust and vendor success in DNMs [9,13]. In-market feedback scores play a more significant role than external signals like forum activity, gradually filtering out low-quality vendors [9]. High-reputation vendors achieve more sales, though revenue generation early on is a stronger predictor of long-term success. Vendors often use marketplace-specific jargon, e.g., fruit-based terms for drugs [31], to appeal to users. Former vendor Sam Bent described building trust by posting over 5,000 supportive comments on Dread, reinforcing the value of community engagement [2]. To preserve identity across platforms, some vendors reuse pseudonyms [3], although PGP key reuse is more secure [2]. Yannikos et al. showed how vendors on White House Market submitted PGP keys—many created years prior—revealing preferred providers like ProtonMail and Gmail [30]. Booij et al. modeled 2,925 vendor careers from 90 DNMs, showing that 80% last only four months with minimal revenue, while a top 2% span multiple markets and generate 31% of total revenue [3]. Further, Ouellet et al. found vendor migration is driven by economic and social incentives [19], while Tai et al. showed that vendors may maintain up to 11 accounts [21]. Wang et al. demonstrated vendor deanonymization via photo fingerprinting, revealing Sybil accounts across markets [25].

4 Entry Requirements for Buyers and Sellers on DNMs

4.1 Login and Registration Process

Most DNMs require users to log in before viewing products. DarkDock and Dark Matter do not follow this rule. The registration process typically mirrors that of clear web sites. A username, a password and an action to solve a CAPTCHA is always required. Unlike on the clear web, no email address is required here [22]. Additional security steps often include setting a six-digit PIN or a unique recovery phrase. After signing up, users receive a mnemonic to recover their account if needed. These procedures vary across markets, as summarized in Table 2. CAPTCHA complexity and frequency also differ. Yannikos and Heeger (2024) categorized various types used on DNMs such as Ab, Ar, MGM, TZ, and WTN, offering a detailed comparison [29]. In a 2022 study, Yannikos et al. noted that CAPTCHAs serve to hinder automated data collection [30]. The CAPTCHAs observed in our study lacked accessibility, often demanding advanced visual, motor, or cognitive skills (see Fig. 2).

Fig. 2. The figure shows a censored example of a login CAPTCHA from the darknet marketplace WeTheNorth. The left side displays the original colored CAPTCHA, while the right side shows an adjusted version with enhanced contrast and saturation for better visibility.

In summary, security measures and registration requirements vary between DNMs. While Wang et al. provide a broad overview of all implemented mechanisms [28], our focus was on the minimum needed for registration and login. Despite differences in setup, the login process itself is consistent across marketplaces.

Vendor Registration. To become a vendor, users must meet specific requirements, which vary across marketplaces. Some platforms, like Abacus and Dark Matter, require an account with no prior purchase history. Dark Matter, in particular, states that this requirement is in place for security reasons. A vendor registration fee is mandatory on all examined DNMs and is deducted from the user's balance. This fee is non-refundable on most platforms (e.g. Abacus, TorZon, WeTheNorth) and serves as a financial safeguard for customer compensation. Dark Matter treats the fee as a refundable bond, returned only after sales activities end or a high vendor level is reached. Most marketplaces assign vendors a ranking level and require submission of a public PGP key for encrypted

Table 2. The table presents the requirements and security mechanisms of the registration and login processes for each marketplace.

Mechanisms	Ab	Ar	DD	DM	MGM	Nx	TZ	WTN
Login								
Login Mask								
Username	✓	✓	✓	✓	✓	✓	✓	✓
Password	✓	✓	✓	✓	✓	✓	✓	✓
CAPTCHA	✓	✓	✓	✓	✓	✓	✓	✓
Entry Queue / Browser Check	✓	✗	✗	✓	✗	✓	✗	✗
DDOS Protection	✓	✗	✗	✓	✗	✓	✓	✗
Phishing Protection	✓	✗	✗	Optional	✗	✓	✓	✓
Registration								
Registration Mask								
Username	✓	✓	✓	✓	✓	✓	✓	✓
Password	✓	✓	✓	✓	✓	✓	✓	✓
Pin	✓	✗	✓	✓	✓	✓	✓	✓
CAPTCHA	✓	✓	✓	✓	✓	✓	✓	✓
Phrase	✓	✓	✗	✓	✗	✗	✓	✗
Mnemonic / Recovery Token	✓	✓	✓	✓	✓	✓	✓	✓

communication except WeTheNorth, where it is only recommended. Two-factor authentication is mandatory on several platforms, including Abacus, Ares, DarkDock, Nexus, and WeTheNorth. Only MGM Grand and TorZon require a motivation letter during registration, with TorZon demanding proof of activity on other markets. These measures are intended to prevent fraudulent vendors. In summary, nearly all darknet marketplace (DNM) examined require a PGP key, active 2FA, and payment of a vendor fee. Details are outlined in Table 3.

Table 3. The table outlines the registration requirements for vendors on selected DNMs, detailing the criteria needed to complete the registration process successfully.

DNM	PGP	2FA	Vendor fee	Option of free vendor registration
Ab	✓	✓	1,250$	✓ no requirements
Ar	✓	✓	1,250$	✓ min. 2 yrs. experiences, >500 sales, >95% positive feedback
DD	✓	✓	1,000$	✓ no further information
DM	✓	✗	346.43$	✓ >20 sales, >90% positive feedback
MGM	✓	✗	200$	✓ personalized (required support contact)
Nx	✓	✓	1,000$	✓ >250 sales
TZ	✓	✗	500$	✗
WTN	✗	✓	211.84$	✓ personalized (required support contact)

Free Vendor Waiver. Experienced vendors from other marketplaces may apply for a fee waiver on all examined DNMs, except DarkDock and TorZon. Requirements vary by platform but typically include proof of prior activity, often verified through consistent use of the same PGP key. Applicants must usually demonstrate a positive sales history via sales data, customer reviews, or both, as shown in Table 3. MGM Grand, WeTheNorth, and Abacus do not list specific criteria, though support contact is still required. In all cases, applications undergo a review and validation process.

4.2 Rules for Vendors

Vendors on all examined DNMs are subject to marketplace rules, which they automatically accept upon registration. These rules often include restrictions on certain products and prohibit behaviors such as sharing confidential or personal information. Violations can result in immediate and permanent bans. The most common regulations across platforms are summarized in Table 4.

Table 4. The table outlines the key rules that vendors must follow on the respective marketplaces, sorted in descending order based on the frequency of each rule's occurrence.

Rules	Ab	Ar	DD	DM	MGM	Nx	TZ	WTN
Always								
No child pornography	✓	✓	✓	✓	✓	✓	✓	✓
Most								
Respectful manner	✗	✓	✓	✗	✓	✓	✓	✗
FE only with permission or required status	✓	✗	✓	✓	✓	✗	✓	✗
No doxing	✓	✓	✗	✓	✓	✗	✓	✓
No scamming	✓	✓	✓	✓	✓	✓	✗	✓
No deals & contact outside the marketplace	✓	✓	✗	✗	✓	✓	✓	✓
No selling fakes / clean product presentation	✓	✓	✗	✗	✓	✓	✓	✓
No weapons	✓	✗	✗	✓	✗	✓	✓	✓
No sale of fentanyl, poisons, murder services	✓	✓	✗	✓	✓	✓	✗	✓ (except poisons)
Frequently								
No feedback manipulation	✗	✗	✗	✓	✓	✓	✓	✓
No prostitution	✓	✗	✗	✗	✗	✓	✓	✓
No threaten or insult anybody	✗	✓	✓	✗	✓	✓	✗	✗
Compliance of adding new products	✓	✓	✗	✗	✓	✗	✓	✗
Occasionally								
Only original & own product pictures	✗	✓	✗	✗	✗	✓	✓	✗
No sharing contact details (in private messages)	✗	✓	✗	✗	✗	✗	✓	✓
Treat particularly customers with respect	✗	✓	✗	✗	✓	✗	✓	✗
Use Escrow	✗	✓	✓	✗	✗	✓	✗	✗

A universal rule across all DNMs is the prohibition of child pornography. Other banned activities include scamming, doxing, selling counterfeit products, and certain goods such as fentanyl, poisons, or murder services. Beyond prohibitions, marketplaces also set behavioral expectations, such as respectful communication and proper product listing practices. Some platforms, like Ares, provide detailed sales etiquette guidelines, advising vendors to stay online daily, offer small bonuses to loyal customers, and maintain engagement throughout transactions.

4.3 Comparison of Entry Requirements

To evaluate entry requirements for buyers and vendors, we compared marketplace security measures and rules, assigning up to three points per category. The categories include the login process, registration process, vendor registration and its requirements, and DNM rules. Distinguishing between user groups is important: the first section covers login and registration, relevant to both buyers and sellers, while the second focuses exclusively on vendor-specific requirements.

Scores were assigned based on the number of checkmarks in Tables 2, 3, and 4. The first area covers login and registration, relevant to both buyers and sellers, while the second focuses on vendor-specific requirements. This distinction is crucial for comparing entry barriers by user group. Login and registration (Table 2) receive a full score (3) for 5âĂŞ6 checkmarks, 2 points for 3âĂŞ4 checkmarks, and 1 point for 2 or fewer.

The same approach was applied to Tables 3 and 4. This resulted in the following classification:

- Registration Requirements and Fee
  - PGP Key: 1 point
  - 2FA: 1 point
  - vendor fee: USD 1,500 - 1,001 (3 points), USD 1,000 - 501 (2 points), USD 500 - 0 (1 point)
- Rules for Vendors
  - 3 points: 16 - 12 rules applied
  - 2 points: 11 - 7 rules applied
  - 1 point: 6 - 0 rules applied

Based on the evaluation scale shown in Table 5, Abacus, Dark Matter, Nexus, and TorZon implement all login and registration measures listed in Table 2. A key difference is their use of CAPTCHAs for DDoS protection or anti-phishing, which increases the time and effort required to access the marketplace. As noted in Subsect. 4.1, these CAPTCHAs may pose accessibility challenges for some users, making the entry barrier higher than in other markets. In the vendor-specific section, Ares stands out due to its extensive rules, with Abacus closely following except in this area, and Nexus ranked third. Overall, Abacus and Ares lead, followed by Nexus. To explore potential correlations, a Pearson correlation coefficient (r) was calculated, where x represents buyer entry hurdles (first section subtotal) and y vendor entry hurdles (second section subtotal).

Table 5. Evaluation and analysis of the entry barriers for each DNM.

Category	Ab	Ar	DD	DM	MGM	Nx	TZ	WTN
Login Process	3	2	2	3	2	3	3	2
Registration Process	3	3	3	3	3	3	3	2
Vendor Registration								
PGP Key	1	1	1	1	1	1	1	0
2FA	1	1	1	0	0	1	0	1
Vendor Fee	3	3	2	1	1	2	1	1
Applied Rules for Vendors	2	3	1	2	3	2	3	2
Total (14)	13	13	10	10	10	12	11	8

The Pearson correlation coefficient r ranges from -1 to 1. A value of 1 indicates a perfect positive correlation, -1 indicates a perfect negative correlation, and 0 suggests no correlation. With a correlation coefficient of 0.204, the result indicates a weak positive correlation between hurdles for buyers (section one) and vendors (section two).

5 Extractable Vendor Related Data

5.1 Information Pool

From related work we know already that researchers have extracted data from DNMs for ten years. Turk et al. describe the current problems researchers face by the anti-scraping mechanisms the administrators implemented in their websites to improve the performance [22]. By doing so, researchers needed more effort to gain data out of DNMs. Nevertheless, we wanted to conclude the data that can possibly be exfiltrated from anonymous marketplaces that are active in 2024.

Homepage of the Markets Website. Here we find a bar to search for a product and a button for digital and physical products to navigate between those two main commodities easily in Abacus, DarkMatter and Nexus. Furthermore, there is the option to select subcategories of both commodities and to display top products as well as vendors. There is a direct link to the markets rules provided on Nexus and WeTheNorth. This is combined with filter options to select desired products. There is the possibility to filter ship from and ship to, the vendor, (again) the commodity, the price range, the accepted cryptocurrencies and multisig as well as FE options. Moreover, Abacus, DarkDock, Dark Matter and MGM Grand offer sorting according to the popularity of products.

Product Page and Vendor Profile. The product pages are similar to each other. Besides general information such as the price of a product, its name and the name of the vendor, the description, policies and reviews, the customer gets information about the minimum order quantity, how many products are in stock, which kind of payment the vendor accepts and which shipping methods he or she uses within MGM Grand and Nexus. WeTheNorth does not provide those information. Nevertheless, WeTheNorth, DarkDock, Dark Matter and MGM Grand show how many times the product got sold within the marketplace. However, Nexus and TorZon do not focus on sales figures of a single product. Instead both marketplaces give insights about how many sales a single vendor has (identificable by using the same PGP key [2, 30]) on each platform he or she has ever sold products. There it is also visible, on which other DNMs a vendor sold its items, how many he or she sold and which reviews the seller has on those marketplaces if available. In TorZon it says *"All feedback has been reviewed and approved by the moderator team."* which should increase the trustworthiness of the data they provide and is shown in Fig. 3.

Fig. 3. Example of a Nexus vendor profile displaying the vendor's activity history.

5.2 Revenue Framework

Our research on the DNMs has uncovered various revenue streams based on the information provided by the marketplaces. Additionally, some DNMs offer incentives and motivations to encourage the recruitment of new users, further enhancing their growth and user engagement.

Sales Commission. A sales commission on the revenue is typically paid by the buyer and vendors to the respective marketplace, which increases the turnover of the operators. We know that all DNMs charge a commission, except for Dark-Dock. DarkDock emphasizes in their FAQ section that, unlike other marketplaces, they do not charge any fees for buyers, but they do not mention the vendors in this context. In our investigation of the selected DNMs, only a few marketplaces like Ares and Dark Matter provided detailed information on whether a commission is charged and, if so, its amount. Ares' commission is 4%, although this percentage may be lower depending on the vendor level. Dark Matter operates in the same way. Here, the commission for vendor Level 1 is 6%. But often exact numbers are hidden somewhere on the website. For example on Nexus you can find in the FAQ section the question *"If an order is canceled, is there still a commission?"*. The answer is *"The market fee will be charged only if the buyer cancels the order himself, if the vendor cancels the order, the market fee will not be charged to the buyer."* Because of that we know there is a commission, but we were unable to determine its exact amount. Some information regarding existing commissions was found in relation to the affiliate program.

Affiliate Program. Through affiliate programs, DNMs like Abacus, Dark Matter, MGM Grand, and WeTheNorth incentivize users to attract new customers. Referrers earn a share of the marketplace's income for each completed order, typically by sharing a referral link or code during user registration. For example, Abacus offers 20% of the vendor's commission or 10% of the buyer's commission.

Dark Matter shares 25% of its total marketplace income earned through referred users, equating to up to 1.5% of total revenue if the full commission is considered profit. WeTheNorth shares 10%, while MGM Grand offers a 50% share of the commission paid by the referred user. Dark Matter also has a special deal for vendors, reducing their commission to 1.5% if they refer users who make a purchase. Ares provides a referral code during registration, but further details on their affiliate program were not found.

6 Most Profitable Vendors

From papers of other authors we know already that the minority of the vendors on DNMs are responsible for the majority of the turnover [3,7,9,20]. More specifically, Soska and Christin analyzed that the top 1% of most successful vendors were responsible for 51.5% of the turnover [20]. These findings we would like to foster by figuring out the top 10 vendors with the highest revenue they gained across all marketplaces on which they were registered as a vendor. Furthermore, our scope is for both, vendors digital and physical goods. This separation is done due the fact that the marketplaces we observed divide their items in those two commodities which we explained in Subsect. 5.1.

Gaining Insights. The calculations in this study are based on data provided by Nexus and TorZon vendor profiles, which include information about the marketplaces where a vendor has been active and the number of sales they have achieved on those platforms. Nexus offering more digital products than TorZon was selected as the primary dataset to identify the top-performing vendors. Nexus lacks a filter option to rank the most popular products. To address this limitation, we focused on vendors appearing within the first three pages of each category (digital and physical goods), with each page displaying 36 products. This approach allowed us to identify 25 vendors of digital goods and 47 vendors of physical goods. As a next step, we manually reviewed all profile pages of these vendors to examine the price of each product they offer. This process resulted in the creation of two manually curated datasets, as automated data collection is not feasible within DNMs [22]. The first dataset contains 1,503 listings of digital goods, while the second includes 1,150 listings of physical products. On the basis of both databases we calculated the revenue for each vendor. We multiplied the average piece price per vendor with the amount of sales the vendor has ever had to get the revenue of a vendor across all marketplaces. Finally, we sorted the vendors by the amount of their revenue which can be seen in Tables 6 and 7.

Result: Top 10 Vendors for Digital Products. Table 6 highlights that *Vendor 1* leads this category with a remarkable sales volume of $5,812,729.57 and a total of 183,698 sales. *Vendor 1* is also the most widely active vendor, being listed on 33 different DNMs. However, he holds the lowest rating among the 25 vendors analyzed in this category, with a rating of just 3.4 out of 5 stars. The second highest-performing vendor in this category, *Vendor 2*, achieves approximately 50% of *Vendor 1*'s revenue but with nearly 20 times fewer sales. *Vendor*

2 has operated on about one-third as many marketplaces as *Vendor 1*, yet his average price per product is eight times higher. Beyond these two top performers, no other vendor in this category reached a turnover exceeding $1 billion. *Vendor 10*, the vendor ranked last in this overview, has yet to surpass a revenue of $100,000.

Table 6. Top 10 vendors for digital products

Vendor	#Sales	#Items	Av. Price	Revenue	#DNMs
1	183,698	70	31.64 $	5,812,729.57 $	33
2	9,540	220	264.16 $	2,520,090.74 $	9
3	4,701	100	119.76 $	562,991.76 $	17
4	3,230	60	109.42 $	353,431.98 $	11
5	6,496	14	50.00 $	324,800.00 $	14
6	5,359	39	35.90 $	192,374.36 $	9
7	14,966	36	9.14 $	136,772.61 $	12
8	1,416	19	94.68 $	134,073.84 $	17
9	1,852	5	61.20 $	113,342.40 $	13
10	137	220	719.44 $	98,564.84 $	3

Result: Top 10 Vendors for Physical Products. In the commodity of physical products, which is predominantly comprised of drugs [6,20], similar patterns emerge as observed in the digital category. *Vendor A* leads this category with the highest revenue, totaling $4,130,009.14. However, *Vendor A* does not hold the highest number of sales; this position belongs to *Vendor I*, who achieved more than twice the sales volume but offers the lowest average price among all top 10 vendors. Five vendors in this category surpassed $1 billion in revenue, while 20 vendors achieved revenues exceeding $100,000. Additionally, the payment method of escrow plays a significant role in this category. Among the 47 analyzed vendors, 27 utilize escrow with an average time frame of seven days.

7 Discussion

7.1 Reflection on Results

The results of our investigation provide valuable insights into the structure and actors on DNMs. The awareness of anonymity and information security is high on DNMs and need appropriate measures to maintain this. We examined, listed, and categorized the entry barriers to the marketplaces and the process of becoming a vendor, which are designed to protect anonymity, information and the marketplaces from external attacks.

Table 7. Top 10 vendors for physical products

Vendor	#Sales	#Items	Av. Price	Revenue	#DNMs
A	14,484	28	285.14 $	4,130,009.14 $	18
B	17,075	35	236.00 $	4,025,452.00 $	19
C	7,761	22	505.77 $	3,925,302.14 $	6
D	2,002	28	976.60 $	1,955,143.19 $	5
E	5,337	40	226.98 $	1,211,365.58 $	8
F	11,485	47	84.13 $	966,206.17 $	8
G	14,507	5	54.40 $	789,180.80 $	22
H	1,484	143	407.97 $	605,425.30 $	12
I	36,728	32	10.19 $	374,166.50 $	20
J	13,518	16	20.33 $	274,837.84 $	4

Entry Requirements. Most marketplaces require user registration for purchases, though exceptions exist—e.g., Dark Matter allows order initiation without login, though completion likely requires authentication. Account deletion is not user-initiated; no visible option was found. Vendors face stricter conditions, including required PGP keys, 2FA, vendor fees, and rule compliance. We observed a moderate correlation: marketplaces with higher entry barriers for buyers also tend to impose medium to high restrictions on vendors, likely reflecting increased operator awareness of security risks.

Rule Book. All examined DNMs prohibit child pornography, likely to reduce legal exposure rather than for moral reasons—a rationale that may also apply to bans on weapons, murder-for-hire, and similar offenses. Interestingly, while hard drugs like heroin and cocaine are permitted, fentanyl is often explicitly banned. This distinction is based on observation and remains open for further research.

Commission Structures. Commission fees—often embedded in vendor rules—represent a major revenue stream for marketplaces, though not always transparently communicated. Only DarkDock explicitly states that it collects no commission. Activities that compromise operational anonymity, such as scamming or doxing, are typically prohibited. However, without acting as sellers, we could not verify rule enforcement practices directly.

Vendor Profile and Revenue. Vendors maintain consistent usernames and PGP keys across markets for recognizability and credibility. While we treat vendors as single entities, team operation cannot be ruled out. Our revenue analysis confirms earlier findings: few vendors achieve significant success, with only a small group generating more than $100,000 [3]. Our methodology supports LEAs by identifying top vendors via cumulative cross-market data, offering a resource-efficient strategy for targeting high-impact actors.

7.2 Limitations

Accessibility of Marketplaces. One of the challenges is the restricted accessibility of DNMs due to DDoS attacks and other events described by Gomez et al. [14]. Furthermore, there are more hidden marketplaces that are accessible only through invitation links or private chat groups, which were not included in our analysis [18]. Researchers face significant limitations here, as purchasing access to a private DNMs would involve buying from darknet vendors, which is illegal and raises ethical and legal concerns.

Trustworthiness of Data. A key limitation is the uncertain trustworthiness of data from DNMs. For example, *Nexus* shows vendor sales across other markets, but it is unclear whether this information is self-reported or provided by administrators. On TorZon, data is reviewed by moderators (*"All feedback has been reviewed and approved by the moderator team."*), which introduces dependency on their integrity. The update frequency and accuracy of such data are unknown. Moreover, sales figures may be artificially inflated, as vendors can manipulate reputation by purchasing their own products and leaving positive reviews.

Specific Dynamics of DNMs. The study's calculation of top vendors for digital and physical goods assumes purchases at the minimum available quantity, excluding potential bulk discounts that could affect results. It is based on the average price of a vendor's products multiplied by their sales on Nexus and other marketplaces. It remains unclear whether vendors offered identical products across markets or how their pricing structures differed. On Nexus, only total sales per vendor are visible, making it impossible to determine which products were sold more frequently, potentially distorting the turnover calculation.

7.3 Future Work

Vendor Practices and Payment Processes. Due to legal barriers, the steps that follow the payment required to become a vendor remain unexplored. Cooperation with LEAs could provide further details. Additionally, broadening the analysis to include a wider range of DNMs, chat groups and invitation only markets could provide a more comprehensive understanding of vendor behavior and marketplace dynamics. Different selling places should be combined with further research about insights into a potential specification of vendors and the goods they offer, a factor that could make them more identifiable. LEAs might benefit from targeting these key players, as previous research indicates that a small percentage of vendors are responsible for the majority of sales on DNMs [3,9].

Identification of Scam-Products. Marketplaces often implement rules to prevent the sale of such items. Further research could investigate the criteria for detecting fake products and estimate their overall prevalence. While the high volume of repeat purchases and positive feedback suggests that the quality of physical goods, such as drugs, meets customer expectations, the situation for digital goods is less clear. For example, it is uncertain whether software tools like the *Pegasus RAT* function as advertised or whether customers receive genuine products. Future studies should also focus on identifying products or vendors that represent significant security threats to society or critical industries.

Verification of Vendor Origin. As outlined in Sect. 2, we examined product descriptions, F.A.Q.s, and marketplace rules to identify linguistic cues hinting at the authors' native language. Combined with metadata—such as stated country of origin in physical goods—these indicators may help refine offender profiles. While we could not verify the accuracy of such origin claims, these combined signals may support law enforcement in identifying actors across multiple marketplaces [10]. Research has shown that targeted interventions, such as account closures, are significantly more effective in disrupting illegal trade than warnings, underscoring the importance of verifying vendor identities [4].

8 Conclusion

This paper provides a systematic and cross-market analysis of vendor-related structures and data within currently active darknet marketplaces. By examining eight DNMs with a focus on DGs, we reveal that these platforms maintain a surprisingly standardized but varied onboarding process for vendors, supported by internal rulebooks, fee structures, and identity verification mechanisms. We contribute a comparative overview of vendor entry requirements, including platform-specific protections and obligations. Our structured documentation of extractable vendor-related data shows that DNMs publicly expose significant operational metadata, including product portfolios, feedback mechanisms, and—in some cases—cross-market activity. Our most impactful contribution is the introduction of a method for quantifying vendor revenue across multiple DNMs. Utilizing unique data available through the Nexus platform, we traced vendors' cumulative turnover even on defunct marketplaces, providing the first empirical estimates of vendor earnings based on validated identifiers rather than approximations. In both digital and physical product categories, the most successful vendors generated revenues of up to $5 million. Together, these findings close important gaps in the current research landscape and establish a foundation for further academic inquiry into DNM vendor ecosystems. They also offer practical value for law enforcement and policy-makers aiming to understand, monitor, and disrupt high-value actors in the cybercrime economy.

References

1. One of the darkweb's largest cryptocurrency laundromats washed out | Europol — europol.europa.eu. https://www.europol.europa.eu/media-press/newsroom/news/one-of-darkwebs-largest-cryptocurrency-laundromats-washed-out. Accessed 14 Apr 2025
2. Bent, S.: DEF CON 30 - Sam Bent - Tor - Darknet Opsec By a Veteran Darknet Vendor — youtube.com. https://www.youtube.com/watch?v=01oeaBb85Xc. Accessed 12 Jul 2024

3. Booij, T.M., Verburgh, T., Falconieri, F., Wegberg, R.S.v.: Get rich or keep tryin' trajectories in dark net market vendor careers. In: 2021 IEEE European Symposium on Security and Privacy Workshops (EuroS&PW), pp. 202–212 (2021)
4. Bradley, C.: On the Resilience of the Dark Net Market Ecosystem to Law Enforcement Intervention. Ph.D. thesis, University College London (UCL) (2019). https://discovery.ucl.ac.uk/id/eprint/10080409/. Accessed 06 May 2025
5. Bradley, C., Stringhini, G.: A qualitative evaluation of two different law enforcement approaches on dark net markets. In: 2019 IEEE European Symposium on Security and Privacy Workshops (EuroS&PW), pp. 453–463 (2019). https://doi.org/10.1109/EuroSPW.2019.00057
6. Broséus, J., Rhumorbarbe, D., Morelato, M., Staehli, L., Rossy, Q.: A geographical analysis of trafficking on a popular darknet market. Forensic Sci. Int. **277**, 88–102 (2017)
7. Christin, N.: Traveling the silk road: a measurement analysis of a large anonymous online marketplace. In: Proceedings of the 22nd International Conference on World Wide Web, pp. 213–224. WWW '13, Association for Computing Machinery, New York, NY, USA (2013). https://doi.org/10.1145/2488388.2488408, https://doi.org/10.1145/2488388.2488408
8. Coldewey, D.: How German and us authorities took down the owners of darknet drug emporium wall street market (2019). https://techcrunch.com/2019/05/03/how-german-and-us-authorities-took-down-the-owners-of-darknet-drug-emporium-wall-street-market/
9. Cuevas, A., Christin, N.: Does online anonymous market vendor reputation matter? In: 33rd USENIX Security Symposium (USENIX Security 24), pp. 4641–4656. USENIX Association, Philadelphia, PA (2024). https://www.usenix.org/conference/usenixsecurity24/presentation/cuevas
10. dosReis, E., Teytelboym, A., ElBahrawy, A., Loizaga, I.D., Baronchelli, A.: Identifying key players in dark web marketplaces through bitcoin transaction networks. Sci. Rep. **14**(2385) (2024)
11. European Monitoring Centre for Drugs and Drug Addiction (EMCDDA) and Europol: Drugs and the darknet: perspectives for enforcement, research and policy (2024). https://www.euda.europa.eu/publications/joint-publications/drugs-and-the-darknet_en
12. Europol: Takedown of notorious hacker marketplace selling your identity to criminals | Europol — europol.europa.eu. https://www.europol.europa.eu/media-press/newsroom/news/takedown-of-notorious-hacker-marketplace-selling-your-identity-to-criminals (2024). Accessed 14 Apr 2025
13. Georgoulias, D., Pedersen, J.M., Falch, M., Vasilomanolakis, E.: A qualitative mapping of darkweb marketplaces. In: 2021 APWG Symposium on Electronic Crime Research (eCrime), pp. 1–15. IEEE (2021)
14. Gomez, G., van Liebergen, K., Caballero, J.: Dark Ending: what happens when a DarkWeb market closes down. In: Proceedings of the 9th International Conference on Information Systems Security and Privacy (2023)
15. Hämäläinen, L.: User names of illegal drug vendors on a darknet cryptomarket. Onoma **50**, 45–71 (2015). https://doi.org/10.34158/ONOMA.50/2015/2, available at: https://onomajournal.org/
16. Kermitsis, E., Kavallieros, D., Myttas, D., Lissaris, E., Giataganas, G.: Dark web markets. In: Dark Web Investigation, pp. 85–118 (2021)
17. Labrador, V., Pastrana, S.: Examining the trends and operations of modern dark-web marketplaces. In: 2022 IEEE European Symposium on Security and

Privacy Workshops (EuroS&PW), pp. 163–172 (2022). https://doi.org/10.1109/EuroSPW55150.2022.00022
18. Lusthaus, J.: Beneath the dark web: excavating the layers of cybercrime's underground economy. In: 2019 IEEE European Symposium on Security and Privacy Workshops (EuroS&PW), pp. 474–480 (2019). https://doi.org/10.1109/EuroSPW.2019.00059
19. Ouellet, M., Maimon, D., Howell, J.C., Wu, Y.: The network of online stolen data markets: how vendor flows connect digital marketplaces. Br. J. Criminol. **62**(6), 1518–1536 (2022)
20. Soska, K., Christin, N.: Measuring the longitudinal evolution of the online anonymous marketplace ecosystem. In: 24th USENIX Security Symposium (USENIX Security 15), pp. 33–48. USENIX Association, Washington, D.C. (2015). https://www.usenix.org/conference/usenixsecurity15/technical-sessions/presentation/soska
21. Tai, X.H., Soska, K., Christin, N.: Adversarial matching of dark net market vendor accounts. In: Proceedings of the 25th ACM SIGKDD International Conference on Knowledge Discovery & Data Mining, pp. 1871–1880 (2019)
22. Turk, K., Pastrana, S., Collier, B.: A tight scrape: methodological approaches to cybercrime research data collection in adversarial environments. In: 2020 IEEE European Symposium on Security and Privacy Workshops (EuroS&PW), pp. 428–437 (2020). https://doi.org/10.1109/EuroSPW51379.2020.00064
23. Ursani, Z., Peersman, C., Edwards, M., Chen, C., Rashid, A.: The impact of adverse events in darknet markets: an anomaly detection approach. In: 2021 IEEE European Symposium on Security and Privacy Workshops (EuroS&PW), pp. 227–238. IEEE (2021)
24. Van Wegberg, R., et al.: Plug and Prey? Measuring the commoditization of cybercrime via online anonymous markets. In: 27th USENIX Security Symposium (USENIX Security 18), pp. 1009–1026 (2018)
25. Wang, X., Peng, P., Wang, C., Wang, G.: You are your photographs: detecting multiple identities of vendors in the darknet marketplaces. In: Proceedings of the 2018 on Asia Conference on Computer and Communications Security, pp. 431–442 (2018)
26. Wang, Y., Hu, Y., Xu, W., Zou, F.: Multi-identity recognition of darknet vendors based on metric learning. Appl. Sci. - AI-Based Image Process. 2nd Edition **14**(4)(1619) (2024)
27. Wouters, R.: Boarding a sinking ship: trust mechanisms in the underground in the face of high market platform volatility (2019)
28. Wang, Y., Arief, B., Julio, H.C.: Analysis of security mechanisms of dark web markets (2024). https://dl.acm.org/doi/pdf/10.1145/3655693.3655700
29. Yannikos, Y., Julian, H.: Captchas on darknet marketplaces: overview and automated solvers. Electron. Imaging **36**(107) (2024)
30. Yannikos, Y., Heeger, J., Steinebach, M.: Data acquisition on a large darknet marketplace. In: Proceedings of the 17th International Conference on Availability, Reliability and Security, pp. 1–6 (2022)
31. Yuan, K., Lu, H., Liao, X., Wang, X.: Reading thieves' cant: automatically identifying and understanding dark jargons from cybercrime marketplaces. In: 27th USENIX Security Symposium (USENIX Security 18), pp. 1027–1041 (2018)

Proceedings of the Ninth International Workshop on Cyber Use of Information Hiding (CUING 2025)

CUING 2025 Preface

It is our great pleasure to introduce research papers presented at the 9th International Workshop on Cyber Use of Information Hiding (CUING 2025), co-located with the 20th International Conference on Availability, Reliability, and Security (ARES 2025). The conference was held in Ghent, Belgium on August 11–14, 2025.

The CUING 2025 workshop focuses on the analysis and countermeasures of information hiding techniques used in cyber attacks, addressing the growing sophistication of threat actors in leveraging stealthy methods to evade detection. As information hiding – such as steganography, covert channels, obfuscation, and anti-forensics – becomes more prevalent in cybercrime, CUING brings together researchers, practitioners, and law enforcement to examine emerging threats and develop novel detection and mitigation strategies. The workshop welcomes work on a wide range of related topics, including AI-enabled hiding methods, privacy-enhancing technologies, stegomalware, traffic obfuscation, and the misuse of legitimate platforms like social media and cloud services. CUING 2025 also encourages discussion on the dual-use nature of these technologies, such as their role in both enabling privacy and facilitating cybercrime.

This year CUING received 14 submissions, of which 50% were accepted. Each paper was peer-reviewed by our experts from the Technical Program Committee (TPC) and, on average, received 3.5 reviews. This year, our TPC consisted of 25 experts from 11 countries around the world (Austria, China, France, Germany, Italy, Israel, Japan, Macedonia, Poland, Spain, and the USA). The whole review process was conducted using double-blind methodology, and assisted by all Workshop Chairs.

August 2025

Philipp Amann
Luca Caviglione
Angelo Consoli
Joerg Keller
Peter Kieseberg
Wojciech Mazurczyk

CUING 2025 Organization

Workshop Chairs

Philipp Amann	Europol EC3, The Netherlands
Luca Caviglione	CNR – IMATI, Italy
Angelo Consoli	Scuola Universitaria Professionale della Svizzera Italiana (SUPSI), Switzerland
Joerg Keller	FernUniversität in Hagen, Germany
Peter Kieseberg	FH St. Pölten, Austria
Wojciech Mazurczyk	Warsaw University of Technology, Poland

Program Committee

Giacomo Benedetti	Institute of Applied Mathematics and Information Technologies, Italy
Krzysztof Cabaj	Warsaw University of Technology, Poland
Michał Choraś	Bydgoszcz University of Science and Technology, Poland
Rémi Cogranne	Troyes University of Technology, France
Marco Cremonini	University of Milan, Italy
Jana Dittmann	Otto-von-Guericke-Universität Magdeburg, Germany
Massimo Guarascio	Institute of HPC and Networking, Italy
Mordechai Guri	Ben-Gurion University, Israel
Stefan Katzenbeisser	University of Passau, Germany
Zbigniew Kotulski	Warsaw University of Technology, Poland
Christian Kraetzer	Otto-von-Guericke-Universität Magdeburg, Germany
Minoru Kuribayashi	Tohoku University, Japan
Daniel Lerch-Hostalot	Universitat Oberta de Catalunya, Spain
David Megías	Universitat Oberta de Catalunya, Spain
Aleksandra Mileva	University Goce Delcev, Macedonia
Marek Pawlicki	Bydgoszcz University of Science and Technology, Poland
Paweł Rajba	University of Wroclaw, Poland
Tobias Schmidbauer	Nuremberg Institute of Technology, Germany
Reza Soosahabi	Keysight Technologies Inc., USA
Avinash Srinivasan	United States Naval Academy, USA
Martin Steinebach	Fraunhofer SIT, Germany

Milad Taleby Ahvanooey	Warsaw University of Technology, Poland
Hui Tian	National Huaqiao University, China
Steffen Wendzel	University of Ulm, Germany
Tanja Zseby	Vienna University of Technology, Austria

Contextual Coherence Evaluation of Perfectly Secure Steganography in Text Documents

Katsuyuki Umezawa[1]([✉])[iD], Toshikatsu Kashima[1], Sven Wohlgemuth[2], and Kazuo Takaragi[3]

[1] Shonan Institute of Technology, Fujisawa, Japan
umezawa@info.shonan-it.ac.jp
[2] Fujisawa, Japan
[3] HISAFE, Ebina, Japan
https://www.shonan-it.ac.jp/

Abstract. Perfectly secure steganography is a technique designed to render the presence of embedded information undetectable by ensuring that the statistical distributions before and after embedding remain perfectly identical, thereby setting the Kullback–Leibler (KL) divergence to zero. However, in terms of textual documents, specific linguistic features, such as dialects or speech patterns associated with elderly individuals, can create noticeable inconsistencies for human readers, potentially revealing the existence of hidden information.

This study aims to evaluate stegotexts generated through perfectly secure steganography by employing alternative metrics beyond KL divergence. This is not a proposal to replace the KL divergence evaluation metric for perfectly secure steganography, but rather a proposal to conduct an additional evaluation using a different metric. Specifically, we utilize latent Dirichlet allocation (LDA) and cosine similarity to assess the coherence of the generated stegotext with a set of documents sharing the same topic. For our experiments, we collected news articles on gaming, sports, and politics from BBC News. The results indicate that gaming-related stegotexts exhibited significantly lower similarity with sports- and politics-related news articles, and a similar trend was observed for politics-related stegotexts. However, for sports-related stegotexts, no significant difference was detected.

Keywords: Perfectly secure steganography · latent Dirichlet allocation · cosine similarity

1 Introduction

Steganography has long been studied as a method for concealing data by embedding it within seemingly harmless content such as images, audio, and text. Unlike traditional security measures such as encryption, which aim to protect the data from decrypting the contents, steganography hides the existence of the communication itself. This makes it a valuable complement to cryptographic technologies. Its applications are varied, encompassing the secure transmission of sensitive information and privacy protection.

Traditional steganographic methods have sought to embed confidential information within a covertext (i.e., content used for steganography to embed data) while minimizing alterations to make detection by third parties challenging. Although these methods can obscure the specific contents of the embedded information when combined with encryption techniques, embedded information may still be statistically detectable. Consequently, the security level provided by traditional steganography has been limited, necessitating more advanced technologies to enhance its effectiveness.

In recent years, a concept referred to as "perfectly secure steganography" has been proposed [1]. This technique aims to modify the covertext in a manner that is statistically undetectable, thus rendering the embedded information imperceptible. Specifically, it requires that the statistical distributions of the covertext and stegotext (i.e., the content containing the embedded information) match perfectly. To achieve this, generative AI technologies, such as GPT-2 and WaveRNN, are used alongside a method called iterative minimum entropy coupling (iMEC) to minimize the Kullback–Leibler (KL) divergence towards zero. This approach effectively hides the fact that information has been embedded.

This study focuses on the steganography of text documents. Although achieving a KL divergence of zero suggests perfect statistical concealment, the possibility that human readers might notice anomalies remains. Detection can occur if the covertext, which may include specific features such as dialects or archaic phrases, reads as unnatural. These discrepancies could inadvertently indicate the presence of embedded information.

We evaluate stegotexts generated through perfectly secure steganography using metrics beyond KL divergence. Specifically, we employ latent Dirichlet allocation (LDA) [2] to model a collection of documents and calculate cosine similarity to assess the similarity between documents. This method helps verify whether the generated stegotexts align with document groups on the same topics. By incorporating this contextual consistency evaluation along with the statistical criteria (KL divergence of zero), we aim to better understand how the texts might be perceived by human readers.

2 Related Work

2.1 Perfectly Secure Steganography

Steganography has gained recognition in the field of information security as a technique that conceals not only the contents of communications but also the act of communication itself. This technology prevents third parties from detecting data modifications, thereby addressing some limitations of cryptographic methods. Notably, information theory-based models, which assess the security of steganography through statistical analysis, are widely employed [3,4].

Cachin's model [5], a foundational approach in steganography, emphasizes the statistical similarity between covertexts and stegotexts. A covertext is defined as natural, inconspicuous data used to embed secret information, such as images, text, or audio. By contrast, a stegotext is the data produced when secret information is embedded within the covertext, designed to ensure that its statistical characteristics align with those of the covertext. This model is intended to completely eliminate the risk of detection by third parties.

As a primary approach to achieving a KL divergence of zero, the minimum entropy coupling (MEC) method has been proposed. MEC is designed to identify the optimal coupling between the distribution of a covertext and that of a stegotext, enabling the statistical properties of the stegotext to closely mirror those of the covertext. Specifically, MEC modifies the entropy structure of the covertext distribution while ensuring that it aligns with the statistical characteristics of the embedded information. This adjustment minimizes discrepancies between the two distributions, effectively avoiding statistical detection.

The emergence of generative AI models such as GPT-2, WaveRNN, and Image Transformer in recent years has significantly improved the performance of steganography. These models can accurately replicate complex covertext distributions, and when integrated with techniques like MEC, they allow for more precise modifications to the entropy structure [1]. This combination greatly enhances the naturalness and secrecy of stegotexts, offering an effective means of reducing KL divergence. In addition, the previously defined method of iMEC has been introduced to improve the alignment between the distributions of covertexts and stegotexts, not only approaching zero KL divergence but also maximizing statistical security. Consequently, the application of MEC alongside generative AI techniques not only boosts the safety of steganography but also enhances its practicality, laying a critical foundation for the advancement of this field.

2.2 Latent Dirichlet Allocation (LDA)

In this section, we describe LDA, which is a method used for topic modeling and cosine similarity analysis.

Topic models operate on the premise that a document encompasses several latent topics, with each keyword either belonging to a specific topic or being produced by that topic. LDA [2] is a method for estimating these latent topics from keywords. It is a language model that assumes the probability distribution of topics (parameter θ of the multinomial distribution) that follow a Dirichlet distribution. In LDA, topics are selected according to the Dirichlet distribution, and words are chosen based on the probability distribution associated with that topic.

LDA can be represented by the graphical model shown in Fig. 1. This figure illustrates the smoothed LDA model. In recent years, the term "LDA" has commonly referred to smoothed LDA, and our implementation follows this formulation.

Here, d represents the document ID, n denotes the word ID of a word in a document, and k indicates the topic ID. The total number of documents is

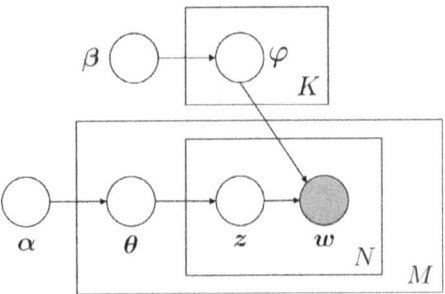

Fig. 1. Graphical model representation of smoothed LDA

M whereas N and K refer to the number of words and topics in a document, respectively. The number of words in document d is given as N_d. The ranges for d, n, and k are specified as $1 \leq d \leq M$, $1 \leq n \leq N_d$, and $1 \leq k \leq K$, respectively. w_{dn} represents the nth word of document d, and z_{dn} represents the latent topic associated with the nth word in document d. The variable θ_{dk} is the mixing ratio for the latent topic k of document d. For example, if document d has three topics with mixing ratios of 10%, 70%, and 20% for topics 1, 2, and 3, respectively, then $\theta_{d1} = 0.1$, $\theta_{d2} = 0.7$, and $\theta_{d3} = 0.2$, reflected as $\boldsymbol{\theta}_d = \{0.1, 0.7, 0.2\}$. In this context, $\boldsymbol{\alpha}$ is the parameter of the Dirichlet prior on the per-document topic distributions, and $\boldsymbol{\beta}$ denotes the parameter of the Dirichlet prior on the per-topic word distribution. φ represents the word distribution for topic k. A collection of documents is referred to as a corpus, denoted as $\boldsymbol{D} = \{\boldsymbol{w}_1, \boldsymbol{w}_2, \cdots, \boldsymbol{w}_M\}$.

In this framework, we observe the word $\boldsymbol{w}_d$ and aim to determine the topic from which these words originated. Specifically, for document d, we calculate and estimate the topic distribution $\boldsymbol{\theta}_d$, the topic assignment for each word $\boldsymbol{z}$, and the word distribution for each topic φ. Various methods, such as the Bayesian method [2], Markov chain Monte Carlo (MCMC) [6], and Gibbs sampling [7] (a specific type of MCMC), have been proposed to estimate these latent variables ($\boldsymbol{\theta}$, $\boldsymbol{z}$ and φ).

2.3 Cosine Similarity

The similarity between documents d and d' can be evaluated by calculating the cosine similarity of $\boldsymbol{\theta}_d$, which is approximately derived using the aforementioned LDA method. The cosine similarity is expressed by the following equation.

$$sim_{cos}(d, d') = \frac{\sum_{k=1}^{K} \theta_{dk} \theta_{d'k}}{\sqrt{\sum_{k=1}^{K} \theta_{dk}^2} \sqrt{\sum_{k=1}^{K} \theta_{d'k}^2}} \qquad (1)$$

3 Proposal

In this study, we utilize LDA to evaluate the similarity and contextual consistency of stegotexts generated through perfectly secure steganography. This approach assesses how well the stegotexts integrate with their respective textual environments, ensuring they maintain a natural appearance while effectively embedding hidden information.

Figure 2 provides an overview of the proposal. It illustrates that articles from three categories, namely, games, sports, and politics, are randomly selected, with 100 articles from each category. The process consists of the following steps: 1) a news article about games is chosen and used as the covertext to generate stegotext through perfectly secure steganography; 2) a topic model is created from news articles across all categories, and this model is used to compute the cosine similarity between the generated stegotext and the articles from each category (games, sports, politics); 3) the similarity is calculated for the sports category; 4) the similarity calculation is repeated for the politics category. This method assesses how effectively the stegotext integrates into the context of each category while preserving its concealed information.

If a high similarity is identified between the stegotext generated from a game-related news article and the original game-related article, it indicates that the stegotext was produced on the same topic. This also holds true for sports and politics. However, even if perfectly secure steganography results in a KL divergence of zero, if the covertext is from the 'game' category and the stegotext is related to 'sports' or 'politics,' readers may notice a discrepancy, as the topic of the stegotext deviates from that of the covertext.

4 Experiment

4.1 Selecting a Dataset

In this study, the dataset consists of articles that were randomly selected from BBC News, with 100 articles from each of the three categories: games [9], sports [10], and politics [11].

4.2 Generation of Stegotext

The stegotext was generated by executing the source code published on GitHub [12]. The main parameters used are shown in Table 1. Table 4 presents the news articles utilized as covertexts, along with the generated stegotexts.

4.3 Creation of the LDA Model

In total, 300 news articles as explained in Sect. 4.1 were used to create the LDA model, with the number of topics, one of the parameters, manually set to eight.

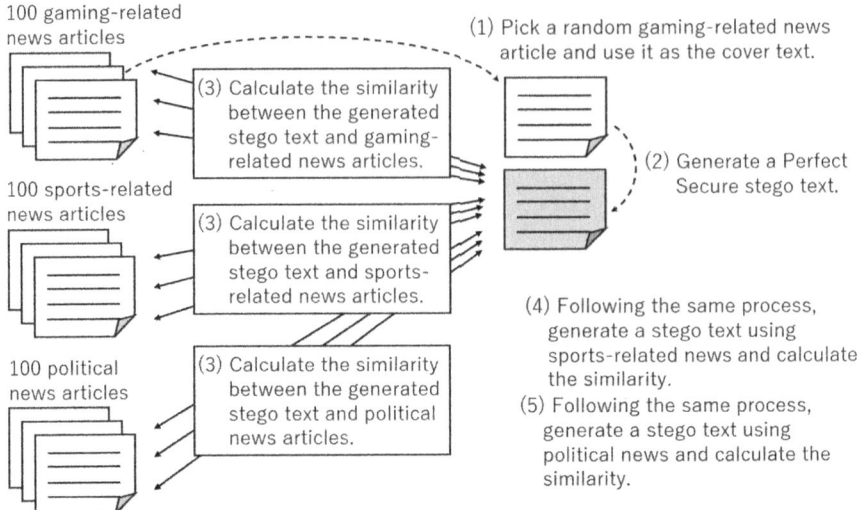

Fig. 2. Overview of the proposal

Table 1. Parameters used when executing perfectly secure steganography.

Parameter	Value
block-size	10
method	imec
top-k	40
message-mode	randombits
repetition	1

4.4 Calculation of Cosine Similarity

First, we calculated the cosine similarity between the stegotext generated using a game-related news article as the covertext and 100 other game-related news articles. We refer to this as game–game similarity. Next, we determined the cosine similarity between the same stegotext and 100 sports-related news articles, which we call game–sports similarity. We also measured the cosine similarity between the same stegotext and 100 politics-related news articles, which we term game–politics similarity. The same methodology was applied to stegotexts generated from sports- and politics-related news.

These terms are summarized in Table 2. A similarity value close to 1 indicates a strong resemblance of the stegotext to articles from that category, whereas a value close to 0 indicates minimal resemblance.

Table 2. Abbreviations for similarities between Articles A and B

Article A	Articles B	Abbreviation
Similarity between the stegotext generated from gaming-related news and	100 gaming-related news articles	game–game similarity
	100 sports-related news articles	game–sports similarity
	100 political news articles	game–politics similarity
Similarity between the stegotext generated from sports-related news and	100 gaming-related news articles	sports–game similarity
	100 sports-related news articles	sports–sports similarity
	100 political news articles	sports–politics similarity
Similarity between the stegotext generated from political news and	100 gaming-related news articles	politics–game similarity
	100 sports-related news articles	politics–sports similarity
	100 political news articles	politics–politics similarity

5 Experimental Results

5.1 Similarity Histogram

The histograms of similarities for game-, sports-, and politics-related content are presented in Figs. 3, 4, and 5, respectively. The horizontal axis in each figure represents the range of cosine similarity (from 0 to 1), whereas the vertical axis indicates the number of texts within each range.

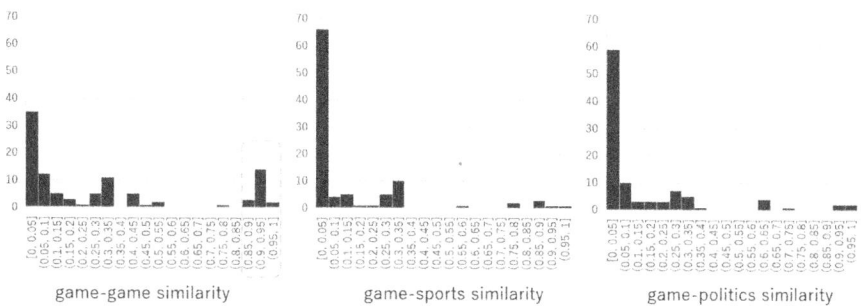

Fig. 3. Histogram of game-related similarities.

From Fig. 3, we observe that game–game similarity generally yields high values, with a significant number of data points in the range above 0.8. This suggests that stegotexts generated through perfectly secure steganography closely resemble news articles in the same category as the covertext. By contrast, game–sports

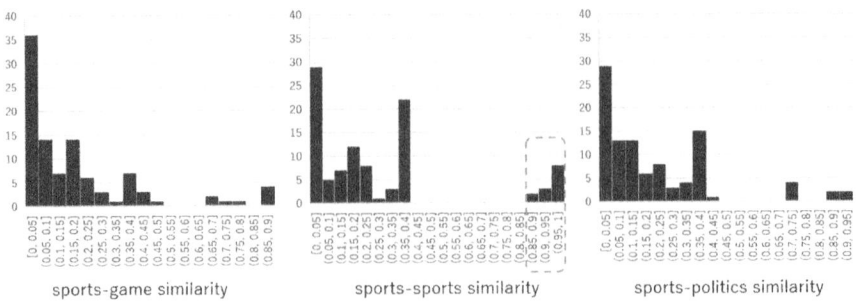

Fig. 4. Histogram of sports-related similarities.

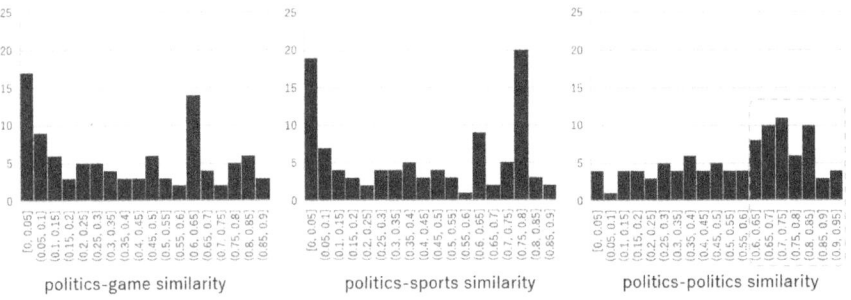

Fig. 5. Histogram of political similarities.

and game–politics similarities are predominantly concentrated below 0.4, with very few instances exceeding a value of 0.8. Notably, this indicates that game stegotexts have minimal similarity with news articles from different categories.

Figure 4 clearly shows that sports–sports similarity generally shows high values, with a significant number of data points in the range above 0.85. By contrast, the similarities between sports–game and sports–politics are mainly concentrated below 0.4, and only a few instances exceed a 0.85. In addition, over 70% of the data is below 0.4, indicating that sports stegotexts have minimal similarity with news articles in the game and politics categories.

Figure 5 illustrates that politics–politics similarity is relatively high, with a significant number of data points above 0.6. Most of the data is concentrated between 0.6 and 0.9, suggesting that stegotexts within the politics category show strong similarity with articles from the same category. By contrast, although politics–game and politics–sports similarities contain data points below 0.2, a significant number of instances are above 0.6. The proportion of data above 0.6 in politics–sports similarity is particularly high, indicating a certain level of association between political stegotexts and sports news. This trend may be due to overlaps in the reporting of politics and sports news.

Table 3 presents the average values of each similarity measure.

Table 3. Average values of each similarity

Category	Similarity	Average value (Mean)
game	game-game similarity	0.293400307
	game–sports similarity	0.126264980
	game–politics similarity	0.135203711
sports	sports–game similarity	0.180721423
	sports–sports similarity	0.274772562
	sports–politics similarity	0.206046409
politics	politics–game similarity	0.384843029
	politics–sports similarity	0.419023576
	politics–politics similarity	0.540932822

6 Analysis and Evaluation

The previous section described the visual assessment conducted in this study. This section describes our statistical verification of the differences between categories. Specifically, we tested whether the average similarity values shown in Table 3 differed significantly.

The histograms from Figs. 3, 4, 5 indicate that the data do not follow a normal distribution. Therefore, we conducted a Wilcoxon rank-sum test, which is a non-parametric test that can be used even when the data does not follow a normal distribution, to assess statistical differences.

The tests were conducted pairwise within each category to determine differences in the mean values. Because a total of nine tests were required, we addressed the issue of multiple testing. To do this, we applied the Bonferroni correction, one of the methods to avoid the issue of multiple testing. Specifically, the significance level, or p-value, was adjusted using the Bonferroni method to a threshold of $0.05/9 = 0.0055556$.

The results of the tests are shown in Fig. 6. As illustrated, stegotexts generated from game news articles exhibited high similarity with other game news articles. The same was true for sports and politics. Significant differences were found between game and politics categories. However, for sports, no significant differences were observed among all similarity measures.

7 Discussion

In this study, we conducted experiments using the LDA model and cosine similarity to assess the theoretical perfection of perfectly secure steganography by evaluating the semantic similarity between stegotexts and news articles. The results indicated that stegotexts related to games and politics exhibited a higher cosine similarity to news articles within the same category than to those from different categories. Notably, strong similarities were observed between game

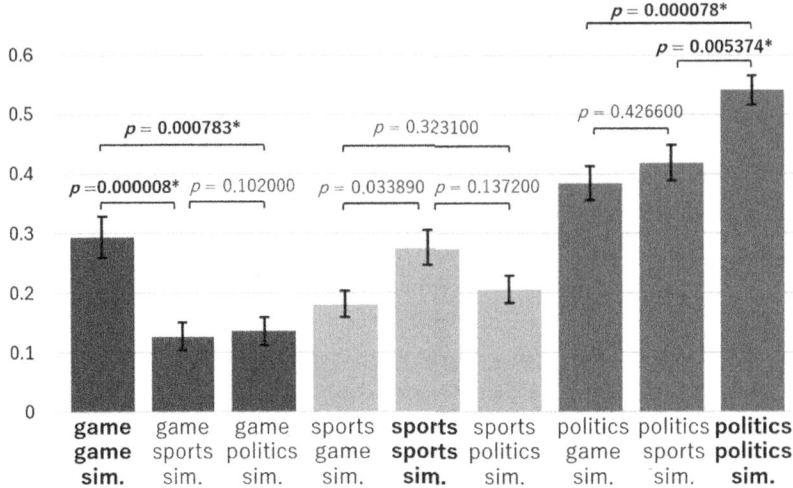

Fig. 6. The results of the tests

stegotexts and game news, as well as between political stegotexts and political news, confirming that the content in these two categories was well-aligned.

By contrast, stegotexts in the sports category showed similarities to articles in other categories, with no statistically significant differences found. This may be attributed to the diversity of vocabulary in sports news and its commonalities with other categories. Specifically, overlapping topics may exist between sports and political news, leading to stegotexts that are not strictly confined to sports content but that also resemble other categories. In addition, the brevity of the news articles or the excessive number of topics defined in the LDA model may have blurred the distinctions between categories. When articles are short, LDA may struggle to extract sufficient features for precise topic estimation, resulting in ambiguous topic distributions. In this study, we set the number of topics for the LDA to eight, which may not have been adequate for clear categorization.

8 Conclusion

In this study, we utilized LDA and cosine similarity to evaluate the similarity between documents, verifying whether the generated stegotexts resembled document groups with shared topics. The results confirmed that stegotexts derived from game-related news articles had significantly lower similarity to news articles in other categories (sports and politics). Likewise, stegotexts generated from political news articles also demonstrated significantly lower similarity to news articles in different categories. However, no significant differences were identified among stegotexts related to sports. Although the findings did not entirely meet expectations across all categories, two out of three categories demonstrated the anticipated similarity levels. These results suggest that perfect secure steganography not only achieves statistical perfection but also produces texts that resemble articles within the same category when read by humans.

In the future, expanding the variety of categories and the lengths of individual news articles is essential. In addition, providing an appropriate number of topics when training the LDA model is critical. Finally, utilizing data such as dialects and archaic phrases is necessary to ensure that the generated documents do not create a sense of incongruity for native speakers. These steps will enhance the accuracy and effectiveness of steganography in preserving the naturalness and relevance of covertexts.

Acknowledgments. Part of the work was supported by JDC Foundation for the Promotion of Academic Research.

A Covertext and Generated Stegotext

Table 4 presents the news articles used as covertexts and the generated stegotexts.

Table 4. The covertext and the generated stego text

Category	Kind	Text
Game	covertext	The forthcoming film comes during a renaissance for gaming films, which were once thought to be almost guaranteed flops. In the 90s, film adaptations of popular video games such as Super Mario Bros and Mortal Kombat were critical and commercial failures when they were released. But Nintendos star-studded Super Mario Bros Movie, which was released earlier this year, became one of the highest-grossing animated films of all time, earning more than $1bn (£800m) at the box office. While Mario was the most successful, it is not a one-off. Films based on Segas Sonic the Hedgehog, starring Jim Carrey, Ben Schwartz and James Marsden, have made hundreds of millions in box office takings, and Nintendos Detective Pikachu, starring Ryan Reynolds as the titular Pokemon, was a box office hit too
	Generated stego text	But with Nintendo, with its huge gaming audience and lucrative licensing deals, the company has been facing tough financial struggles. In the last ten years it has been embroiled in a string of scandals that led to massive losses, most famously for its gaming assets. In May 2015, the film released the first-ever leak of sensitive information about the Nintendo Switch console
Sports	covertext	Meanwhile, Naomi Osaka retired from the final of the Auckland Classic with an abdominal injury. The four-time Grand Slam winner, who was playing in her first WTA final for three years after taking a 15-month break and giving birth to her first child midway through 2023
	Generated stego text	with a populist and anti-immigration message that included references to the euro, free trade and the end of collective bargaining, despite his staunch support for the party. "I think we're a very different country from Germany", he said, "but I also think the world needs to realize how Germany is more than a German colony". But at the end, the talk was dominated by the two
Politics	covertext	Elon Musk took his endorsement of Germanys far-right party to the next level on Thursday, hosting a live chat with its frontwoman, Alice Weidel. The 74-minute conversation ranged across energy policy, German bureaucracy, Adolf Hitler, Mars and the meaning of life. The worlds richest man unequivocally urged Germans to back Alternative f_r Deutschland (AfD) in forthcoming elections. Its the tech billionaires latest controversial foray into European politics. Thered been a considerable build-up to this discussion as Elon Musk faced accusations of meddling in Germanys snap election
	Generated stego text	with a populist and anti-immigration message that included references to the euro, free trade and the end of collective bargaining, despite his staunch support for the party. "I think we're a very different country from Germany", he said, "but I also think the world needs to realize how Germany is more than a German colony". But at the end, the talk was dominated by the two

References

1. Schroeder de Witt, C., Sokata, S., Kolter, Z., Forester, J., Strohmeier, M.: Perfectly Secure Steganography using Minimum Entropy Coupling, Published as a Conference Paper at ICLR 2023 (2023)
2. Blei, D., Ng, A., Jordan, M.: Latent Dirichlet Allocation. J. Mach. Learn. Res., 1107–1135 (2003)
3. Sallee, P.: Model-based steganography. In: Kalker, T., Cox, I., Ro, Y.M. (eds) Digital Watermarking. IWDW 2003. Lecture Notes in Computer Science, vol. 2939. Springer, Berlin, Heidelberg (2003). https://doi.org/10.1007/978-3-540-24624_12
4. Chhikaraa, S., Kumarb, R.: An information theoretic image steganalysis for LSB steganography. Acta Cybernet. **24**(2020), 593–612 (2020). https://doi.org/10.14232/actacyb.279174
5. Cachin, C.: An information-theoretic model for steganography. In: Aucsmith, D. (ed.) IH 1998. LNCS, vol. 1525, pp. 306–318. Springer, Heidelberg (1998). https://doi.org/10.1007/3-540-49380-8_21
6. Griffiths, T., Steyvers, M.: Finding scientific topics. In: Proceedings of the National Academy of Science, pp. 5228–5235 (2004)
7. Teh, Y., Newman, D., Welling, M.: A collapsed variational bayesian inference algorithm for latent Dirichlet allocation. In: Proceedings of Advances in Neural Information Processing Systems 19, NIPS '07, Cambridge, MA, pp. 1353–1360 (2007)
8. Spooky_Maskman, Topic analysis by LDA with Gensim. https://qiita.com/Spooky_Maskman/items/0d03ea499b88abf56819. Accessed 6 Jun 2025
9. BBC Gaming. https://www.bbc.com/news/topics/c008ql15vdxt. Accessed 6 Jun 2025
10. BBC SPORT. https://www.bbc.com/sport. Accessed 6 Jun 2025
11. BBC politics. https://www.bbc.com/search?q=politics&edgeauth=eyJhbGciOiAiSFMyNTYiLCAidHlwIjogIkpXVCJ9.eyJrZXkiOiAiZmFzdGx5LXVyaS10b2tlbi0xIiwiZXhwIjogMTczODExMDk5OSwibmJmIjogMTczODExMDYzOSwicmVxdWVzdHVyaSI6ICIlMkZzZWFyY2glM0ZxJTNEcG9saXRpY3MifQ.nvt2u8NmlOLjrAzzFiW_ScVYJlGQrijzbNqAoqEjv8g. Accessed 6 Jun 2025
12. GITHUB: perfectly-secure-steganography. https://github.com/schroederdewitt/perfectly-secure-steganography. Accessed 6 Jun 2025

Robust Hashing Meets Inpainting

Martin Steinebach[(✉)][iD] and York Yannikos[iD]

Fraunhofer Institute for Secure Information Technology (SIT) National Research Center for Applied Cybersecurity (ATHENE), Rheinstr. 75, 64295 Darmstadt, Germany
`{martin.steinebach,york.yannikos}@sit.fraunhofer.de`

Abstract. Robust image hashing algorithms are designed to produce similar or equal hash values for image variants despite benign transformations like resizing or compression. However, modern generative techniques like image inpainting undermine this robustness by introducing semantically meaningful content changes that are imperceptible at the pixel level. This paper demonstrates how such inpainting attacks can exploit perceptual hash functions, causing significant semantic alterations to go undetected or, conversely, generating false positives that overload detection systems. We evaluate several widely used hashing schemes including Blockhash, rHash, ISCC, and PhotoDNA and show that they struggle to detect inpainting-based manipulations while remaining overly sensitive to trivial changes like cropping. These findings reveal a critical trade-off in hash function design: the balance between robustness to benign edits and sensitivity to malicious content alteration. We discuss the implications for systems relying on hash-based content detection, such as those targeting child sexual abuse material (CSAM), and highlight the potential for denial-of-service and strike inflation attacks. Our results underscore the urgent need for semantically aware image hashing solutions capable of withstanding adversarial generative modifications.

Keywords: Robust Hashing · Inpainting · Injection Attack

1 Motivation

Robust image hashing techniques are widely used for tasks such as image retrieval, content-based indexing, and near-duplicate detection. The core premise of robust hashing is that semantically similar images should yield similar hash values, even under common transformations such as resizing, compression, or minor occlusions. However, emerging generative techniques, particularly image inpainting, pose a significant challenge to this assumption.

Inpainting methods are capable of modifying localized regions within an image while preserving its overall structure, style, and low-level features. While such alterations may appear subtle at the pixel level, they can lead to profound semantic shifts in content. For example, an image of a person holding a firearm could be modified via inpainting to depict a person holding a similar-sized object such as a power drill as shown in Fig. 1. Likewise, explicit content may be replaced with modest variants by altering specific regions, leaving the background and general appearance unchanged.

These kinds of modifications exploit the very robustness that hashing algorithms are designed to provide. If the inpainted image yields a hash value close to the original, systems relying on hash similarity may fail to detect the semantic alteration, leading to vulnerabilities in content moderation, copyright enforcement, or forensic analysis. Conversely, if the hash changes drastically, it undermines the algorithm's robustness to benign edits.

This highlights a fundamental tension in the design of robust hashing algorithms: the need to balance invariance to benign modifications with sensitivity to content-level manipulations. Inpainting challenges existing assumptions about what constitutes a "minor" or "acceptable" image transformation. It underscores the need for reevaluating robustness in the context of modern generative manipulation techniques, and for developing methods that can detect content-level alterations even when they are localized and stylistically coherent with the original image.

Fig. 1. Inpaiting example: man holding a gun changed to holding a power drill.

2 Risk

The ability to generate images with significantly altered semantic content while preserving robust hash similarity introduces a critical vulnerability in systems that rely on perceptual hashing for content identification. This risk is particularly pronounced in domains such as the detection of child sexual abuse material

(CSAM), where even minimal failures in identification accuracy can have serious legal, ethical, and operational consequences.

One widely discussed application of robust hashing is client-side scanning for known CSAM, as proposed in initiatives such as the European Commission's Chatcontrol framework. In these systems, a local hash-based matching algorithm is employed to detect known illicit images on user devices before they are transmitted. If an adversary can alter a CSAM image in such a way that it becomes non-problematic – e.g., by digitally "dressing" a nude victim through inpainting – yet still triggers a hash match, the modified image may be incorrectly flagged as CSAM by the client-side detector. Figure 2 shows an example. The image of a bare chested dancer has been changed by inpainting into a dancer wearing a vest. Both a standard blockhash [23] and a version optimized for avoiding collisions [13] only produce one bit difference. The overall hash size is 256 bit.

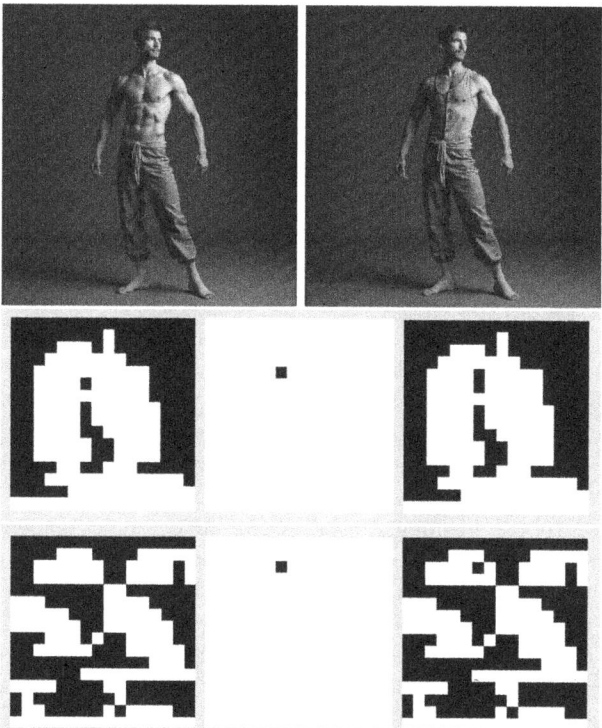

Fig. 2. An example of dressing a nude body part. Top Left: original, Right: Inpainting of vest Mid: Blockhash comparison with only one bit difference, Bottom: Optimized blockhash comparison also with one bit difference.

The implications of this kind of attack are twofold. First, institutions tasked with reviewing flagged content would face an increased burden of manual inspection for images that are no longer illegal or harmful, constituting a denial-of-service (DoS) vector. The effort required to verify these false positives could overwhelm moderation systems, exhaust legal oversight resources, and erode public trust in automated detection technologies.

Second, in scenarios where alerts are only triggered after a predefined threshold of suspicious content is detected – commonly employed to avoid false positives and preserve user privacy – an attacker could mount a strike inflation attack. By repeatedly distributing benign images that are hash-similar to known CSAM, the attacker could artificially inflate a user's suspicion score without ever transmitting actual illegal content. Such a strategy would be particularly insidious if it leads to unjustified escalation, such as wrongful investigation or reporting to authorities.

These risks expose a fundamental shortcoming in current robust hashing paradigms: a lack of semantic awareness. While perceptual similarity is preserved by design, the failure to distinguish between semantically benign and harmful alterations undermines the integrity and utility of hash-based detection in adversarial settings.

3 State of the Art

This work discusses the possibility of inpainting as an attack on robust hashing. We therefore briefly introduce both techniques here.

3.1 Robust Hashing

Hash-based algorithms are widely used in applications such as image retrieval, duplicate detection, and image authentication [4,5,9,17]. This work assumes the reader is familiar with the distinction between cryptographic and robust hashing. Briefly, cryptographic hashes are sensitive to any input modification, producing uncorrelated outputs even under minor transformations.

In contrast, robust hashing preserves similarity under non-semantic transformations such as compression or scaling. Classical methods achieve this via perceptual features [19–22], while recent approaches leverage deep learning to learn transformation-invariant, content-preserving hash codes [2,3,12].

A critical limitation of robust hashing – and related content recognition systems – is their design assumption of a benign environment. While robust to natural distortions, these systems lack defenses against adversarial manipulation. In multimedia security, this motivates a key distinction: robustness denotes invariance to benign transformations; security refers to resilience against intentional attacks [7]. This gap has been addressed with neural hashing systems such as Apple's NeuralHash [18], which are vulnerable to bidirectional attacks: evasion (altering an image to avoid detection) and injection (modifying an image to match a target hash). Thus, robustness does not imply adversarial robustness. Attacks on widely deployed systems such as Microsoft's PhotoDNA and

Facebook's PDQ confirm this vulnerability. Preimage attacks can yield perceptually distinct images with identical hashes, undermining hash-based semantic verification [11].

In this work, we use four robust hash methods for evaluation. We investigate their response to content-altering image modifications made with inptainting:

- Blockhash [23]: An image is downscaled to 16×16 pixels and converted to grayscale. A 256 bit hash is calculated by comparing the pixel values to their median.
- rHash [13]: Based on Blockhash, the hash introduces 4 subsections of the 16×16 pixels to render it more sensitive to local characteristics of the image.
- PhotoDNA [8]: The image is down scaled and divided into overlapping blocks on which edge detection is applied. The results is a list of bytes describing positive and negative edge strength in vertical and horizontal direction
- ISCC image content code[1]: Included here because it is widely used in ISCC codes. It aims to preserve the similarity of image objects. A discrete cosine transform a 32×32 downsized grayscale version of the image is calculated. Then the values from the top left of the DCT matrix are compared with their median values to set the hash bits.

3.2 Inpainting

Inpainting was first introduced as a method of image restoration [6]. Today it is widely used to modify image sections. In this work, a particular feature is important: one can define a mask and then use a text prompt to change the image content in the masked area, leaving the rest of the image untouched. This allows local, content-changing manipulations that are perfectly matched to the rest of the image in terms of style, color space and brightness. The result is an image that has been altered in terms of its content, but which appears innocuous to the human observer.

Deep learning has improved the ability to modify images without detailed knowledge and experience of image editing. Image inpainting has changed the process of image manipulation from traditional pixel-based methods to semantically-driven, context-aware generation tasks. Prompt-guided inpainting, where natural language prompts are used to guide the generation of content within missing or masked regions of an image, is available for many text-to-image frameworks. At the heart of this development is the integration of generative models – in particular diffusion models and transformers – that are trained to understand and synthesize visual data conditioned by textual input. A milestone in this area is GLIDE (Guided Language-to-Image Diffusion for Generation and Editing) [10] which demonstrated that text-based diffusion models can produce high-quality image annotations guided by natural language prompts. InstructPix2Pix [1] fine-tunes diffusion models to follow natural language instructions for local image editing, including inpainting. This approach emphases following

---

[1] https://core.iscc.codes/units/content/code_content_image/.

instructions rather than static text prompts, allowing for a more interactive and adaptive image manipulation workflow.

4 Concept

An evaluation of robust image hashing methods under semantic changes requires a structured pipeline encompassing three components: the generation of image datasets, the application of targeted inpainting-based manipulations, and the systematic comparison of hash outputs.

First, it is necessary to generate high-quality, diverse base images using a generative model. These images should reflect a range of attack subjects to serve as anchors for evaluating perceptual sensitivity.

Next, controlled modifications must be introduced via inpainting. This involves masking salient image regions and altering their semantic content through prompt changes, simulating plausible but adversarial content shifts. The process should include a manual or automated filtering step to ensure the validity of generated variants, discarding visually inconsistent outputs or unchanged. Table 1 shows examples of the prompts used for the original and the modified images.

Finally, to evaluate the robustness of hashing methods, various perceptual hash algorithms – both classical and learning-based – should be applied to the original and altered images. Hash similarity metrics (e.g., Hamming or Euclidean distance) must be used to quantify both intra-class stability and inter-class separability. This will enable a precise assessment of each method's resilience to content-preserving yet semantically adversarial edits. Additionally, hash distances to standard operations like JPEG lossy compression and limited cropping should be applied to the test images. Thereby a realistic comparison between expected operations and inpainting can be executed, comparing the distances of both sets of hashes. Based on this comparison it can be determined whether inpainting produces hash distances that are large enough to be over the threshold of common robustness expectations of the hash functions.

Table 1. Comparison of prompts used in evaluation.

Example	Original Prompt	New Prompt
ballerina	10 year old female ballet dancer wearing white ballet dress, black background, spotlight on dancer	20 year old female ballet dancer wearing white ballet dress, black background, spotlight on dancer
dancer	bare-chested male ballet dancer wearing historical pants	male ballet dancer wearing historical pants and skin-colored vest
female	bare-chested female ballet dancer wearing historical pants	female ballet dancer wearing historical pants and corsage
juice	bottle of whiskey on kitchen table	bottle of apple juice on kitchen table

5 Implementation

The implementation of our evaluation is based on the generation of test material and the inpainting attacks on the resulting images as well as the generation and comparison of the different robust hashing methods.

For the generation of the test material, we used forge via pinokio[2]. First we generated 10 example images with fitting prompts and the following parameters: Steps: 20, Sampler: Euler, Schedule type: Simple, CFG scale: 1, Distilled CFG Scale: 3.5, Seed: 832881156, Size: 1032 × 1024, Model hash: bea01d51bd, Model: flux1-dev-bnb-nf4-v2, Version: f2.0.1v1.10.1-previous-633-ge073e4ec. Resulting image size was 1032 × 1024.

Then we used the inpainting option and masked relevant objects in the image. We changed the prompt to modify the masked object, with the following parameters: Steps: 20, Sampler: Euler, Schedule type: Simple, CFG scale: 1, Distilled CFG Scale: 3.5, Seed: 2091049022, Size: 1032 × 1024, Model hash: bea01d51bd, Model: flux1-dev-bnb-nf4-v2, Denoising strength: 0.75, Mask blur: 4, Version: f2.0.1v1.10.1-previous-633-ge073e4ec.

Thereby, an image showing a "bottle of whiskey on kitchen table" was changed to showing a "bottle of apple juice on kitchen table", similar to the examples given in Figs. 1 or 2. As the inpainting function sometimes produced erratic outputs like unchanged masked regions or masked regions filled with colorful patterns, we selected suitable "attack candidates" by hand, deleting all unwanted results. For each of the 10 test images, we aimed at generating 16 variants.

For robust hash evaluation, we implemented both Blockhash and rHash as described in the papers and also included PhotoDNA and the ISCC imaged content code. Hash distances were calculated using the Hamming distance for Blockhash, rHash and ISCC and the Euclidean distance for PhotoDNA as described in the respective publications. For robustness comparison, we apply cropping between 1 and 50 lines and columns of the test images and JPEG lossy compression between quality factor 100 and 50.

6 Experiments

In this section, we give examples and provide results of the evaluation discussed in the previous sections. The inpainting of the images always changed one central aspect of the images: a nude chest was replaced with a dressed upper body, a bottle of whiskey was replaced with a bottle of apple juice. In no case multiple objects were modified.

The main results are presented in Tables 2 and 3. It can be seen that the hash differences between the original image and the inpainted image are small overall, but vary from image to image. The image "Ballerina" shows almost no hash difference, while "bigjuice" causes large differences compared to the rest of the results. Hash methods react differently to inpainting changes, depending on the image content and the size of the masked area changed. Figure 3 shows

---

[2] https://github.com/pinokiofactory/stable-diffusion-webui-forge.

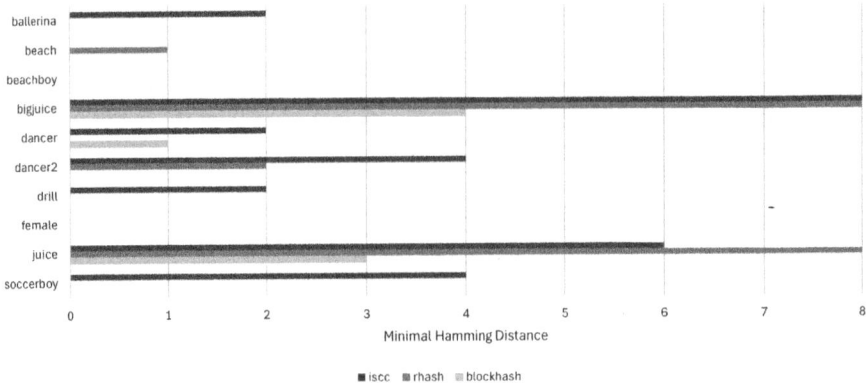

Fig. 3. Minimal hamming distances for the three hashes using hamming distance.

the distribution of minimum distances for Blockhash, rHash and ISCC. The minimum distance is the smallest distance found for a given set of inpainting versions of a given test image. An attacker using inpainting to distribute images with altered content but matching hashes could expect to achieve this distance by creating 16 inpainting versions and selecting the best match. The hash size for blockhash and rHash is 256, for ISCC image code it is 64. Therefore, the absolute differences have different relevance: for blockhash and rHash, a hash difference below 10 can be interpreted as a reliable match of the images. Since the ISCC hash size is a quarter of the blockhash and rHash, a minimal difference of 8 as in "bigjuice" could be interpreted as a failed attack as the inpaintings all caused a relatively high ISCC code distance.

Figure 4 shows the test image "dancer2" as well as examples of the inpaintings made for this image, with detailed hash differences listed in Table 4. The zoom in this picture is only applied for convenience in this paper. The hash comparison was executed on the whole image as shown in Fig. 4 (top). PhotoDNA produces small differences for the inpaintings where the vest is almost the color of the skin, and larger differences for stronger color changes. It can be assumed that this is due to the change in edge strength. The Blockhash is 0 for most examples, the rHash varies between 2 and 8, showing that the goal of being more responsive to local image changes than the standard Blockhash is achieved.

6.1 Robustness Against Common Attacks

As discussed in the concept section, we also executed a number of standard robustness tests with the test images and the hash functions. Tables 5, 6 and 7 provide examples of these results. We applied JPEG compression quality factors (QF) 100, 90, 85, 80, 75, 70, 60 and 50 as well as cropping of 1, 2, 5, 10, 25 and 50 lines and rows from the upper left of the test images. JPEG lossy compression with QF 80 only leads to small hash differences as expected. But the differences are the same or larger than inpainting in some cases. An example: JPEG QF 80

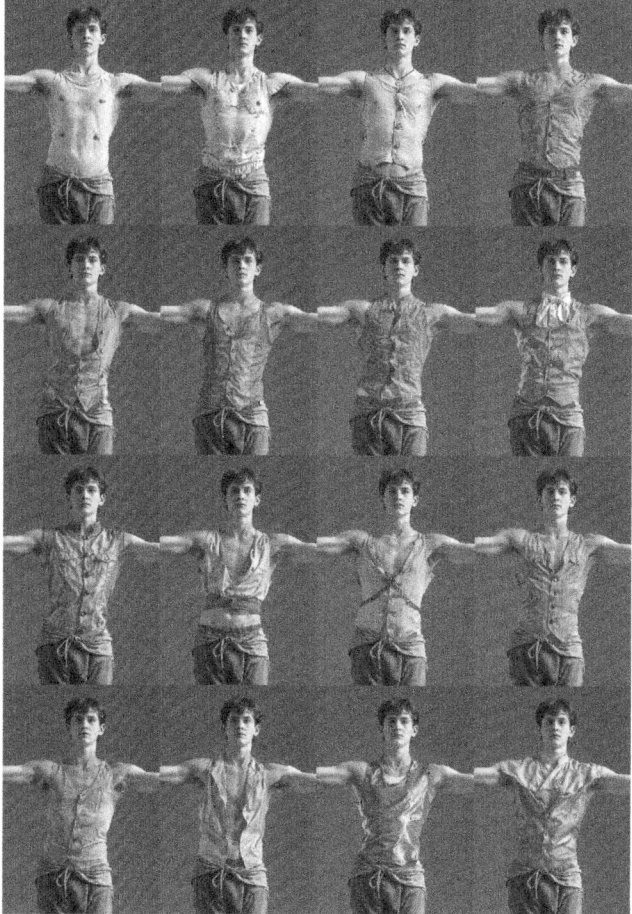

Fig. 4. Top: Original image. Prompt: bare-chested male ballet dancer wearing historical pants, Steps: 20, Sampler: DPM++ 2M, Schedule type: Karras, CFG scale: 1, Seed: 826878541, Size: 1032 × 1024, Model hash: 39903ba05f, Model: flux1-schnell-fp8, Version: f2.0.1v1.10.1-previous-633-ge073e4ec. Bottom: Zoomed regions of example image inpaintings.

Table 2. Summary of Blockhash and rHash statistics for each evaluation folder

Folder	Blockhash				rHash			
	Min	Max	Mean	Median	Min	Max	Mean	Median
ballerina	0	0	0.00	0.0	0	6	2.09	2.0
beach	0	6	2.88	5.0	1	7	3.50	3.0
beachboy	0	4	0.50	0.0	0	5	0.94	0.0
bigjuice	4	12	6.88	6.5	8	23	14.69	14.0
dancer	1	11	8.45	9.0	0	5	3.40	4.0
dancer2	0	6	0.88	0.0	2	9	6.29	6.0
drill	0	1	0.12	0.0	0	2	1.19	1.0
female	0	1	0.16	0.0	0	4	2.22	3.0
juice	3	13	7.06	6.0	8	21	12.88	13.0
soccerboy	0	6	2.21	2.0	0	10	3.36	3.0
Overall	0	13	2.91	0.0	0	23	5.06	3.0

Table 3. Summary of PhotoDNA and ISCC statistics for each evaluation folder

Folder	PhotoDNA				ISCC			
	Min	Max	Mean	Median	Min	Max	Mean	Median
ballerina	26.80	84.82	57.14	56.13	2	6	3.83	4.00
beach	33.24	114.14	59.07	54.92	0	8	3.88	4.00
beachboy	14.18	74.93	42.72	44.63	0	6	3.75	4.00
bigjuice	74.11	121.66	95.14	92.91	8	14	10.25	10.00
dancer	27.82	125.73	82.13	81.69	2	10	6.60	6.00
dancer2	53.35	261.52	172.55	187.49	4	8	5.65	6.00
drill	23.64	85.72	44.08	39.69	2	6	3.38	3.00
female	28.04	104.18	55.27	52.60	0	4	2.19	2.00
juice	52.75	121.55	83.69	82.14	6	16	11.38	12.00
soccerboy	28.98	109.55	60.79	61.24	4	10	5.03	4.00
Overall	14.18	261.52	75.26	58.69	0	16	5.59	4.00

of "female" produces a rHash difference of 7, minimal inpainting distance is 0, maximal difference is 4. This means: if the hash is to be robust against JPEG QF 80, it requires a threshold of at least 7. This would include all inpaiting variants of "female". No change would be detected.

Cropping has a greater effect on the hash distances. rHash is more sensitive to cropping than blockhash. Cropping 2 lines of images 1024 pixels wide means a reduction in size of 0.2%, cropping 5 lines 0.5%. The Table 7 clearly shows that if the hashes are to be robust against this amount of cropping, most inpainting attacks will be below the hash thresholds. PhotoDNA gives the best discrimina-

Table 4. Hash distance comparison of selected images against original image, images from 4(bottom), sorted left to right, row by row.

Filename	Blockhash	rHash	PhotoDNA	ISCC
00000-629034090.png	1	2	55.62	4
00004-629034094.png	0	4	63.33	6
00013-629034103.png	0	6	53.35	4
00044-826878542.png	0	6	236.47	6
00045-826878543.png	0	7	187.49	6
00046-826878544.png	0	7	136.32	6
00048-826878546.png	0	6	162.28	6
00050-826878548.png	0	5	141.65	6
00051-826878549.png	0	7	120.62	6
00052-826878550.png	0	8	143.77	6
00053-826878551.png	0	8	150.94	6
00054-826878552.png	0	6	177.88	6
00055-826878553.png	0	6	144.79	6
00056-826878554.png	0	6	128.36	6
00057-826878555.png	0	6	151.15	6
00058-826878556.png	0	6	140.09	6

tion between inpainting and cropping, with only "Beachboy" and "Drill" having a smaller distance for inpainting than for crop5. But as soon as 1% cropping is allowed, the required threshold of PhotoDNA is also above for all test images except "bigjuice", as shown in the Table 8.

7 Discussion

Our experiments reveal a fundamental challenge in the design of robust perceptual hash functions: the very robustness that makes them insensitive to benign image transformations (such as mild JPEG compression or slight cropping) also renders them ineffective at detecting malicious inpainting-based content modifications. In several test cases, blockhash, rHash and the ISCC content code all produced zero Hamming distance changes for some test images when inpainting was applied – despite the fact that visually perceptible content had been altered. This suggests that these hash functions, by prioritising stability under common image operations, inherently discard the fine-grained spatial information needed to flag localised pixel-level edits.

PhotoDNA, often praised for its strong discriminatory capabilities [14], performed only marginally better. Although it registered non-zero distances in response to our inpainting tests, these distances were consistently smaller than the changes caused by cropping the image by just 10 pixels out of 1024×1024.

Table 5. Hash differences PNG to JPEG(80) images

Name	Blockhash	rHash	PhotoDNA	ISCC
ballerina	0	3	3.00	0
beach	0	3	4.24	2
beachboy	0	1	4.36	0
bigjuice	0	2	3.74	0
dancer2	0	5	6.86	2
dancer	1	5	6.32	2
drill	0	2	4.80	2
female	1	7	8.66	0
juice	0	2	3.74	0
soccerboy	0	10	3.46	2

Table 6. Hash differences for cropped (crop2) image pairs, grouped by original image name

Name	Blockhash Diff	rHash Diff	PhotoDNA Diff	ISCC Diff
ballerina	0	0	10.25	6
beach	1	7	11.58	2
beachboy	0	6	10.34	6
bigjuice	4	7	16.46	2
dancer2	1	11	12.08	4
dancer	6	115	11.79	0
drill	1	4	13.82	8
female	1	6	11.40	2
juice	4	7	16.46	2
soccerboy	2	21	11.96	2

In practical terms, this means that a benign cropping operation can move an image's PhotoDNA hash further from its original value than a targeted inpainting attack, undermining any scheme that would flag large hash differences as indicators of tampering. Put another way, if a system is tuned to ignore differences below the threshold required to detect mild cropping, it will also miss more significant semantic changes introduced by inpainting.

These findings highlight a key limitation: robust perceptual hashes cannot reliably detect inpainting-based manipulations if they also have to tolerate common image operations. Their robustness thresholds must be set high enough to avoid false positives on benign transformations, but it is this tolerance window that swallows the subtle but semantically significant distortions introduced by modern inpainting algorithms. As a result, relying on a single robust hash approach leaves a blind spot for content-aware editing techniques.

Table 7. Hash differences for cropped (crop5) image pairs, grouped by original image name

Name	Blockhash Diff	rHash Diff	PhotoDNA Diff	ISCC Diff
ballerina	0	0	24.12	6
beach	3	11	27.24	2
beachboy	0	7	24.37	8
bigjuice	2	10	37.62	4
dancer2	3	52	29.22	4
dancer	6	111	27.66	4
drill	2	8	31.35	6
female	2	121	25.40	2
juice	2	10	37.62	4
soccerboy	3	19	26.85	6

Table 8. Side-by-side comparison of PhotoDNA (crop10) versus minimum PhotoDNA inpainting minimum per test image

Name	crop10	Inpaint Min.	Name	crop10	Inpaint Min.
ballerina	47.80	26.80	beachboy	48.05	14.18
beach	54.00	33.24	bigjuice	64.47	74.11
dancer	55.48	27.82	dancer2	59.99	53.35
drill	62.51	23.64	female	51.64	28.04
juice	64.47	52.75	soccerboy	50.86	28.98

This limitation has serious real-world implications. Consider automated "chat control" or content monitoring systems that rely on known image databases of CSAM: An adversary could take a known CSAM image, apply inpainting to replace or remove the illicit content, and then redistribute the variant. Because robust hashes remain unchanged (or change less than they would with simple cropping), these inpainted variants will cause false positives. This could lead to the inundation of authorities tasked with monitoring CSAM. However, in the case of multi-strike solutions, where an internal counter is used that is incremented when a known CSAM is found, and authorities are only notified when the counter is above a certain threshold, the manipulation of this counter with false positives could also be a serious risk.

8 Future Work

Manipulating the hash algorithms presented in this work can pose a substantial risk in certain scenarios. Therefore, strategies should be developed to counter such attacks. The challenge is to find approaches that are robust against accepted changes yet sensitive to content changes that resemble the original image.

One strategy that likely would be more sensitive to lokal changes of an image would be the combination of image segmentation and hashing of the individual objects. We suggested approaches for this in previous works [15,16]. The goal there was to recognize objects after image montages combined with rotation. But as image 5 shows, the strategy could also help to mitigate the effects of inpainting.

A more generic approach could be designing an intelligent hash that focuses on image elements important for the task to which the hash is applied. For example, if the task is to identify child pornography, a cropping algorithm could remove everything in an image that does not show a minor. This would lead to similar focusing effects as the image segmentation described in the last paragraph. However, there would be no need to hash additional objects in the images.

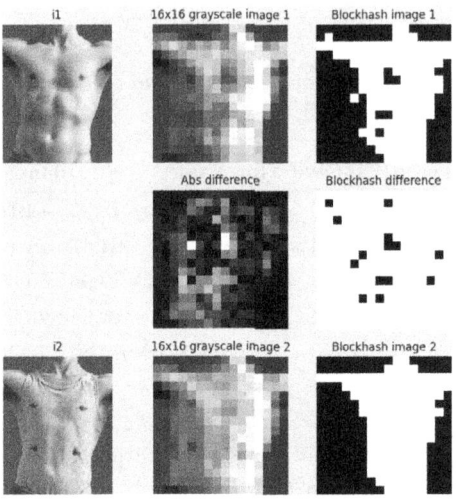

Fig. 5. Hashing of relevant objects increases the chance of detection of changes caused by inpainting. Screenshot from rHash comparison tool.

Acknowledgments. This research work was supported by the National Research Center for Applied Cybersecurity ATHENE. ATHENE is funded jointly by the German Federal Ministry of Research, Technology and Space and the Hessian Ministry of Science and Research, Arts and Culture.

References

1. Brooks, T., Holynski, A., Efros, A.A.: Instructpix2pix: learning to follow image editing instructions. In: Proceedings of the IEEE/CVF Conference on Computer Vision and Pattern Recognition, pp. 18392–18402 (2023)

2. Buchko, O., et al.: Classification of confidential images using neural hash. NaUKMA Res. Papers Comput. Sci. **5**, 68–71 (2022)
3. Desai, V., Rao, D.: Image hash using neural networks. Int. J. Comput. Appl. **63**(22) (2013)
4. Drmic, A., Silic, M., Delac, G., Vladimir, K., Kurdija, A.S.: Evaluating robustness of perceptual image hashing algorithms. In: 2017 40th International Convention on Information and Communication Technology, Electronics and Microelectronics (MIPRO), pp. 995–1000. IEEE (2017). https://doi.org/10.23919/MIPRO.2017.7973569
5. Du, L., Ho, A.T., Cong, R.: Perceptual hashing for image authentication: a survey. Signal Process. Image Commun. **81**, 115713 (2020). https://doi.org/10.1016/j.image.2019.115713
6. Guillemot, C., Le Meur, O.: Image inpainting: overview and recent advances. IEEE Signal Process. Mag. **31**(1), 127–144 (2013)
7. Hao, Q., Luo, L., Jan, S.T., Wang, G.: It's not what it looks like: manipulating perceptual hashing based applications. In: Proceedings of the 2021 ACM SIGSAC Conference on Computer and Communications Security, pp. 69–85 (2021)
8. Ith, T.: Microsoft's photodna: protecting children and businesses in the cloud. Retrieved from Microsoft News Center: https://news.microsoft.com/features/microsoftsphotodna-protecting-children-and-businesses-inthe-cloud (2015)
9. Nguyen, D.T., Alam, F., Ofli, F., Imran, M.: Automatic image filtering on social networks using deep learning and perceptual hashing during crises. http://arxiv.org/pdf/1704.02602v1
10. Nichol, A., et al.: GLIDE: towards photorealistic image generation and editing with text-guided diffusion models. arXiv preprint arXiv:2112.10741 (2021)
11. Prokos, J., et al..: Squint hard enough: evaluating perceptual hashing with machine learning. Cryptology ePrint Archive, Paper 2021/1531 (2021). https://eprint.iacr.org/2021/1531
12. Qin, C., Liu, E., Feng, G., Zhang, X.: Perceptual image hashing for content authentication based on convolutional neural network with multiple constraints. IEEE Trans. Circuits Syst. Video Technol. **31**(11), 4523–4537 (2020)
13. Steinebach, M.: Robust hashing for efficient forensic analysis of image sets. In: Gladyshev, P., Rogers, M.K. (eds.) ICDF2C 2011. LNICSSITE, vol. 88, pp. 180–187. Springer, Heidelberg (2012). https://doi.org/10.1007/978-3-642-35515-8_15
14. Steinebach, M.: An analysis of PhotoDNA. In: Proceedings of the 18th International Conference on Availability, Reliability and Security, ARES 2023, Benevento, Italy, 29 August 2023- 1 September 2023, pp. 44:1–44:8. ACM (2023). https://doi.org/10.1145/3600160.3605048
15. Steinebach, M., Berwanger, T., Liu, H.: Towards image hashing robust against cropping and rotation. In: Proceedings of the 17th International Conference on Availability, Reliability and Security, pp. 1–7 (2022)
16. Steinebach, M., Berwanger, T., Liu, H.: Image hashing robust against cropping and rotation. J. Cyber Secur. Mobility, 129–160 (2023)
17. Steinebach, M., Liu, H., Yannikos, Y.: Efficient cropping-resistant robust image hashing. In: 2014 Ninth International Conference on Availability, Reliability and Security, pp. 579–585. IEEE (2014). https://doi.org/10.1109/ARES.2014.85
18. Struppek, L., Hintersdorf, D., Neider, D., Kersting, K.: Learning to break deep perceptual hashing: the use case neuralhash. In: Proceedings of the 2022 ACM Conference on Fairness, Accountability, and Transparency, pp. 58–69 (2022)

19. Sun, R., Zeng, W.: Secure and robust image hashing via compressive sensing. Multimedia Tools Appl. **70**(3), 1651–1665 (2012). https://doi.org/10.1007/s11042-012-1188-8
20. Tang, Z., Chen, L., Zhang, X., Zhang, S.: Robust image hashing with tensor decomposition. IEEE Trans. Knowl. Data Eng. **31**(3), 549–560 (2019). https://doi.org/10.1109/TKDE.2018.2837745
21. Tang, Z., Yang, F., Huang, L., Zhang, X.: Robust image hashing with dominant DCT coefficients. Optik **125**(18), 5102–5107 (2014). https://doi.org/10.1016/j.ijleo.2014.05.015, https://www.sciencedirect.com/science/article/pii/S0030402614005853
22. Tang, Z., Zhang, X., Dai, X., Yang, J., Wu, T.: Robust image hash function using local color features. AEU - Int. J. Electron. Commun. **67**(8), 717–722 (2013). https://doi.org/10.1016/j.aeue.2013.02.009, https://www.sciencedirect.com/science/article/pii/S1434841113000629
23. Yang, B., Gu, F., Niu, X.: Block mean value based image perceptual hashing. In: Proceedings of the 2006 International Conference on Intelligent Information Hiding and Multimedia, pp. 167–172. IIH-MSP '06, IEEE Computer Society, USA (2006)

Combining Different Existing Methods for Describing Steganography Hiding Methods

Steffen Wendzel[1]( ), Christian Krätzer[2], Jana Dittmann[2], Luca Caviglione[3], Aleksandra Mileva[4], Tobias Schmidbauer[5], Claus Vielhauer[2,6], and Sebastian Zander[7]

[1] Ulm University, Ulm, Germany
steffen.wendzel@uni-ulm.de
[2] Otto-von-Guericke University Magdeburg, Magdeburg, Germany
{dittmann,kraetzer}@ovgu.de
[3] Institute for Applied Mathematics and Information Technology, Genoa, Italy
luca.caviglione@ge.imati.cnr.it
[4] Goce Delcev University, Stip, North Macedonia
aleksandra.mileva@ugd.edu.mk
[5] Technische Hochschule Nürnberg Georg Simon Ohm, Nuremberg, Germany
tobias.schmidbauer@th-nuernberg.de
[6] Brandenburg University of Applied Sciences, Brandenburg, Germany
claus.vielhauer@th-brandenburg.de
[7] Murdoch University, Perth, Australia
s.zander@murdoch.edu.au

Abstract. The proliferation of digital carriers that can be exploited to conceal arbitrary data has increased the number of techniques for implementing steganography and other forms of information hiding. As a result, the literature overlaps greatly in terms of concepts and terminology. Moreover, from a cybersecurity viewpoint, the same hiding mechanism may be perceived differently, making harder the development of a unique defensive strategy or the definition of practices to mitigate risks arising from the use of steganography. To mitigate these drawbacks, several researchers introduced approaches that aid in the unified description of steganography methods and covert channels.

Understanding and combining all descriptive methods for steganography techniques is a challenging but important task. For instance, researchers might want to explain how malware applies a certain steganography technique or categorize a novel hiding approach. Consequently, this paper aims to provide an introduction to the concept of *descriptive methods for steganography*. The paper is organized in the form of a tutorial, with the main goal of explaining how existing descriptions and taxonomy objects can be combined to achieve a detailed categorization and description of hiding methods. To show how this can effectively help the research community, the paper also contains various real-world examples.

Keywords: Steganography · Information Hiding · Covert Channels · Science of Security · Taxonomy · Terminology · Systematization

1 Introduction

The expanding diffusion of digital objects increases the opportunities for hiding data. For instance, the need for enforcing copyright, tracking the diffusion of information, or preventing that data is ingested without a suitable consent, culminated in a vast array of *watermarking* mechanisms [49]. At the same time, the massive softwarization of services in combination with the complexity of modern software supply chains required the design of new watermarks for concealing control information. As an example, software artifacts should be traceable to guarantee provenance and early detect tampering that may cause outages or data breaches [10]. In parallel, the ubiquitous diffusion of AI opened up new challenges. Information needs to be hidden in datasets and models to support licensing schemes, protect large monetary investments, and track quality in AI-as-a-Service frameworks [42].

However, the process of hiding information is not always performed for legitimate purposes. This is the case with malware endowed with steganographic capabilities. In essence, this class of malicious software tries to prevent detection or bypass security countermeasures by cloaking configuration data, offensive attack routines, or optional payloads within multimedia assets. As a result, malware is no longer monolithic, but is implemented through a multi-stage architecture, which reduces its footprint [6]. Another offensive approach concerns the creation of *covert channels*, i.e., parasitic communication paths that can be used to exchange data in a secret and unauthorized manner. Even with real-world attacks abounding in *carriers* that can be abused for the covert communication (e.g., patterns of syscalls or hardware behaviors), the most effective approaches take advantage of network traffic [47].

As a result, the works dealing with information hiding and steganography largely overlap both in terms of terminology and concepts. In some cases, the same idea is reinvented multiple times, wasting resources and complicating the retrieval of knowledge. For instance, hiding secret information in the least significant bits (LSB) of an image file is a steganography technique since many decades, see, e.g., [15,21,40], but also applied in network information hiding.

Another major issue is rooted within the double-edged nature of mechanisms devoted to cloak data. On one hand, they have proven their effectiveness for tracking and copyright purposes (e.g., watermarks). On the other hand, they are definitely becoming an important resource in the toolbox of attackers (e.g., to implement stegomalware). This causes a "mismatch" in the perception of the various steganographic approaches, as some ideas may require to be designed contextually with a proper defensive strategy. Moreover, different backgrounds and use cases hinder the possibility of developing general countermeasures. For instance, the mitigation of network covert channels requires preventing ambiguities that could be exploited by an attacker early on, i.e., during the design stage. Unfortunately, this conflicts with the need for offering techniques to mark packet flows and control their route through the Internet, such as for traffic engineering goals [7].

To cope with the aforementioned pitfalls, several authors introduced different approaches for a *unified description* of steganography methods and network covert channels. This paper explains how existing steganography taxonomy and description objects can be used jointly to achieve a unified and clear explanation. The goal here is to provide a solid foundation for the scientific literature on steganography and covert channels. Our paper is accompanied by an inter-active online tool: https://patterns.omi.uni-ulm.de/desrcovert/.

In summary, the main contribution of this work is to provide an introduction to concepts related to *descriptive methods for steganography*. The paper provides a tutorial on how existing descriptions and taxonomy objects can be combined for designing precise descriptions of several hiding methods.

The remainder of this paper is structured as follows. We discuss the existing concepts in Sect. 2 and then describe how these can be combined in Sect. 3. We provide tutorial examples in Sect. 4 and a brief discussion in Sect. 5. Finally, Sect. 6 concludes.

2 Related Work and Fundamentals

This section reviews previous approaches on how steganographic methods and techniques for the creation of covert channels can be organized or described in terms of hiding patterns. For the sake of brevity, this section does not embrace the literature on information hiding on a *tout court* manner. Rather, it should be considered as a complement of more comprehensive works, see, e.g., [5] for a general overview of cloaked/abusive communication paths.

Hiding Patterns. For the specific case of taxonomies, several authors already categorized information hiding and steganography methods. As a result, a relevant corpus of works has emerged [4,11,15,22,23,25,28,29,34,39,41,54–56]. However, the existing categorizations have either focused on high-level aspects or have been tailored to specific domains. For instance, many works only consider network steganography or image steganography.

In 2015, the concept of *hiding patterns* has been introduced to provide a generic taxonomy on the hiding process [52]. In essence, hiding patterns describe hiding methods in an abstract fashion. Until recently, the description of hiding patterns still has been domain-specific: the original taxonomy was tailored for network steganography [52] but an analysis of the taxonomy in the context of cyber-physical systems exists as well [20].

More recently, a *generic pattern-based taxonomy for all steganography domains* has been introduced [50]. Based on this taxonomy, hiding patterns either describe how a secret message is *embedded* in a carrier (so-called *embedding patterns*) or how the secret message is *represented* (so-called *representation patterns*). Representation patterns are derived from embedding patterns. The enumeration and nomenclature is driven by clear rules. Two major types of embedding hiding patterns exist: (1) those that modulate a state or value, e.g., the pattern E1.3. LSB STATE/VALUE MODULATION[1] subsumes LSB-based methods; (2) those that modify the occurrence of some element, e.g., the pattern E2.1. ELEMENT ENUMERATION encodes secret information through the number of some element (e.g., byte count of a file or size of a network packet) [50]. A brief overview on the major patterns is given by Table 1. Note that patterns can be media-specific, e.g., E1.3N1. NETWORK LSB STATE/VALUE MODULATION or E1.3T1. TEXT LSB STATE/VALUE MODULATION for network and text steganography, respectively.

Table 1. Overview of core hiding patterns of [50].

Pattern	Brief Description
E1. STATE/VALUE MODULATION	Some state (e.g., of an actuator) or value (e.g., bit in a file) is modulated to hide a secret message.
E1.1. RESERVED/UNUSED STATE/VALUE MOD.	Sub-variant where reserved or unused states/values (e.g., padding bits) are modulated to embed a secret message
E1.2. RANDOM STATE/VALUE MOD.	Sub-variant that covers the modulation of random values (e.g., cryptographic hashes)
E1.3. LSB STATE/VALUE MOD.	Sub-variant covering all forms of LSB steganography
E1.4. CHARACTER STATE/VALUE MOD.	Sub-variant covering textual character modulations, e.g., changing the case of letters
E1.5. REDUNDANCY STATE/VALUE MOD.	Sub-variant that covers hiding methods that change redundancy (to embed secret data), e.g., transcoding steganography
E2. ELEMENT OCCURRENCE	Some element's occurrence is changed in some way (e.g., a network packet *appears*)
E2.1. ELEMENT ENUMERATION	Sub-variant covering methods where the number of elements is modulated to encode a secret message (e.g., number of bytes of a file)
E2.2. ELEMENT POSITIONING	Sub-variant covering methods where the location of an element in a cover object is used to encode a secret message (e.g., position of a specific pixel in an image or time of appearance of a signal)

Local and Distributed Channels. Local steganography channels do not rely on distributing the secret message over multiple cover objects nor do they apply multiple hiding methods to the same cover object. The following terms were proposed in [52] to describe distributed hiding methods using patterns: *Pattern variation* refers to techniques that apply the same hiding pattern to different carrier objects, e.g., least significant bit modulation to a field in the IPv4 and the IPv6 header, without needed a whole new implementation. *Pattern combination* applies multiple hiding patterns to the same carrier object (e.g., embedding a secret bit into the least significant bit of a timestamp in a file's metadata

---

[1] In this paper, we will use a highlighted font to indicate our proposed nomenclature, including the patterns introduced in [50].

while embedding additional secret data into unused metadata bits). Finally, *pattern hopping* refers to the (pseudo-randomized) alternation of hiding methods [52]. Mazurczyk *et al.* slightly extended these terms in [32] by further splitting pattern variation into *host-, flow-* and *protocol-based scattering*, which represent approaches specific for network steganography. The core idea is to distribute secret message bits to different hosts, through multiple flows or through multiple protocols.

Direct and Indirect Channels. Some steganography methods, including network techniques for the creation of covert channels, are designed to establish indirect paths for secret messages, i.e., the covert sender does not directly send data to the covert receiver [54,55]. For instance, personal cloud storage services can be used to implement an encoding for transferring secret information. In this case, file operations (e.g., copying and renaming) can be grouped into patterns and are used to generate suitable signaling flows to convey secret data to the intended recipients [8].

When the covert communication path does *not* behave in a direct end-to-end flavor and is based on the (involuntary) integration of a third-party node, such as a network host or a process on a local system, the channel can be described by two indirect hiding patterns that have been introduced by Schmidbauer and Wendzel: *redirector* or *broker*, with the broker having the two sub-patterns *proxy* and *dead drop*) [43]. A brief description of these indirect hiding patterns is summarized in Table 2.

Active and Passive Channels. Covert senders do not necessarily need to create their own cover objects to embed data into, nor must covert receivers necessarily be the overt recipients of a cover object [58]. In this perspective, an *active* channel is one where the covert sender creates the cover object and the covert receiver is the overt recipient. In contrast, a *passive* channel would require a covert sender to modify a third-party cover object to embed the secret message into and the covert receiver to recognize the embedded message (e.g., as an on-path attacker). It is also possible to create channels of mixed form (*semi-active* [24] as introduced by Lamshöft and Dittmann; *semi-passive* as introduced by Zander [54]). In some cases *fully-passive* channels can be created (as introduced by Wendzel *et al.* [51]). In such cases, the cover object is untouched by sender and receiver. Instead, the sender solely *points* to the cover object and the receiver observes the traffic through eavesdropping or as a broadcast receiver.

Multi-level Steganography. Multiple authors proposed nesting steganographic objects inside other steganography objects, leading to multiple levels (or layers) of steganography. Multi-level steganography can be found in different domains, including filesystem steganography [30] and network steganography [14]. Multi-level steganography can be used to reach a plausible deniability, where the outer steganography level is presented to an observer, but inner levels are not revealed and kept secret.

Table 2. Summary of indirect hiding patterns as introduced in [43]; descriptions have been generalized to remove the network-specific context.

Indirect Hiding Pattern	Brief Description
REDIRECTOR	A sender forces a third-party node to unintentionally redirect steganography objects to a covert receiver. Example: a covert sender transmits steganography objects as payload within a spoofed network packet. The packet contains a request (e.g., ICMP or IGMP) and is sent to a third-party node that responds to the spoofed address (which is the one of the covert receiver) [43].
BROKER	In comparison to the REDIRECTOR, a broker does not redirect steganography objects but manipulates the third-party node so that these steganography objects can be extracted by a covert receiver [43]. A BROKER is either a PROXY or a DEADDROP.
PROXY	Sub-variant of the BROKER where a covert sender influences a third-party node in such a way that the influence can be recognized by a covert receiver. Example: A local covert sender process might cause heavy load on a third-party process handling his requests. This load influences the third-party process' performance and can be measured by a covert receiver's process. The influence on the performance represents the secret message.
DEAD DROP	Sub-variant of the BROKER where the steganography object is stored on a third-party node. Example: a sender might influence the network protocol's cache of a third-party node to embed a secret message. The cache's content is then read by the covert receiver [43].

A similar concept introduced by Ogiela and Koptyra is called *multi-secret steganography* [36]. Instead of nesting one layer inside another, multi-secret steganography embeds a set of secret messages into the same carrier. Several of these messages are *false stego-objects* that are comparably easy to detect while the actual secret message is more challenging to detect.[2]

Pointers to "Historic" and "Future" Data. A steganography transmission can embed the actual secret message or a *pointer* that refers to the desired secret message, so that only a small fraction of the information is used instead of transferring the entire message [51]. In the case of a pointer, one can refer to either already existing data (called historic data, even if it was *just* created, e.g., a few CPU cycles ago) or to anticipated future data (e.g., expected regular ARP requests).

---

[2] Multi-secret steganography could alternatively be considered a special variant of the previously-mentioned *pattern combination* [52] as multiple hiding methods are combined to add secret message (fragments) to the same cover object.

Unified Description Method. In 2016, a *unified description method* (UDM) was introduced for network information hiding methods, which was slightly modified in 2025 to fit all domains of steganography and better integrate the updated patterns taxonomy [50, supplemental material Sect. A.6]. The UDM covers several attributes that are described in a comparable manner, including the application scenario, the hiding patterns of a hiding method, the required properties of a cover object that are necessary to realize the steganography channel, and the channel properties (e.g., robustness, countermeasures, and capacity). Finally, optional information can be provided on a channel-internal protocol. The UDM has been designed to improve the replicability, comparability, and identification of research gaps in the steganography literature.

3 Proposal for a Combination of Description Methods

Figure 1 shows the general structure of our naming convention. Following the recent steganography taxonomy [50], here we apply the proposed pattern naming convention for "hiding patterns" (see the most-right component in the figure). At the same time, we also adjust it to incorporate the surrounding terms for categorization (see the remaining boxes in the figure). A dash (-) indicates a default category, i.e., it can be omitted if a channel does not contain a specific feature. In particular, it must not be mentioned explicitly that a steganography channel is non-distributed, direct, active, uses solely a single level of embedding, or when the steganography data is embedded into the object itself (present-focused) rather than referring to history or anticipated (future) data.

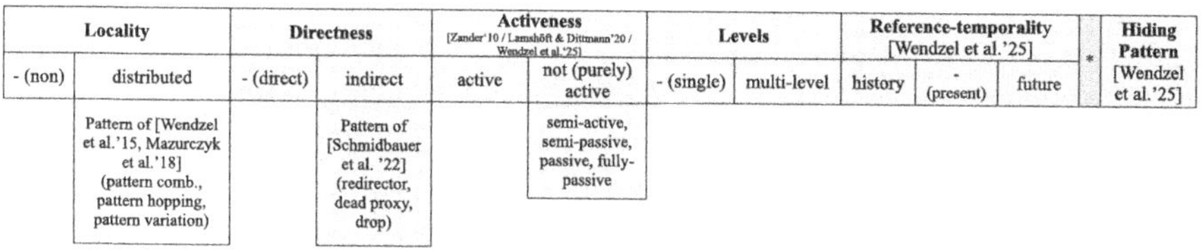

Locality		Directness		Activeness [Zander'10 / Lamshöft & Dittmann'20 / Wendzel et al.'25]		Levels		Reference-temporality [Wendzel et al.'25]			*	Hiding Pattern [Wendzel et al.'25]
- (non)	distributed	- (direct)	indirect	active	not (purely) active	- (single)	multi-level	history	- (present)	future		
	Pattern of [Wendzel et al.'15, Mazurczyk et al.'18] (pattern comb., pattern hopping, pattern variation)		Pattern of [Schmidbauer et al. '22] (redirector, dead proxy, drop)		semi-active, semi-passive, passive, fully-passive							

Fig. 1. Proposed Naming Convention.

All components of our naming convention are additionally explained by our inter-active online tool: https://patterns.omi.uni-ulm.de/desrcovert/

3.1 Naming Components in Detail

Referring to Fig. 1, we now discuss the components that can be used to develop the proposed naming convention. The naming components are described below.

Locality. This clarifies whether a steganography hiding method is local or distributed. To this end, the first (but optional) component of the naming can be "distributed", followed by the distribution pattern (e.g., "pattern combination") enclosed in brackets [32,52]. Such methods might employ different hiding patterns simultaneously. As will be detailed later in Sect. 4.2, multiple methods should be mentioned jointly.

Directness. This clarifies if the hiding method represents a direct or indirect channel. The optional attribute "indirect" would be followed by the name of the particular *pattern* of Schmidbauer and Wendzel [43] in brackets, e.g., "redirector". Multiple examples featuring such indirect patterns will be provided in Sect. 4.

Activeness. This defines whether the channel is *active* (must not be mentioned explicitly) or *passive* [58]. Here, the above-mentioned passivity terms (*semi-active, semi-passive, fully-passive*) can be be placed in brackets behind the "passive" attribute.

Level Characteristic. This denotes whether the steganography method establishes a multi-level steganography system, or not. The attribute should be omitted if it is a single-level system.

Reference-Temporality. This attribute can be used to specify if secret data is "moved" through the channel by means of pointers, that is if the channel points to previously found/written data (history covert channel) or to anticipated (future) data as introduced in [51].

Star-Property (*). This attribute is a star property (*) that allows arbitrary details to be added. For instance, one might employ terms like *cover selection* [15] or *coverless steganography* [26,57]. Another option is to state whether a channel is a unidirectional, bidirectional, or broadcast channel. If desired, one might explicitly mention robustness criteria, e.g., whether the channel is *noisy* or *noise-free* or if the cover is *predictable, variable* or *randomized* as mentioned by Zander [54]. Finally, one might state that a hiding method is *reversible* [9,19,31,44], i.e., if an (intermediate) covert receiver can restore the cover object to its status before a secret message was embedded.

Hiding Pattern. This attribute must mention the hiding pattern of the 2025 taxonomy of steganography hiding methods [50]. This is a very important aspect, as this attribute contributes to aligning the various concepts within the literature towards a common knowledge.

3.2 Describing Sophisticated Methods

In general, the aforementioned *seven* attributes already provide some flexibility to describe sophisticated methods. For example, one might apply the distributed *host-based scattering* method introduced in [32] by using an indirect communication through *dead drops* [43] that serve as nodes for storing the secret data.

The actual hiding method might be a network-based LSB state-value modulation. To this end, we would call such a method a DISTRIBUTED (HOST-BASED SCATTERED) INDIRECT (DEAD DROP) E.1N1. NETWORK LSB STATE/VALUE MODULATION.

However, if the steganography method *utilizes different hiding patterns*, each must be named separately. For instance, one might be LSB and the other reserved/unused state/value modulation, so we would gain two descriptions, (a) and (b): DISTRIBUTED (HOST-BASED SCATTERED) INDIRECT (DEAD DROP) (A) E1.3N1. NETWORK LSB STATE/VALUE MODULATION AND (B) E1.1N1. NETWORK RESERVED/UNUSED STATE/VALUE MODULATION).

Unfortunately, methods might also apply *multi-level steganography*, i.e., nesting stego objects inside other stego objects. This requires more elaborate naming, but the availability of a solid convention/taxonomy makes the process simple and reduces ambiguities. In this case, each stego-layer could utilize a *different* hiding pattern. For instance, a multi-layer filesystem steganography method might be classified as MULTI-LEVEL (A) E1.3F1. FILESYSTEM LSB STATE/VALUE MODULATION, (B) E1.1F1. FILESYSTEM RESERVED/UNUSED STATE/VALUE MODULATION AND (C) E1.2F1. FILESYSTEM RANDOM STATE/VALUE MODULATION).

This means that the outermost layer performs LSB state/value modulation, while the middle layer performs reserved/unused state/value modulation, and the innermost layer is LSB state/value modulation on filesystem data.

It would also be reasonable to have a multi-*level*-multi-*media* approach. For instance, network steganography might hide data inside network packets, and embedded data could contain a second layer featuring digital image steganography data. An example of such a case would be MULTI-LEVEL (A) E1.1N1. NETWORK RESERVED/UNUSED STATE VALUE MODULATION, (B) E1.3D1. DIGITAL MEDIA LSB STATE/VALUE MODULATION.

Allowing such multi-media descriptions also contributes to fill a gap identified by the latest taxonomy [50, cf. Fig. 1]. Especially, hiding methods have been described until now as belonging to only *one* domain, i.e., neglecting another domain if they utilize objects or hiding methods from multiple domains.

3.3 Utilization of the Unified Description Method

In case our nomenclature cannot capture all the nuances of the targeted steganography approach, the missing details can be covered by borrowing ideas from the UDM [50, cf. electronic supplement]. Figure 2 shows the structure of the UDM. As shown, such a unified framework foresees that a steganography method is described by using hiding patterns as its core component as well as by several additional attributes. These additional attributes (application scenario, required properties of the cover object, etc.) leave room for a structured description of typical attributes.

Handling Representation Patterns. Some steganography methods utilize a different embedding and representation pattern. In this case, the attribute "representation hiding pattern" of the UDM can be used to mention the representation

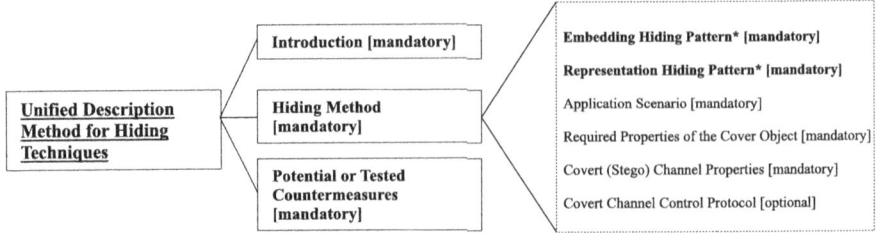

Fig. 2. The UDM of [50]. Our nomenclature is used within the attributes specifying the patterns (indicated by *).

pattern, also following our nomenclature (see example in Sect. 4.2). In other cases where the representation pattern is simply the representing variant of the embedding pattern, the UDM attribute "representation hiding pattern" can just state "representation variant of embedding pattern".

4 Examples

This section describes existing steganography methods by using our combined approach. Table 3 provides an overview on our examples. We start with a simple network-specific technique, followed by two indirect/hybrid network steganography techniques. Afterwards, we cover an example from digital media steganography, one from cyber-physical systems steganography, and one from text steganography.

Table 3. Overview on provided examples

Ex.	Scenario	Description
1	Simple Network Method	E1.1N1. NETWORK RESERVED/UNUSED STATE/VALUE MODULATION
2	Hybrid Hiding Method	(1) INDIRECT (PROXY) E1N1. NETWORK STATE/VALUE MODULATION, (2) INDIRECT (PROXY) R2.2N1. NETWORK ELEMENT POSITIONING
3	Indirect Dead-drop	INDIRECT (DEAD DROP) E1.1N1. NETWORK STATE/VALUE MODULATION
4	(History-focused) LSB Audio Steganography	(HISTORY-FOCUSED) E1.3D1. DIGITAL MEDIA LSB STATE/VALUE MODULATION
5	(Distributed) OPC UA Steganography	(DISTRIBUTED) E1.3C1. CPS LSB STATE/VALUE MODULATION
6	Text Steganography	(1) E2.1T1. TEXT ELEMENT ENUMERATION, (2) (SEMI-ACTIVE) E2.1T1. TEXT ELEMENT ENUMERATION, (3) INDIRECT (DEAD-DROP) E2.1T1. TEXT ELEMENT ENUMERATION

4.1 Simple Network Steganography Method

In network steganography, secret data is hidden inside the content of network packets (e.g., overwriting unused bits or replacing values in header fields) or by modulating temporal characteristics of the traffic (e.g., influencing packet occurrence or flow duration) [34,52,55]. The first methods for network steganography (or: network covert channels) have been described in the late1980 s e.g., [16,53]. Recently, network steganography has become a major branch of steganography-capable malware [6,47].

In this first example, we assume that a covert sender hides data within the unused "reserved" bit of the IPv4 header. Without any additional sophisticated characteristics, such as multi-level steganography or an indirect manipulation of values, the whole description consists of the pattern E1.1N1. NETWORK RESERVED/UNUSED STATE/VALUE MODULATION. As the covert receiver interprets the same reserved bit of the IPv4 header, the representation pattern is *R1.1n*.

4.2 Hybrid Hiding Method

Spiekermann *et al.* [46] present a migration covert channel. They propose that a covert sender migrates a virtual machine from one server to another, e.g., from Europe to Australia, so that a covert receiver can measure a different round trip time (RTT). While the embedding hiding pattern to migrate the virtual machine is a E1N1. NETWORK STATE/VALUE MODULATION (commands in a protocol are transferred so that the migration is triggered), the covert receiver must measure the RTT with probe traffic or by conducting some measurements. In particular, the time of occurrence of a response packet is measured to obtain the RTT, which is R2.2N1. NETWORK ELEMENT POSITIONING (the network element (=packet) is "positioned" in time [50]).

To map the underlying patterns of this "migration" channel into the proposed nomenclature, we utilze Fig. 1 as a guide. The hiding method is *not* distributed, but it is an indirect method following the "proxy" pattern [43]. The method is an active method without multi-level component, and no history/future reference, i.e., these three aspects must not be mentioned explicitly. Thus, we call this hybrid method as follows: INDIRECT (PROXY) E1N1. NETWORK STATE/VALUE MODULATION (the embedding pattern) and INDIRECT (PROXY) R2.2N1. NETWORK ELEMENT POSITIONING (the representation pattern). Note that the indirect attribute is included in both, embedding and representation patterns.

4.3 Network-Based Indirect Dead-Drop Hiding Method

Velinov *et al.* introduced an indirect method that allows the establishment of a bidirectional network covert channel in the MQTT protocol, which has been described as "ICC.1" in [48]. The channel is also referred to as "MQTT.1" in [43]. MQTT is specialized in conveying information between IoT devices, the clients of the MQTT server, via topics. Such topics may have numerous subtopics and can be subscribed to by clients. To achieve indirect covert communication, the covert sender and covert receiver (i.e., clients of the MQTT server) must agree on one first-level topic. The covert receiver has to subscribe to all subtopics of this first-level topic. The covert sender now embeds covert information in one of the subtopics that is stored by the MQTT-server. Due to subscription, the MQTT-server notifies the covert receiver and sends the embedded covert information, which can be extracted at the target of the covert channel. Due to the storing of information on the MQTT server, [43] considers this concept to be a so-called dead drop. For such an implementation, the covert channel is split into three phases: manipulation, storing, and extraction. Each phase may utilize different hiding methods, but in the case of this example, each phase uses the patterns E1n1. and R1n1. for embedding and representation of covert information, respectively.

In the proposed nomenclature, this covert channel can be defined as *non-distributed* but "indirect" (using the "dead drop" pattern). Furthermore, the method is active, does not apply multi-level steganography, and does not employ a history/future component. Thus, the complete categorization is INDIRECT (DEAD DROP) E1.1N1. NETWORK STATE/VALUE MODULATION.

4.4 Audio Hiding Method

Despite dating back to the late1990 s Least Significant Bit (LSB) modification is still one of the most relevant hiding methods used in audio steganography. From the approximately 800 audio steganography repositories currently available on Github, an estimated 70% features LSB modification based hiding methods, such as LSB Replacement (LSBR) and also one of the few audio stego-malware cases reported in the wild features LSBR as the embedding method [6,47].

Technically, in LSBR parts of the least significant bit plane of an uncompressed audio or image sample is adapted to match the bits in a secret message. In compact disc (CD) compliant pulse code modulated (PCM) WAV audio files, every sample value is encoded by a 16 bit value per channel. In that case, the lowest bit-plane value is modified, producing minimal changes in the audio content that are much below the hearing threshold of a human being, even if introduced into silent parts of the audio content. In general, LSBR for image and audio is considered to be easily detectable if high embedding rates ($>20\%$ of potential hiding places) are used since the message embedding in those cases overwrites/destroys the underlying characteristics of the cover signal. For very low embedding rates (i.e., very short messages hidden in long covers) the introduced embedding artifacts have been shown to be statistically indistinguishable from the cover statistics and therefore undetectable.

Due to the prominence of this method in digital media steganography the pattern E1.3D1. DIGITAL MEDIA LSB STATE/VALUE MODULATION has been proposed [50]. A hiding method would simply be described by its pattern if no sophisticated approach is given.

Instead, if a hiding method would only embed pointers to previously recorded data in a cover object, it would be categorized as HISTORY-FOCUSED E1.3D1. DIGITAL MEDIA LSB STATE/VALUE MODULATION.

4.5 OPC UA Hiding Method

Neubert *et al.* present and analyze three methods for steganographic embedding of hidden messages in OPC UA data packets [35]. OPC UA is a cross-platform, open-source protocol for Cyber-Physical Systems (CPS), in particular for Industrial Control System (ICS) network communication, and is developed by the OPC Foundation [37]. The goal of Neubert *et al.* is to generate and evaluate steganographic OPC UA network traffic including packets generated by simulation of a corrupted Programmable Logic Controller (PLC) within an ICS network. The PLC generates OPC UA packets with slight timestamp modifications in micro- and nanosecond range to embed hidden messages. OPC UA timestamps are composed in the format "$T_i = hh : mm : ss : mmm\ \mu\mu\mu\ nnn$", where h,m,s,m,μ and n stand for hour, minute, second, millisecond, microsecond and nanosecond respectively. All three methods make use of the least two digits of the microsecond timestamp and all three digits of the nanosecond values. This results in timestamps such as "$T_i = 10:00:00.123\ 4$ **56 789** " for each modified packet, where the five potentially modified digits are marked in bold, *"56"* representing the lower 2 digits of the microseconds and *"789"* the three digits for the nanoseconds. The three algorithms vary with respect to their strategy for constructing the actual embedding pattern and its position. The first and simplest method generates patterns by embedding two distinct digit values as embedding symbols for 1 and 0 for each hidden message bit in all three positions for the microsecond timestamp of three subsequent OPC UA packets (i.e. positions of *"456"* in the above example) in the communication flow. A second method involves basically the same scheme, but performs an embedding key-based permutation of the embedding symbols, as well as the embedding digit positions. The third method additionally involves the timestamp values at positions not considered for modification to generate patterns and uses XOR encryption.

All three examples fall in the category E1.3C1. CPS LSB STATE/VALUE MODULATION because the least significant digits (although not exactly bits!) of timestamp elements are modulated.

All other properties can be omitted, as they fall into the default categories, because the payload is bit-wise directly represented, all channels are active (due to the assumption of a compromised PLC component), do not consider multi-level steganography and carry the message directly. Thus, the directness, activeness, level characteristic, and reference-temporality properties can be omitted. As a result, the simplest method can be described as NON-DISTRIBUTED E1.3C1. CPS LSB STATE/VALUE MODULATION, whereas the remaining two methods fall into the category of DISTRIBUTED E1.3C1. CPS LSB STATE/VALUE MODULATION. The two distributed methods utilize a key-based permutation of the embedding position of each single numeric symbol within the 5 potential least significant numeric positions (i.e., *"56789"* in the above example) across subsequent data packets. The description for the pattern combination of the two distributed methods can be formulated as *"key-based symbol, embedding position and cover data permutation"* using the *-property of Fig. 1.

4.6 Text Hiding Method

Most of the methods applied in text steganography are simple. For example, repeating white space characters in a text (open space method) [2,3] is a form of the pattern E2.1T1. TEXT ELEMENT ENUMERATION. However, these methods can be applied in heterogeneous scenarios, with different naming components, such as directness and activeness. For example, Mileva *et al.* [33] suggest three different applications of the open space method and the pattern E2.1T1 using DICOM files as covert carriers. DICOM (*Digital Imaging and Communications in Medicine*, cf. [12]) is a standard for the digital handling of medical images, containing several attributes that can be filled with textual content.

In the first scenario, a covert sender and a covert receiver are the actual sender and receiver, which means that the created covert channel is active and direct, so we can describe it simply as E2.1T1. TEXT ELEMENT ENUMERATION. The second scenario covers a direct channel in which the covert sender is the actual sender, while covert receiver(s) monitor the network traffic intended for other receivers to extract the hidden message. This covert channel can be described as SEMI-ACTIVE E2.1T1. TEXT ELEMENT ENUMERATION. The last scenario is an example of an indirect active channel in which the covert sender (as the actual sender) stores the cover DICOM file in an archive (utilized as third-party intermediate component), while the covert receiver(s) can request some services regarding that DICOM file from the archive and extract the hidden message. Thus, this hidden communication mechanism can be described as INDIRECT (DEAD-DROP) E2.1T1. TEXT ELEMENT ENUMERATION.

5 Discussion

The examples provided here do not cover the full extent of existing hiding methods, such as steganography in filesystems [13,18], AI models [27,38,45], air-gapped covert channels [5,17] or covert channel-based traffic obfuscation for censorship circumvention [1]. However, we believe that our methodology can be easily extended to these domains, especially since the patterns taxonomy [50] already foresees many of them. At the same time, we are also aware that our work might be limited due to the lack of some categorizations and subtaxonomies of information hiding topics. However, the proposed approach and the related corpus of works at the basis of [50] are solid, thus making improvements and adjustments easier. As our work becomes accepted by the community, routine "maintenance" operations will be easier. In this perspective, information hiding topics that may emerge in the future due to the utilization of new technologies not yet invented or not yet relevant could be added when needed. As an example, the vivid area of tracking AI-generated content was completely unforeseeable ten years ago but now drives vast research directions. This reinforces the need of having multiple and flexible attributes to describe how the steganography area evolves.

Another limitation of our work is that it does not cover countermeasures; they are solely an attribute of the UDM. However, since our work is focused on the categorization and description of hiding methods instead of the categorization and description of countermeasures to detect, limit, or prevent steganography, we consider the description of countermeasures as a separate project.

Future developments are notoriously difficult to predict. For this reason, our approach might be considered an intermediate step that allows extension in areas where it is needed (due to its *-property in Fig. 1).

6 Conclusion

We have introduced a meta-view on description and taxonomy approaches in steganography that several researchers focusing on information hiding have constructed over the years. Our combination of existing methodologies allows for a comprehensive description of steganography methods in a unified and comparable fashion. As a result, scientific re-inventions could be reduced and the knowledge between different fields (e.g., defensive watermarking and detection of stegomalware) could be exchanged much more effectively. Our provided interactive online tool aids the understanding of our methodology. Additionally, the tool can be used for didactic settings.

Future work will focus on the development of a similar methodology for countermeasures against threats endowed with some form of steganographic capabilities. Specifically, we are working towards the definition of a suitable abstraction/taxonomy to prevent ambiguities and imperfect isolation issues that may lead to exploitable hiding patterns.

Acknowledgments. We like to thank the anonymous reviewers for their constructive feedback. We further like to express our gratitude to co-authors of previous works that helped paving the way to this paper: Wojciech Mazurczyk, Jörg Keller, Krzysztof Cabaj, Laura Hartmann, Sebastian Zillien, Tom Neubert, Bernhard Fechner, and Christian Herdin. Finally, we like to thank Tobias Wendzel and for supporting the development of the interactive tool.

The work of Luca Caviglione has been partially supported by Project SERICS (PE00000014) under the NRRP MUR program funded by the EU - NGEU.

Disclosure of Interests. The authors have no competing interests to declare that are relevant to the content of this article.

References

1. DomEye: Detecting network covert channel of domain fronting with throughput fluctuation. Comput. Sec. **144** (2024). https://doi.org/10.1016/j.cose.2024.103976

2. Ahvanooey, M.T., Li, Q., Hou, J., Rajput, A.R., Chen, Y.: Modern text hiding, text steganalysis, and applications: A comparative analysis. Entropy **21**(4), 355 (2019)
3. Bender, W., Gruhl, D., Morimoto, N., Lu, A.: Techniques for data hiding. IBM Syst. J. **35**(Nos3&4), 313–336 (1996)
4. Bennett, K.: Linguistic steganography: Survey, analysis, and robustness concerns for hiding information in text. Tech. Rep. 2004-13, CERIAS Tech Report, Purdue University (2004)
5. Carrara, B., Adams, C.: Out-of-band covert channels–a survey. ACM Comput. Surv. (CSUR) **49**(2), 1–36 (2016)
6. Caviglione, L., Mazurczyk, W.: Never mind the malware, here's the stegomalware. IEEE Sec. Priv. **20**(5), 101–106 (2022)
7. Caviglione, L., Mazurczyk, W.: You can't do that on protocols anymore: analysis of covert channels in ietf standards. IEEE Netw. **38**(5), 255–263 (2024)
8. Caviglione, L., Podolski, M., Mazurczyk, W., Ianigro, M.: Covert channels in personal cloud storage services: the case of Dropbox. IEEE Trans. Industr. Inf. **13**(4), 1921–1931 (2017)
9. Chang, C.C., Lin, C.Y.: Reversible steganography for VQ-compressed images using side matching and relocation. IEEE Trans. Inform. Forens. and Sec. **1**(4), 493–501 (2006)
10. Dey, A., Bhattacharya, S., Chaki, N.: Software watermarking: progress and challenges. INAE Lett. **4**, 65–75 (2019)
11. Dhawan, S., Gupta, R.: Analysis of various data security techniques of steganography: a survey. Inform. Sec. J. Global Perspective **30**(2), 63–87 (2021)
12. DICOM: The DICOM standard (2025). https://www.dicomstandard.org/
13. Eckstein, K., Jahnke, M.: Data hiding in journaling file systems. In: Digital Forensic Research Workshop (2005)
14. Fraczek, W., Mazurczyk, W., Szczypiorski, K.: Multi-level steganography: Improving hidden communication in networks. J. Univ. Comput. Sci. (J. UCS) **18**(14), 1967–1986 (2012). https://doi.org/10.3217/jucs-018-14-1967
15. Fridrich, J.: Steganography in Digital Media: Principles, Algorithms, and Applications. Cambridge University Press (2009). https://doi.org/10.1017/CBO9781139192903
16. Girling, C.G.: Covert channels in LAN's. IEEE Trans. Software Eng. **13**, 292–296 (1987)
17. Guri, M., Monitz, M., Mirski, Y., Elovici, Y.: BitWhisper: covert signaling channel between air-gapped computers using thermal manipulations. In: 2015 IEEE 28th Computer Security Foundations Symposium, pp. 276–289 (2015). https://doi.org/10.1109/CSF.2015.26
18. Han, J., Pan, M., Gao, D., Pang, H.: A multi-user steganographic file system on untrusted shared storage. In: 26th ACSAC, pp. 317–326. ACM (2010). https://doi.org/10.1145/1920261.1920309, https://doi.org/10.1145/1920261.1920309
19. Heßeling, C., Keller, J., Litzinger, S.: Reversible network covert channel by payload modulation in streams of decimal sensor values. In: 2023 IEEE 19th International Conference on e-Science (e-Science). IEEE Computer Society, Los Alamitos, CA, USA (2023). https://doi.org/10.1109/e-Science58273.2023.10254946
20. Hildebrandt, M., Lamshöft, K., Dittmann, J., Neubert, T., Vielhauer, C.: Information hiding in industrial control systems: An opc ua based supply chain attack and its detection. In: Proceedings of the 2020 ACM Workshop on Information Hiding and Multimedia Security, pp. 115–120 (2020)

21. Johnson, N.F., Jajodia, S.: Exploring steganography: seeing the unseen. Computer **31**(2), 26–34 (1998). https://doi.org/10.1109/MC.1998.4655281
22. Johnson, N.F., Katzenbeisser, S.: A survey of steganographic techniques. In: Information hiding, pp. 43–78 (2000)
23. Knöchel, M., Karius, S.: Text steganography methods and their influence in malware: A comprehensive overview and evaluation. In: Proceedings of the 2024 ACM Workshop on Information Hiding and Multimedia Security, pp. 113–124 (2024)
24. Lamshöft, K., Dittmann, J.: Assessment of hidden channel attacks: Targetting Modbus/TCP. IFAC-PapersOnLine **53**(2) (2020). https://doi.org/10.1016/j.ifacol.2020.12.258
25. Li, B., He, J., Huang, J., Shi, Y.Q.: A survey on image steganography and steganalysis. J. Inf. Hiding Multim. Signal Process. **2**(2), 142–172 (2011)
26. Liu, H., et al.: To deliver more information in coverless information hiding. Multim. Tools Appl. **83**(3), 7215–7229 (2024)
27. Liu, T., Liu, Z., Liu, Q., Wen, W., Xu, W., Li, M.: Stegonet: Turn deep neural network into a stegomalware. In: Proc. ACSAC 2020, pp. 928–938. ACM (2020). https://doi.org/10.1145/3427228.3427268
28. Lubacz, J., Mazurczyk, W., Szczypiorski, K.: Principles and overview of network steganography. IEEE Commun. Mag. **52**(5), 225–229 (2014)
29. Majeed, M.A., Sulaiman, R., Shukur, Z., Hasan, M.K.: A review on text steganography techniques. Mathematics **9**(21), 2829 (2021)
30. Masud, M.A., Akter, S., Sultana, N., Yousuf, M.A., Uddin, M.Z.: Multi-layered password-based steganography: A novel approach for tiered information hiding. techxiv (2024). https://doi.org/10.36227/techrxiv.173397886.68744435/v1
31. Mazurczyk, W., Szary, P., Wendzel, S., Caviglione, L.: Towards reversible storage network covert channels. In: Proc. ARES 2019, pp. 1–8
32. Mazurczyk, W., Wendzel, S., Cabaj, K.: Towards deriving insights into data hiding methods using pattern-based approach. In: Proc. ARES 2018, pp. 10:1–10. ACM (2018). https://doi.org/10.1145/3230833.3233261
33. Mileva, A., Caviglione, L., Velinov, A., Wendzel, S., Dimitrova, V.: Risks and opportunities for information hiding in dicom standard. In: CUING, ARES 2021: Proceedings of the 16th International Conference on Availability, Reliability and Security (2021). https://doi.org/10.1145/3465481.347007
34. Mileva, A., Panajotov, B.: Covert channels in TCP/IP protocol stack-extended version. Open Comput. Sci. **4**(2), 45–66 (2014)
35. Neubert, T., Peuker, B., Schueler, E., Ullrich, H., Buxhoidt, L., Vielhauer, C.: An analysis framework for steganographic network data in industrial control systems. In: Proc. SECURWARE 2024. IARIA (2024)
36. Ogiela, M.R., Koptyra, K.: False and multi-secret steganography in digital images. Soft. Comput. **19**(11), 3331–3339 (2015). https://doi.org/10.1007/s00500-015-1728-z
37. OPC Foundation: official website (2025). https://opcfoundation.org
38. Pan, X., Zhang, S., Zhang, M., Yang, M.: House of cans: covert transmission of internal datasets via capacity-aware neuron steganography. In: Advances in Neural Information Processing Systems (2022)
39. Petitcolas, F., Anderson, R.J., Kuhn, M.G.: Information hiding-a survey. Proc. of the IEEE **87**(7), 1062–1078 (1999)
40. Petitcolas, F., Anderson, R., Kuhn, M.: Information hiding - a survey. Proc. IEEE **87**(7), 1062–1078 (1999)
41. Provos, N., Honeyman, P.: Hide and seek: an introduction to steganography. IEEE Sec. Priv. **1**(3), 32–44 (2003)

42. Regazzoni, F., Palmieri, P., Smailbegovic, F., Cammarota, R., Polian, I.: Protecting artificial intelligence ips: a survey of watermarking and fingerprinting for machine learning. CAAI Trans. Intell. Technol. **6**(2), 180–191 (2021)
43. Schmidbauer, T., Wendzel, S.: SoK: a survey of indirect network-level covert channels. In: Proc. 17th Asia Conf. Computer and Communications Security (ASIA-CCS), pp. 546–560. ACM (2022). https://doi.org/10.1145/3488932.3517418
44. Song, C., Zhang, Y., Lu, G.: Reversible data hiding in encrypted images based on image partition and spatial correlation. In: Proc. International Workshop On Digital Watermarking (IWDW), pp. 180–194 (2018)
45. Song, C., Ristenpart, T., Shmatikov, V.: Machine learning models that remember too much. In: Proc. ACM CCS 2017, pp. 587–601. ACM (2017). https://doi.org/10.1145/3133956.3134077
46. Spiekermann, D., Keller, J., Eggendorfer, T.: Towards covert channels in cloud environments: a study of implementations in virtual networks. In: International Workshop on Digital Watermarking, pp. 248–262. Springer (2017). https://doi.org/10.1007/978-3-319-64185-0_19
47. Strachanski, F., Petrov, D., Schmidbauer, T., Wendzel, S.: A comprehensive pattern-based overview of stegomalware. In: Proc. ARES 2024 (2024). https://doi.org/10.1145/3664476.3670886
48. Velinov, A., Mileva, A., Wendzel, S., Mazurczyk, W.: Covert channels in the MQTT-based Internet of Things. IEEE Access **7**, 161899–161915 (2019). https://doi.org/10.1109/ACCESS.2019.2951425
49. Wan, W., et al.: A comprehensive survey on robust image watermarking. Neurocomputing **488**, 226–247 (2022)
50. Wendzel, S., et al.: A generic taxonomy for steganography methods. ACM Comput. Surv. **57**(9), 1–37 (2025). https://doi.org/10.1145/3729165
51. Wendzel, S., Schmidbauer, T., Zillien, S., Keller, J.: DYST (did you see that?): an amplified covert channel that points to previously seen data. IEEE Trans. Dependable Sec. Comput. (TDSC) (2024). https://doi.org/10.1109/TDSC.2024.3410679
52. Wendzel, S., Zander, S., Fechner, B., Herdin, C.: Pattern-based survey and categorization of network covert channel techniques. Comp. Surveys **47**(3) (2015). https://doi.org/10.1145/2684195
53. Wolf, M.: Covert channels in LAN protocols. In: Berson, T.A., Beth, T. (eds.) LANSEC 1989. LNCS, vol. 396, pp. 89–101. Springer, Heidelberg (1989). https://doi.org/10.1007/3-540-51754-5_33
54. Zander, S.: Performance of selected noisy covert channels and their countermeasures in IP networks. Ph.D. thesis, Swinburne Univ. (2010)
55. Zander, S., Armitage, G., Branch, P.: A survey of covert channels and countermeasures in computer network protocols. Commun. Surv. Tutorials **9**(3), 44–57 (2007)
56. Zhiyong, C., Yong, Z.: Entropy based taxonomy of network convert channels. In: Proc. 2nd Int. Conf. on Power Electronics and Intelligent Transportation System (PEITS), pp. 451–455 (2009)
57. Zhou, Z., Mu, Y., Wu, Q.: Coverless image steganography using partial-duplicate image retrieval. Soft. Comput. **23**(13), 4927–4938 (2019)
58. Zi, X., Yao, L., Pan, L., Li, J.: Implementing a passive network covert timing channel. Comput. Sec. **29**(6), 686–696 (2010). https://doi.org/10.1016/j.cose.2009.12.010

Open Access This chapter is licensed under the terms of the Creative Commons Attribution 4.0 International License (http://creativecommons.org/licenses/by/4.0/), which permits use, sharing, adaptation, distribution and reproduction in any medium or format, as long as you give appropriate credit to the original author(s) and the source, provide a link to the Creative Commons license and indicate if changes were made.

The images or other third party material in this chapter are included in the chapter's Creative Commons license, unless indicated otherwise in a credit line to the material. If material is not included in the chapter's Creative Commons license and your intended use is not permitted by statutory regulation or exceeds the permitted use, you will need to obtain permission directly from the copyright holder.

Calyptography: Secure Secret Storage Inspired by Cryptography and Steganography

Daniel Lerch-Hostalot[1(✉)], Jordi Puiggalí[2], and David Megías[1]

[1] Internet Interdisciplinary Institute (IN3), CYBERCAT-Center for Cybersecurity Research of Catalonia, Universitat Oberta de Catalunya (UOC), Barcelona, Spain
{dlerch,dmegias}@uoc.edu
[2] SecretsVault.xyz - Limitless Technologies and Applications, S.L., Barcelona, Spain
jordi.puiggali@secretsvault.xyz

Abstract. This paper introduces calyptography, a novel method for secure secret storage that combines principles from steganography and cryptography without altering the carrier media. Unlike traditional cryptographic systems, which rely solely on passphrases or keys, or steganographic systems, which embed data into a cover medium, calyptography links a secret to an unmodified image via a robust perceptual hash. The proposed system derives encryption and decryption keys from both a user passphrase and the perceptual features of a reference image, allowing secure storage while resisting typical image transformations such as compression, filtering, or rescaling. A detailed method based on DCT-based image hashing and randomized patch extraction is presented, alongside error correction techniques that preserve key robustness without reducing entropy. Experimental results show the method's high robustness against common image manipulations compared to traditional perceptual hashing schemes, making calyptography a promising alternative for secure and user-friendly secret management.

Keywords: Secure storage · Perceptual hash · Robust hash · Image processing

1 Introduction

The secure storage of sensitive information, often referred to as "secrets," is a fundamental challenge in information security. The need to protect data from unauthorized access has driven the development of various techniques, broadly categorized under cryptography [6] and steganography [12].

Cryptography, derived from the Ancient Greek words χρψπτός (kryptós), meaning "hidden" or "secret," and γράφειν (gráphein), meaning "to write" is the practice and study of techniques for secure communication, particularly in the presence of adversaries. At its core, cryptography involves transforming plaintext (the original message) into ciphertext (an unintelligible form) through a process called encryption. This transformation is controlled by a cryptographic key, a piece of secret information known only to the authorized parties. The reverse process, decryption, uses the same (in symmetric cryptography) or a related (in asymmetric or public-key cryptography) key to recover the original plaintext from the ciphertext. The security of cryptographic systems fundamentally relies on the difficulty of an unauthorized party deducing or obtaining the (decryption) key and, consequently, decrypting the ciphertext (Fig. 1). A general diagram of cryptographic processes is shown in Fig. 1a.

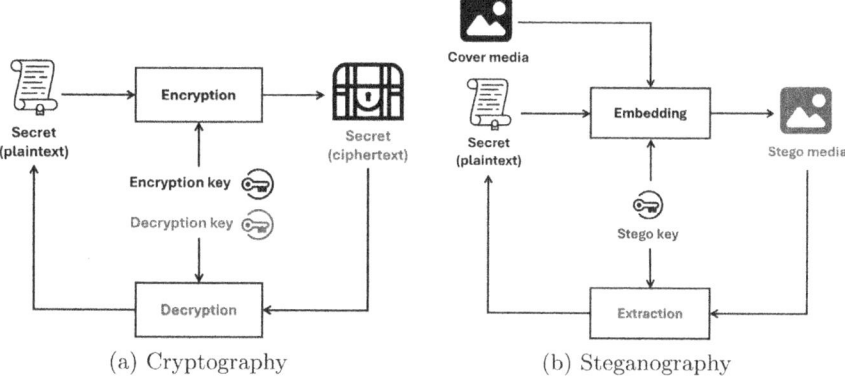

(a) Cryptography   (b) Steganography

Fig. 1. Diagram of the standard cryptographic and steganographic processes.

Steganography, derived from the Ancient Greek words στεγανός (steganós), meaning "covered" or "sealed," and, again, γράφειν (gráphein), is the art and science of concealing the very existence of communication. Unlike cryptography, which focuses on rendering a message unintelligible, steganography aims to embed the secret message within a seemingly innocuous carrier (cover), such as an image, audio file, video, or text, or even the network protocols. The goal is to make the presence of the hidden message undetectable to an observer who is not aware of the steganographic technique being employed. Steganographic methods achieve this by exploiting redundancies or making small variations within the carrier medium to store the secret data, inevitably introducing subtle changes to the cover object. These alterations, even if imperceptible, can be statistically analyzed or detected using machine learning techniques in a field known as steganalysis. Critically, for steganography, the mere detection of the existence of a hidden message is considered a successful attack, even if the message itself remains unrecovered. A diagram of this process is presented in Fig. 1b.

To mitigate the inherent vulnerability of traditional steganography to steganalysis, researchers have explored alternative approaches. Coverless steganography [13], as proposed in recent years, aims to achieve covert communication without modifying a cover object. Instead, the secret information is represented by inherent properties of the carrier itself, such as, in the context of images, pixel brightness values, color, texture, edges, contours, or high-level semantics. This approach bypasses the process of embedding data within the carrier, allowing the carrier to directly represent the secret information. This offers the potential for undetectability by existing steganalysis tools, as no alterations are made to the stego image. Steganography by cover selection [20], on the other hand, also avoids modifying any single cover object but does so by selecting a suitable cover from a pool of available options to represent the secret message. In some variations of cover selection with images, this involves searching for an existing image where the desired secret message is already represented, albeit unintentionally, within specific pixel values or transform coefficients. The sender and receiver agree upon a method to interpret these existing image features as the message. However, it must be noted that finding a suitable image for cover selection in this manner is practically limited to encoding very small messages due to the extremely low probability of a given image perfectly matching the required encoding. While these techniques offer resistance against steganalysis by eliminating or minimizing modifications to individual carriers, they introduce new challenges related to capacity and security in different scenarios.

1.1 Contribution and Plan of the Paper

This paper focuses on a specific application of data hiding: the secure storage of secrets. Unlike traditional steganography, which is often employed for covert communication between parties, the primary concern here is not the transmission of a secret message from sender Alice to receiver Bob. Instead, we address the scenario where a user wishes to securely store a secret and associate it with a readily available and easily memorable reference media, such as an image, on their own device or within a trusted storage environment.

In this paper, we introduce calyptography, a novel approach to secret storage that draws inspiration from both cryptography's use of keys and steganography's association with media, but diverges from both in its core mechanisms. The term "calyptography" is derived from the Ancient Greek words καλύπτō (kalýptō), meaning "to cover" or "to conceal," and γράφειν (gráphein), meaning "writing" or "representation," reflecting the method's focus on using an image as a means to cover or represent the hidden secret. The goal is to provide a method for protecting the secret from unauthorized access at rest, leveraging the image as a key or reference for retrieval while avoiding modifications that could compromise its integrity or attract attention, or facilitate the detection of the secret storage by using steganalysis.

The particular method proposed in this paper[1] uses a robust image hash together with a calyptographic key to derive the encryption and decryption keys used to securely store the secret. This is just one of the many possible realizations of calyptography, which may become a new branch in data hiding and data protection schemes.

The rest of the paper is organized as follows. Section 2 reviews the relevant background on perceptual image hashing, robust hashing algorithms, and coverless steganography, situating the proposed method within the broader landscape

---

[1] A patent application related to this work has been filed EP24382864.

of secure information hiding. Section 3 presents the core architecture of the proposed approach, detailing the perceptual hash generation process, its randomized expansion, and the integration with cryptographic primitives and error correction mechanisms. Section 4 reports experimental results evaluating the robustness of various hashing strategies under typical image transformations. Finally, Sect. 5 summarizes our findings and outlines potential directions for future work.

2 Related Work

This section presents an overview of perceptual and robust image hashing, as well as coverless steganography, which are the main techniques related to the calyptographic solution proposed in this work.

In today's digital world, images are shared, edited, and distributed more than ever before. While this brings numerous benefits, it also raises significant concerns about the authenticity and integrity of visual content. Traditional cryptographic hashes, though effective for exact data integrity verification, are overly sensitive to even the slightest modification, rendering them inadequate for tasks involving visually similar content.

Perceptual image hashing addresses this limitation by generating compact representations of images based on features that align with human visual perception. These hashes are designed such that similar images yield similar hash values, enabling efficient comparison despite minor alterations such as resizing, filtering, or lossy compression. The core idea is to extract visual features that are invariant to common manipulations while maintaining sensitivity to perceptual differences.

One of the simplest and most established methods is the Average Hash (A-Hash) [3,5], which converts the image to grayscale, reduces its resolution, and generates a binary sequence by comparing each pixel value to the mean luminance. An alternative is the Difference Hash (D-Hash), which enhances sensitivity to gradient information by evaluating the difference between adjacent pixel intensities along rows. A more sophisticated technique is the Perceptual Hash (P-Hash) [3,5,18], which applies a Discrete Cosine Transform (DCT) to the image, extracting low-frequency coefficients that correlate with the human visual system's sensitivity to brightness and contrast changes. Another method, the Singular Value Decomposition Hash (SVD-Hash), relies on matrix decomposition to capture global geometric features from overlapping image blocks, although it tends to be less robust against manipulations. Similarly, the Wavelet Hash (W-Hash) [3,5] operates in the frequency domain but uses the Discrete Wavelet Transform (DWT), offering strong robustness against localized structural changes.

Over the years, a wide range of perceptual hashing techniques have been proposed, leveraging diverse strategies from both spatial and frequency domains [4]. These include local and global feature extraction, invariant transformations, statistical modeling, and machine learning-based methods. Some approaches exploit keypoint descriptors such as the Scale-Invariant Feature Transform (SIFT) or

Speeded-Up Robust Features (SURF), while others rely on moment invariants, wavelet transforms, or deep neural networks. This diversity reflects the multifaceted nature of the perceptual similarity problem and the broad spectrum of application requirements. Perceptual image hashing thus serves as the foundation for the approach proposed in this work, enabling images to act as stable references to hidden data without requiring modification of the media itself.

Among the many directions in perceptual hashing research, a prominent focus has been the development of robust hashing algorithms [15], specifically designed to extract hash values stable under a wide range of benign image transformations. Unlike traditional visual descriptors, robust image hashing aims to capture perceptual essence while suppressing the influence of compression, filtering, geometric distortions, and noise, making it suitable for applications such as image provenance or multimedia forensics.

Some well-known perceptual hashing algorithms, such as A-Hash, D-Hash, P-Hash, and W-Hash [3], already exhibit moderate robustness to common manipulations. Further advances include quaternion-based hashing methods [8,17], Gabor filters combined with dithered lattice vector quantization [9], and learning-based approaches [11,16], such as convolutional neural networks trained to extract invariant features from visual data. Hybrid models, like DCT-SVD or DWT-SVD [7], have also been proposed to balance robustness and discrimination across diverse manipulation types. This evolving landscape of robust hashing methods strengthens their applicability in calyptography, where the image's perceptual integrity must remain sufficiently stable even after transformations like compression, resizing, or filtering.

Another area conceptually related to calyptography is coverless steganography [10,20], a class of techniques where the message is not embedded into a carrier object, but instead inferred from the selection or structure of the media itself. This approach eliminates alterations to the cover, thereby reducing vulnerability to statistical steganalysis.

In some methods, specific images are selected from a database to match message codes, using feature descriptors or robust hashes. For instance, approaches such as robust hash-based selection [20] or SIFT feature orientation methods [19] associate secret information with naturally occurring properties of the image without modifying its content. Although coverless steganography shares the general principle of not altering the carrier, its goal is covert communication, whereas calyptography focuses on secure storage. In calyptography, the image serves not as a transmitter of information but as an auxiliary secret necessary for unlocking the hidden data.

3 Proposed Method

Building upon the concepts of perceptual image hashing and the indirect use of media as reference material, this work introduces a novel approach to secure secret storage, termed *calyptography*. Unlike conventional cryptographic systems that rely solely on user-defined keys, or image steganographic systems that embed messages into visual content, calyptography uses the perceptual characteristics of an image as part of the access mechanism, without altering the image itself. The main properties of calyptography for secure storage, compared to cryptography and steganography, are outlined in Table 1.

Table 1. Comparison of Cryptography, Steganography, and Calyptography for Secure Storage

Feature	Cryptography	Steganography	Calyptography
Goal	Securely store information by making it unintelligible	Hide the existence of the stored information	Securely store information by associating it with a reference medium
Secrecy	Ciphertext is illegible without the key	Hidden information is difficult to detect	Encrypted secret is stored separately; association with the reference medium is hidden
Security Focus	Confidentiality of data at rest	Concealment of data's presence	Confidentiality and integrity of data at rest, potentially concealment of association
Robustness	Strength of the encryption algorithm, key management	Capacity of the cover medium, undetectability of embedding	Strength of key derivation, robustness of reference medium features, secure storage of ciphertext
Vulnerabilities	Key compromise, algorithm weaknesses	Steganalysis, cover medium compromise	Reference medium compromise, key derivation flaws
Advantages	Strong confidentiality, proven algorithms	Covertness, difficult detection	Potentially easier key management (using reference medium), no modification of reference medium
Disadvantages	Key management complexity, potential for algorithm weaknesses	Limited capacity, susceptibility to steganalysis, carrier medium modification	Complexity of association between medium and secret, potential for key derivation flaws

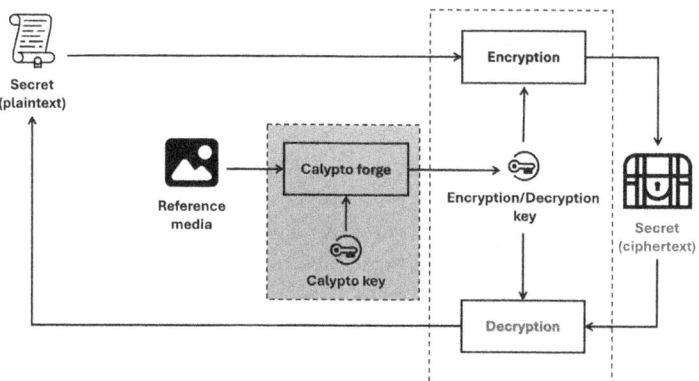

Fig. 2. Diagram of the calyptographic processes.

The core idea is to bind a secret to an auxiliary image by using its perceptual hash as a cryptographic component. In this approach, the perceptual hash of an image becomes part of the key used to encrypt or decrypt a message. This means that, in addition to knowing a passphrase, the user must also possess a specific image, or at least a visually similar one. As a result, the image itself becomes a second factor of protection, enhancing security through a combination of something the user knows and something the user has. A diagram of calyptographic processes is shown in Fig. 2, where the "Calypto forge" block takes the reference image and a calypto key as inputs to derive (forge) an encryption/descryption key that is used to protect the secret. The term "forge" is inspired from the process of transforming a metal object (the calypto key) into another metal object (the encryption/decryption key) using some kind of fuel (the reference image). Although the diagram suggests symmetric cryptography, for simplicity, it could also apply to public-key encryption.

In the following, we present the architecture of the proposed method in detail, covering the generation and use of perceptual hashes, the construction of the encryption and decryption procedures, and the incorporation of mechanisms to handle errors that may arise during hash extraction due to benign image alterations such as compression, scaling, or the application of image enhancement filters.

3.1 Computation of the Image-Based Hash

Ideally, a perceptual hash used as a reference in secure storage systems should remain stable under a wide range of image transformations. In practice, however, achieving full invariance to all possible modifications is unfeasible. Instead, it is more realistic—and more useful—to focus on robustness against the most common transformations that occur during the typical life cycle of an image in digital environments.

In this context, our method targets robustness to transformations that are especially prevalent when images are shared or stored through platforms such as social networks or messaging applications. These platforms often apply automatic processing to uploaded media, either for optimization or standardization purposes. Consequently, the ability of the hash to survive such processing becomes critical.

The most frequent transformation introduced by these systems is lossy compression, most notably JPEG compression. This operation often alters fine image details and frequency components, making it the primary threat to hash stability. Therefore, our first and most important requirement is that the image hash remains stable under moderate to high levels of JPEG compression.

A second, less frequent but still relevant transformation is the application of filters or enhancements by the platform, either automatically or by user interaction. While this is not as widespread as compression, some services apply subtle sharpening, contrast adjustment, or color enhancement, which can slightly alter the visual content and affect the hash.

Finally, we also consider robustness to rescaling. This occurs when platforms downsample very large images before storing or transmitting them. Though less common, this transformation can change spatial resolutions and pixel arrangements in ways that are perceptually insignificant to humans but impactful for pixel-based hashing algorithms.

In light of these constraints, selecting a perceptual hash algorithm that can tolerate compression, minor filtering, and rescaling is essential.

3.2 Bit Extraction from Visual Data

There are multiple strategies for extracting binary information from visual content, each designed to balance robustness, simplicity, and perceptual relevance. In A-Hash, the image is resized and converted to grayscale, and each bit is determined by comparing pixel values to the global mean luminance. D-Hash improves sensitivity to local changes by computing differences between adjacent pixels in each row, encoding relative brightness variations. P-Hash, on the other hand, operates in the frequency domain by applying the DCT and comparing each low-frequency coefficient to the mean of a selected subset.

The proposed method computes the image-based hash by applying the DCT to the image, specifically using 8×8 non-overlapping blocks, mirroring the same structure employed in JPEG compression. This design choice is motivated by the need to align the hash computation process with the transformation most likely to affect the image during storage or transmission. By operating in the same frequency domain and spatial granularity as JPEG, the hash captures perceptual information that is less likely to be discarded or significantly altered by compression artifacts. As discussed in the experimental section, various hashing strategies were evaluated under different compression settings, and this block-wise DCT-based approach consistently demonstrated superior robustness against JPEG compression.

Unlike A-Hash or P-Hash, which typically rely on comparisons against a mean value, our method derives each bit by directly comparing the DC coefficients obtained from two distinct image blocks. Specifically, for two DC coefficients, v_i and v_{i+1}, extracted from image blocks B_i and B_{i+1} respectively (the ordering of block selection is detailed below), each bit b_i is determined by the relationship between these coefficients: $b_i = 1$ if $v_i > v_{i+1}$, and $b_i = 0$ otherwise.

This pairwise comparison approach preserves robustness while introducing greater entropy into the resulting hash, enabling the use of the binary sequence not only as a perceptual signature, but also as a component of a secure key in downstream cryptographic applications. By relying on relative magnitudes rather than absolute thresholds, this method achieves greater robustness against subtle photometric variations commonly introduced by compression, filtering, or post-processing.

3.3 Hash Expansion via Randomized Mapping

To support cryptographic applications that require binary keys of arbitrary length, the proposed method includes a mechanism for hash expansion based on a randomized mapping strategy. Unlike conventional cryptographic hashes, where even a single-bit error can render the entire output unusable, our approach maintains robustness by structuring the expanded hash in a way that tolerates some variations in the image content. This is achieved through the use of a pseudorandom generator initialized with a seed derived from the user-provided passphrase.

The random seed governs two key aspects of the process. First, it determines the spatial locations from which image content is extracted. Specifically, the grayscale image is resized to a common minimum dimension to ensure consistency across inputs. Then, using the seeded generator, a fixed number of large patches (e.g., 512 × 512 pixels) are selected at random from the image. This randomization ensures that the same image combined with different passphrases will yield different hash outputs, effectively binding the image to the passphrase in a nontrivial way.

Second, the same seed is used to shuffle the resulting set of DCT-derived coefficients prior to bit extraction. Each selected patch is first resized to a smaller dimension (e.g., 32 × 32), then divided into non-overlapping 8 × 8 blocks. The DC coefficient of each block is computed using a 2D DCT, yielding a sequence that captures low-frequency structural information. A deterministic shuffle, seeded by the passphrase, is then applied to this sequence to decorrelate spatial structure and enhance the entropy of the resulting bitstream.

Finally, the hash is constructed by comparing consecutive elements in the shuffled list of DC coefficients. Because the shuffle is seeded by the passphrase, this stage acts as a passphrase-dependent mapping from perceptual content to binary output. Unlike traditional cryptographic hash functions, where a single-bit change in the input leads to a completely different output due to the avalanche effect, the proposed method exhibits graceful degradation: small perturbations in the image or the extracted coefficients result in a limited number of bit flips in the final hash. This means that isolated errors during hash extraction do not propagate catastrophically, but instead translate into a proportional and predictable bit error rate (BER). The expanded binary hash can be made arbitrarily long by adjusting the number of selected patches or the number of comparisons performed, while preserving this key property of error tolerance.

Beyond robustness and extensibility, the use of randomized patch selection and coefficient shuffling introduces beneficial side effects. It reduces the likelihood that perceptually similar images produce similar hashes, thereby mitigating risks associated with collision attacks or reverse-engineering attempts. Furthermore, by standardizing input dimensions through resizing and random sampling, the implementation becomes less sensitive to image resolution or aspect ratio, simplifying deployment across heterogeneous media sources. While this added randomness slightly weakens the purely perceptual interpretation of the hash, it provides a favorable trade-off between conceptual clarity, practical robustness, and security.

Therefore, this sequence can be safely used to encrypt a secret of arbitrary length, as any extraction errors will manifest as a roughly constant bit error rate across the entire key, allowing the design of error correction codes tailored to the expected BER for reliable recovery.

3.4 Error Correction Without Key Space Reduction

As discussed in the previous section, the structure of the proposed hash allows for the presence of bit errors without catastrophic failure, since small perturbations in the image or its encoding result in a predictable and bounded BER. This characteristic opens the door to the use of error correction codes (ECC) to recover the encrypted message reliably, even when the extracted hash is not perfectly identical to the original.

Given a target BER tolerance, the error correction scheme can be selected or designed to provide the necessary redundancy for successful decoding. Standard block codes such as BoseâĂŞChaudhuriâĂŞHocquenghem (BCH) [1] or Reed-Solomon [14] are suitable for this purpose, although more efficient schemes may be used depending on the characteristics of the expected errors. Importantly, the ECC is applied only to the encrypted message and not to the hash itself, preserving the full entropy and size of the key space. This ensures that the strength of the cryptographic protection is not reduced by the introduction of redundancy.

The ability to tune the ECC parameters based on empirical measurements of BER in typical scenarios (e.g., JPEG compression, filtering, or rescaling) makes the method adaptable to different application requirements. In practice, once the expected error profile has been established, a code with appropriate correction capacity can be chosen to maximize reliability without incurring unnecessary overhead. This separation between the perceptual hash and the error-corrected message allows the system to maintain both robustness and security without compromising either.

3.5 Method Outline

The proposed method, grounded in the principles of calyptography, enables the secure storage and retrieval of a secret by linking it to both a passphrase and an image, without altering the image in any way. The system combines two key components: a perceptual hash generation process that derives a binary identifier from the image, and a cryptographic module that uses this identifier, together with the passphrase, to encrypt or decrypt the message. To improve robustness against minor variations in the extracted hash, the scheme incorporates ECC, allowing for reliable decryption even when the image has undergone mild transformations.

Algorithm 1: Image-based Hash Generation

Input: RGB image I, passphrase P
Output: Binary hash string H
// Preprocessing
$I \leftarrow \text{grayscale}(I)$
$I \leftarrow \text{resize\_to\_min}(I, \text{MIN\_IMAGE\_SIZE})$
$seed \leftarrow \text{sha256}(P)$
$\text{init\_prng}(seed)$
// Patch extraction and transformation
$patches \leftarrow \text{random\_patches}(I, \text{LARGE\_PATCH\_SIZE}, N)$
$V \leftarrow$ empty list
foreach $patch \in patches$ **do**
  $patch \leftarrow \text{resize}(patch, \text{SMALL\_PATCH\_SIZE}, \text{SMALL\_PATCH\_SIZE})$
  $blocks \leftarrow \text{divide}(patch, 8 \times 8)$
  foreach $block \in blocks$ **do**
    $D \leftarrow \text{dct2}(block)$
    $V \leftarrow V \cup \{D_{0,0}\}$
  end
end
// Hash generation
$V \leftarrow \text{shuffle}(V, seed)$
$H \leftarrow \text{compare\_pairs}(V)$
return H

The first stage involves computing a perceptual hash from the input image in a way that is tolerant to benign transformations such as compression, filtering, or slight rescaling. As shown in Algorithm 1, the image is first converted to grayscale and resized to ensure consistent spatial coverage. A fixed number of patches are then randomly sampled from the image using a seed derived from the passphrase. Each patch is resized and processed block-wise using the DCT, and the low-frequency (DC) components are extracted. After applying a seed-based shuffle to decorrelate the coefficients, a binary hash is generated by comparing consecutive values. The resulting hash captures perceptual characteristics of the image and serves as a key-dependent fingerprint. In the comparison of consecutive (after shuffling) DC values, we have used each DC value twice, i.e., b_i is obtained from v_i and v_{i+1} and b_{i+1} is obtained from v_{i+1} and v_{i+2}.

In the second stage, shown in Algorithm 2, this binary hash is used in combination with the passphrase to derive a cryptographic key. In encryption mode, the message is first encoded with an error correction scheme to increase resilience against slight variations in the input hash, and then encrypted using a bitwise XOR operation with the derived key. In decryption mode, the reverse process is applied: the ciphertext is decrypted using the bitwise XOR with the reconstructed key and passed through a decoder to correct potential errors introduced by hash instability. The length of the key is adjusted to match the size of the encoded message. This design ensures that access to the secret requires both knowledge of the passphrase and possession of an image that is perceptually close to the original, enabling a practical and secure two-factor binding mechanism.

Note that the use of XOR or a similar encryption method is required to make the error correction operation possible. The bitwise XOR mechanism preserves the positions of the bit errors in the derived key, making the error correction properties of the scheme work. Instead of bitwise XOR, any other encryption/decryption method that preserves the errors at the same (bit) locations could be used. Otherwise, the error correction would not work properly.

It may be argued that bitwise XOR encryption is not highly secure and that this undermines the security of the scheme, but this is not the case for different reasons:

– First, the key generated with the proposed approach can be extremely long before any repetition. This ensures that, in most practical cases, there is no repetition of the key for the encryption of different fragments of the message.
– Second, the method is intended to protect just one secret, and not a collection of different messages. If the method were to be used for different messages, it could be easily modified, for more security, as detailed below.
– Third, in case that the scheme was to be used for really long messages or for multiple encryptions, the message to encrypt using XOR, instead of being the secret itself, may be the key of a secure encryption method (such as AES) that is used for encrypting the actual secret. The modifications in Algorithm 2 are straightforward, just adding a new encryption or decryption step after the bitwise XOR operation. In fact, this is exactly how the LTA Labs company offers this service under the Secret Vaults[2] brand.

Algorithm 2: Encrypt/Decrypt using Image-Based Hash and ECC

Input: Hash H, passphrase P, message M, mode $\in$ {encrypt, decrypt}
Output: Encrypted or decrypted message
// Key derivation
$seed \leftarrow$ sha256(P)
init_prng($seed$)
$key \leftarrow$ hash_to_key($H, seed$)
if $mode = encrypt$ then
    // Apply error correction encoding
    $M_{ecc} \leftarrow$ encode_ecc(M)
    // Encrypt the message with the derived key
    $C \leftarrow$ bitwise_XOR(M_{ecc}, key)
    return C
else
    // Decrypt the ciphertext
    $M_{ecc} \leftarrow$ bitwise_XOR(M, key)
    // Attempt to correct errors
    $M' \leftarrow$ decode_ecc(M_{ecc})
    return M'
end

3.6 Implementation Details

To demonstrate the feasibility of the proposed method, we have implemented a prototype system using a fixed set of parameters. Although not necessarily optimal for all scenarios, they illustrate the method's behavior under realistic conditions and provide a reproducible reference.

The grayscale input image is resized to ensure a minimum dimension of MIN_IMAGE_SIZE = 2048 pixels (in its smallest dimension) using nearest-neighbor

---

[2] https://secretsvault.xyz/.

interpolation. Then, N = 32 patches of size LARGE_PATCH_SIZE = 512 are randomly sampled. Each patch is resized to SMALL_PATCH_SIZE = 32 with Lanczos interpolation to preserve frequency characteristics. The resized patches are divided into 16 non-overlapping 8 × 8 blocks, and the DC coefficient of each block is extracted.

The list of DC coefficients is shuffled using the Fisher-Yates algorithm, seeded by a passphrase-derived pseudorandom generator, producing a deterministic, passphrase-dependent ordering to enhance entropy.

Encryption is performed using only the bitwise XOR operation for simplicity, avoiding the need for traditional symmetric modes or key padding in the case of using the more secure two-step encryption mode described above. To tolerate small deviations in the extracted hash, BCH error correction codes are applied to the message before encryption. Their correction capacity is tuned based on the expected BER, depending on image manipulations such as compression, filtering, or scaling.

These parameters are consistently used throughout the experimental section, offering a practical balance between robustness, security, and computational efficiency.

4 Experimental Results

In this section, we present a series of experiments conducted to evaluate the robustness of the image-based hash used in our method. The primary goal is to compare the behavior of different perceptual hashing algorithms under common image transformations, and to analyze several variations of our proposed approach in order to identify the most resilient configuration. These experiments are focused exclusively on the hash generation process described in Algorithm 1, and do not assess the performance of the encryption or error correction components. Robustness is a critical property in our setting, as it determines the system's ability to recover the original hash—even when the image has undergone compression, filtering, or geometric modifications—ensuring successful decryption in the presence of typical image alterations. To ensure comparability across methods, all evaluations are performed using the (percent) BER between the original and transformed hashes, providing a unified metric to quantify robustness under varying conditions.

For BER calculation, hashes were truncated to 128 bits if their base length was 128 or more, and to 64 bits if shorter. The exception is Sect. 4.5, where all hashes were truncated to 64 bits for comparison with traditional methods.

4.1 Image Database

The experiments in this study were conducted using a subset of high-quality RAW images from the ALASKA steganography detection challenge dataset [2]. This dataset is well-suited for evaluating perceptual image hashing methods due to its diversity in content and image characteristics, as well as its uncompressed format, which avoids introducing prior artifacts that could affect the results.

For our experiments, a total of 5,000 images were randomly selected from the available pool. To ensure uniformity in spatial dimensions, each image was center-cropped to extract the largest possible square region and then resized to a resolution of 1080 × 1080 pixels. This preprocessing step guarantees consistent input size for all hashing methods under evaluation, facilitating fair and reproducible comparisons.

4.2 Robustness to JPEG Compression

Table 2 presents the results of an experimental evaluation of the robustness of different hashing strategies against JPEG compression. The goal is to assess how the BER of each method evolves when the image is compressed at increasingly aggressive levels—namely, quality factors of 100, 80, 70, and 50.

The table rows represent various configurations of the hashing method. The **"Operation"** column shows the transformation used for hash computation: DCT, DWT, SVD, or simple averaging ("AVG"). If the operation is not DCT, the values v_i and v_{i+1} for embedding or extracting the hidden bit b_i differ from the DC coefficient (which only applies to DCT). Specifically, averaging uses the average pixel value, DWT uses the first LL sub-band coefficient, and SVD uses the first singular value, normalized by the sum of all singular values.

But the average value of pixels—when the operation is averaging— the first coefficient of the LL sub-band (for the DWT), or the first singular value (normalized by the sum of all the singular values)—for the SVD.

The **"Mode"** column specifies whether the image was processed in grayscale or color, while **"Patches"** describes whether the full image was used (value 1) or if it was subdivided into multiple smaller regions. In most cases, the image (originally 1080 × 1080 pixels) was divided into non-overlapping patches of fixed size, except for the row labeled "Random 512×512", where patches were sampled randomly and may overlap.

The **"Large Patch"** column indicates the size of the extracted patches from the original image, while **"Small Patch"** refers to the dimensions to which each patch was resized before being processed. This resizing step affects the spatial resolution of the hash computation and plays a role in balancing detail retention and compression robustness. The **"Hash Base"** column shows the number of bits extracted before applying any further expansion.

Table 2. BER [%] under different JPEG compression levels

Operation	Mode	Patches	Large Patch	Small Patch	Hash Base	Quality Factor			
						100	80	70	50
DCT	Color	1	Full image	64 × 64	64	0.04	0.07	0.10	0.12
DWT	Color	1	Full image	64 × 64	64	0.06	0.13	0.19	0.27
DCT	Color	1	Full image	32 × 32	16	0.03	0.06	0.08	0.10
DCT	Color	1	Full image	16 × 16	4	0.03	0.04	0.08	0.08
SVD	Grayscale	1	Full image	64 × 64	64	0.25	0.48	0.65	0.87
AVG	Grayscale	1	Full image	64 × 64	64	0.04	0.07	0.10	0.12
DCT	Grayscale	1	Full image	64 × 64	64	0.04	0.07	0.10	0.12
DCT	Grayscale	1	Full image	128 × 128	256	0.05	0.09	0.13	0.17
DCT	Grayscale	4	540 × 540	64 × 64	256	0.05	0.10	0.15	0.19
DCT	Grayscale	4	540 × 540	32 × 32	64	0.03	0.06	0.09	0.12
DCT	Grayscale	4	540 × 540	16 × 16	16	0.03	0.05	0.07	0.09
DCT	Grayscale	9	360 × 360	16 × 16	36	0.03	0.05	0.08	0.12
DCT	Grayscale	1	Full image	160 × 160	400	0.05	0.10	0.15	0.21
DCT	Grayscale	24	Random 512 × 512	32 × 32	384	0.05	0.11	0.15	0.20

The last four columns report the BER values, expressed as percentages, observed when comparing the hash of the original image to the hash extracted after applying JPEG compression at the specified quality levels. Since the raw BER values tend to be very small, representing them as percentages improves readability and facilitates comparison across methods. Lower BER percentages indicate greater robustness to compression.

As shown in the table, methods based on the DCT generally perform well across compression levels, especially when smaller patches are used or when more patches are combined to increase redundancy. In contrast, methods like SVD show higher BERs, suggesting lower tolerance to lossy compression. Notably, the final row—corresponding to the proposed configuration using 24 random patches and resizing to 32 × 32—shows competitive robustness across all compression settings, highlighting its suitability for real-world usage where compressed images are prevalent.

4.3 Robustness to Filters

Table 3 summarizes the impact of common image enhancement filters on the stability of the hash. These filters are often applied automatically by social media platforms or photo editing tools and can introduce subtle photometric variations that affect pixel values and frequency components. The tested filters include a standard grayscale conversion, a sepia tone filter, and three popular stylized filters—Clarendon, Lark, and Juno—commonly found in mobile applications. The BER is reported for each configuration when comparing the hash of the original image against its filtered version.

Table 3. BER [%] under image enhancement filters

Operation	Mode	Patches	Large Patch	Small Patch	Hash Base	Filter				
						Grayscale	Sepia	Clarendon	Lark	Juno
DCT	Grayscale	1	Full image	128 × 128	256	0.02	0.48	0.68	0.47	0.47
DCT	Grayscale	4	540 × 540	64 × 64	256	0.01	0.52	0.68	0.48	0.72
DCT	Grayscale	4	540 × 540	32 × 32	64	0.02	0.48	0.68	0.47	0.47
AVG	Grayscale	1	Full image	64 × 64	64	0.01	0.54	0.77	0.50	0.54
DWT	Color	1	Full image	64 × 64	64	0.03	0.45	0.66	0.47	0.44
DCT	Grayscale	1	Full image	160 × 160	400	0.02	0.46	0.66	0.47	0.45
DCT	Grayscale	24	Random 512 × 512	32 × 32	384	0.01	0.60	0.80	0.56	0.62

Results show that grayscale conversion causes minimal disruption to most configurations, as expected. However, stylized filters such as Clarendon and Juno introduce more significant changes, with some methods—particularly those using fewer patches or larger block sizes—experiencing substantial increases in BER. The proposed configuration (last row) exhibits a somewhat lower robustness resulting in a higher BER compared to most alternatives, though the difference is not substantial. However, its key advantage lies in its ability to generate hashes of arbitrary length. By selecting a larger number of patches, the hash size can be extended as needed, a flexibility not offered by the other configurations that produce a fixed hash size. This arbitrary length makes it possible to adapt the scheme to unknown message sizes, which is the primary reason for selecting this specific configuration over alternatives with slightly better BER performance.

4.4 Robustness to Image Rescaling

Table 4 reports the BER observed when the input image is rescaled by various factors before hashing. This scenario simulates common preprocessing operations applied by platforms that downsample or upscale images to match display or storage constraints. The tested scale factors range from 1.5 (upsampling) to 0.5 (significant downsampling), and the BER is computed by comparing the hash of the original image to that of its resized version. As in previous evaluations, configurations vary in terms of patch sampling, block size, and hash base size.

The results indicate that moderate rescaling has a relatively small impact on BER, particularly for configurations that use smaller patches or spatially

Table 4. BER [%] under image rescaling

Operation	Mode	Patches	Large Patch	Small Patch	Hash Base	Rescaling Factor			
						1.5	0.9	0.7	0.5
DCT	Grayscale	1	Full image	128 × 128	256	0.04	0.05	0.06	0.08
DCT	Grayscale	4	540 × 540	64 × 64	256	0.04	0.05	0.06	0.08
DCT	Grayscale	4	540 × 540	32 × 32	64	0.03	0.04	0.04	0.05
AVG	Grayscale	1	Full image	64 × 64	64	0.03	0.04	0.05	0.06
DWT	Color	1	Full image	64 × 64	64	0.05	0.07	0.08	0.11
DCT	Grayscale	1	Full image	160 × 160	400	0.04	0.07	0.07	0.09
DCT	Grayscale	24	Random 512 × 512	32 × 32	384	0.04	0.06	0.07	0.09

distributed sampling. Downsampling to 50% begins to noticeably degrade performance for most methods, although the degradation is gradual.

4.5 Comparison with Traditional Hashing Methods

To compare our method's performance against established techniques, we evaluated it across various image transformations using common algorithms: A-Hash, D-Hash, P-Hash, and W-Hash. The selected configuration for the proposed method is the one corresponding to the last row of Tables 2, 3, and 4, which is not the most robust but provides an adjustable hash size. Table 5 summarizes the BER under JPEG compression, common image enhancements, and rescaling.

Table 5. BER [%] of different hashing methods under JPEG compression, filtering, and rescaling

Method	Quality Factor				Filter					Rescaling Factor			
	100	80	70	50	Grayscale	Sepia	Clarendon	Lark	Juno	1.5	0.9	0.7	0.5
A-Hash	0.16	0.21	0.25	0.33	0.78	1.16	1.28	0.95	1.21	0.14	0.18	0.19	0.22
D-Hash	0.47	0.65	0.77	1.04	1.94	1.84	2.30	1.65	1.87	0.41	0.51	0.55	0.62
P-Hash	0.34	0.46	0.56	0.62	0.48	2.50	3.07	1.80	2.61	0.30	0.36	0.40	0.42
W-Hash	0.11	0.20	0.22	0.30	0.03	0.62	0.72	0.61	0.56	0.08	0.11	0.15	0.17
Proposed	**0.05**	**0.11**	**0.15**	**0.20**	**0.01**	**0.60**	**0.80**	**0.56**	**0.62**	**0.04**	**0.06**	**0.07**	**0.09**

Under JPEG compression, the proposed method consistently achieves the lowest BER, especially at higher compression levels (quality factors 70 and 50), outperforming both spatial-domain (A-Hash, D-Hash) and frequency-domain (P-Hash, W-Hash) baselines. This supports the design goal of maximizing robustness to compression by aligning the hash computation with JPEG's internal transform domain.

When subjected to popular image filters (*e.g.,* Sepia, Clarendon, Lark), traditional hash functions suffer significant degradation. Notably, P-Hash and D-Hash exhibit a marked drop in stability, whereas W-Hash maintains relatively low BERs thanks to its multi-resolution frequency representation. Our method achieves comparable or superior robustness across all filter types, particularly in the grayscale scenario.

In terms of rescaling, the proposed method again demonstrates strong performance, with BER values remaining below 0.10 even under 50% downscaling. This is in contrast to D-Hash and P-Hash, whose BERs rise steadily with increased resizing severity. Only W-Hash approaches the robustness of the proposed method in this setting, confirming its strength in handling geometric distortions.

5 Conclusions

This paper introduces calyptography, a novel paradigm for secure secret storage inspired by principles from cryptography and steganography, but fundamentally different from both. Instead of embedding secrets into carrier media or relying solely on secret keys, calyptography associates secrets with unmodified reference images (or other media) via robust perceptual hashes.

The proposed DCT-based patch extraction and randomized hashing method demonstrates high resilience to common image transformations (JPEG compression, filtering, rescaling) while ensuring full entropy in key derivation. Integrated error correction enables practical and reliable secret recovery despite moderate distortions, without altering reference media or compromising security. Experimental results confirm its robustness under realistic conditions, supporting its use in applications requiring media integrity and naturalness. Calyptography, thus, offers a promising framework for secure, media-linked secret storage beyond traditional encryption and steganographic methods.

Future work will focus on the development and integration of perceptual hashing techniques robust not only against compression, filtering, and scaling, but also more complex geometric transformations such as rotations, cropping, and slight affine distortions. Enhancing robustness to these operations would further strengthen the practical resilience of calyptographic systems in uncontrolled or adversarial environments. Although we have already conducted preliminary comparisons with state-of-the-art robust image hashing methods, the results are omitted here due to space constraints. Future work will include a more comprehensive evaluation, with a focus on deep learning-based approaches such as CNNs and transformers, to assess their robustness, efficiency, and suitability.

Acknowledgments. The authors acknowledge the funding obtained by the "SECURING" (PID2021-125962OB-C31) grant funded by the Ministry of Science and Innovation through the State Research Agency (AEI) and the European Regional Development Fund (ERDF), as well as the ARTEMISA International Chair of Cybersecurity (C057/23) and the DANGER Strategic Project of Cybersecurity (C062/23), both funded by the Spanish National Institute of Cybersecurity through the European Union – NextGenerationEU and the Recovery, Transformation and Resilience Plan.

References

1. Bose, R., Ray-Chaudhuri, D.: On a class of error correcting binary group codes. Inf. Control **3**(1), 68–79 (1960)
2. Cogranne, R., Giboulot, Q., Bas, P.: The ALASKA steganalysis challenge: a first step towards steganalysis. In: Proceedings of the ACM Workshop on Information Hiding and Multimedia Security, pp. 125–137. IH&MMSec'19, Association for Computing Machinery, New York, NY, USA (2019)
3. Drmic, A., Silic, M., Delac, G., Vladimir, K., Kurdija, A.S.: Evaluating robustness of perceptual image hashing algorithms. In: 2017 40th International Convention on Information and Communication Technology, Electronics and Microelectronics (MIPRO), pp. 995–1000 (2017)
4. Du, L., Ho, A.T., Cong, R.: Perceptual hashing for image authentication: a survey. Signal Process. Image Commun. **81**, 115713 (2020)

5. Hamadouche, M., Zebbiche, K., Guerroumi, M., Tebbi, H., Zafoune, Y.: A comparative study of perceptual hashing algorithms: application on fingerprint images (2021). https://api.semanticscholar.org/CorpusID:235963864
6. Katz, J., Lindell, Y.: Introduction to Modern Cryptography: Principles and Protocols. Chapman and Hall/CRC (2007)
7. Kozat, S., Venkatesan, R., Mihcak, M.: Robust perceptual image hashing via matrix invariants. In: 2004 International Conference on Image Processing, 2004. ICIP '04, vol. 5, pp. 3443–3446 (2004)
8. Li, Y.N., Wang, P., Su, Y.T.: Robust image hashing based on selective quaternion invariance. IEEE Signal Process. Lett. **22**(12), 2396–2400 (2015)
9. Li, Y., Lu, Z., Zhu, C., Niu, X.: Robust image hashing based on random Gabor filtering and dithered lattice vector quantization. IEEE Trans. Image Process. **21**(4), 1963–1980 (2011)
10. Meng, L., Jiang, X., Sun, T.: A review of coverless steganography. Neurocomputing **566**, 126945 (2024)
11. Peng, Y., Zhang, J., Ye, Z.: Deep reinforcement learning for image hashing. IEEE Trans. Multimedia **22**(8), 2061–2073 (2020)
12. Petitcolas, F., Anderson, R., Kuhn, M.: Information hiding-a survey. Proc. IEEE **87**(7), 1062–1078 (1999)
13. Qin, J., Luo, Y., Xiang, X., Tan, Y., Huang, H.: Coverless image steganography: a survey. IEEE Access **7**, 171372–171394 (2019)
14. Reed, I.S., Solomon, G.: Polynomial codes over certain finite fields. J. Soc. Ind. Appl. Math. **8**(2), 300–304 (1960)
15. Venkatesan, R., Koon, S.M., Jakubowski, M., Moulin, P.: Robust image hashing. In: Proceedings 2000 International Conference on Image Processing (Cat. No.00CH37101), vol. 3, pp. 664–666 vol.3 (2000)
16. Wu, L., Wang, Y., Ge, Z., Hu, Q., Li, X.: Structured deep hashing with convolutional neural networks for fast person re-identification. Comput. Vis. Image Underst. **167**, 63–73 (2018)
17. Yan, C.P., Pun, C.M., Yuan, X.C.: Quaternion-based image hashing for adaptive tampering localization. IEEE Trans. Inf. Forensics Secur. **11**(12), 2664–2677 (2016)
18. Zauner, C.: Implementation and Benchmarking of Perceptual Image Hash Functions. Master's Thesis, Upper Austria University of Applied Sciences, Hagenberg Campus (2010). https://api.semanticscholar.org/CorpusID:17075066
19. Zheng, S., Wang, L., Ling, B., Hu, D.: Coverless information hiding based on robust image hashing. In: Huang, D.S., Hussain, A., Han, K., Gromiha, M.M. (eds.) Intelligent Computing Methodologies, pp. 536–547. Springer International Publishing, Cham (2017)
20. Zhou, Z., Sun, H., Harit, R., Chen, X., Sun, X.: Coverless image steganography without embedding. In: Huang, Z., Sun, X., Luo, J., Wang, J. (eds.) ICCCS 2015. LNCS, vol. 9483, pp. 123–132. Springer, Cham (2015)

An Independent Secure Authentication System Against False Positive/Negative Attacks in SVD-Based Watermarking: Design and Implementation

Tanya Koohpayeh Araghi[(✉)] and David Megías

Internet Interdisciplinary Institute (IN3), Universitat Oberta de Catalunya (UOC),
CYBERCAT-Center for Cybersecurity Research of Catalonia, Rambla del Poblenou,
154-156, 08018 Barcelona, Spain
{tkoohpayeharaghi,dmegias}@uoc.edu

Abstract. The False Positive Problem (FPP) is one of the main concerns in Singular Value Decomposition (SVD) based image watermarking schemes. In the SVD transform, an image is decomposed into three matrices: U and V (singular vectors) and S (singular values). The coefficients within S are excellent candidates for watermark insertion due to their stability against signal processing and geometric attacks. However, this embedding is not applicable for copyright protection since attackers can misuse of FPP. In this paper, we designed and implemented an independent full package as an authentication system to investigate the authenticity of watermark extractors and ensure FPP elimination. This authentication system can be added to all SVD based image watermarking schemes suffering from FPP to eliminate it and to ensure security with minimum degradation in imperceptibility and robustness. The distinction of the proposed system is that it can be offered as a separate and independent package for authentication without tangible consequence on quality of the watermarked images which is especially useful for all watermarking schemes susceptible to FPP to correct false positive and avoid false negative problems.

Keywords: False Positives · Digital Watermarking · Authentication System · SVD · Digital Signatures

1 Introduction

Digital image watermarking defines as hiding digital signals into multimedia covers like image, video or audio to minimize the degradation of their quality and keep the secret symbols in an imperceptible manner [9,20]. Protection of digital media is crucial since they can be easily tampered by illegitimate access [6]. Digital image watermarking is used to prevent unlawful access or illegal alteration of the digital Images. Among transform-domain techniques, the hybrid DWT-SVD approach has a strong reputation. This is due to several key advantages:

a) the scattering of the watermark throughout the cover image, b) the stability of S coefficients against geometric and signal processing distortions, and c) separability, which refers to the difference between the correlation of the original watermark and the highest correlation of the watermark after attacks. Together, these characteristics make the hybrid DWT-SVD technique an excellent candidate for watermark embedding [5].

Singular Value Decomposition (SVD) has been a very attractive issue in information hiding and image watermarking, since it provides high imperceptibility and robustness in comparison to other proposed watermarking schemes. However, this technique is not secure caused by failure to detect and protect false positive problem (FPP). FPP refers to the situation in which an attacker claims illegitimate ownership of the watermark image. To avoid such situation, we designed and implemented an authentication system to detect and protect not only false positive, but also the false negative problem. The distinction of this authentication system is being independent from the embedding and extraction of any watermark scheme means that it can be added to each SVD based and even non SVD based scheme to fight against false positive situation and to increase security with minimum effect on imperceptibility of the scheme. The essence of the work is based on a decision maker that analyzes the output of our two tests as digital signature known as T1 and a hashing test as T2. Since in traditional digital signatures, correct extraction of complete bits exposed on severe attacks is rarely possible, security of digital signature in SVD based schemes is threatened. To guarantee this security, another test (T2) is added to our proposed authentication system and the result of the two tests is sent to be decoded by a decision maker. Experimental result shows that the proposed authentication system can accurately detect both false positive and false negative problems with less than 0.001 possibility of fault rate.

The rest of this paper is organized as follows: in Sect. 2, related works, SVD surgery and false positive effect has been explained. In Sect. 3, the process of design and implementation of the proposed authentication system is clarified. Section 4, is assigned to show the results. In Sect. 5, comparison to authentication policies of the other researchers has been made, and finally in Sect. 6, the conclusions are drawn.

2 Related Work

FPP is one of the major predicaments of the researchers in using SVD; thus, although some solutions have been proposed to address this problem, it still remains an open issue. Several SVD based schemes embed either the S coefficients of the watermark or the watermark itself into the singular values of the host image. In other schemes, the watermark image is directly embedded into the singular values of the host while, other researchers employed the S coefficients of the watermark to be embedded into the singular values of the host [18]. Later, we explain that all of such schemes suffer from FPP. Trying to avoid this situation, different solutions were employed by researchers. Some of them, such as [3,19], embed principal components of watermark into S coefficients of the host image after DWT transform. These solutions usually affect on imperceptibility. Others benefit hash functions as a solution against FPP [17] and the third group utilized digital signatures [4,7,18,23]. However, using conventional digital signatures and hash functions are not robust enough to severe signal processing and geometric attacks since a small distortion causes a big change in achieving correct DS or hash statement. Recently, another approach has been shown to solve FPP especially for IoT based medical image applications, in which the watermark image would be decrypted by Arnold transform or cryptographic functions [10–12,24], this solution needs another layer of protection because if an insider attacker access to the key cryptography can embed its own watermark and threaten the integrity of the image.

2.1 SVD Surgery and False Positive Problem

FPP refers to the situation in which a false watermark can be extracted from the watermarked image because the watermarked image carries insignificant parts of the watermark, so the attackers can inject most considerable portions of their own watermark to extract a fake one.

Considering matrix A as an image, after SVD transformation, it can be shown based on multiplying three elements of U (left singular vector, $M \times M$), S (singular value, $M \times N$) which is a diagonal matrix, and V^T (right singular vector, $N \times N$). Left and right singular vectors U and V^T include vectors representing all the geometric specifications of each element from the matrix A, while S just contains a set of diagonal coefficients free from any distance or vector characteristics. As a result, if matrix A represents an image, after SVD, the S matrix carries out the luminance of the image while U and V^T consist of the geometric specifications of the image. Hiding a watermark is possible in each of these three matrices, but S matrix offers more imperceptibility and robustness because of stability of S coefficients against geometric distortions and small noise disturbance. The experimental and mathematical judgments to prove this claim are explained and shown in [15]. However, a big drawback of false positive effect is involved in SVD based image watermarking schemes. The reason as mentioned above is that, in SVD all geometric characteristics are carried by the U and V^T vectors and the S coefficients just carrying the luminance of the image, so that attackers can simply inject their own U and V^T vectors with an intangible effect on the luminance. FPP occurs in two situations which are explained in the following:

– Inserting S coefficients of the watermark in the S coefficients of the host image: In this situation, the host image is decomposed to SVD. Consider host image I_H after the SVD transform we have:

$$I_H = U_H S_H V_H^T. \qquad (1)$$

Also, considering watermark image as I_w, after SVD:

$$I_w = U_w S_w V_w^T. \qquad (2)$$

Watermark embedding is done by adding the singular values of the host with the singular values of the watermark multiply by a scaling factor α as below:

$$S' = S_H + \alpha S_w. \tag{3}$$

The new S' is replaced with S_H in Eq. (1) and the watermarked image $I_{Watermarked}$ is obtained by using S' multiplying with U_H and V_H^T:

$$I_{Watermarked} = U_H S'_H V_H^T.$$

Watermarked extraction: Now, imagine an attacker wants to extract the watermark image without knowing or accessing to the singular vectors of U_w and V_w^T. So they inject their own U and V^T. Assume these singular vectors as U' and V'^T. In order to extract the watermark image, attackers calculate S_w from Eq. (3):

$$S_w = \frac{(S' - S_H)}{\alpha}. \tag{4}$$

In the current situation, attackers use their own U' and V'^T instead of U_w and V_w^T in Eq. (2) and S_w in Eq. (4) multiplying them to achieve I'_w. If the watermarking scheme was free from false positive, even when attackers find SW, they could not calculate the watermark image I_w successfully; thus, normally $I_w \neq I'_w$ if false positive situation would not exist, but here when attacker tries to calculate I_w in Eq. (2):

$$I_w = U' S_w V'^T_w.$$

They face that:

$$I_w = I'_w. \tag{5}$$

Equation (5) represents the existence of false positive effect, because it means the equality of the extracted watermark with the original watermark and consequently proves the ownership of the watermark by attackers. The reason is due to mathematical justification of assigning geometric specifications to singular vectors U_w and V_w^T. Hence, in spite of participation of the S coefficients of the diagonal matrix of watermark image in watermark embedding, they cannot be extracted carefully since they just carryout the luminance of the image and variation in luminance does not have significant effect on accuracy in watermark extraction since the most fundamental parts of the image are represented by the singular vectors of U_w and V_w^T.

- Another type of false positive situation can be occurred when in Eq. (3), the whole watermark multiplies with the scaling factor instead of SW as below:

$$S' = S_H + \alpha W.$$

Again for the same mentioned reasons the watermark extraction will face false positive effect. Some researchers try to address this problem by involving principal components of SVD (one of singular vectors) to Eq. (3), for example:

$$S' = S_H + \alpha U_W S_W.$$

But this solution remarkably degrades PSNR. Thus, the problem is: "how to propose an authentication system that helps us hide the watermark or its diagonal matrix S_W into the S coefficients of the host in order to achieve high imperceptibility and robustness while eliminating false positive problem?" In other words, we try to devise a situation in which we can embed the W or S_W, to the host according to Eq. (3) such that the Eq. (5) does not hold.

2.2 Solution Approach

Hash functions preserve the integrity of a message. Thus, one way in solving false positive problem in SVD is to hash U and V^T singular vectors with a secret key and send them to receiver. In this case if attackers inject their own U' and V'^T singular vectors, the hash values of U' and V'^T injected by the attackers must be equal to the hash values of original U and V^T in the receiver, otherwise permission of watermark extraction is not granted to unauthenticated users. This is also possible to hash the whole watermark image instead of just U and V^T singular vectors and embed this hash value as a digital signature in addition to the watermark into the host image.

Taking into consideration that a small change in input data before hashing makes a tremendous difference in output after hashing, while the watermarked image is under exposure of a large number of attacks with various intensities, there is a high probability in changing the value of the hash image or hash values of U and V^T singular vectors taken from the attacked watermarked. Hence, the traditional hashing functions like SHA1, SHA 2 and MD 5 and etc. does not work here properly for watermarked images under attack.

To solve this problem authors in [16,21] proposed other hashing mechanisms working exactly for images to recognize whether the hash value belongs to an image under severe attacks or to a completely different image. In their proposed technique, the most important features of an image is extracted by dividing it into overlapped rectangles such that their locations and sizes are chosen pseudo-randomly, and then a secondary image based on these elaborated features is constructed. These features roughly capture semi-global geometric specifications of the image. From this secondary image, the ultimate features would be extracted to build the hash value. In fact, the 2D image matrix would be dimensionally reduced to two 1D hash vectors incorporating the semi global geometric characteristics of the main image. The gist of the research is to capture the essence of geometric content of information in one hand and achieving dimensionally reduction with enough randomness on the other hand. Different types of transforms like discrete wavelet transform (DWT), discrete cosine transforms (DCT), or singular value decomposition (SVD) are used to extract the robust features from images. The method is examined for 5000 images and the result shows robustness of the produced hash values under extensive attacks. In this paper we referred two types of DWT-SVD and SVD-SVD hashing algorithms respectively to hash our watermark image as test T2 and to create a Digital Signature (DS) for increasing both security and performance in our proposed authentication system.

3 Design and Implementation

As mentioned before, FPP is regarded as a security threat in which attackers employ their own eigenvectors to claim fake ownership.

To prevent such situation, an authentication system constitutes of two tests of T1 and T2 is devised. 'A' and 'B' are two parameters resulting from the tests of T1 and T2 respectively. In test T1, the watermark image is authenticated before watermark extraction process. At first, in T1 test, the watermark image is hashed and a unique digital signature is generated to embed into the host image. The signature embedding process is the last step of the watermark embedding procedure. On the detection side, first the embedded signature is extracted and is compared with the generated signature at the user side. If they matched, the watermark image is authenticated and T1 is passed. Consequently, the A parameter is assigned by 1 meaning that the watermark extraction process is allowed to continue for checking T2.

T2 is an auxiliary test to avoid false negative detection. False negative is referred to a situation in which the digital signature cannot be extracted properly because of attacks severity. As a result, the permission of watermark extraction is not granted to user or the user is introduced as an attacker. To avoid such situation, we used the Kozat's hashing method [16] named 'hash by SVD' to hash our watermark image and call it the T2.

In this test, after decomposing the watermark image to SVD, the singular vectors of U and V that carry the most important geometric specification of the image are being hashed. Since in the proposed scheme we used 'S' singular values, this test is very useful as it gives an opportunity to the U and V singular vectors to be hashed and hence the whole watermark image is participated in the T2 test.

In this research, we used wavelet hashing function by [21] for creating the digital signature or T1 test and SVD hash function by [16, 21, 22] for T2 test. The reason for this selection is that in spite of traditional hashing functions, these hashing functions are not very sensitive to image manipulation. Sensitivity of traditional hashing functions against image manipulation is very high such that changing even one bit in the input causes a huge modification in the output of the hash values. Since in digital image watermarking the watermarked image is exposed to various modifications or attacks like filtering, cropping and also noise attacks stemming from transmission channel, these novel hashing functions could be more useful for image identification after attacks. The distinction of these image hashing functions (wavelet and SVD hashing) is robustness in which the created signature based on them is invariant to trivial and insignificant changes while it detects the malicious tampering of the image.

Figure 1 shows the architecture of the designed authentication system including two levels of authentications as T1 and T2. In the first leve (T1), the watermark image will be hashed and changed to a digital signature added to the host image as well as the watermark image itself. In the process of watermark extraction, first, it is requested to the user to enter the image that he is going to extract. The entered image is then hashed and the generated signature is checked with the extracted signature hidden in the cover image. If the created signature is the same as extracted hidden signature, it means that the image is authenticated and verified or it might be a false positive situation. In this case the value of 1 is assigned to variable 'A' (A=1), otherwise the digital signature is not extracted properly and the value of 0 is assigned to 'A'. It can be interpreted as two situations.

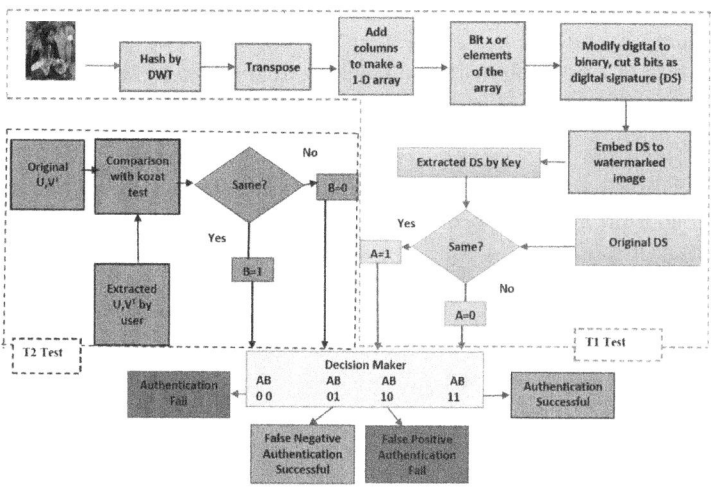

Fig. 1. Architecture of the Designed Authentication System.

The first situation interprets that user is not an authenticated user and intends to misuse of false positive detection based on his own watermark. As a result, the user is known as an adversary. The second situation is that user does not intend to attack and the entered watermark by the user is the same as original watermark, but regarding attack severity, the digital signature cannot be extracted properly leading to incorrect recognition or the false negative problem in which the user is mistakenly known as adversary.

To avoid this condition, an extra controlling procedure is added in the proposed authentication system calling T2 test. In fact, this extra test controls the authenticity of the watermark image when the watermarked image is confronted with very severe attacks in which the digital signature is partly or totally distorted because of the attack's intensity

3.1 Design and Implementation of a Digital Signature (T1)

Figure 2 shows details of generating the Digital Signature. In Fig. 2, the watermark image is hashed by DWT and is changed into a two dimensional array. To create the digital signature from this array, it is first transposed and added the columns to change into a 1-D array. The transposition is done to make difficulty

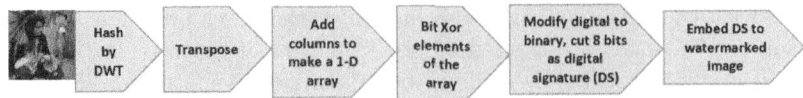

Fig. 2. Signature Generation.

and confusion for the attackers. Then, all of the elements of this array are bitwise XORed together and the produced value is changed from digital to binary and eight first bits of this binary array are selected to generate the digital signature. The following steps are performed to generate the digital signature:

- Step 1: Hash the watermark picture using the "hash by wavelet" method [21].
- Step 2: Transform the hash value from 2-D to 1-D arrays by adding the values of each column and transpose it, if the hashed value itself is a 1-D array only transpose it.
- Step 3: Bitwise XOR between the elements of the Digest image (the hashed watermark image), and then convert it into its corresponding binary digits.
- Step 4: For authentication intentions, choose the first 8-bits of the result as the digital signature bits stream.

3.2 Signature Embedding

After embedding the watermark to the host image, there is another process to embed the digital signature to the watermarked image. In fact this is the final step of the image watermarking process. On the detection side, the signature is extracted and compared to the signature that is generated at the user side based on the received watermark image. If they matched, the watermark image will be authenticated, and the watermark extraction process is allowed to go to the next level. In the following the details of implementation is described.

Before description of the embedding process, it is useful to consider some hints. First, the stream of the digital signature should be embedded to some of the pixels of the cover image such that the robustness of the watermarked image is not affected. In order to achieve this purpose, we benefit from the SVD transform specifications which make it the ideal selection for embedding the digital signature. In order to embed the signature the first column entries of the V components of SVD are chosen.

Theoretical and empirical investigations show that the second rows of the first columns elements of the orthogonal vector V has the optimum characteristics to resist against image digital signal processing and geometric attacks [13].

On the other hand, the embedded signature should not sensibly affect the image imperceptibility. Hence, DWT is selected before performing SVD transform. Simplicity and security are two other reasons to select the DWT as the other transform domain technique to embed the digital signature. Therefore, in order to embed the DS, first DWT is performed on the watermarked image and divide LL sub band into 4×4 non overlapped blocks and with a secret key 8 blocks are chosen and performing SVD in these 8 blocks to hide DS. The reason for dividing the LL sub band into 4×4 blocks is that when a level of DWT is exerted on the image, the size of the image is divided into two. For example, the image size of 512×512 is changed to 256×256. Dividing this image to 4×4 blocks gives us the opportunity to consider 64 places of LL sub bands to randomly select target bits for hiding the signature. Thus, this randomness decreases the chance of finding places carrying the DS by the attacker with resulting high security. Signature embedding process is performed based on the following instructions:

- Step 1: Perform one level DWT on the watermarked image.
- Step 2: Divide the LL sub band into 4×4 blocks.
- Step 3: With the help of a secret key select eight blocks randomly.
- Step 4: Perform SVD for each chosen block.
- Step 5: Multiply absolute values of $V_{2,1}$ by 100 and change the integer part to the nearest integer less than or equal to itself. Then change the value to binary by separating the integer part from decimal.
- Step 6: If the signature bit is equal to one, change the second LSB of the binary value produced by last level to 0, otherwise change it to 1.
- Step 7: Modify the new binary value to integer and add it with the decimal part that was separated before and divide this new value of $V_{2,1}$ by 100.
- Step 8: Perform ISVD for all selected blocks and then Perform inverse DWT (IDWT).

Figure 3 shows embedding signature following the mentioned instructions. In Fig. 3, first $V_{2,1}$'s from each selected block are gathered into a matrix for simplicity and then each element of this matrix is multiplied by 100. The produced values are fixed and the integer and decimal parts are separated. The integer value should not be equal to zero; otherwise the other $V_{2,1}$ value will be selected. Then this value is changed to binary. If signature bit is equal to zero, then the second LSB value will be modified to one; otherwise, if the signature bit is one, then the second LSB of the binary value will be modified by 0. This situation will be checked for the whole bits of the digital signature.

3.3 Signature Extraction

Signature extraction is performed based on the following instructions:

- Step 1: Perform one level DWT on possibly distorted watermarked image.
- Step 2: Divide the LL sub band into 4×4 blocks.
- Step 3: Select 8 blocks based on the secret key.
- Step 4: for i=1 to 8 do steps 4 to 6: Perform SVD on each 4×4 block and gather $V_{2,1}$'s in a matrix.
- Step 5: Multiply absolute values of $V_{2,1}$ by 100 and check and change the integer part to binary.

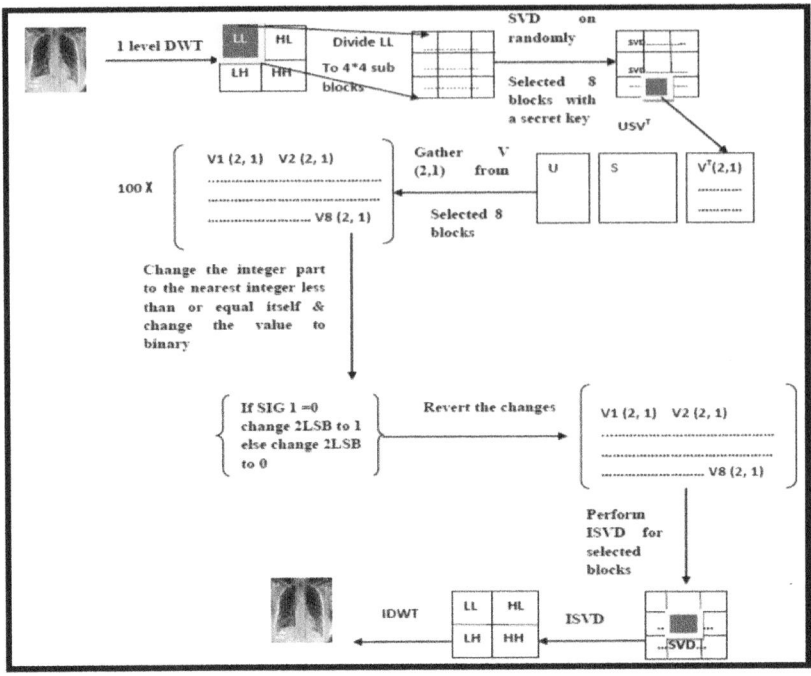

Fig. 3. Embedding Signature.

- Step 6: Check the second LSB bit (LSB_2) and extract the signature based on the instruction (Fig. 4):

$$\text{Sig}(i) = \begin{cases} 0, & \text{if } LSB_2 = 1, \\ 1, & \text{if } LSB_2 = 0. \end{cases}$$

3.4 T2 Test

Image hash functions map an image to a binary string based on the image's appearance to the human eye. Particularly, a perceptual image hash function should have the property that two images that look the same to the human eye map to the same hash value, even if the images have dissimilar digital illustrations [22].

In spite of the T1 test in which the whole watermark is hashed and only 8 bits by a secret key are selected for DS, in T2 both Eigen vectors of U and V will be hashed by SVD-SVD hashing function according to [16, 22]. In this case, when the T1 test fails, T2 test is performed. The result of this test is important because if two tests fails means neither DS stemming from hash value of the watermark nor the Eigen vectors V, U of the original watermark are similar to the user's watermark which clearly shows that the user's watermark is fake and

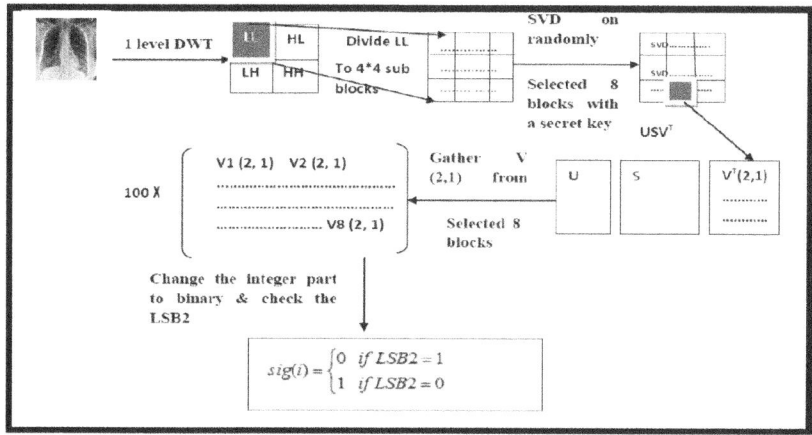

Fig. 4. Signature Extraction.

he is an illegitimate user therefore extraction permission is not granted to him. But when both T1, T2 are passed, it is understandable that both Eigen vectors and DS are belonged to a unique watermark which confirms the authenticity of the user for watermark extraction.

Modifications in bits of DS after severe attacks are usually possible. In case of such situation T2 compensates the flaws of T1, while the reverse situation is rarely happen. That is why we chose different hashing algorithms for T1 and T2.

3.5 Test and Analysis of False Positive Detection

In this section we test our proposed authentication system as following. Figure 5 shows cover, the original and fake watermark images. As it is depicted in this figure, the cover image is medical image X-ray and the real watermark image is Cameraman.

To test the authentication system and prevent false positive detection, the original watermark image 'Cameraman' is embedded into the cover image 'X-ray'. In the extraction process the attacker tries to extract his own watermark, showed as (c) in Fig. 5.

The result of this examination is shown in Fig. 5 (d) in which an attacker tries to misuse the false positive detection and intends to extract his own watermark. Then a digital signature is created by taking the specifications of the fake image. This digital signature is compared with the extracted digital signature which is hidden into the watermarked image. The output of this comparison is called 'A' situation, which would be 0 meaning that two signatures are not the same. Then T2 test is performed on the fake image to hash its V and U singular vectors and check them with the hash parameters of the original watermark. The T2 test analyses fake watermark image to its singular vectors and judges on situation B

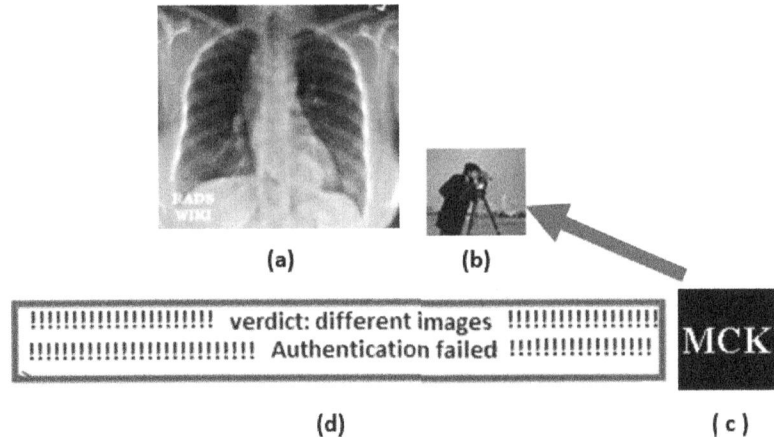

Fig. 5. (a) Cover image, (b) Real watermark, (c) Fake watermark, (d) Ultimate Results of the Proposed Authentication System.

for sending the result to the decision maker. The specifications of the fake image are asked from the user to hash the fake watermark's singular vectors. Based on both situations A and B, the authentication system is judged to determine whether the extraction permission is given to the user or not. Figure 5 (d) shows the results of this judgment.

4 Experimental Results

In order to analyze the performance of the proposed authentication system, it needs to be added to a separate watermarking scheme. In this paper the designed authentication system is implemented on a DWT+SVD2 watermarking scheme [8] to show the effect of this system on imperceptibility, robustness and capacity. In the following the result of using this system on cover images "Pepper", is shown. We also test our proposed authentication system on medical images. Table 1 represents the details of 12 types of attacks, on image "Pepper". It can be clearly seen that the proposed authentication system does not have tangible effect on robustness because of achieving highly robust results. Results of the proposed authentication system are brought on columns T1 and T2, and authentication test which present highly trustable level of authenticity. Table 2 shows the test of imperceptibility after implementation of the proposed authentication system and clearly high imperceptibility is achieved. So our proposed authentication system has a subtle effect on PSNR for either medical or non-medical images.

Table 1. Attack Details and Results on the Proposed System for Image "Pepper"

Row	Attack	Parameters	T1	T2	Authentication Test	NC
1	Average Filter	Window size: 9×9	A=1	B=1	Passed	0.9973
2	Median Filter	Window size: 9×9	A=1	B=1	Passed	0.9980
3	Gaussian Noise	Density: 0.1	A=1	B=1	Passed	0.9562
4	Salt and Pepper	Density: 0.1	A=1	B=1	Passed	0.9730
5	Speckle	Density: 0.1	A=1	B=1	Passed	0.9818
6	Gamma Correction	Value:0.8	A=0	B=1	FN/Passed	0.9970
7	Scale	512→128→512	A=1	B=1	Passed	0.9974
8	Crop	256 rows (0.5)	A=1	B=1	Passed	0.9999
9	Rotation	30°C	A=0	B=1	FN/ Passed	0.9987
10	Rotation	100°C	A=0	B=1	FN/Passed	0.9988
11	Rotation	270°C	A=0	B=1	FN/Passed	0.9987
12	Histogram Equalization	—	A=1	B=1	Passed	0.9994

Table 2. PSNR Test for the Proposed System with Two Types of Medical and Non-medical Images

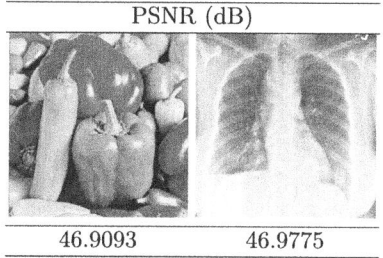

PSNR (dB)	
46.9093	46.9775

5 Comparison and Discussion

In this section, the robustness achieved by implementing our authentication system is compared with several schemes and the results shown in Table 3.

In order to analyze the efficiency of our proposed authentication system, a comparison is made among 10 secure schemes which have been presented to solve FPP. The result of this analysis is depicted on Table 5. In this table, some parameters are considered to compare the proficiency of each scheme to resist FPP. In the following, explanation for some of parameters is given to make it clear.

In Table 5, Accuracy means the ability of authentication mechanism to recognize both false positive and negative problems. Speed means the time considered for authentication which means that whether authentication in performed before watermark extraction or after it. In some of the schemes the watermark extraction is done but watermark is not extracted correctly for unauthorized users.

Since emphasize is on authentication system, we do not consider time of watermark embedding or extraction. The aim is to analyze speed of authentication technique.

Portability means that whether proposed system for false positive and watermark embedding/extraction are related to each other or not. In other words, authentication is done during watermark embedding like those schemes using principal components of SVD or not?

Dependency of robustness, capacity and imperceptibility means that using authentication mechanism affects on capacity, robustness or imperceptibility. To answer this question, we should investigate how many bits are used for this mechanism. For example how many bits used for Digital Signature (DS)? Or, has it an impact on imperceptibility or robustness? In the following, we briefly explained about each of these schemes and their used techniques against FPP. We have also an analysis and a comparison among all these schemes and our proposed system in terms of trustable authentication.

One solution against FPP is watermark encryption. Awashti [10], proposed a scheme based on lifting wavelet transform (LWT) and SVD for security of medical images. For their authentication mechanism they used AES encryption for the watermark image in which firstly the watermark extracted and checked by the decrypt-ed AES watermark image given to the trusted users in the hospital. If they were similar then the authentication is granted. The speed of the authentication is weak since the watermark should be extracted and then checked with the decrypted version. Also the scheme is vulnerable to FPP if the attack is done from internal users since only S components of the watermark and cover are chosen for hiding the watermark. The same problem is for Begum [11], Zeng [24] and Chaudhary [12] because of their similar watermark embedding policy and using Arnold transform only for water-mark encryption.

DS based authentication algorithms are other authentication mechanisms proposed in [18,23]. The base of these algorithms is hashing U and V singular vectors to combine them then selecting some bits as a digital signature and embed DS in addition to the watermark to check legal authenticity. The speed of the authentication in these algorithms is fast because of checking authenticity by extracting DS before watermark extraction, but, depending on the selected hashing algorithm (if it is conventional hash function like SHA or MD5), they cannot resist against severe attacks because DS bits may be changed during the intensive signal processing and geometric attacks. So these authentication algorithms are not enough to prevent both FPP and the false negative problem (FNP), which decreases accuracy and need additional capacity for embedding DS.

The third group of authentication mechanisms is proposed by [1,3,18]. To prevent FPP, in these schemes the principal components US or SV are hidden into S coefficients of the host image. The drawback of these schemes is dependency of scheme on imperceptibility and robustness such that in comparison to other schemes they provide less imperceptibility or robustness. To solve this problem [3], used artificial bee colony (ABC) as optimization algorithm. Self-adaptive differential evolution (SDE) used by [23], a firefly photinus approach proposed in [2] and finally multi objective ant colony optimization (MOACO) proposed by [19] to select an optimum multiple zoom in factor (MZF). Bear in mind that these optimization techniques are used just for finding an optimal scaling factor to enhance imperceptibility.

Low speed is also the other vulnerability of these schemes such that unauthenticated user is not recognized at the very primary steps and watermark extraction is done in every situation but in case of accessing unauthenticated users the incorrect watermark will be extracted. The strength point of them is accuracy in detection of both FPP and FNP.

In [14], authors used fast Walsh-Hadamard transform (FWHT) for watermark embedding leading to low computational complexity. Authors also used singular values of SVD for key mapping to increase the robustness. However, security analysis established by them is not pointed on FPP and how to solve it. With high probability, it is guessed that their scheme is not effective for detection and prevention of FPP/FNP because of using singular values for key mapping.

Our proposed authentication system is a hybrid of DS in addition to hash U and V components in which we did not used conventional hashing functions. The other distinction is using two different unconventional hashing functions for T1 and T2, so if the DS was not retrieved because of attacks intensity, T2 can detect and prevent from unauthenticated access. The DWT-SVD and SVD-SVD hashing functions are used respectively for T1 and T2 tests. Experimental results disclosed that the authentication system acts accurately since it is tested for not only 5000 images, but also for a lot of linear arrays. Hundreds of linear arrays were manipulated and sent to this system, the error rate is estimated below 0.001.

Table 3. Comparison of NC for cover image "X-Ray" (proposed scheme)/ Pepper and watermark "Cameraman" AVG:Average filtering, MD: Median filtering, GN:Gausian noise, SP: salt and pepper, GC: Gamma correction, Sc: Scaling, Cr: Crop,R: Rotation, HE: Histogram equalization

Attacks	Ahmadi [1]	Awashti [10]	Makbol [19]	Vali [23]	Begum [11]	Zeng [24]	Khanam [14]	Chaudhary [12]	Proposed
No attack	0.9443	1	1	1	1	1	1	1	1
AVG 2*2	NA	0.9541	NA	NA	0.9431	NA	NA	NA	0.9999
MD 2*2	0.9633	0.9964	0.9969	0.9434	0.9789	0.9847	0.9541	0.50	0.9999
GN 0.05	0.9335	0.9983	0.9208	0.8020	0.9911	0.9880	0.9823	NA	0.9644
SP 0.05	0.9241	0.9995	0.9433	0.8072	0.9915	0.9644	0.9931	0.95	0.9773
Speckle 0.05	0.9829	NA	0.9977	0.8085	0.9916	NA	0.9292	0.97	0.9760
GC 0.6	0.9861	NA	0.9956	0.9901	NA	NA	NA	NA	0.9993
Sc 512-64-512	0.8810	NA	0.9720	0.7060	0.9934	0.9980	NA	NA	0.9994
Cr 80, 80	0.9861	NA	0.9757	0.9872	NA	0.9636	0.7821	NA	0.9999
R 60	0.9671	0,9451	NA	0.8769	NA	0.8722	0.5132	NA	0.9997
R 170	0.9620	NA	0.9507	0.8311	NA	NA	NA	NA	0.9998
R 200	NA	NA	NA	0.8548	NA	NA	0.7544	NA	0.9995
HE	0.9741	0.9269	0.9405	0.9889	NA	NA	NA	NA	0.9996

Table 4. PSNR Comparison

Ahmadi [1]	Zeng [24]	Makbol [19]	Begum [11]	Chaudhary [12]	Awashti [10]	Khanam [14]	Ansari [3]	Araghi [5]	Proposed
44.1172	46.5558	42.9477	48.9688	49.86	37.1628	49.78	38.4833	46.7493	46.9775

Table 5. Comparative analysis of authentication mechanisms to avoid FPP and FN

Authors	Accuracy	Type of transform	Type of optimisation	Speed	Cover size	Watermark size	Portability	In dependency of PSNR	In dependency of capacity	In dependency of robustness	Type of authorization mechanism
Ahmadi et al. [2]	NA	DWT+SVD	Firefly photons	Weak	512×512	32×32	NA	NA	NA	NA	NA
Makbol et al. [19]	Yes	IWT+SVD	MOACO+MZF	Weak	256×256	256×256	NA	NA	NA	NA	Principal components U
Ansari et al. [3]	NA	DWT+SVD	ABC	Weak	512×512	128×128	NA	NA	NA	NA	Principal components US
Voli et al. [23]	NA	RDWT+SVD	SDS	Fast	512×512	512×512	NA	Negligible	NA	Yes	DS
Khanam et al. [14]	NA	SVD	FWHT	Weak	256×256	32×32	NA	NA	NA	Yes	Key mapping
Ahmadi et al. [1]	Yes	DWT+HVS+SVD	PSO	Weak	256×256	32×32, 64×64	NA	Yes	NA	Yes	Principal components UV+ Arnold transform
Zeng et al. [24]	NA	NSCT+DWT+SVD	NA	Weak	512×512	32×32	NA	NA	NA	NA	Arnold cat map
Awashti et al. [10]	NA	LWT+SVD	PSO+JAYA	Weak	512×512	256×256	NA	NA	NA	NA	AES encryption
Begum et al. [11]	NA	DWT+SVD	NA	Weak	512×512	64×64	NA	NA	NA	NA	Arnold cat map
Chaudhary et al. [12]	NA	DWT+HMD+SVD	NA	Weak	512×512	64×64	NA	NA	NA	NA	Arnold cat map
Proposed scheme	Yes	DWT+SVD2	NA	Fast	Unlimited N×N	Equal to cover	Yes	Negligible	NA	Yes	DS + Hash U, V

6 Conclusion

In this paper, we investigated the hybrid SVD schemes in terms of effectiveness to overcome FPP for rightful ownership. The state-of-the-art solutions against FPP are divided to 4 groups of DS, one way hash functions and principal components and watermark encryptions. We also pointed out to vulnerabilities and distinctions of each groups. An independent authentication system was proposed, designed and implemented. Our authentication system does not apply conventional hashing functions which are vulnerable against signal processing and geometric attacks. Moreover, we used two different unconventional hash functions which are quite robust against both signal processing and geometric attacks. Effectiveness of the system is tested for thousands of both images and even one dimensional arrays and the experimental results prove that our proposed system has a very high ability to recognize FPP with less than 0.001 error rate.

Furthermore, it can be used as an independent package and can be added to those vulnerable schemes against FPP, since it is shown in this paper its effect on imper-ceptibility, capacity and robustness is barely small while making these unreliable schemes to be trustful and secure for rightful ownership. Therefore all unauthorized schemes mentioned in the literature of this paper can be changed to authorized scheme by using our proposed authentication system.

Acknowledgements. The authors acknowledge the funding obtained from the "SECURING" project (PID2021-125962OB-C31) funded by the Ministry of Science and Innovation, the Agencia Estatal de Investigación, and the European Regional Development Fund (ERDF), and by the ARTEMISA International Chair of Cybersecurity (C057/23) and the DANGER Strategic Project of Cybersecurity (C062/23), both funded by the Spanish National Institute of Cybersecurity through the European Union âĂŞ Next GenerationEU and the Recovery, Transformation, and Resilience Plan.

References

1. Ahmadi, S., Zhang, G., Rabbani, M., Boukela, L., Jelodar, H.: An intelligent and blind dual color image watermarking for authentication and copyright protection. Appl. Intell. **51**, 1701–1732 (2021)
2. Alomoush, W., et al.: Improved security of medical images using dwt-svd watermarking mechanisms based on firefly photinus search algorithm. Discover Appli. Sci. **6**(7), 366 (2024)
3. Ansari, I.A., Pant, M.: Multipurpose image watermarking in the domain of dwt based on svd and abc. Pattern Recogn. Lett. **94**, 228–236 (2017)
4. Araghi, T.K.: Digital image watermarking and performance analysis of histogram modification based methods. In: Arai, K., Kapoor, S., Bhatia, R. (eds.) SAI 2018. AISC, vol. 858, pp. 631–637. Springer, Cham (2019). https://doi.org/10.1007/978-3-030-01174-1_49
5. Araghi, T.K., Abd Manaf, A., Araghi, S.K.: A secure blind discrete wavelet transform based watermarking scheme using two-level singular value decomposition. Expert Syst. Appl. **112**, 208–228 (2018)
6. Araghi, T.K., Alarood, A.A., Araghi, S.K.: Analysis and evaluation of template based methods against geometric attacks: a survey. In: Saeed, F., Mohammed, F., Al-Nahari, A. (eds.) IRICT 2020. LNDECT, vol. 72, pp. 807–814. Springer, Cham (2021). https://doi.org/10.1007/978-3-030-70713-2_73
7. Araghi, T.K., Manaf, A.A.: An enhanced hybrid image watermarking scheme for security of medical and non-medical images based on dwt and 2-d svd. Futur. Gener. Comput. Syst. **101**, 1223–1246 (2019)
8. Araghi, T.K., Megías, D.: Analysis and effectiveness of deeper levels of svd on performance of hybrid dwt and svd watermarking. Multimedia Tools Appli. **83**(2), 3895–3916 (2024)
9. Araghi, T.K., Megías, D., Garcia-Font, V., Kuribayashi, M., Mazurczyk, W.: Disinformation detection and source tracking using semi-fragile watermarking and blockchain. In: Proceedings of the 2024 European Interdisciplinary Cybersecurity Conference, EICC 2024, pp. 136–143. Association for Computing Machinery, New York (2024). https://doi.org/10.1145/3655693.3655718
10. Awasthi, D., Srivastava, V.K.: Hessenberg decomposition-based medical image watermarking with its performance comparison by particle swarm and jaya optimization algorithms for different wavelets and its authentication using aes. Circ. Syst. Signal Process. **42**(8), 4953–4984 (2023)
11. Begum, M., et al.: Image watermarking using discrete wavelet transform and singular value decomposition for enhanced imperceptibility and robustness. Algorithms **17**(1), 32 (2024)
12. Chaudhary, H., Garg, P., Vishwakarma, V.P.: Enhanced medical image watermarking using hybrid dwt-hmd-svd and arnold scrambling. Sci. Rep. **15**(1), 9710 (2025)
13. Fan, M.Q., Wang, H.X., Li, S.K.: Restudy on svd-based watermarking scheme. Appl. Math. Comput. **203**(2), 926–930 (2008)
14. Khanam, T., Dhar, P.K., Kowsar, S., Kim, J.M.: Svd-based image watermarking using the fast walsh-hadamard transform, key mapping, and coefficient ordering for ownership protection. Symmetry **12**(1), 52 (2020)
15. Koohpayeh Araghi, T., Abd Manaf, A., Alarood, A., Zainol, A.B.: Host feasibility investigation to improve robustness in hybrid dwt+ svd based image watermarking schemes. Adv. Multimedia **2018**(1), 1609378 (2018)

16. Kozat, S.S., Venkatesan, R., Mihçak, M.K.: Robust perceptual image hashing via matrix invariants. In: 2004 International Conference on Image Processing, ICIP 2004, vol. 5, pp. 3443–3446. IEEE (2004)
17. Loukhaoukha, K., Nabti, M., Zebbiche, K.: A robust svd-based image watermarking using a multi-objective particle swarm optimization. Opto-Electron. Rev. **22**(1), 45–54 (2014)
18. Makbol, N.M., Khoo, B.E.: A new robust and secure digital image watermarking scheme based on the integer wavelet transform and singular value decomposition. Digital Signal Process. **33**, 134–147 (2014)
19. Makbol, N.M., Khoo, B.E., Rassem, T.H., Loukhaoukha, K.: A new reliable optimized image watermarking scheme based on the integer wavelet transform and singular value decomposition for copyright protection. Inf. Sci. **417**, 381–400 (2017)
20. Malanowska, A., Mazurczyk, W., Araghi, T.K., Megías, D., Kuribayashi, M.: Digital watermarking–a meta-survey and techniques for fake news detection. IEEE Access (2024)
21. Monga, V.: Perceptually based methods for robust image hashing. The University of Texas at Austin (2005)
22. Monga, V., Mihcak, M.K.: Robust image hashing via non-negative matrix factorizations. In: 2006 IEEE International Conference on Acoustics Speech and Signal Processing Proceedings, vol. 2, pp. II–II. IEEE (2006)
23. Vali, M.H., Aghagolzadeh, A., Baleghi, Y.: Optimized watermarking technique using self-adaptive differential evolution based on redundant discrete wavelet transform and singular value decomposition. Expert Syst. Appl. **114**, 296–312 (2018)
24. Zeng, F., Bai, H., Xiao, K.: Blind watermarking algorithm combining nsct, dwt, svd, and hvs. Sec. Priv. **5**(4), e223 (2022)

Entropy-Aware Secret Data Embedding for Network Storage Channels

Paweł Rajba[1]([✉]), Jörg Keller[2], and Wojciech Mazurczyk[3]

[1] University of Wrocław, Wrocław, Poland
`pawel@cs.uni.wroc.pl`
[2] FernUniversität in Hagen, Hagen, Germany
`Joerg.Keller@fernuni-hagen.de`
[3] Warsaw University of Technology, Warsaw, Poland
`wojciech.mazurczyk@pw.edu.pl`

Abstract. Information hiding techniques are currently increasingly utilized by cybercriminals for various nefarious purposes. That is why, from the defenders' perspective, it is essential to investigate how such methods can be used to bypass security countermeasures so the countermeasures can be further improved. Thus, in this paper, we address the challenge of embedding secret data into network traffic while preserving the statistical properties of the carrier stream, particularly Shannon entropy. In particular, we focus on storage-based network steganography, and we introduce two novel embedding strategies that significantly reduce detectability by entropy-based network wardens. The first technique employs an inverse Huffman-inspired encoding scheme, which encodes encrypted secret messages in a way that closely mimics the entropy distribution of the cover traffic while maximizing bandwidth. The second method is designed to precisely match the entropy of the carrier traffic, allowing tunable trade-offs between stealth and bandwidth. Extensive experimental evaluations across synthetic and real-world network distributions demonstrate that the proposed schemes achieve superior performance in maintaining entropy while offering higher steganographic bandwidth than conventional techniques. This research advances the state of covert communications by quantifying entropy-bandwidth trade-offs and delivering practically implementable, entropy-aware embedding methods.

Keywords: Network Steganography · Network Warden · Shannon Entropy · Bandwidth Optimization · Information Hiding

1 Introduction

Embedding a secret message into a stream of network packets is known as network steganography [15], and it creates a parasitic covert channel within the innocent-looking transmissions. In such cases, a "carrier" is defined as the normal, overt network traffic, i.e., the sequence of packets exchanged between legitimate endpoints into which a covert message is hidden. Network steganography is mainly used for malicious purposes [1,5], e.g., to enable the compromised host to covertly communicate with the attacker's Command & Control (C&C) server. That is why a frequently used solution is to use a dedicated entity called a *warden* [14], which is capable of monitoring the passing network traffic in search for anomalies and reacting accordingly by either detecting the presence of secret transfers, eliminate them, limit their bandwidth and/or audit them [25]. Yet the steganographers are designing the covert channels so they are stealthy in order to avoid detection by a warden [4].

One of the most common network steganography group of methods are covert storage channels. Such techniques exploit fields in the protocol that are either unused/reserved, are not inherent for the correct forwarding of the packets or whose modification does not significantly impact the transmission quality.

Introducing secret data bits into header values may impact the entropy of the packet and the flow of packets. In this case, three scenarios are possible depending on the characteristics of values that are carried in such a field: *(i)* the field carries only a single fixed value, *(ii)* the values in the field vary over a small known set of values, and *(iii)* a field that already carries pseudo-random values. In the first case, when a header bit or flag is never used by regular protocols—hiding data forces that field to flip unpredictably, injecting maximum new randomness where there was none before and creating a stark anomaly that is easy to spot. In the second case, when a header element legitimately cycles through a handful of well-known states, overwriting it with covert bits increases unpredictability. Still, only up to the size of that small alphabet, and an observer who knows the typical usage patterns may still detect deviations. Finally, in the third case, when the field naturally holds high-entropy, seemingly random numbers—replacing its contents with hidden data produces only a subtle disturbance, blending almost imperceptibly into existing variability; this makes detection very difficult, though it also limits how much secret information can be safely carried.

From the perspective of secret data exchange, we will define anomaly as a change in the Shannon entropy [18] of the packet stream. There is a well-known trade-off between the bandwidth and the stealthiness of a covert channel [15]. We try to address this problem quantitatively by defining our attack model and specifying requirements and assumptions that we consider fulfilled beyond looking at entropy. For example, we assume that the embedding of a piece of secret message in a header field of a network packet should not use a symbol that is not used in this header field in normal traffic, as this would allow easy detection even if such action might help to bound the change in entropy.

Therefore, the main novel contributions of this work are as follows:

– Next to standard means to reduce entropy change, such as using only every t-th packet for steganographic purposes or restricting the number of secret message bits per packet, we propose an embedding for encrypted secret messages based on inverse Huffman encoding.
– We introduce an embedding that matches a required entropy value exactly, yet without looking at carrier symbol frequencies and with lower bandwidth than inverse Huffman encoding.

– We experimentally demonstrate that for similar changes in entropy, our embedding achieves higher bandwidth than other proposals, and for similar bandwidth, our embedding achieves smaller changes in entropy.

The remainder of this article is structured as follows. Section 2 summarizes network steganography, possible countermeasures, and Shannon entropy. Section 3 specifies the attack model together with the requirements and assumptions that should be fulfilled when embedding a secret message into the header field of a network packet. Section 4 presents our Inverse Huffman-based embedding and compares it with different approaches to embedding a secret message into a stream of network packets without changing carrier entropy too much. Section 5 presents an experimental evaluation via several header fields of TCP/IP packets. Section 6 concludes our research.

2 Background and Related Work

In this section, we first describe the fundamentals of network covert channels (a.k.a. network steganography), summarize state-of-the-art efforts related to their detection, and explain Shannon entropy.

2.1 Network-Based Data Hiding Basics

In this study, we address the topic of network steganography, which has been extensively characterized in [15]. Establishing a covert channel necessitates embedding hidden information within the traffic flow exchanged between at least two endpoints. Owing to the vast number of coexisting protocols employed for Internet service delivery, the opportunities for data concealment are virtually limitless. Nevertheless, the steganographic process must ensure that it does not interfere with standard traffic behavior or introduce discernible anomalies.

In the literature, various classifications of information-hiding techniques in network traffic have been proposed [21,23,25]. However, the most common one is where the network steganographic techniques are divided into the following categories [15]: *(i)* covert storage methods, which embed hidden data within unused or dedicated sections of network protocol structures. These methods exploit fields that are either unassigned or reserved, utilizing bits that are not ordinarily anticipated during regular communication or fields that are in use but whose modification will not prevent the network packet's transmission, although the quality of communication may be lowered; *(ii)* covert timing methods, which involve transmitting hidden information through the manipulation of event timing and packet transmission delays. For instance, the deliberate alteration of packet dispatch intervals to encode information exemplifies this approach. Note that these two types of steganographic methods can also be utilized concurrently, in which case the resulting technique is typically referred to as hybrid [15].

Irrespective of the specific hiding technique employed, the performance of a covert channel is predominantly influenced by three critical factors [15]. The first is *steganographic bandwidth*, quantifying the amount of hidden data that can be transmitted within a given timeframe. The second is *robustness*, defined as the extent to which the covert channel can tolerate modifications without becoming ineffective. The third is *undetectability*, which refers to the degree to which the presence of hidden information remains concealed within the overt network traffic.

These indicators are interconnected, as optimizing one metric without negatively impacting the others is impossible. For example, increased steganographic bandwidth typically leads to a higher probability of the hidden information becoming detectable.

2.2 Shannon Entropy and Entropy-Based Encoding

Shannon entropy was introduced by Claude E. Shannon in 1948 in the seminal paper *A Mathematical Theory of Communication* [18]. It is a foundational concept in information theory that quantifies the average level of "information" or "uncertainty" inherent in the possible outcomes of a random variable. For a discrete random variable X on a finite sample space (also called symbol set Σ) of size n with a probability distribution $P = \{p_1, p_2, \ldots, p_n\}$, the Shannon entropy $H(X)$ is defined as:

$$H(X) = -\sum_{i=1}^{n} p_i \log_2 p_i \quad (1)$$

This expression represents the expected number of bits required to optimally encode the outcome of X, assuming the probability distribution is known. The entropy reaches its maximum $\log_2 n$ when the distribution is uniform, i.e., when all outcomes are equally likely, and is minimized (equal to zero) when the result is certain. Instead of $H(X)$, we also write $H(P)$ when the context is clear. Shannon entropy has broad applicability across fields, including data compression, cryptography, statistical mechanics, and machine learning. It establishes the theoretical limit for lossless data compression and is the foundation for entropy-based coding algorithms such as Huffman coding [6].

Given a symbol set Σ with probability distribution P, entropy-based coding assigns a codeword, i.e., a bit string, to each symbol such that a message over Σ can be encoded symbol by symbol and can be uniquely decoded again (mostly by ensuring that codewords for different symbols are prefix-free). Furthermore, the bit length of the encoded message in relation to the number of symbols in the message, i.e., the average number of bits per symbol, is as close as possible to the entropy of a random variable with sample space Σ and distribution P.

Huffman coding [9] is an algorithm to derive such a set of codewords for given Σ and P. The algorithm starts with a list of the symbols $i \in \Sigma$, together with their probabilities p_i. Repeatedly, the two symbols (or pseudo-symbols in later stages) with the lowest probabilities in the list are removed from the list and merged into a pseudo-symbol with combined probability, which is added to the list. This stops when only one pseudo-symbol (with combined probability 1) is left. The algorithm thus produces a binary tree where the symbols are the leaves, and each merge operation produces an inner node representing a pseudo-symbol connected to the two symbols that have been merged, with the last pseudo-symbol being the tree root. The two edges leaving an inner node are annotated with 0 and 1, respectively. The sequence of annotations on the unique path from the root to a symbol constitutes the codeword for this symbol. As paths that diverge at an inner node will lead to codewords that differ in at least this position, and as a path to a symbol never passes another symbol because symbols are only represented by leaves, a codeword can never be the prefix of another codeword. Therefore Huffman codes are prefix-free and uniquely decodable.

2.3 Entropy-Based Detection

Below, we review the most notable approaches to entropy-based detection of anomalies and cyber threats. Then, we move to characterizing how entropy was used in information-hiding-related research.

In 2007, Lyda and Hamrock [11] focused on Portable Executable (PE) file analysis using bintropy tools. By establishing baseline entropy levels for legitimate Windows DLLs (typically 6.2-6.8 bits/byte), analysts can flag files exceeding 7.2 bits/byte as potentially packed or encrypted. This approach reduced malware analysis time by 73% in comparative studies.

Next, Tellenbach et al. [19] presented the entropy telescope, a comprehensive framework for detecting and classifying network anomalies by examining how traffic feature distributions change over time. Central to their approach is the use of Tsallis entropy, computed across a range of sensitivity parameters, which they further refine by isolating the portions of each distribution that contribute most to the entropy measure. This pruning step reduces unwanted correlations and makes the resulting features more discriminative. By feeding these generalized-entropy features into established detection methods (Kalman filtering, PCA, KLE) and an SVM classifier, they show—through both controlled injections of diverse anomaly models and analysis of real backbone data—that their refined entropy metrics yield substantially higher detection and classification accuracy than traditional Shannon-based techniques.

Then, Liu et al. [10] proposed a two-stage method combining Shannon entropy with Renyi cross-entropy to analyze Snort IDS alerts. They computed entropy distributions across five alert attributes (source/destination IPs, threat scores, packet length), then used cross-entropy differences to identify coordinated attack patterns in campus network data, achieving a 96% detection rate. Berezinski et al. [3] proposed entropy analysis for network anomaly detection by applying Shannon, Renyi, and Tsallis entropy to traffic features like packet size distributions and protocol usage patterns. Their method identifies deviations from baseline entropy thresholds, flagging botnet command-and-control traffic that exhibits irregular communication patterns. Analyzing a labeled dataset containing nine attack types demonstrated entropy's sensitivity to volumetric DDoS attacks and stealthy exfiltration.

In [16], Menendez Benito et al. developed Entropy Time Series (EnTS), which applies wavelet transforms to entropy signatures of executable binaries. By treating entropy as a temporal sequence and analyzing amplitude variations, EnTS detects packed malware with 93.9% accuracy while maintaining linear time complexity. This approach outperformed 56 commercial antivirus engines in detecting encryption-based polymorphism during testing. Recent work in [2] revealed critical vulnerabilities in entropy-based ransomware detectors. Attackers can create hybrid files that defeat threshold-based detection systems by strategically blending high-entropy malicious payloads with low-entropy benign content. This evasion technique reduced detection accuracy by 41% in controlled experiments.

Regarding information-hiding-related research, several works have tried to design covert channels to bypass entropy-based detectors or propose using entropy to detect them. Walls and Wright [20] designed the Liquid covert timing channel to bypass entropy-based detection by strategically adjusting inter-packet delays (IPDs). By allocating a subset of IPDs to "smooth" entropy irregularities while encoding data in others, they maintained undetectability (Shannon entropy of ca. 7.2 bits/symbol) against Gianvecchio's CEN/CCE tests [8]. Then, Mali et al. [12] embedded data in JPEG blocks with high local entropy (>7.5 bits/pixel) using DCT mid-band coefficients. High-entropy blocks mask payloads better due to natural texture complexity, achieving 98% undetectability against histogram-based steganalysis. Next, Darwish et al. [7] applied multi-scale entropy analysis to IPD streams, identifying covert channels by detecting entropy minima at specific time scales (e.g., 32ms bins). Hierarchical entropy improved detection accuracy by 22% compared to flat entropy methods. Finally, in [24], the authors leveraged Shannon entropy optimality to create steganographic encodings indistinguishable from cover distributions. They achieved perfect secrecy with 12% higher payload capacity than prior LSB methods.

While entropy-based methods have been used in some steganographic domains (e.g., digital image steganography), they have only been found to be used in network steganography for timing channels. Hence, this work explores using entropy-based methods for network storage channels. In particular, we investigate how such channels may try to evade detection methods by trading some steganographic bandwidth for a better match of entropy with the entropy of a carrier communication.

3 Attack Model, Requirements, Assumptions

We consider a carrier or overt communication realized by a stream of network packets, for instance, but not restricted to TCP/IP packets, that flow from an overt sender to an overt receiver. A covert sender, which might be residing with the overt sender or may be on the communication path, embeds an encrypted secret message into this carrier piece by piece via modifying the content of a header field[1] in each or a subset of the packets. The header field is chosen so that the modification does not disturb or corrupt the communication mechanism, i.e.,

---

[1] Similar considerations for payload modifications are possible but future work.

the packets will still be delivered to the overt receiver. The covert receiver that resides either with the overt receiver or on the communication path can eavesdrop on the communication, thus can read the modified header field content and can extract from it the pieces of the secret message, which it can then re-assemble into a message, and finally decrypt it to obtain the secret message in plaintext.

We assume that the covert sender and receiver have previously exchanged a key and agreed on the embedding details, such as which packets the cover sender will use. We also assume that the communication is robust. We do not assume that the covert receiver can or attempts to reconstruct the original contents of the packets' header fields that had been used for embedding the secret message, i.e., we are not focussing on reversible covert channels, as in the following, we will consider the stream of packets as seen by an entity on the communication path between the covert sender and receiver, and not as seen by the overt receiver.

We assume a passive warden on the communication path between CS and CR, which can inspect each packet header, more exactly each header field in each packet, for any value not occurring in normal carrier traffic, and for entropy on byte or field level over a window of packets. It might sound more general if the warden would check the whole header, however then all byte values will generally occur, as each field has different field-specific typical values, so the check for unusual values would fail. Moreover, checking for entropy changes is difficult over the whole header. The header of an IPv4 packet has 20 bytes (plus up to 40 optional bytes), and the header of an IPv6 packet has 40 bytes. The TCP header that follows the IP header again has 20 bytes (without optional bytes). If only a single field, i.e., one byte, is modified, then the change in entropy will be marginal as byte value frequencies will only change slightly. Thus, the change in entropy might disappear in the normal variations of carrier traffic entropy.

Consequently, the checks that we assume are quite rigorous, leading to the following strict requirements for the covert channel if it should have a chance to go unnoticed. First, embedding the secret message may not lead to unusual values, necessitating the covert sender to monitor the overt traffic to learn which values are "normal" in the targetted header field. Second, the value distribution in the embedding must be such that it does not deviate much from the entropy of this field in the carrier traffic. This again necessitates that the covert sender monitors the overt traffic to learn the frequencies of values in the targetted header field over a window of packets.

Both requirements exclude, among other things, the use of a reserved or unused field as there, only one value will occur with frequency 100%, and the entropy of this field will be 0, i.e., there is no chance to embed a secret message, even with small steganographic bandwidth, in that field.

Our research aims to see which steganographic bandwidth can still be achieved despite these constraints and how this bandwidth varies depending on the allowable deviation of entropy.

Once more, we note that we assume that the secret message is encrypted, i.e., bits have 50% value 0 and 50% value 1, and values of different bits are independent. This assumption is not artificial as steganography only makes a message stealthy but not confidential. Furthermore, we assume that the warden does not know precisely how the covert sender embeds the secret message and hence can only check for unusual values and entropy change. Still, allowing the warden to check each header field is a very strong assumption that raises the bars for the covert channel relatively high. Finally, we assume that the covert sender can monitor the carrier traffic for some time or choose a header field where he can be sure that the value distribution is relatively stable. Also, the covert sender must be able to send this distribution and/or all design decisions that he derives from it to the covert receiver before exchanging secret messages. This assumption is at least easily fulfilled for header fields where value distribution is relatively stable over more extended periods, such as the Type of Service (ToS) field[2] in the IPv4 header that we will use as an example in our experiments.

4 Strategies for Stealthy Embedding

In the following, we assume a header field that has k bits, i.e., can assume any value in $B_k = \{0,1\}^k \equiv \{0,\ldots,2^k - 1\}$ where $\equiv$ denotes isomorphism via k-bit binary representation of integers.

We assume that the covert sender and receiver know the distribution of values in the targetted header field from (e.g., historical) observations of the carrier which models situations with stable traffic, while dynamic traffic will require distribution and resulting encoding updates. Thus, value $i \in B_k$ occurs with probability $0 \leq p_i \leq 1$, so that $\sum_{i \in B_k} p_i = 1$. As we will not use any value that does not occur in practice (cf. Sect. 3), we define S as the set of symbols with non-zero probability, i.e., $S = \{i \in B_k \mid p_i > 0\}$. We might even restrict set S further to values with probabilities above a certain threshold. In any case, set S must have at least two elements.

We denote the elements of S via $S = \{s_0, \ldots, s_{|S|-1}\}$ and assume they are indexed in descending order of probability, i.e., $p_{s_i} \geq p_{s_{i+1}}$ for $i = 0, 1, \ldots, |S|-2$. There is a mapping $\pi : S \to B_k$ to denote, for each element of S, which element of the original symbol set B_k it represents. When the relation is evident from the context, we might omit π and write e.g. p_{s_i} instead of $p_{\pi(s_i)}$.

4.1 Conventional Embeddings

If the size of set S is between 2^l and 2^{l+1}, then l bit of the secret message can be embedded by using the 2^l most frequent symbols, i.e., we interpret bits $b_0 \cdots b_{l-1}$ of the secret message $m = b_0 b_1 \ldots$ as the binary representation of an integer z with $0 \leq z < 2^l$ and use symbol $\pi(s_z)$ to embed these bits.

---

[2] Note that the 8-bit ToS field in the IPv4 header was redefined and replaced by a 6-bit Differentiated Services (DS) field (in RFC 2474, December 1998) and a 2-bit Explicit Congestion Notification (ECN) field (in RFC 3168, September 2001). However, in the remainder of this work, to avoid adding additional complexity to this research, we treat it jointly as an 8-bit field and thus further refer to it as ToS.

The probability of each symbol $i' = \pi(s_i)$ in the covert channel traffic is 2^{-l} instead of $p_{i'}$ in the normal carrier traffic. Thus, the covert channel entropy, which is now l, will be higher than the carrier entropy in many cases. Also, the covert channel bandwidth is l.

To get a lower entropy, one can only embed $l - \delta$ bits of the secret message for $\delta = 1$ (or 2 is possible), using only $2^{l-\delta}$ symbols and achieving entropy $l - \delta$ in the covert channel. The covert bandwidth is $l - \delta$, too.

To bring the covert channel entropy closer to the normal carrier entropy, one can only use every t-th packet for embedding, where $t = 1, 2, 3, \ldots$. Then the probability of symbol s_i is

$$p'_{s_i} = \begin{cases} \frac{1}{t} \cdot 2^{-(l-\delta)} + \frac{t-1}{t} \cdot p_{s_i} & \text{if } i < 2^{l-\delta} \\ \frac{t-1}{t} \cdot p_{s_i} & \text{otherwise}, \end{cases}$$

and the covert channel entropy is given by $H_{conv,l,\delta,t} = H(\{p'_i\})$. The bandwidth achieved is $BW_{conv,l,\delta,t} = (l - \delta)/t$.

In the following, we present two encodings that result in a covert channel that closely matches the carrier entropy yet has a higher steganographic bandwidth than the previously known methods.

4.2 Embedding Inspired by Inverse Huffman Encoding

To present our first new embedding approach, we arrange the symbols of S in a Huffman-tree [9], i.e., repeatedly merge the two (pseudo-)symbols with the lowest probabilities into a new pseudo-symbol with combined probability, cf. Sect. 2.2. The sequence of annotations on the path from the root to a leaf symbol s_i is denoted by $e_i \in \{0, 1\}^+$. The e_i form a Huffman code, i.e., a prefix-free code. Yet, in contrast to the normal use of Huffman encoding that encodes a symbol $s_i \in S$ by binary codeword e_i, we encode a piece e_i of the secret message $m = b_0 b_1 \cdots$ by a symbol in S. Therefore, we coin our procedure *inverse* Huffman coding-inspired.

To encode a piece of the secret message, we search for the codeword e_i that matches $b_0 \cdots b_{|e_i|-1}$ and encode this piece of the secret message by the symbol represented by s_i, i.e., by $\pi(s_i) \in B_k$.

In the next packet, we do the same encoding for the rest of the secret message starting from $b_{|e_i|}$. When we reach the end of the secret message while still at an inner node of the Huffman tree, we assume that the secret message is padded with zeroes so that the last encoding can occur. We assume that the covert sender and receiver have agreed in advance on set S, mapping π and the codewords e_i. The covert receiver thus extracts the secret message by observing the sequence of symbols from B_k present in the stream of network packets. Upon receiving a symbol $s \in \pi(S) \subset B_k$, it looks up $s_i = \pi^{-1}(s)$, which is possible because π is a mapping, i.e., injective, and transforms it into the corresponding codeword e_i. The sequence of these codewords comprises the encrypted secret message, possibly including a padding. The padding can be removed as the secret message is assumed to be encrypted, i.e., its bit length will be a multiple of the block length of the encryption algorithm used, such as 128-bit for AES. Furthermore, the actual message can be preceded by two bytes specifying the number of blocks the encrypted message has. This avoids fixing secret message lengths in advance or signaling message lengths between covert sender and receiver via an out-of-band channel. Please note that we assume that the covert sender and receiver have agreed in advance when the secret message will be transmitted, as this is a problem to be solved in any network steganographic transmission and not specific to our research. The following Lemma 1 guarantees that there always exists a unique codeword that matches the first part of the secret message.

Lemma 1. *Let S be a set of symbols in descending order of probabilities p_i, let e_i, where $i = 0, \ldots, |S| - 1$, be the codewords of a Huffman code for S and let $m = b_0 b_1 \cdots 00 \cdots$ be a padded secret message. Then, exactly one of the codewords e_i will match the beginning of message m.*

Proof. To find at least one e_i that matches the beginning of message m, we start at the root node of the Huffman tree. As S comprises at least two symbols, the root is an inner node of the Huffman tree. By constructing the Huffman tree (cf. Sect. 2.2), each inner node has two outgoing edges annotated with 0 and 1, respectively. Hence, one can follow the edge with annotation b_1. This is repeated with b_j for $j = 2, 3, \ldots$ as long as another inner node is reached. Finally, a leaf node, i.e., a symbol s_i will be reached, and by design, the sequence of edge annotations from the root to the symbol s_i is equal to e_i, which in turn means that $b_0 \cdots b_{|e_i|-1} = e_i$, i.e. the existence of a codeword that matches the beginning of the message m is guaranteed.

Now assume that there exist two codewords e_i and $e_{i'}$ that would match the beginning of message m. As a Huffman code is injective, $e_i \neq e_{i'}$. So if both would still match the beginning of message m, one must be a prefix of the other. However, as the Huffman code is prefix-free, this cannot occur. □

The computational effort to construct the Huffman tree is linear in the size of S, i.e., not heavy, and it is done only once and could be spread over a longer time. The encoding effort per packet, i.e., per symbol, only comprises following the Huffman tree from root to leaf (see above proof) and thus is also possible for restricted or weak devices. The use of heuristic methods with pre-computed tables that check frequent patterns first will even be faster.

Although our heuristic assigns short codewords to high-probability symbols, the probabilities generated from embedding the secret message m will not be equal to the distribution P in carrier communication. We assume that the secret message is encrypted and that each bit b_j has values 0 or 1 with probabilities 50%, respectively, and all bits are independent. Then, e_i will be matched with probability $\tilde{p}_i = 2^{-|e_i|}$ (by the construction of the Huffman tree, $\sum_{s_i \in S} \tilde{p}_i = 1$) and encode $|e_i|$ bits of the secret message. Therefore, on average, the bandwidth of this encoding method is

$$BW_{invH} = \sum_{s_i \in S} |e_i| \cdot 2^{-|e_i|} \qquad (2)$$

bits per packet. Note that by the construction, $-\log_2 \tilde{p}_i = |e_i|$ and, therefore, the entropy $H_{invH} = H(\{\tilde{p}_i\})$ of the covert channel corresponds to the (average) bandwidth.

The probability of symbol $i' = \pi(s_i)$ is now $2^{-|e_i|}$ instead of probability $p_{i'}$ in the normal carrier traffic. Still, by the Huffman tree constructions, symbols i with higher probability p_i in the carrier traffic will be assigned shorter codes and thus higher probabilities also in the covert channel traffic. Therefore, the entropies of this header field in the carrier traffic and the covert channel will generally be close to each other, as the evaluation in the next section will confirm.

We illustrate our encoding with a toy example. Let $S = \{s_0, \ldots, s_3\}$ with probabilities $12/25, 6/25, 4/25, 3/25$, that correspond to a Zipf distribution [26] which to some extent models the frequency of characters in texts [17]. The entropy of this header field is 1.792. The codewords computed via the Huffman tree on the carrier distribution and the codeword and thus symbol probabilities in the covert channel are shown in Table 1, resulting in entropy 1.75, i.e., close to the carrier entropy. As explained above, the steganographic bandwidth is identical to the entropy, i.e., 1.75 bits per packet.

Table 1. Codewords with probabilities, for example, carrier symbol distribution.

symbol	codeword	prob. $\tilde{p}_i$
s_0	0	1/2
s_1	10	1/4
s_2	111	1/8
s_3	110	1/8

In contrast, when using the conventional methods of Sect. 4.1 with $l = 2$, $\delta = 0, 1$ and $t = 1, 2, 3$, i.e., embedding 1 or 2 bits into every or every 2nd or every 3rd packet, the entropies and bandwidths are given in Table 2. Only one of the achieved bandwidths supersedes the capacity of the proposed embedding, while all entropies except embedding 1 bit every 3rd packet (with very low bandwidth, only 0.33 bit per packet) are pretty far apart from the carrier entropy, even for much lower bandwidth.

Table 2. Bandwidth and entropy of conventional embeddings.

Scenario	using every packet		every 2nd packet		every 3nd packet	
	2 bit	1 bit	2 bit	1 bit	2 bit	1 bit
Bandwidth	2	1	1	0.5	0.67	0.33
Entropy	2	1	1.947	1.570	1.906	1.671

We might refine our method when the probability of the most frequent symbol s_0 is notably larger than 0.5 in the carrier. In this case, symbol s_0 will receive prefix $e_0 = 0$ and thus probability 0.5 in the covert channel. To increase this probability, we can modify our protocol to send $k = 2$ packets with the symbol $\pi(s_0)$ instead of one packet. It will increase the probability of symbol s_0 in the covert channel from $1/2$ to $k/(k+1) = 2/3$ and reduce all other symbol probabilities by a factor $2/(k+1) = 2/3$. Thus, the probabilities (especially the probability of s_0) will be closer to the probabilities in the carrier traffic, and hence, the entropy

$$H_{invH,k} = H\left(\left\{\frac{k}{k+1}, \frac{2\tilde{p}_{i:i\geq 1}}{k+1}\right\}\right)$$

will be closer, too. For a symbol s_0 with high probability in the carrier traffic, we might even send $k = 3$ or more packets with symbol $\pi(s_0)$ in the covert channel traffic instead of one packet, reducing bandwidth further but getting covert channel entropy closer to the carrier entropy. The choice of k is a design decision where the covert sender can trade stealthiness for steganographic bandwidth.

Alternatively, we can combine the inverse Huffman-inspired encoding with the last conventional encoding, i.e., use only every t-th packet to embed a symbol.

4.3 Embedding to Match Carrier Entropy

As a further contribution, we propose an embedding method that can be parameterized to match the carrier entropy exactly, yet possibly at the cost of some steganographic bandwidth compared to the inverse-Huffman-inspired embedding. We assume that $|S| = 2^l + 1$ symbols are used in the carrier traffic (otherwise, we only use the first $2^l + 1$ symbols) and that they are not equi-distributed (in that case, the conventional embedding would be used.) The entropy of the carrier traffic is assumed to be $H_{carrier} \in [0; l]$.

When embedding the secret message, we use the symbol s_0 as a marker that does not carry any information from the secret message but whose frequency $\hat{p}_0$ is adapted to achieve the desired entropy. The remaining symbols $s_1, \ldots, s_{2^l}$ are used with equal probabilities $\hat{p}_i = (1 - \hat{p}_0)/2^l$ to encode the next l bit of the secret message. The entropy of the covert channel traffic is

$$H_{cc} = -p_0 \cdot \log_2 p_0 - 2^l \cdot ((1 - p_0)/2^l) \cdot \log_2((1 - p_0)/2^l). \quad (3)$$

The range for H_{cc} is 0 to l depending on $\hat{p}_0$, and H_{cc} is continuous in $\hat{p}_0$ (for fixed l). Thus, we can set the right-hand side of Eq. (3) equal to $H_{carrier}$ and solve numerically for a value of $\hat{p}_0$ so that $H_{matchCC} = H_{carrier}$. The steganographic bandwidth, in this case, is $BW_{matchCC} = (1 - \hat{p}_0) \cdot l$.

As an example, we use a carrier that uses 17 symbols. Figure 1 depicts the entropy and steganographic bandwidth of the entropy-matching embedding for different values of $\hat{p}_0$ in the range 0.1 to 0.9, together with the entropy and steganographic bandwidth of the extended inverse Huffman-inspired embedding on the rather harsh assumption that the carrier symbol distribution was identical to the distribution used by the entropy-matching embedding. In all cases, the steganographic bandwidth of the inverse Huffman-inspired embedding is higher than the steganographic bandwidth from the entropy-matching embedding, and the entropy is always close by.

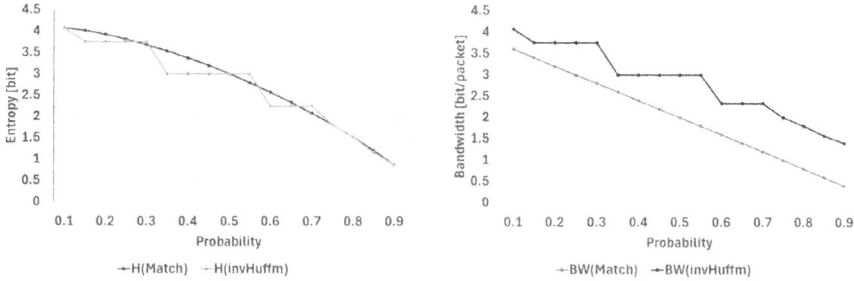

Fig. 1. Entropy (left) and steganographic bandwidth (right) of the entropy-matching embedding for various values of p_0 and of the corresponding inverse-Huffman inspired embedding.

5 Evaluation

The primary purpose of the evaluation is to ensure that the proposed method works in practice and check how closely the entropy of the covert channel matches the entropy of the carrier compared to conventional approaches of Sect. 4.1. We consider several distributions and sizes of the alphabet to apply the method proposed in the previous section for different variants. In general, the schema of the experiment for a specific character distribution is defined as follows:

- Define a symbol alphabet and distribution, i.e., characters and probability of occurrence in a header field of the carrier communication (as the actual alphabet does not matter, we refer to symbols as s_i in the following);
- Generate a Huffman Tree and obtain codewords e_i, which the symbols above shall represent;
- Generate 1000 random bit streams (representing encrypted secret messages) of length 1000 bits each (in all our experiments, we use once-generated test data, so results are in some sense comparable and reproducible)
- Encode each of the above streams by turning it into a sequence $e_{i_1} e_{i_2} \cdots$ of codewords and corresponding symbols (on top of that, we also decode the encoded stream to ensure the correctness)
- Analyze the frequencies of symbols in the encoded string and calculate the distance between obtained values and the defined distribution, i.e., compare the entropies of the carrier distribution and the covert channel distribution.

Analysis from the last point is performed as follows. Based on the assumed distribution, we have symbols s_i and probabilities p_i. After encoding a bitstream with e_i and obtaining an encoded message, we calculate frequency $\hat{p}_i$ for each symbol s_i. We leave smaller window sizes for computing entropies as future work. Having that we define $dist_i = |p_i - \hat{p}_i|$ for each s_i. Finally, we calculate the mean and the standard deviation values for the set of values $\{dist_i\}$ and then calculate the mean and the standard deviation for all 1000 streams again, obtaining a single mean value and single standard deviation value for the whole data set. Beyond, we compute entropies of distributions $\{p_1, \ldots, p_n\}$ (carrier) and $\{\hat{p}_1, \ldots, \hat{p}_n\}$ (covert channel). Please note that we only analyze the entropy of a single header field, while wardens mostly investigate the entropy of complete headers.

In the further analysis, we consider synthetic data from uniform distribution which is well-known and from a distribution where probabilities are randomly chosen from a given interval. Additionally, we use a distribution inspired by real network traffic (i.e., ToS field of the IPv4 header). For the synthetic symbol distributions, we considered alphabets of 3 sizes: 16 (power of 2), 30 (close to the power of 2), and 50 (between powers of 2), where especially the latter check the capability of the Huffman encoding—even for uniform distributions. We analyze the above distributions to ensure the feasibility and practical efficiency of the method.

5.1 Uniform Distribution

This is a fundamental distribution, and assuming sizes of alphabets 16, 30, and 50, we obtain the following probabilities, respectively: 0.0625, 0.0333, 0.02.

Following all steps of the experiment described earlier, we obtain the results presented in Table 3.

Table 3. Mean and standard deviation values for distances between expected and actual symbols frequencies, entropy based on distribution probabilities, mean and standard deviation values for entropies based on actual data (for uniform distributions).

Size	Distance		Entropy		
	Avg.	StdDev.	Distr.	Avg.	StdDev.
16	0.0124	0.0088	4.0000	3.9553	0.016
30	0.0112	0.0093	4.9034	4.7687	0.0367
50	0.0095	0.0074	5.6439	5.3488	0.0561

We can easily observe that the method is very effective and that both mean values and deviations for distances are negligible. Moreover, the values obtained for entropies are also very promising.

5.2 Random Distribution

This is a distribution where the probability for each symbol occurrence has been randomly generated. In our consideration, these values are presented in Table 4.

For this distribution and the alphabet of size 16, we additionally present a visualization of the Inverse Huffman Tree (Fig. 2). This type of tree is generated for each use case as explained in the experiment steps (tree is used for obtaining codes e_i).

Following all steps of the experiment described earlier, we obtain the results presented in Table 5.

Table 4. Random distribution values for size 16, 30, and 50.

Size	Values
16	0.11, 0.08, 0.07, 0.1, 0.1, 0.03, 0.09, 0.07, 0.05, 0.06, 0.03, 0.02, 0.03, 0.01, 0.06, 0.1
30	0.06, 0.03, 0.01, 0.04, 0.06, 0.05, 0.04, 0.04, 0.04, 0.03, 0.02, 0.01, 0.06, 0.01, 0.01, 0.05, 0.05, 0.06, 0.04, 0.05, 0.03, 0.01, 0.02, 0.05, 0.01, 0.04, 0.01, 0.06, 0.01, 0.01
50	0.009, 0.036, 0.021, 0.004, 0.011, 0.004, 0.013, 0.033, 0.032, 0.026, 0.02, 0.017, 0.004, 0.013, 0.014, 0.019, 0.024, 0.036, 0.036, 0.023, 0.016, 0.012, 0.013, 0.015, 0.027, 0.012, 0.011, 0.022, 0.028, 0.033, 0.007, 0.007, 0.033, 0.016, 0.036, 0.033, 0.011, 0.029, 0.025, 0.031, 0.024, 0.008, 0.033, 0.01, 0.013, 0.035, 0.017, 0.01, 0.014, 0.022

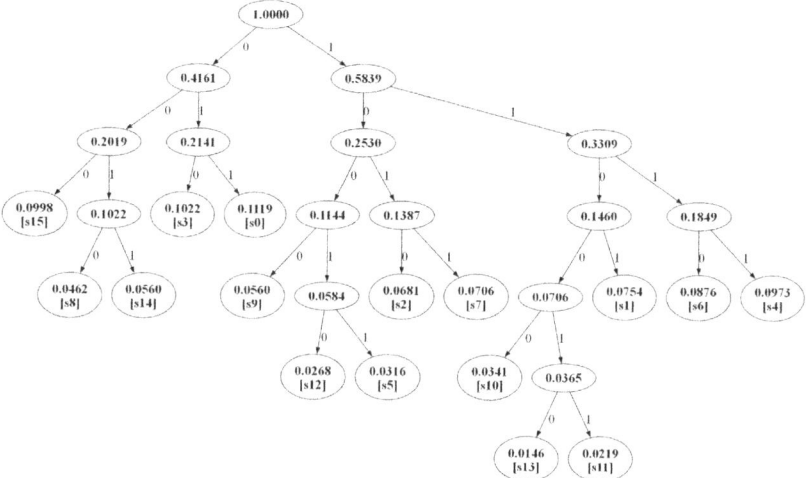

Fig. 2. Huffman Tree for a random distribution for size 16.

We can easily observe that the method is very effective and that both mean values and deviations for distances are negligible. Moreover, the values obtained for entropies are also very promising. Therefore, we also did not conduct any further analysis and visualization (e.g., box plot diagram).

5.3 ToS Inspired Distribution

This is a distribution where the probability for each symbol occurrence has been determined based on the ToS field values distribution. This is an example of distribution inspired by a practical use case for steganography. In our consideration, these values are

$$[0.935, 0.014, 0.006, 0.002, 0.007, 0.009, 0.015, 0.010, 0.002]$$

and values are based on the data collected on 2024-07-01 and available as a PCAP file in the MAWI dataset [13]. As this distribution is very uneven, it is

Table 5. Mean and standard deviation values for distances between expected and actual symbols frequencies, entropy based on distribution probabilities, mean and standard deviation values for entropies based on actual data (for random distributions).

Size	Distance		Entropy		
	Avg.	StdDev.	Distr.	Avg.	StdDev.
16	0.0162	0.0133	3.8154	3.7408	0.0474
30	0.0107	0.0090	4.6621	4.5071	0.0608
50	0.0083	0.0069	5.4564	5.2516	0.0635

interesting to see how the method works in such a case. Following all experiment steps described earlier, we obtain the results presented in Table 6.

Table 6. Mean and standard deviation values for distances between expected and actual symbols frequencies, entropy based on distribution probabilities, mean and standard deviation values for entropies based on actual data (for ToS inspired distribution).

Size	Distance		Entropy		
	Avg.	StdDev.	Distr.	Avg.	StdDev.
9	0.0969	0.1251	0.5256	2.3317	0.0731

Here, we can see that results are slightly different than previous use cases. The average mean distance is ca. 9 times bigger, and the standard deviation is even more than 10 times bigger. Let us include here box plot diagrams both for uniform distribution and currently considered one for comparison in Fig. 3. We can see that the shape and structure are very similar, but the range of values is different, as discussed. Moreover, we can see that the difference between distribution-based entropy and calculated one is much bigger than previously observed, as we did not implement the refined version with $k \geq 2$, cf. Section 4.2, which would have resulted in an entropy of about 0.53253. However, these values are stable and predictable, considering the standard deviation value.

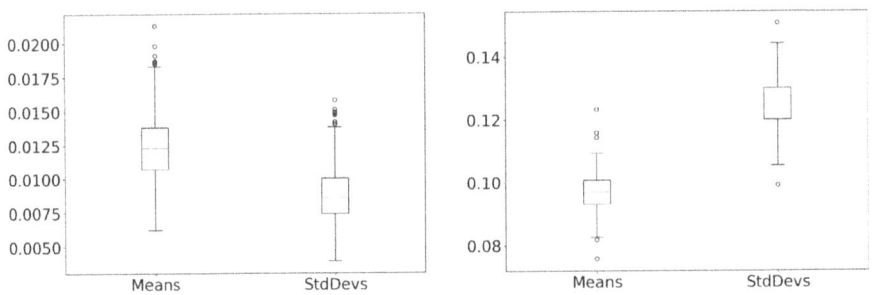

Fig. 3. Box plot diagram for results for uniform distribution for size = 16 (left) and ToS inspired distribution (right).

To sum up, the obtained values are not as ideal as previously observed, but they still make the proposed method feasible and efficient. Finally, we must keep in mind that we consider here a very uneven distribution that obviously strongly impacts encoding methods.

6 Conclusions

In this work, we addressed the long-standing trade-off between steganographic bandwidth and detectability in network storage channels by explicitly accounting for changes in Shannon entropy. After defining a realistic attack model and outlining the warden's monitoring capabilities, we introduced two entropy-aware embedding schemes. The first scheme uses an inverse Huffman‐inspired encoding to map encrypted message bits onto packet header symbols in a way that naturally mirrors the carrier's symbol distribution, yielding an average bandwidth equal to the covert-channel entropy and consistently outperforming conventional fixed-rate and sparse-packet approaches. The second scheme matches the carrier's entropy by adjusting the frequency of a designated marker symbol, providing a guaranteed zero net entropy deviation at the cost of reduced bandwidth. Through extensive experiments on both synthetic distributions (uniform and random) and real-world header-field distributions (i.e., IPv4 ToS field) and across various alphabet sizes, we demonstrated that both methods keep entropy fluctuations well within normal traffic variations while delivering 40–60 percent higher bandwidth than comparable traditional embeddings under the same entropy constraints. In cases where a single symbol dominates the carrier distribution, we showed that a simple packet-duplication extension to the inverse Huffman method can further refine entropy alignment.

As future work, we will adapt the proposed schemes for reversible embeddings so that original header-field values can be perfectly restored, which benefits scenarios requiring payload integrity. Also, we will explore hybrid channels that combine storage-based and timing-based methods to exploit their complementary stealth characteristics. Implementing adaptive strategies that continuously update the embedding model by using, e.g., a micro-protocol [22] in response to traffic drift could address dynamic network traffic and also strengthen resistance against advanced, learning-based wardens. Finally, extending the entropy-preservation framework to payload-level or application-layer embeddings may broaden its applicability. By providing the first quantitative methodology for trading off bandwidth against entropy deviation in network steganography, this work equips both attackers and defenders with principled tools to design, analyze, and counter covert channels under realistic monitoring conditions.

References

1. Badar, L.T., Carminati, B., Ferrari, E.: A comprehensive survey on stegomalware detection in digital media, research challenges and future directions. Signal Process. **231**, 109888 (2025)

2. Bang, J., Kim, J.N., Lee, S.: Entropy sharing in ransomware: bypassing entropy-based detection of cryptographic operations. Sensors **24**(5) (2024)
3. Bereziński, P., Jasiul, B., Szpyrka, M.: An entropy-based network anomaly detection method. Entropy **17**(4), 2367–2408 (2015)
4. Caviglione, L., et al.: Tight arms race: overview of current malware threats and trends in their detection. IEEE Access **9**, 5371–5396 (2021)
5. Caviglione, L., Mazurczyk, W.: Never mind the malware, here's the stegomalware. IEEE Sec. Priv. **20**(5), 101–106 (2022)
6. Cover, T.M., Thomas, J.A.: Elements of Information Theory. Wiley-Interscience, 2nd edn. (2006)
7. Darwish, O., Al-Fuqaha, A., Anan, M.: Hierarchical entropy analysis for covert timing channel detection. In: IWCMC, pp. 153–159 (2015)
8. Gianvecchio, S., Wang, H.: Detecting covert timing channels: an entropy-based approach. In: Conference on Communications and Network Security, CCS 2007, pp. 307–316 (2007)
9. Huffman, D.A.: A method for the construction of minimum-redundancy codes. Proc. IRE **40**(9), 1098–1101 (1952)
10. Liu, T., Wang, Z., Wang, H., Lu, K.: An entropy-based method for attack detection in large scale network. Int.l J. Comput. Comm. **7**(3), 509–517 (2012)
11. Lyda, R., Hamrock, J.: Using entropy analysis to find encrypted and packed malware. IEEE Sec. Priv. **5**(2), 40–45 (2007)
12. Mali, J., Sonawane, V., Awale, R.: Image steganography using block-level entropy thresholding. IJERA **3**, 412–415 (2013)
13. Mawi, W.G.T.A.: Packet traces from WIDE backbone. https://mawi.wide.ad.jp/mawi/ (2025), Accessed 10-May-2025
14. Mazurczyk, W., Wendzel, S., Chourib, M., Keller, J.: Countering adaptive network covert communication with dynamic wardens. Future Gener. Comput. Syst. **94**(C), 712–725 (2019)
15. Mazurczyk, W., Wendzel, S., Zander, S., Houmansadr, A., Szczypiorski, K.: Information hiding in communication networks: fundamentals, mechanisms, and applications. IEEE Ser. Inf. and Comm. Netw. Security, Wiley, Hoboken, NJ (2016)
16. Menendez Benito, H., Crawford, T.: The arms race: adversarial search defeats entropy used to detect malware. Expert Syst. Appl. **109**, 1–15 (2016)
17. Piantadosi, S.: Zipf's word frequency law in natural language: a critical review and future directions. Psychon. Bull. Rev. **21**(5), 1112–1130 (2014)
18. Shannon, C.E.: A mathematical theory of communication. Bell Syst. Tech. J. **27**(3), 379–423 (1948)
19. Tellenbach, B., Burkhart, M., Schatzmann, D., Gugelmann, D., Sornette, D.: Accurate network anomaly classification with generalized entropy metrics. Comput. Netw. **55**(15), 3485–3502 (2011)
20. Walls, R.J., Kothari, K., Wright, M.: Liquid: A detection-resistant covert timing channel based on ipd shaping. Comput. Netw. **55**(6), 1217–1228 (2011)
21. Wendzel, S., et al.: A generic taxonomy for steganography methods. ACM Comput. Surv. (2025)
22. Wendzel, S., Keller, J.: Low-attention forwarding for mobile network covert channels. In: De Decker, B., Lapon, J., Naessens, V., Uhl, A. (eds.) CMS 2011. LNCS, vol. 7025, pp. 122–133. Springer, Heidelberg (2011). https://doi.org/10.1007/978-3-642-24712-5_10
23. Wendzel, S., Zander, S., Fechner, B., Herdin, C.: Pattern-based survey and categorization of network covert channel techniques. ACM Com. Sur. **47**(3) (Apr 2015)

24. de Witt, C.S., Sokota, S., Kolter, J.Z., Foerster, J.N., Strohmeier, M.: Perfectly secure steganography using minimum entropy coupling. In: 11th International Conference on Learning Representations, ICLR 2023. OpenReview.net (2023)
25. Zander, S., Armitage, G., Branch, P.: A survey of covert channels and countermeasures in computer network protocols. IEEE Com. Sur. & Tut. **9**(3), 44–57 (2007)
26. Zipf, G.K.: The Psychobiology of Language. Houghton-Mifflin, New York (1935)

ReWaP: Reversible Watermarking and Paillier Encryption Approach for Privacy-Preserving Smart Meter

Farzana Kabir[1]([✉]) [iD], Krzysztof Cabaj[2] [iD], Tanya Koohpayeh Araghi[1] [iD], and David Megías[1] [iD]

[1] Internet Interdisciplinary Institute (IN3), Universitat Oberta de Catalunya (UOC), CYBERCAT-Center for Cybersecurity Research of Catalonia, Rambla del Poblenou, 154-156, 08018 Barcelona, Spain
{fkabir,tkoohpayeharaghi,dmegias}@uoc.edu
[2] Warsaw University of Technology, plac Politechniki 1, 00-661 Warszawa, Poland
krzysztof.cabaj@pw.edu.pl

Abstract. Smart meters generate detailed information about the energy consumption patterns of the consumer, increasing the risks of data breaches, identity theft, and other forms of cyberattacks. Many existing solutions still suffer from computational complexity, time consumption, and security vulnerabilities. To address these issues, this paper presents ReWaP, a Reversible Watermarking and Paillier encryption-based privacy-preserving scheme to ensure data confidentiality, integrity, and authenticity in smart meter systems. This unique approach protects user privacy and maintains the security of the meter reading. A comprehensive security analysis verifies the resilience of the proposed scheme against multiple known attacks. The implementation using a RIOT OS and Nucleo microcontroller board resulted in low computational overhead and minimal impact on communication bandwidth. The experimental results and performance analysis demonstrate that the proposed scheme effectively balances data privacy, system reliability, and operational efficiency, making it an effective solution for modern smart metering infrastructures.

Keywords: Smart Meter · Security · Privacy · Watermarking · Cryptography

1 Introduction

Given the increasing energy demands of the twenty-first century, it is essential that we create more convenient ways to produce, distribute, and transmit energy. The significant advancement of smart grid technology within the Internet of Things (IoT) sector offers promising solutions [13]. The smart meter market tracker forecasts these IoT devices to achieve 54% adoption of the overall global electricity meter market by 2030 [7]. Some advantages of smart grid technology include increased mutual communication, more efficiency, and the ability to include renewable energy sources, all of which contribute to its predicted growth in popularity [14]. However, when energy usage data is being transmitted, smart meters may endanger user privacy by revealing specific data on electricity use from several devices [12], hence raising critical concerns about data security and user confidentiality. There may be instances where a hostile attacker tries to gather the meter reading of a user and extract relevant information concerning, for example, living behaviors or financial status [12,20]. Many cryptographic and steganographic techniques have been proposed to enhance privacy preservation in the smart metering system. However, these existing solutions often face several challenges, including high computational costs associated with cryptographic methods and insufficient security in data-hiding techniques [4]. In addition, reliance on trusted third parties and the lack of real-world experiments can be considered common drawbacks for such systems [8,11].

After acknowledging all these concerns, this paper presents a new updated Reversible Watermarking and Paillier encryption (ReWaP) scheme for smart metering systems data aggregation. Unlike previous approaches, it does not rely on external servers or third-party entities. This scheme is implemented and tested on the RIOT operating system, leveraging its built-in cryptographic libraries optimized for ARM Cortex-M microcontrollers (*e.g.*, STMicroelectronics' Nucleo boards with Cortex-M3) [2]. It is well-suited for secure, lightweight data handling in smart metering systems as it provides cryptographic support for public-key cryptography [5,18]. The Nucleo board maintains a balance between performance and energy efficiency, providing sufficient computational power for complex encryption tasks while maintaining low energy consumption. The proposed scheme combines reversible watermarking and Paillier encryption to achieve resource efficiency, lightweightness, and effectiveness. The main contributions of this research are:

- A privacy-preserving scheme for smart meters has been proposed using reversible watermarking based on LSB shifting and Paillier homomorphic encryption.
- A comparative study of the most recent research works is provided to verify that the presented schemes meet all requirements, taking into account security and privacy requirements as well as resilience to possible attacks.
- The proposed scheme is proven efficient and reliable by the experimental results obtained from a real hardware implementation using the Nucleo development board and the RIOT operating system.

The rest of the paper is organized as follows: Sect. 2 briefly reviews recent studies on privacy-preserving data aggregation in smart meters. Section 3 describes the overall representation of the ReWaP scheme in detail, including architecture and methodologies as well as the security and privacy analysis. Section 4 evaluates the experimental results and the performance analysis. Finally, Sect. 5 concludes the paper by summarizing the outcome and achievements of the proposed scheme and indicating some future directions.

2 Related Work

Security and privacy challenges in smart meters have received substantial attention in recent years from a variety of communities, including network engineers, computer scientists, and academic researchers.

Kathrine et al. [6] have investigated the utilization of the extended Merkle Signature Scheme (XMSS) in combination with using blockchain technology to improve the smart grid's security. The combination of blockchain technology and XMSS can improve the security, dependability, and efficiency of smart grids.

A novel authentication management model with a combination of two-level security methods has been proposed by Parvez et al. [16], with data encryption and node authentication. In this configuration, one server handles data encryption between the meter and the control center/central database, while the second server manages data transmission in a random sequence. Packet randomization and data encryption ensure enhanced data security.

Singal et al. [19] designed and implemented a robust blockchain-based architecture for smart meters that encrypts data using AES-256 encryption and enables the blockchain to carry out the majority of computations directly on encrypted information to ensure user privacy and confidentiality of smart meter information in a smart grid.

A security-focused smart energy meter design was suggested by Hseiki et al. [3] following a detailed comparative analysis of current methods and their characteristics. The solution prevents distributed denial of service (DDoS) attacks, data integrity challenges, data privacy violations, and energy theft.

The Quantum-Secure Privacy-Preserving Smart Meter Authentication (Q-Secure-P2-SMA) protocol is presented by Prateek et al. [17]. It enables quantum-resistant metered data transfer by using a hash function and semi-quantum key distribution. It can resist potential attacks, including replay attacks and impersonation attacks, and also provides privacy, anonymity, and message unlinkability.

A lightweight privacy-preserving data aggregation scheme in smart grid IoT networks is proposed by Wang et al. [21] to encrypt metering data with specified encryption keys generated by non-interactive key negotiation. It prevents attacks, including eavesdropping, collusion, and malicious Control Center (CC) and greatly reduces communication complexity.

Zhang et al. [22] proposed a novel privacy-enhancing data aggregation scheme based on proxy reencryption and asymmetric scalar product-preserving encryption. The suggested method is ideal for network scenarios involving a large number of resource-constrained devices like smart meters because it effectively eliminates time-consuming exponentiation and pairing processes.

A privacy-preserving smart meter data storage (SMDS) model is proposed by Kumar et al. [9] that aggregates smart meter data at the fog node using Paillier homomorphic encryption. Additionally, a secure processing framework is implemented to handle the two distinct types of queries—time-based and ID-based—which results in better performance.

Lei et al. [10] presented an efficient blockchain-based data aggregation scheme with privacy-preserving on the smart grid (EC-ASPG) using ElGamal encryption that preserves privacy on the smart grid and enhances system security by implementing a supervised mechanism for the lazy leader node. Comprehensive analyses show its superiority to other schemes in terms of security, functionality, and performance evaluations.

A lightweight, verifiable, certificate-based P2DA scheme (LV-P2DA) is designed by Zhu et al. [23] utilizing additive homomorphic encryption, modifying the traditional PKI-based elliptic curve ElGamal scheme to accommodate the certificate-based cryptosystem. It is proven to be more convenient for resource-constrained smart meters, achieving very low computational and communication costs.

3 ReWaP Scheme

This section describes the overall architecture and methodology of the proposed ReWaP-reversible watermarking and Paillier encryption based privacy-preserving smart meter scheme—in detail, including algorithms and theorems.

3.1 Scheme Architecture

Smart meter data contains detailed information regarding the energy consumption (water, gas, or electricity) of the smart home. The information offers insights into patterns of energy usage, which is gathered either in real-time or at regular intervals (*e.g.*, daily, hourly, or every 15 min). Smart meter data may contain user identity or the smart meter ID used for power supplies and payment. Timestamp is another content, which is the exact date and time when the data was recorded. The ReWaP scheme starts by protecting both the user identity and power consumption. To preserve user privacy, each smart meter is given an anonymous identity to transmit power consumption. This way, an attacker cannot link power consumption to the actual identity. Smart meters use Paillier homomorphic encryption and reversible watermarking to resist popular attacks and ensure the security of energy consumption data. No other entities in the system can obtain fine-grained power consumption and the real identity of the users. As a result, this scheme can defend not only against external attacks but also internal attacks while protecting user privacy. The key generation and sharing are done in a cryptographically secure way by the system entities, which removes the necessity of any trusted third party or any external entity.

3.2 Scheme Model

There are three entities in this scheme, including smart meters (SMs), a data aggregator (DA), and a control center (CC). Our scheme considers a residential area with n smart homes, each of which sends power consumption periodically

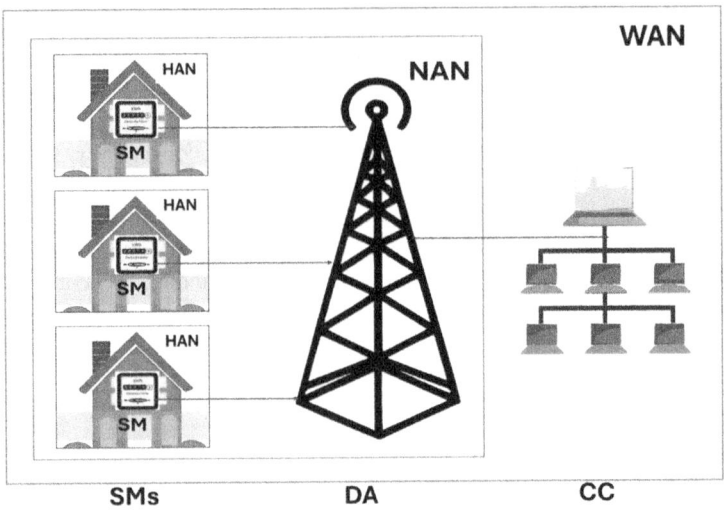

Fig. 1. System Model for ReWaP.

to the DA using a smart meter SM. Each region contains a DA that sends aggregated data to the CC, as shown in Fig. 1.

SM: A total of n users (SMs) are included in a residential area in this scheme model, and data are collected for m timeframes. Each smart home is equipped with a SM that collects the energy consumption in real time and periodically sends the watermarked encrypted power consumption to DA at fixed time intervals t_j ($i = 1, 2, 3, \ldots, n$ and $j = 1, 2, 3, \ldots, m$).

DA: The data aggregator acts as a middle point to aggregate the encrypted information received from n SMs in bulk to ensure data integrity during transmission and forwards it to CC after the aggregation process completes.

CC: The control center is the final destination unit with higher computing power and is responsible for verifying, decrypting, and processing the aggregated meter data sent by DA. CC manages the daily operations of the distribution network.

3.3 Security Requirements

The ReWaP scheme must fulfill the following major security and privacy requirements for smart metering systems:

- R1 (Data confidentiality): Energy consumption data must be protected from disclosure to any unauthorized party during transmission and aggregation, and the fine-grained consumption data of individual users must remain secret even from the data aggregator and control center.
- R2 (Data integrity): Any unauthorized alteration of consumption data must be detectable. The accuracy and consistency of the aggregated data must be ensured by the system.

- R3 (System scalability): The collection and aggregation of SM data must comply with any number of SMs and any frequency of data generation.
- R4 (Entity authenticity): SMs and DA must be properly authenticated by CC, registering themselves before sending any sensitive data. The system must prevent impersonation of legitimate devices or communication media.
- R5 (User anonymity): The real identity of the consumer must be protected. Energy consumption patterns must not be traced back to particular homes or users because aggregated energy data is sufficient for dynamic billing, load forecasting, and demand response for small residential areas.

3.4 Threat Model

In our threat model, both CC and DA are considered to be dishonest. SMs are presumed to function in a secure and honest manner. Additionally, there is a chance that adversaries may intercept communications between the DA and the CC, as well as between SMs and the DA, and subsequently capture the transmitted data. The intruder can try to determine the individual SM readings.

3.5 Scheme Process

This section explores the fundamental steps of the proposed scheme, followed by an in-depth description elaborating on the design, algorithms, and processes phase by phase.

Initialization Phases

The initialization phase performs the following tasks:

System Registration: The SMs must complete a registration process with CC before offering household electricity management services. The DA initiates its registration with the CC before being responsible for managing all the SMs within a designated area.

Key Generation and Sharing: The ReWaP scheme employs a key generation and sharing approach combining asymmetric Paillier encryption for secure data aggregation and symmetric AES keys for secure key transmission. Keys are generated and distributed during system initialization to ensure confidentiality, integrity, and authenticity as follows:

1. The Control Center (CC) generates a Paillier key pair (P_k, S_k), where $P_k = (N, g)$ is the public key (with N being an RSA modulus and g a generator), and $S_k = (\lambda, \alpha)$ is the private key used for decryption [15].
   This property makes it suitable for secure aggregation of encrypted smart meter readings without revealing individual values. CC also generates a cryptographically secure random key (K_w), which is used as a secret key in a keyed-hash message authentication code (HMAC) based on SHA-256 to generate the watermark. CC also generates a unique random seed $Seed_{i,j}$ for each SM to generate a pseudorandom number.

2. SM downloads the Paillier public key from CC. This communication is unencrypted as follows:
   - SM →CC: SM sends request ReqT1 for public key P_k;
   - CC →SM: CC responds with RespT1 containing unencrypted Paillier public key P_k;
3. SM downloads the key for the watermark and the initial seed as follows:
   - SM generates a random AES session key (AES_k), encrypts it using Paillier public key (P_k) and sends it to the CC using ReqT2 message;
   - After receiving the request from SM, CC decrypts AES_k using the Paillier private key (S_k) and later encrypts the watermark key(K_w) and $Seed_{i,j}$, using AES_k. After that, CC sends a response (RespT2) to the SM with the encrypted key and seed.
   - After receiving the encrypted data from CC, SM decrypts K_w and $Seed_{i,j}$ using the session key (AES_k).
4. DA downloads the Paillier public key P_k from CC in the same manner as SM. The key is needed to aggregate encrypted data.

Scheme Phases

In this section, the step-by-step procedure of the ReWaP scheme is described, including the flow diagram in Fig. 2

Smart Meter Phase: When considering a total of n SMs and m time frames, each smart meter SM_i sends its energy consumption data, $d_{i,j}$, at each time period, t_j, where $i = 1, 2, 3, \ldots, n$. and $j = 1, 2, 3, \ldots, m$.

At each measurement interval t_j, the smart meter SM_i performs the following operations:

- Data collection and processing: SMs record energy consumption measurements $d_{i,j}$ with timestamp t_j. Prior to watermark embedding, each floating-point smart meter reading $d_{i,j}$ is transformed into an integer. This is accomplished by multiplying $d_{i,j}$ by 1,000. This conversion ensures that all ensuing averages and differences stay integers.
- Watermark generation and embedding: For each timeframe t_j, the watermark W_j is generated using the SHA256 hash function and the symmetric key. After generation of the HMAC, $H_j \leftarrow SHA256(t_j, K_w)$, the first 6 bits are taken as the watermark bits. $W_j \leftarrow LSB_6(H_j)$. 6 bits provide sufficient protection for tamper detection while minimizing data distortion. For the same t_j, every SM computes the same W_j. Thus, no collisions occur (all SMs agree on W_j). Now, these 6 watermark bits are embedded into the last 6 least significant bits (LSBs) of the meter data $d_{i,j}$ as follows:

$$d'_{i,j} \leftarrow d_{i,j} \cdot p + w_j.$$

Here, the modulus p is used to distinguish the watermark from the host data. As we are embedding 6 bits of watermark, the range of values for a 6-bit watermark is: $w_i \in [0, 2^6 - 1] = [0, 63]$. With n smart meters, the maximum total watermark could be $63 \cdot n$. As a result, p must be less than $63 \times n$ in order to preserve reversibility. We can simply represent it with a fixed formula based on the number of SMs as follows: $p = 2^{\lceil \log_2(63 \cdot n + 1) \rceil}$, which represents the smallest power of 2 greater than $63 \cdot n$. According to this formula, For 100 SMs ($n = 100$), the minimum value of p that avoids overlap is 8,192. As we are considering a single residential area with n SMs and 1 DA, the maximum number of n would not cross 1,000 in a practical scenario. Even for maximum $n = 1000$, the bit overhead will be minimal (still efficient for Cortex-M microcontrollers) with no added cost for HMAC-SHA256.

- PRNG addition and Paillier encryption: The state of the pseudo-random number generators is initialized using the corresponding seed after receiving the RespT2 message as follows:

$$\text{state}_{i,j} \leftarrow \text{initState}(\text{seed}_{i,j}).$$

Here, the *initState* function initializes a deterministic PRNG using the seed Seed$_{i,j}$. This ensures that each SM generates the same sequence of pseudorandom values for verification at the CC at each timeframe. The pseudorandom number $R_{i,j}$ is generated for each SM$_i$, which is specific for each time frame t_j using the following equation:

$$R_{i,j} \leftarrow \text{PRNG}(\text{state}_{i,j}).$$

After generating $R_{i,j}$, the PRNG state is updated for the next time frame, t_{j+1}, which allows the PRNG to produce new pseudorandom values at each time frame

$$\text{state}_{i,j+1} \leftarrow \text{UpdateState}(\text{state}_{i,j}).$$

This $R_{i,j}$ is only shared between SM$_i$ and CC, and DA has no access to this. $R_{i,j}$ is encrypted in the watermarked data to add an extra layer of security:

$$d''_{i,j} \leftarrow d'_{i,j} + R_{i,j},$$

and, finally, the output is encrypted using the Paillier encryption which is a probabilistic partial homomorphic encryption. If the text is $d''_{i,j} \in Z_n$ and r is a random number $r \in Z_n^*$, the ciphertext can be generated as:

$$E_{i,j} = \text{Enc}_{P_k}(d''_{i,j}) = g^{d''_{i,j}} \cdot r^N \pmod{N^2}.$$

- Transmission: Each smart meter SM$_i$ transmits the encrypted watermarked data, $E_{i,j}$, to the DA using the request ReqT3 carried by a UDP datagram.

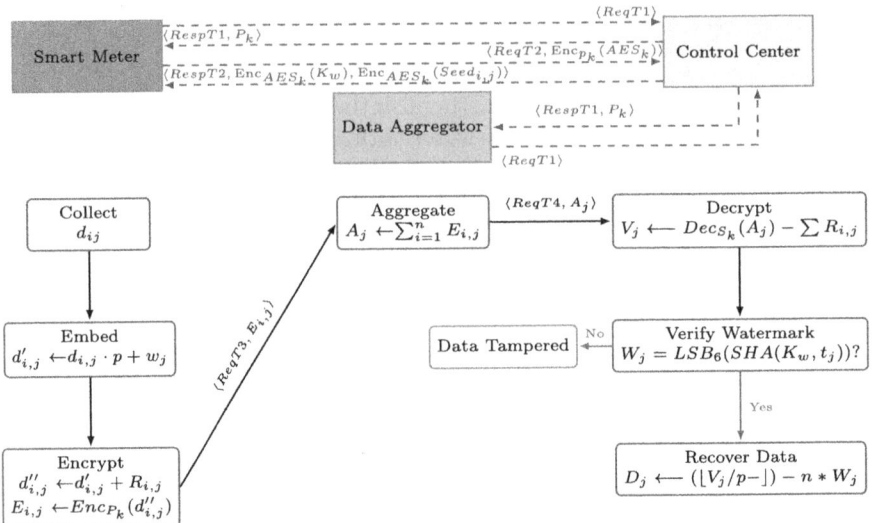

Fig. 2. Data flow diagram.

Data Aggregator Phase: Upon receiving the request ReqT3 from all SMs, DA aggregates all the n watermarked encrypted data $(E_{i,j})$ aligning with Paillier's additive homomorphism for data aggregation. This aggregation is performed via modular multiplication, leveraging Paillier's following homomorphic property:

$$A_j \leftarrow \sum_{i=1}^{n} E_{i,j} \pmod{N^2}.$$

Here N is part of the Paillier public key, $\mathsf{P_k}$. DA transmits the homomorphically aggregated data to the CC using request, ReqT4.

Control Center Phase: CC receives the aggregated data A_j, decrypts it using the private key applies Paillier decryption, which is given by:

$$\text{Dec}_{\mathsf{S_k}}(A_j) \leftarrow L\left(A_j^\lambda \pmod{N^2}\right) \cdot \mu \pmod{N},$$

where

$$L(x) = \frac{x-1}{N},$$

and λ, μ are the private key parameters.

After that, CC subtracts the sum of the pseudorandom values $(R_{i,j})$ to retrieve the original watermarked data as follows:

$$V_j \leftarrow \text{Dec}_{\mathsf{S_k}}(A_j) - \sum_{i=1}^{n} R_{i,j}.$$

To verify the watermark, we first isolate the 6-bit watermark from the LSBs:

$$W'_j \leftarrow V_j \pmod{p}.$$

Then the watermark W_j is recomputed using K_w and t_j:

$$W_j \leftarrow \text{LSB}_6(\text{SHA256}(K_w, t_j)).$$

If $W_j = W'_j$, the aggregated plaintext is generated as follows:

$$D_j \leftarrow \lfloor V_j/p \rfloor, \text{ where } D_j = \sum_{i=1}^{n} d_{i,j}.$$

In a modern dynamic billing system, the control center does not need to have access to individual fine-grained energy consumption to distribute the bills. Most of the utility service providers use dynamic pricing based on time of day or peak demand rather than individual usage data for each customer. Even load forecasting at a macro level (*e.g.*, predicting total energy demand for a region or system) and demand response do not require individual customer-level data because aggregated data provides sufficient information for accurate predictions.

3.6 Scheme Analysis

In this section, we analyze our proposed scheme from two aspects: a) security and privacy analysis and b) resistance of the scheme against six common types of attacks.

Security and Privacy Analysis

The ReWaP scheme uses cryptographic and watermarking algorithms to meet all five security requirements (R1-R5) mentioned in Sect. 3.3. We explain how each requirement is met in the following:

- **R1 (Data confidentiality)**: Each smart meter encrypts its energy consumption $d_{i,j}$ using the Paillier public key $\mathsf{P_k}$. Given that Paillier is semantically secure, it prevents unauthorized entities (including the DA) from decrypting individual meter readings. Even if an adversary intercepts encrypted data, the additional pseudorandom value $R_{i,j}$ (known only to the CC) prevents leakage of private information. Only the CC can decrypt the aggregated ciphertexts using the private key, $\mathsf{S_k}$, ensuring fine-grained data remains confidential (even to the CC).
- **R2 (Data integrity)**: The 6-bit hash-derived watermark W_j is embedded into the LSBs of $d_{i,j}$ by applying the reversible watermarking process, which protects data integrity. Any tampering alters the watermark, which the CC detects during verification. The CC recomputes the watermark from the decrypted sum and compares it to the expected W_j. If they do not match, CC rejects the data immediately.
- **R3 (System scalability)**: Paillier encryption allows DA to aggregate the encrypted values linearly without individual decryption, making the scheme scalable to thousands of smart meters. Each smart meter phase consists of

three operations in constant time concerning the frequency of transmission and the number of SMs, making them computationally feasible for high-frequency smart meters. Furthermore, the Control Center only performs one decryption per aggregated report. These properties ensure that the ReWaP scheme can scale enough to support large numbers of SMs reporting at high rates.
- **R4 (Entity authenticity):** Each smart meter and the Data Aggregator must authenticate with the Control Center during initial registration using the Paillier public key infrastructure. CC distributes cryptographic keys (watermark key K_w, and PRNG seed $Seed_{i,j}$) in a secure manner using an AES session key AES_k. Moreover, the watermark verification at the CC ensures that the consumption data comes from an authorized entity.
- **R5 (User anonymity):** Because of the semantic security of the Paillier cryptography, the individual SM data can not be linked to the original identity of the user. Even after decryption at the CC, it can only recover the aggregated real data, which keeps the identity of individual smart meter users anonymous.

Attack Resistance Analysis

The architecture of the ReWaP scheme is carefully designed to counter both active and passive cyberattacks that usually pose a danger to smart metering systems. This section is extended and clarified for greater understanding below:

- **Eavesdropping:** The scheme fundamentally prevents exposure of individual consumption data through multiple layers of security. Each SM_i reading $d_{i,j}$ undergoes three transformations before transmission: 1) watermark embedding, 2) pseudorandom masking, 3) Paillier encryption. Since the DA only receives ciphertexts $E_{i,j}$ and lacks the private key S_k, as well as the watermark key k_w, it cannot decrypt individual readings. Paillier's semantically secure public-key cryptosystem is used to encrypt $d_{i,j}$. Ciphertext $E_{i,j}$ cannot be decrypted by eavesdroppers without the private key S_k.
- **Data tampering:** The LSBs of $d_{i,j}$ contain the 6-bit hash-derived watermark, W_j and any alteration to this W_j results in a failure to verify at the CC. CC recomputes W_j using k_w after decryption to match this with the retrieved watermark. Any mismatches trigger immediate rejection of tampered data. Moreover, it aggregates ciphertexts via additive homomorphism but cannot decrypt or modify plaintext values. Any manipulation of $E_{i,j}$ or A_j corrupts the embedded watermark W_j in the decrypted aggregate. Verification occurs through the relation $W'_j = V_j \pmod{p}$. Since the DA cannot compute W_j (it lacks K_w), it cannot forge tamper-proof ciphertexts. In ReWaP, the watermark verification process ensures that any attempt to alter even a single smart meter's data $(d'_{i,j})$ will be caught—even if the attacker somehow guesses the correct W'_j because W'_j and $V_j \pmod{p}$ will not match.

- **Replay attacks:** The combined use of time-bound watermarks and stateful pseudorandom generator nullifies replay attempts. Every watermark W_j is produced using the respective time frame t_j, guaranteeing that it is distinct at a time. If state t_j is replayed, it does not pass verification. Hence, any attempt of a replay attack will be unsuccessful. Simultaneously, the pseudorandom number $R_{i,j}$ evolves per timeframe through PRNG state updates. These mechanisms ensure that replayed transmissions fail verification at multiple levels: 1) timestamp t_j mismatches the current interval, 2) the recomputed value W_j differs from the embedded value, and 3) the expected value of $R_{i,j}$ diverges due to PRNG progression.
- **Impersonation attacks:** SMs and DA prevent impersonation attacks by registering with CC at the initialization phase. During key distribution, the watermark key (K_w) and Paillier key (P_k) are exchanged only after successful registration, preventing unauthorized entities from interfering with the network. In addition, the next phases are protected with Paillier encryption and data aggregation. Additionally, if an attacker tries to send fake data by pretending a legitimate SM, then $Seed_{i,j}$ and the watermark W_j will not match at the CC during verification. Hence, the system will be protected from impersonation.
- **Collusion attacks:** The threat model assumes that DA and CC can be dishonest, whereas SMs are considered as fully trusted. Hence, DA and CC are the primary collusions to consider. If DA colludes with CC to decrypt individual SM readings or infer user identities, it will not be possible because of the homomorphic aggregation in the encrypted domain without decryption. Collusion between DA and CC cannot regain fine-grained SM data $d_{i,j}$, as aggregation eliminates granularity.
- **False data injection (FDI):** $d_{i,j}$ is encrypted with the Paillier public key P_k, so attackers cannot forge valid ciphertexts without it while attacking SM or DA. Another point is that aggregated data retains the embedded watermark. Any tampering disrupts, causing CC to reject invalid data. Even any attack in the CC will not disclose anything but the aggregated sum, keeping the real SM reading protected from FDI.
- **Man-in-the-Middle (MitM):** ReWaP provides robust protection against MitM attacks through cryptographic binding of keys to system entities and time-based verification mechanisms. The only unencrypted transmission is the Paillier public key P_k, which is intentionally non-sensitive. All subsequent critical exchanges use cryptographic chaining. An MitM attack attempting injection or modification would inevitably corrupt this chain, causing verification failure at the CC during aggregate processing. Specifically: 1) altered ciphertexts would invalidate the watermark check, 2) replayed transmissions would exhibit timestamp mismatches, and 3) tampered $R_{i,j}$ would desynchronize the PRNG state progression.

Table 1. Comparative analysis

Method	Independent of any third party	Implemented in real hardware	Scalable for high-frequency SMs
SMDS [9]	✗ TA generates parameters of Paillier homomorphic encryption	✗ Sofware-only simulation using Celeron CPU with Ubuntu 20.04 OS	✗ Not scalable for high-frequency SMs due to storage concern
LV-P2DA [23]	✗ KGC (key generation center) is used for generating secret key	✓ Use a Raspberry Pi Zero W device to simulate the SM	✗ Scalability is not proven
LFTDA [21]	✗ TA generates the system parameters and exports the global encryption key (GEK)	✗ Software-only simulation using Intel Core i5 CPU and Ubuntu OS	✓ Provides clear empirical evidence of scalability
EC-ASPG [10]	✗ TTP is responsible for key sharing and user authentication	✗ Software-only simulation using Intel Core i5	✗ NOT suitable for High-Frequency SMs
Q-Secure-P2-SMA [17]	✓ No external entity is needed	✗ Software-based simulation using Qasm Simulator in Intel Core i5 CPU and Windows OS	✗ Indicates poor scalability or high cost per message
ReWaP [proposed scheme]	✓ Independent of any external entities	✓ Real-hardware simulation on STM32 Nucleo microcontroller boards using linux server	✓ Low-end ARM Cortex-M3\M4 microcontrollers makes it scalable for high-frequency SMs

Comparative Analysis

In this section, some of the recent works mentioned in Sect. 2 are compared with the ReWaP protocol. We have focused on some noticeable limitations of the existing techniques and tried to mitigate them in the proposed protocol. Firstly, the use of a trusted third party or semi-trusted third party in the system for key generation and sharing purposes can be a concern for privacy-conscious users. Secondly, the lack of real-world implementation of some works makes them unsure about the practicality. Lastly, making the method scalable for high-frequency smart meters is a big challenge, which was successfully overcome in the proposed ReWaP scheme. Table 1 shows the comparison among different research works in terms of these three limitations.

4 Experimental Results and Performance Analysis

In this section, we experimentally prove the effectiveness of the proposed ReWaP scheme. For this purpose, we developed a proof-of-concept system using STM32 Nucleo microcontroller boards, RIOT OS system [2], and the Relic [1] cryptographic library. Figure 3 presents the topology of our testbed. The deployed testbed system uses Nucleo-F207zg and Nucleo-F439zi boards both for SMs and the data aggregator. Sample boards used in the testbed are shown in Fig. 4. The control center was implemented as a Linux server running on a virtual machine. All devices are connected with a switch, forming a LAN testbed.

The most important parameters of the used Nucleo boards, which could influence performance, are presented in Table 2. We divide our research into two parts. In the first part, we evaluate the performance of the smart meter implementation. The second part of the evaluation concerns the data aggregator, which was also deployed in the microcontroller platform.

In the first part of the research, concerning smart meter performance, we developed dedicated functions that calculate watermarks, encrypt data, and copy it to the output buffer. Moreover, the function allows measurement of the elapsed

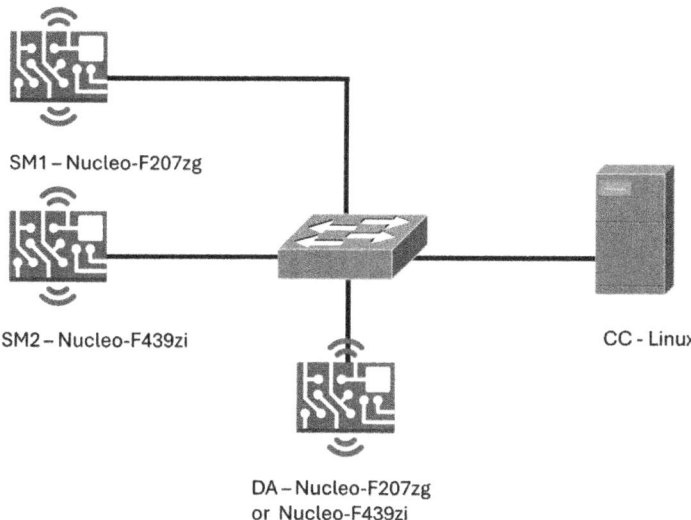

Fig. 3. Deployed ReWaP test-bed topology.

Table 2. Description of used boards' important parameters

Feature	Nucleo-F207zg	Nucleo-F439zi
MCU family	Cortex-M3	Cortex-M4
CPU frequency	120 MHz	180 MHz
RAM size	128 KiB	256 KiB
Flash size	1 MiB	2 MiB

time after a certain number of watermark and encryption iterations. What is important is that this test function does not provide any output to the user. Our initial research shows that the generation of user output could increase operation time from around 8% to more than 40%, depending on the amount of information and the type of device used. Results concerning the performance of choosing Nucleo boards as SMs are presented in Table 3. The results concerns times of adding watermarks and Paillier encryption for both used boards. To achieve representative results calculations are repeated 10, 100 and 1,000 times. Moreover, for easy comparison calculation of average time of one operation is presented.

The most important conclusion from the presented data is that our proposed ReWaP scheme could be used with Nucleo boards even for high-frequency smart meters. It should be emphasized that the use of low-end ARM Cortex-M3 or Cortex-M4 microcontrollers in the experiments enabled power consumption reporting at intervals of just a few times per minute.

The second part of the conducted research, concerning the data aggregator, is carried out similarly, using a dedicated measurement function. This test function

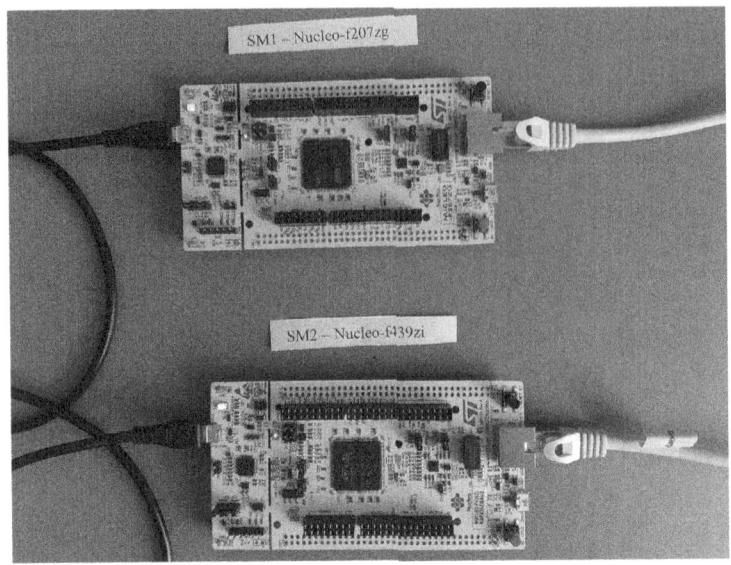

Fig. 4. Sample boards used to deploy ReWaP proof of concept system.

Table 3. Computational Time (ms) - Smart Meter Phase

Board	10 times	Average	100 times	Average	1,000 times	Average
Nucleo-F207zg	3,302	330	33,195	332	334,160	334
Nucleo-F439zi	1,942	194	19,524	195	196,528	197

repeats a given number of times operations performed by DA in normal circumstances. However, data are not received from the network but taken from the memory buffer. To prove that data aggregation works, after calculations, when time measurement is ended, final data are sent to the Control Center. Gathered results are presented in Table 4.

Table 4. Computaional Time (ms) - Data Aggregator Phase

Board	10 times	Average	100 times	Average	1,000 times	Average
Nucleo-F207zg	7	0.7	81	0.8	822	0.8
Nucleo-F439zi	4	0.4	50	0.5	501	0.5

As can be easily seen from the table, in both used boards, the average of adding new data from SM in the DA is well below 1 ms. This proves that using low-end ARM Cortex-M3 or Cortex-M4 microcontrollers for DA could aggregate data from more than one thousand SMs in one second. This proves the scalability of the scheme, which allows deploying DA even for high-frequency smart meters using cheap, low-end Cortex-M microcontrollers.

Another important advantage to be mentioned is that, while initialization involves multiple steps, its one-time execution and absence of recurring overhead make it fundamentally efficient. The design shifts complexity to provisioning time, not operational runtime—a deliberate tradeoff for long-term efficiency in resource-constrained environments. Seeds are distributed by CC once during SM registration. Each SM stores its seed locally and autonomously generates pseudorandom numbers without involving CC. Moreover, no recurring key updates unless a reset occurs (rare in practice). Hence, this one-time initialization should not significantly impact operational complexity.

5 Conclusion and Future Work

This paper proposes and implements a lightweight and resource-efficient privacy-preserving protocol for smart meters in the RIOT operating system by applying a joint technique combining reversible watermarking and Paillier cryptography called ReWaP. This unique approach ensures that sensitive, fine-grained meter data remains inaccessible to unauthorized attackers. Most significantly, this scheme is proven to be scalable in Nucleo boards, even for high-frequency smart meters that report energy consumption frequently, for example, each minute. The computational efficiency of the proposed scheme is demonstrated through systematic experiments conducted in the Nucleo microcontroller in the RIOT OS. The results derived from the real-hardware implementation highlight the practicality of the ReWaP scheme for real-world applications, as it not only stands out in terms of computational cost but also successfully implements robust security measures to defend against a variety of potential threats. The results evidently indicate that the proposed protocol surpasses existing methods, making it a better choice for privacy-preserving data aggregation in smart metering systems.

For future work, the focus will be on enhancing the watermarking technique by increasing the embedded bits and applying more lightweight and modern cryptographic techniques to make it more suitable for resource-constrained smart meters.

Acknowledgements. The authors acknowledge the funding obtained from the "SECURING" project (PID2021-125962OB-C31) funded by the Ministry of Science and Innovation, the Agencia Estatal de Investigación, and the European Regional Development Fund (ERDF), and by the ARTEMISA International Chair of Cybersecurity (C057/23) and the DANGER Strategic Project of Cybersecurity (C062/23), both funded by the Spanish National Institute of Cybersecurity through the European Union – Next GenerationEU and the Recovery, Transformation, and Resilience Plan, and the Mobility PW programme agreement no. CPR-IDUB/266/Z09/2024 funded by Warsaw University of Technology.

References

1. Aranha, D.F., Gouvêa, C.P.L.: RELIC is an Efficient LIbrary for Cryptography. http://code.google.com/p/relic-toolkit/
2. Baccelli, E., et al.: Riot: An open source operating system for low-end embedded devices in the iot. IEEE Internet Things J. **5**(6), 4428–4440 (2018)
3. Hseiki, H.A., El-Hajj, A.M., Ajra, Y.O., Hija, F.A., Haidar, A.M.: A secure and resilient smart energy meter. IEEE Access **12**, 3114–3125 (2024)
4. Kabir, F., Araghi, T.K., Megías, D.: Privacy-preserving protocol for high-frequency smart meters using reversible watermarking and paillier encryption. Comput. Electr. Eng. **119**, 109497 (2024)
5. Kabir, F., Megias, D., Cabaj, K.: Riot-based smart metering system for privacy-preserving data aggregation using watermarking and encryption. arXiv preprint arXiv:2501.06161 (2025)
6. Kathrine, G.J.W., Krittikka, P., Johnraja, I., Kirubakaran, S., Salaja, S., Arunkumar, K.: Enhancing smart grid security with xmss-based blockchain technology. In: 2023 International Conference on Emerging Research in Computational Science (ICERCS), pp. 1–6. IEEE (2023)
7. Krishnan, A.: Smart electricity meter market 2024: Global adoption landscape. IoT Analytics (2024)
8. Kua, J., Hossain, M.B., Natgunanathan, I., Xiang, Y.: Privacy preservation in smart meters: current status, challenges and future directions. Sensors **23**(7), 3697 (2023)
9. Kumar, J., Singh, A.K.: A secure paillier cryptosystem based privacy-preserving data aggregation and query processing models for smart grid. Clust. Comput. **27**(6), 7389–7400 (2024)
10. Lei, L., Wang, F., Zhao, C., Xu, L.: Efficient blockchain-based data aggregation scheme with privacy-preserving on the smart grid. IEEE Trans. Smart Grid (2024)
11. Lin, H.-Y., Tzeng, W.-G., Shen, S.-T., Lin, B.-S.P.: A practical smart metering system supporting privacy preserving billing and load monitoring. In: Bao, F., Samarati, P., Zhou, J. (eds.) ACNS 2012. LNCS, vol. 7341, pp. 544–560. Springer, Heidelberg (2012). https://doi.org/10.1007/978-3-642-31284-7_32
12. Liu, H., Peng, Y., Liu, Y., Zeng, Z.: Privacy-preserving multidimensional data aggregation for diverse electricity data users. J. Syst. Architect., 103363 (2025)
13. Liu, W., Chen, C., Wang, Z., Zhang, X., Zhai, G., Zheng, W.: Consistency evaluation of iot smart meter's metering accuracy considering ambient temperature and load current. In: 2023 5th International Conference on System Reliability and Safety Engineering (SRSE), pp. 547–552. IEEE (2023)
14. Nagpal, T., Sharma, P.: Smart grids: Sources of security intimidations, challenges, and opportunities. Cyber Security Solutions for Protecting and Building the Future Smart Grid, pp. 25–61 (2025)
15. Paillier, P.: Public-key cryptosystems based on composite degree residuosity classes. In: Stern, J. (ed.) EUROCRYPT 1999. LNCS, vol. 1592, pp. 223–238. Springer, Heidelberg (1999). https://doi.org/10.1007/3-540-48910-X_16
16. Parvez, I., Aghili, M., Riggs, H., Sundararajan, A., Sarwat, A.I., Srivastava, A.K.: A novel authentication management for the data security of smart grid. IEEE Open Access J. Power Energy (2024)
17. Prateek, K., Das, M., Surve, S., Maity, S., Amin, R.: Q-secure-p^2-sma: quantum-secure privacy-preserving smart meter authentication for unbreakable security in smart grid. IEEE Trans. Netw. Serv. Manage. **21**(5), 5149–5163 (2024)

18. Rzepka, K., Szary, P., Cabaj, K., Mazurczyk, W.: Performance evaluation of dtls implementations on riot os for internet of things applications. In: Proceedings of the 17th International Conference on Availability, Reliability and Security, pp. 1–9 (2022)
19. Singhal, D., Ahuja, L., Seth, A.: Posmeter: proof-of-stake blockchain for enhanced smart meter data security. Int. J. Inf. Technol. **16**(2), 1171–1184 (2024)
20. Tariq, U., Ahmed, I., Bashir, A.K., Shaukat, K.: A critical cybersecurity analysis and future research directions for the internet of things: a comprehensive review. Sensors **23**(8), 4117 (2023)
21. Wang, Z., Zhang, F., Zhang, A., Chang, J.: Lftda: a lightweight and fault-tolerant data aggregation scheme with privacy-enhanced property in fog-assisted smart grid. Comput. Commun. **220**, 35–42 (2024)
22. Zhang, J., Shi, C.: Efficient secure data aggregation for real-time smart grid monitoring: a lightweight privacy-preserving approach. IEEE Trans. Comput. Soc. Syst. (2024)
23. Zhu, F., et al.: Lightweight verifiable privacy-preserving data aggregation for smart grids. IEEE Internet of Things J. (2024)

Author Index

A
Agel, Marc Leon 171
Araghi, Tanya Koohpayeh 309, 346

B
Baggili, Ibrahim 60
Bardhan, Rajon 113
Bistarelli, Stefano 153
Breitinger, Frank 113

C
Cabaj, Krzysztof 346
Caviglione, Luca 271
Choraś, Michał 205

D
Dittmann, Jana 271
Domingues, Patricio 5
Dorai, Gokila 113
Drury, Dan 78

F
Frade, Miguel 5

G
Gocał, Piotr 205
Graner, Lukas 171

H
Hargreaves, Christopher 42, 78
Heeger, Julian 171
Hennelová, Zuzana 131
Hilgert, Jan-Niclas 23

K
Kabir, Farzana 346
Kanta, Aikaterini 42
Karapapas, Christos 187
Kashima, Toshikatsu 243
Keller, Jörg 327

Kozik, Rafał 205
Kramer, Julia 221
Krätzer, Christian 271

L
Lambertz, Martin 23
Lerch-Hostalot, Daniel 290

M
Mahr, Axel 23
Marková, Eva 131
Mazurczyk, Wojciech 327
McGibney, Jimmy 96
Megías, David 290, 309, 346
Mileva, Aleksandra 271

N
Negrão, Miguel 5
Niemietz, Marcus 221

O
Onik, Abdur 60

P
Patsakis, Constantinos 187
Pittaras, Iakovos 187
Polyzos, George C. 187
Puiggalí, Jordi 290

R
Rad, Pouria 113
Rajba, Paweł 327
Ramasamy, Vijayalakshmi 113
Rizvi, Syed 96
Rovira, Joshua 60

S
Santini, Francesco 153
Scanlon, Mark 96
Schmidbauer, Tobias 271

Sheppard, John 96
Sokol, Pavol 131
Spinosa, Trevor 60
Steinebach, Martin 171, 255
Streicher, Anne 221

T
Takaragi, Kazuo 243
Tavassi, Edoardo Toma 153

U
Umezawa, Katsuyuki 243

V
Vielhauer, Claus 271

W
Wendzel, Steffen 271
Wohlgemuth, Sven 243

Y
Yannikos, York 171, 255

Z
Zander, Sebastian 271

Made in the USA
Monee, IL
03 May 2026